The
Charlton
Standard Catalogue of

ROYAL
DOULTON
FIGURINES

Third Edition

By
Jean Dale

Introduction
by
Louise Irvine

W. K. Cross
Publisher

The Charlton Press
Birmingham, Michigan
Toronto, Ontario

ISBN 0-88968-111-2
ISSN 0228-6947

Printed in Canada

The Charlton Press

Editorial Office
2010 Yonge Street
Toronto, Ontario. M4Z 1E9

EDITORIAL

Editor	Jean Dale
Editorial Assistant	Mary Cross-Dolph
Layout	Frank van Lieshout
Advertising Manager	Donald Lorimer

COVER PHOTOGRAPH

Cover illustration, **The Princess, HN 392,** by courtesy of Nick Tzimas, Managing Director of U.K. International Ceramics.

SPECIAL THANKS

The publishers would like to thank Louise Irvine for writing the introduction to the Third Edition of the Charlton Standard Catalogue of Royal Doulton Figurines. Louise Irvine is an independant writer and lecturer on Royal Doulton's history and products and is not connected with the pricing of this catalogue.

CONTRIBUTORS

The following contributors graciously supplied photographs, price lists, data and other invaluable information for the third and past editions for which we offer a profound Thank You:

DEALERS

Arnie and Judi Berger, Yesterday's South, Miami, Florida; **Nicki and Al Budin,** Gourmet Antiques, Inc., Worthington, Ohio; **Laura Campbell,** Site of the Green, Dundas, Ontario; **Anthony Cross,** Anthony Cross The Englishman, Blackburn, England; **Charles and Joanne Dombeck,** Plantation, Florida; **Arnold and Margaret Krever,** Marnalea Antiques, Campbellville, Ontario; **Dick and Alison Nicholson,** The British Toby, Markham, Ontario; **Ed Pascoe,** Pascoe and Company, Miami, Florida; **Tom Power,** The Collector, London, England; **Nick Tzimas,** U.K. International Ceramics, Suffolk, England; **Stan Worrey,** Colonial House Antiques and Gifts, Berea, Ohio

COLLECTORS

Joseph Hess, Brooklyn, N.Y.; **Emil Kovach, Peter McKinnon,** Ontario; **Robert Puleo,** Canton, MA; **Lucy Weizer,** Florida

A SPECIAL NOTE TO COLLECTORS

We welcome and would appreciate any comments or suggestions in regard to the Charlton Standard Catalogue of Royal Doulton Figurines that you might have. If you would like to participate in pricing or supplying new data, such as information on unlisted figures or varieties, please call Mary Cross or Jean Dale at (415) 488-4653.

HOW TO USE THIS CATALOGUE

The Listings

On the pages that follow Royal Doulton figurines are listed, illustrated, described and cross-referenced in numerical order by HN and M numbers. Their names immediately follow their numbers.

When two or more figures have the same name - but different physical modelling characteristics - they are listed as **Style One, Style Two** and so on after their names. Such figures will also have different HN numbers.

When known, the figurine's modeller or **Designer** is listed next.

What then follows is the figure's **Height**, given in inches and centimeters.

The actual **Colour** (or colours) of the figure is listed next. The date (or dates) when the figure was **Issued** then follows.

The HN numbers of all **Varieties** are then listed. Only colour differences, other minor decorative alterations and slight changes in size due to firing constitute varieties. Different physical modelling characteristics constitute different styles, dictating different HN numbers and so are not called varieties

If the figure is part of a **Series**, that series name is given next.

The final listing gives the **Price**, the current market value of the figure described. The price appears in U.S. funds, then Canadian dollars and then pounds sterling.

Although the publisher has made every attempt to obtain and photograph all figurines and their varieties, several pieces, naturally, have not come into the publisher's possession. In a number of cases, then, photographs of some figures have been used to represent unobtainable varieties of that particular pice. The reader is cautioned, then, that photographs are to be used for design characteristics only. The more specific details of a figurine (i.e.: colourway) should be determined from the actual information printed below the specific figure.

A Word on Pricing

The purpose of this catalogue is to give readers the most accurate, up-to-date retail prices for Royal Doulton figurines in the United States, Canada and the United Kingdom.

To accomplish this, The Charlton Press continues to access an international pricing panel of Royal Doulton experts who submit prices based on both dealer and collector retail price activity as well as current auction results in the U.S., Canadian and UK markets. These market figures are carefully averaged to reflect accurate valuations for the Doulton figurines listed herein in each of these three markets.

Please be aware that prices given in a particular currency are for figurines in that particular country. The prices published herein have not been calculated using exchange rates - they have been determined solely by their supply and demand within the country in question.

A necessary word of caution. No pricing catalogue can be, or should be, a fixed price list. This catalogue, therefore, should be considered as a guide only - showing the most current retail prices (based on market demand within a particular region) for the various figurines.

Current figurines, however, are priced differently in this catalogue. Such pieces are priced according to the manufacturer's suggested retail price in each of the three market regions. For example, **Gardening Time** (HN 3401) has been priced at $250 in the U.S., $330 in Canada and £99.95 in the UK as this is how it is priced by the three Doulton divisions themselves. It should be noted, however, it is likely dealer discounting from these prices will occur.

The prices published herein are for figures in mint condition. Collectors are cautioned that a repaired or restored piece may be worth as little as 50 percent of the value of the same figurine in mint condition. The collector interested strictly in investment potential will avoid damaged figurines.

Doulton has produced the HN series of figurines for a period of 79 years. Over this period, changes in trademarks (or backstamps as they are often called) and other base markings have naturally occurred. Earlier examples of figurines manufactured basically unchanged over the years will become available. The **Old Balloon Seller** for example, was issued from 1929 to the present. Older examples of such figures may have unique markings on their bases. These markings often dictate an earlier date of manufacture. Prices in this catalogue are for figurines without regard to any special marks on their bases - such as hand written script titles and HN numbers, designer's signatures or the phrase 'Potted by Doulton & Co.'. These older (and often harder to find) markings are illustrated and discussed in detail on page 17 under 'A Guide to Backstamps and Dating'.

In this regard, of the figurines that have enjoyed long production periods, the advanced collector will naturally prefer older examples of the same model. Such figures are not marked with their year of production, but the knowledgeable collector will recognize older pieces by their unique marks and their special workmanship that can include careful and subtle painting, delicate flesh tones and more detailed modeling that can be seen in individual flower bouquets, balloon clusters and so on.

Rarity, age and artistry are the characteristics that most often make the value of one figurine greater than another. It is generally thought that many of the early discontinued figures were produced in quantities of less than 2,000. Usually, figures manufactured more recently have been made in quantities greater than this. However, it is a Royal Doulton business practice to limit production by systematically discontinuing figures at the same time as they introduce new ones. According to the latest published lists, over 300 different Royal Doulton figurine versions are currently in production.

A further word on pricing. As mentioned elsewhere, this is a catalogue giving prices for figurines in the currency of a particular market (Canadian dollars for the Canadian market; U.S. dollars for the American market; and Sterling for the UK market.) The bulk of the prices given herein are not determined by currency exchange calculations but by actual market activity in the market concerned.

An exception, however, occurs in the case of current figurines and very recent limited editions issued in inly one of the three markets. Since such items are priced by Doulton only in the country of sale, their value in other markets has been determined using exchange rates at the time of publications. These prices are noted with an asterisk.

Additionally, collectors must remember that all relevant information must be known to make a proper valuation. When comparing auction prices to catalogue prices, collectors and dealers must remember two important points.

First, to compare 'apples and apples', be sure that auction prices realized for figures include a buyer's premium if one is due. Prices realized for figures in auction catalogues may not include these additional costs. Secondly, if a figure is restored or repaired, this fact may not be noted or explained in the listings and as a result, its price will not be reflective of that same piece in mint condition. Please beware of repairs and restorations and the effect they may have on values.

Insuring Your Figurines

As with any other of your valuables, making certain your figurines are protected is a very important concern. It is paramount that you display or store any porcelain items in a secure place - preferably one safely away from traffic in the home.

Your figurines are most often covered under your basic homeowner's policy and there are generally three kinds of such policies - standard, broad and comprehensive. Each has its own specific deductible and terms.

Under a general policy, your figurines are considered 'contents' and are covered for all of the perils covered under the contractural terms of your policy (fire, theft, water damage and so on).

However, since figurines are extremely delicate, breakage is treated differently by most insurance companies. There is usually an extra premium attached to insure figures against accidental breakage by or carelessness of the owner. This is sometimes referred to as a 'fine arts' rider.

You are advised to contact your insurance professional to get all the answers.

In order to help you protect yourself, it is critical that you take inventory of your figurines and have colour photographs taken of all your pieces. This is the surest method of clearly establishing, for the police and your insurance company, the items lost or destroyed. It is also the easiest way to establish their replacement value in the event of a tragedy.

HN and M Number Sequencing

In an effort to help readers understand the numbering rationale of Royal Doulton, we have included a chart on the following page outlining the sequencing of all existing HN and M series numbers. It shows the existing gaps in numbering when HN and M numbers have been used for items not listed in this catalogue (animals, birds, wall masks, bookends, napkin rings and so on). It also contains additional notes.

In the text of this catalogue, an asterisk (*) in the lower left corner of a listing indicates that one or more of the following HN or M numbers was either not issued or used for a piece other than a figurine. A black Square (■) in a listing indicates there is additional information to be found in the chart below.

The black and white photographs in this publication identify figurines in shape and overall design only. Colours, patterns and glazes may differ within individual figurines.

MISCELLANEOUS AND UNISSUED HN NUMBERS

An asterisk (*) in the lower left corner of a listing signifies that one or more of the following HN or M numbers was not issued. It can also denote items produced but not included in this catalogue (animals, birds, wall masks, bookends, napkin rings, etc.). A square (■) in the lower left corner of a listing signifies further information.

HN 100-299
Animal and Bird Figures
HN 360 - Not Issued

Page 32 - Note: HN 423, 423A - E; Due to the size of these figures the HN number is not recorded on the base. However the model number is incised and thus this style can be identified by the model number.

HN Number	Model Number
423	291
423A	295
423B	296
423C	299
423D	300
423E	301

HN 452 - Not Issued

Page 45 - Note: HN 529 to 541 and 544, 545 and 546 were discontinued in 1932 as HN numbers and renumbered as M numbers.

HN 574 - Not Issued
HN 602 - Not Issued
HN 607 - Not Issued
HN 737 - Not Issued
HN 800-1200 - Animal and Bird Figures
HN 1239-1241 - Bird Figures
HN 1381-1386 - Not Issued
HN 1403 - Not Issued
HN 1415 - Not Issued
HN 1477 - Not Issued
HN 1590-1597 - Wall Masks
HN 1601-1603 - Wall Masks
HN 1608-1609 - Wall Masks
HN 1611-1614 - Wall Masks
HN 1615-1616 - Bookends
HN 1623-1625 - Bookends
HN 1630 - Wall Mask
HN 1658-1661 - Wall Masks
HN 1671-1676 - Wall Masks
HN 1733 - Wall Mask

HN 1779 - Bird Figure
HN 1781-1786 - Wall Masks
HN 1787-1790 - Not Issued
HN 1816-1817 - Wall Masks
HN 1823-1824 - Wall Masks
HN 2083 - Not Issued
HN 2124 - Not Issued
HN 2164 - Not Issued
HN 2182 - Not Issued
HN 2187-2190 - Not Issued
HN 2194-2195 - Not Issued
HN 2198-2201 - Not Issued
HN 2219 - Not Issued
HN 2232 - Not Issued
HN 2241 - Not Issued
HN 2285-2286 - Not Issued
HN 2288-2303 - Not Issued
HN 2350-2351 - Not Issued
HN 2353-2355 - Not Issued
HN 2357-2358 - Not Issued
HN 2360 - Not Issued
HN 2363-2367 - Not Issued
HN 2402-2407 - Not Issued
HN 2409 - Not Issued
HN 2411-2416 - Not Issued
HN 2447-2454 - Not Issued
HN 2456-2459 - Not Issued
HN 2462 - Not Issued
HN 2464 - Not Issued
HN 2486 - Not Issued
HN 2488-2491 - Not Issued
HN 2493 - Not Issued
HN 2495-2498 - Not Issued
HN 2500-2501 - Animal Figures
HN 2503-2519 - Animal Figures
HN 2522-2541 - Animal Figures
HN 2548-2553 - Bird Figures
HN 2556-2670 - Animal and Bird Figures
HN 2672-2676 - Not Issued
HN 2681-2682 - Not Issued
HN 2684-2692 - Not Issued
HN 2730 - Not Issued
HN 2766 - Not Issued
HN 2777-2778 - Not Issued

HN 2785-2787 - Not Issued
HN 2812-2813 - Not Issued
HN 2817 - Not Issued
HN 2819-2823 - Not Issued
HN 2847-2850 - Not Issued
HN 2852-2854 - Not Issued
HN 2880 - Not Issued
HN 2886 - Not Issued
HN 2904-2905 - Not Issued
HN 2947-2951 - Not Issued
HN 2973 - Not Issued
HN 2982-2987 - Not Issued
HN 3022-3023 - Not Issued
HN 3055 - Not Issued
HN 3063-3065 - Not Issued
HN 3081 - Not Issued
HN 3101-3104 - Not Issued
HN 3111-3114 - Not Issued
HN 3131 - Not Issued
HN 3146-3154 - Not Issued
HN 3158 - Not Issued
HN 3171 - Not Issued
HN 3193-3194 - Not Issued
HN 3222 - Not Issued
HN 3224-3225 - Not Issued
HN 3227 - Not Issued
HN 3237-3243 - Not Issued
HN 3287-3288 - Not Issued
HN 3291-3292 - Not Issued
HN 3323-3334 - Not Issued
HN 3339-3340 - Not Issued
HN 3361-3367 - Not Issued
HN 3380-3387 - Not Issued
HN 3403-3407 - Not Issued
HN 3414 - Not Issued
HN 3421-3427 Not Issued
HN 3430-3438 - Not Issued
HN 3441-3458 - Not Issued

Page 313 - Note: M 41-56 were originally issued 1922-1932 as HN 529-541, 544, 545 and 546.
M 57-62 - Napkin Rings
M 63 - Not Issued

CONTENTS

HN 2081 PRINCESS BADOURA

THE HISTORY OF ROYAL DOULTON FIGURES
By Louise Irvine

INTRODUCTION

The history of Royal Doulton dates back to 1815 when John Doulton became involved in a little pottery in Lambeth on the banks of the River Thames in London. Trading as Doulton and Watts, they made general stonewares, such as ink wells and ginger beer bottles for daily use. When John's son, Henry, joined the firm in 1835 the business expanded rapidly producing chemical and industrial ceramics. The young entrepreneur also set up a new factory supplying drainpipes to service major cities around the world. The success of this sanitary ware business eventually enabled Henry Doulton to pursue more artistic interests and in 1867 he employed a young sculptor, George Tinworth, to establish an art pottery studio in Lambeth. Tinworth's monumental sculptures and decorative vases quickly focussed public attention on this new venture and more artists were recruited until, by the mid 1880s, there were over 300 young men and women producing vases, figures and other ornaments for the Victorian home.

(Fig. 1) Doulton figures were made at the company's Burslem factory in Stoke-on-Trent from the early 1890s. This vellum style figure of a Water Carrier was modelled by Charles Noke in 1893. It is marked DOULTON BURSLEM, height 18 inches (45.7 cm)

During his long career at the Lambeth studio, Tinworth modelled a wide range of figures, mainly of chubby children at play and animals in human situations. The medium he used is known as salt glaze stoneware, a high-fired clay body, literally glazed with salt. Tinworth's colleague John Broad also used this material as well as terracotta to produce royal portraits, military figures and female studies in classical style. He was a very versatile artist and his figures could range from six inches for the mantlepiece to six feet in height for the garden. He also introduced some fashionable ladies modelled in white bisque porcelain, as did fellow artist Mark Marshall.

The last modeller of note to join the Lambeth studio was Leslie Harradine who contributed a variety of stoneware figure subjects in the early 1900s, some of which were slip-cast in small editions. During the 1920s several of his Lambeth figures, including his Dickens characters, were reproduced in the famous HN collection at Doulton's other factory in Burslem, Stoke-on-Trent.

Henry Doulton invested in the Nile Street pottery at Burslem in 1877 in order to manufacture tableware and ornamental ware at the centre of the British ceramic industry. Charles Noke, an experienced modeller from the Worcester factory, was recruited in 1889 to model exhibition vases but within a few years he had also produced a range of figures. These Vellum figures, as they are now known, are very different in style from the examples sold in china shops today. They are much larger than contemporary models, some nearly 20 inches tall, and they are much less colourful. Most have an ivory body with tinted and gilded decoration by the leading studio artists and they bear a strong resemblance to the figures produced at Worcester.

Noke's first figure, introduced in 1892, was an extraordinary double-sided model depicting Mephistopheles and Marguerite from Faust, as played by the great Victorian acting duo, Henry Irving and Ellen Terry. The theatre, and these actors in particular, inspired many of Noke's early studies and his interest in the stage continued throughout his career. A selection of the early Vellum figures was shown at the Chicago exhibition of 1893 but they do not seem to have captured the public imagination, perhaps because they were very expensive. Despite their disappointing reception, Charles Noke continued to add occasional figures to the collection and by 1900 he had produced 21 free-standing figures and 4 wall-mounted models. Only a very limited number of each design was ever produced making them extremely hard to find today and until recently they were not well documented. However, serious collectors are gradually recognizing the desirability of these distinctive models.

In the opening years of the 20th century, Charles Noke was preoccupied with the development of other Doulton ranges and no new figures were produced. He did, however, experiment with smaller sizes and brighter colours for his existing designs to widen their appeal. For example, his early study of a **Jester** was given a suit of motley colours and it eventually became one of the most popular figures in the collection.

Noke was convinced that a revival of the 18th century Staffordshire figure tradition was desirable and feasible at the Doulton studio but he was aware that he could not achieve his goal alone. Accordingly, in 1909, he began to invite well-known independent sculptors to submit designs that they thought would be suitable for reproducing as small scale ceramic figures. By 1912 he had accumulated the nucleus of a collection and he decided to launch the new range during King George and Queen Mary's visit to the factory in 1913. The Queen was very impressed with the figures, particularly a study of a little child in a nightgown by Charles Vyse. Apparently she exclaimed "isn't he a darling" and the figure was later named **Darling** in her honour and given the first number in the collection, HN1. The 'HN' refers to Harry Nixon who was in charge of the new figure painting department, which comprised three artists in the early years. The HN numbering system is still used today and the company has issued over 3,000 numbers although they are not all new models: some are assigned to colourways of existing figures and some to animal subjects.

(Fig. 2) Jesters were a favourite subject of Charles Noke who was responsible for introducing figures at the Burslem factory. This example was modelled in 1892 and was given a parchment coloured glaze, which is now known as the Vellum style. It is marked DOULTON BURSLEM ENGLAND, height 9 5/8 inches (24.5 cm).

Between the Royal visit and the end of the decade, 80 figures were introduced and their relative popularity is recorded in some surviving production statistics for the years 1913-17. During this period 680 figures were produced, an average of 3 a week, and **Darling** (HN1) was by far the most popular with 148 sold, compared with 51 orders for the **Crinoline** (HN8) the first 'fair lady' figure, which was modelled by George Lambert, an Australian artist working in England. Doulton's first 'street vendor' figure **Madonna of the Square** (HN10), by London sculptor Phoebe Stabler, sold 35 in the first three years whilst there were 40 orders for **A Spook** (HN50) by the talented in-house artist Harry Tittensor. Less than a dozen copies of some subjects were produced making these amongst the rarest figures to buy today. According to the records there were only 7 orders for Noke's **Pedlar Wolf** (HN7) in these early years, which explains why it is particularly elusive today along with his other bizarre subjects **Boy on a Crocodile** (HN373) and **Child on a Crab** (HN32).

Noke continued to draw upon the ideas and talents of other artists, most significantly Leslie Harradine who had worked for Doulton's factory in Lambeth from 1902-12. He left to farm with his brother in Saskatchewan, Canada but the First World War interrupted their new life and, after fighting in Europe, Harradine eventually returned to England. When Noke heard of his return he endeavoured to persuade him to work in the Potteries but Harradine valued his new found independence too much and agreed instead to work on a freelance basis, first from his studio in Kent and then from the Channel Islands. His first figure **The Princess** (HN391) was introduced in 1920 along with **Contentment** (HN395), which was purchased by Queen Mary at the British Industries Fair that year.

For more than 30 years, Harradine sent at least one model a month to Stoke, sometimes two or three, and they ranged from stylish ladies dressed in the latest fashions, such as **The Sunshine Girl** (HN1344) or **Scotties** (HN1281), to penetrating studies of Dickens' characters. Some of his figures from the 1920s are still being made today, for example **The Flower Seller's Children** (HN1342) of 1921 and the **Old Balloon Seller** (HN1315) of 1929. Such was the demand for Harradine's figures that the painting department was expanded to 10 artists by 1927, many of whom were transferred from painting bone china vases and dessert services following a slump in that market. Thus some of Doulton's most talented artists, including the bird painter Harry Allen and the game painter Charles Hart, introduced their considerable expertise to the decoration of Doulton figures. Many alternative colourways were produced during this decade and most involved several firings to achieve the subtle shaded effects. By the end of the decade nearly 200 new figures had been introduced, most of them the work of Leslie Harradine.

Harradine also dominated the output of the 1930s and in 1937 he introduced his most popular figure ever **Top of the Hill** (HN1833). Many of his most successful pretty ladies were also introduced in a miniature size between 1932 and 1939, enabling collectors with limited display space to enjoy a wide range of his work. Some of the miniatures figures were mounted on ash-trays, calendars and book-ends so that they could be useful as well as decorative whilst the larger ladies were incorporated in electric lamps with complimentary shades.

Harradine's 1930s lady figures, for example **Aileen** (HN1645) and **Rhythm** (HN1903), reflect the sophisticated elegance of the period with glamorous evening gowns, as worn in the Hollywood movies by Greta Garbo and others. Gone were the boyish fashions of the 1920s with their short tube-like dresses and cropped hairstyles. As the decade progressed, more famous porcelain artists joined the figure decorating department, notably the flower painter Percy Curnock, so that by 1939 there were 27 painters at work on the collection. The influence of these master painters can be seen most clearly in the faces of the 1930s fair ladies which have much more expression than the earlier models. Instead of the dark 'button' eyes of the 1920s, the iris and pupil are clearly delineated and the lips are brightly painted in one of the fashionable lipstick shades. This more detailed approach to face painting began around 1934 and can be used as a guide to dating figures.

(Fig. 3) Royal Doulton figures have often been very representative of the era that produced them. An interesting comparison in this regard is that between the ample nude on the left called the BATHER and a typical Roaring 20's type, and the modest and lithe DAWN on the right, created 10 years later during a much more self-conscious and sobering decade of history.

The Second World War limited the production of figures as luxury goods could only be made for export and, in addition, many of the experienced artists joined the armed forces. It was a time of assessment and appraisal and many of the early figures were discontinued between 1941 and 1949. Charles Noke retired in 1941 but Peggy Davies, who had been engaged as an assistant modeller before the war, decided to set up her own studio and produce figures on a contract basis for Royal Doulton. Her first, in 1946, was **Christmas Morn** (HN1992) which is still being made today and this was followed by **Minuet** (HN2019), a delightful study of a dancer in Regency costume. Peggy was fascinated with fashion and history and enjoyed all the research necessary to produce realistic, accurate figures. One of her most successful early collections portrayed eight illustrious ladies from English history and these are very sought after today.

From the mid 1950s Peggy worked with the new art director Jo Ledger and produced several figures in a contemporary style, mostly teenagers with pony tails and flat pumps. Her most significant piece from this era was the **Marriage of Art and Industry** (HN2261), which was designed for the Brussels exhibition of 1958. Only 12 copies of this prestigious figure were made and they were not on public sale. Peggy rapidly proved her diversity as an artist producing historical characters, fair ladies, ballerinas and other dancers, child studies and later prestige collections. More and more she dominated the collection as Harradine prepared for retirement, contributing his last figure **Dimity** (HN2169) in 1956.

A new talent, Mary Nicoll, appeared on the scene in the mid 1950s. Her father had been illustrating books for the company and he effected an introduction. It soon became apparent that this young artist had tremendous potential as a character figure modeller. In 1955 she began to contribute a wide range of nautical personalities, street entertainers and historical characters, which she modelled in her Devon studio and sent to Stoke on a regular basis. During the 1950s and 60s nearly all the figures were produced by Mary Nicoll and Peggy Davies. Although Peggy was primarily concentrating on crinoline ladies at this time, she also undertook some ambitious large scale subjects, including the **Matador and Bull** (HN2324), the **Indian Brave** (HN2376) and the **Palio** (HN2428) all of which raised the potential of the ceramic medium to its limits, so intricate and complex were her designs.

Peggy continued this prestige work in the 1970s with several extremely popular limited edition collections. **The Lady Musicians, Femmes Fatales** and **Dancers of the World**, were produced under the supervision of the new Director of Sculpture, Eric Griffiths. He had joined the company in 1972 and his early training as a portrait painter soon became evident in his choice of famous subjects for the figures collection. Good examples are the actor Laurence Olivier and various members of the British Royal family. Eric Griffiths preferred working on a larger scale than the average 8 inch tall Doulton figure and in 1974 he introduced a collection of figures, around 12 inches tall, entitled **Haute Ensemble**. He also advocated the use of a matt finish, believing that a shiny glaze obscured some of the finer points of detail and several of Mary Nicoll's character studies were issued in the matt style.

Sadly, Mary died in 1974, but the character figure range was continued by Bill Harper, a versatile modeller with considerable experience in the ceramic industry. He has been responsible for such perennial favourites as the **Punch and Judy Man** (HN2765) and **Thanks Doc** (HN2731), which is essentially a self portrait. Amongst the other sculptors who worked for the collection during the 1970s were Robert Jefferson, Douglas Tootle, Peter Gee, Alan Maslankowski and Robert Tabbenor. Most of these artists still work for the company today.

Not surprisingly after some 90 years of figure production Royal Doulton had a 'huge' collector following and in 1978 the first book to document the HN range, **Royal Doulton Figures**, was written by Desmond Eyles and Richard Dennis. Prior to this reference work there had been no concept of rarity on the secondary market and all the figures had sold in the region of $75 - $100. Now it was apparent that some figures were more desirable that others, depending on how attractive they were and how long they had been in production. Some models had not been found in time for illustration in the first edition of the book and the hunt was on for these elusive pieces, with prices escalating accordingly. A second edition was published in 1989, including many of the rare commissions as well as all the new models produced during the 1980s.

(Fig. 4) By specializing in figurines of children, a Royal Doulton collector could form a most beguiling display.

The five examples illustrated here are based on nursery rhymes: 'She Loves Me Not,' 'Mary, Mary,' 'Mary Had a Little Lamb,' 'Wee Willie Winkie,' and 'He Loves Me.'

In response to the new collecting boom of the 1980s, Royal Doulton introduced many new series of figures appealing to different tastes and budgets. Several featured children, such as **Characters from Childrens' Literature** and **Childhood Days**. For those interested in royalty and history there were portraits of the current Royal family as well as historical **Queens of the Realm** and for collectors of the crinoline ladies there was the modestly priced **Vanity Fair** range of figures that were very simply decorated. A new contemporary look was achieved in 1981 with the **Images** range of stylised, symbolic sculptures in black basalt or white bone china. In 1987 the **Reflections** range of attenuated figures in fashionable pastel shades was launched.

To keep collectors abreast of all these new developments a Collectors Club was established in 1980 and many figures were commissioned exclusively for members, notably **Prized Possessions** (HN2942) by Robert Tabbenor. This piece features a lady collector consulting the figures book with her latest acquisition by her side. Another popular club commission was **Sleepy Darling** (HN2953) by Pauline Parsons, inspired by Doulton's first figure in the HN collection. Like most of the members' exclusives, it was only made for a six month period. Pauline Parsons has produced other models for the Club and is now one of the foremost modellers of the 'fair lady' figures following Peggy's retirement in 1984. Eric Griffiths also retired at the end of 1990 and a new era has begun with the appointment of Amanda Dixon, Doulton's first female art director. It will be interesting to see what the future holds under this new direction as Royal Doulton enters its second century of figure production.

BUILDING A COLLECTION

Since 1892, more that 2,000 figures have been added to the range and these are now avidly collected in many parts of the world. It would be virtually impossible to acquire them all, even if space and budget allowed, but there is plenty of scope to build interesting collections, based on artist, period, style or theme.

Collecting by Artist

New collectors quickly gravitate towards a particular style of figure and often discover that they favour the work of a specific artist. In the early years the artist was acknowledged on the base of the figures and collectors could appreciate the diverse modelling skills of artists such as Charles Noke, Harry Tittensor and others. After a gap of many years, this practice was revived in 1984 when the artist's facsimile signature was incorporated into the backstamp, making identification as easy as it had been previously.

The work of each Doulton artist has a distinctive quality, even though their figures might be classified with many others as 'fair ladies' or 'character studies'. An experienced eye can quickly spot the difference between a Peggy Davies crinoline lady and one by Leslie Harradine. Similarly Mary Nicoll's nautical figures are quite distinct from Bill Harper's. Each of these artists has a wide following and the scope for collecting their work is often vast and varied, particularly in the case of Peggy Davies, who produced about 250 figures in her 40 year career with Royal Doulton.

Collecting by Period

It has been said of Royal Doulton figures that they are a reflection of the times in which they are made. Certainly, with many of the subjects it is possible to attribute them to a particular period, based on costume, fabric designs and hair styles. The bright young things of the 1920s, such as **Lido Lady** (HN1200) and **Angela** (HN1204) with their negligees and lounging pyjamas, are amongst the most appealing of these period figures but collections can also be formed from other decades. The glamorous style of the 1930s, inspired by the Hollywood stars, is represented in figures such as **Gloria** (HN1488) and **Clothilde** (HN1598) whilst the teenage trends of the 1950s can be seen in **Faraway** (HN2133) and **Sweet Sixteen** (HN2231).

(*Fig. 5) These figurines are particularly good examples of the period costumes to be seen on Royal Doulton fair ladies. VIRGINIA, left, is typical of the 18th century with her elbow-length sleeves, low neckline and gown open in front to reveal a petticoat. BON JOUR, right, is garbed in characteristic mid 19th century style with a flounced skirt, shawl and bonnet.*

For the fashion conscious, it is possible to create a cat-walk of costumes through the ages from the Medieval period to the 20th century. Some collectors focus exclusively on 18th century style costumes, as worn by **Antoinette** (HN1850) and **Kate Hardcastle** (HN1861), which were notable for their wide hooped skirts adorned with ribbons, bows and ruffles of lace. Others prefer Victorian dresses with their flounced skirts and frothy petticoats, represented by such pieces as **Spring Morning** (HN1922) and **Chloe** (HN1470). Whether it be hats (from wimples to poke bonnets), or fluttering fans, even ladies' fashionable accessories have inspired collections.

Collecting by Subject

Child Studies

Darling, the first figure in the HN collection, was so successful that it was soon followed by many more child studies. Consequently, there is plenty of scope to form a delightful collection, whether it includes the sort of children who were 'seen but not heard' in Victorian times, like **Monica** (HN1467) or **Lily** (HN1798), or the mischievous kids of today like **Pillow Fight** (HN2270) and **Lights Out** (HN2262). There are many popular series inspired by childhood, including Leslie Haradine's **Nursery Rhymes** figures and the recently introduced **Age of Innocence** series. Many of the latest child studies incorporate animals and the special relationship young children enjoy with their pets would be an interesting theme to explore with both new and discontinued figures. As well as puppies and kittens, Doulton children also play with teddies, dolls and other toys. It would be fun to track down a representative collection, although there will be competition from serious Teddy Bear collectors. **Sleepyhead** (HN2114), cuddling her teddy, would be a very exciting discovery whilst **Nanny** (HN2221), mending her charge's teddy, is still readily available in the shops.

Fair Ladies

There are more fair ladies than any other type of Doulton figure so it is a good idea to specialize at an early stage. Collecting by artist has already been discussed and, as well as the great names of the past, such as Leslie Harradine and Peggy Davies, there are many talented modellers to look for today. Recently Pauline Parsons has portrayed many famous **Queens of the Realm** and Peter Gee has been inspired by the famous paintings of **Gainsborough** and **Reynolds** ladies. The latest recruits to the studio are Nada Pedley and Valerie Annand who have given us romantic interpretations of Victorian and Edwardian fashions.

Faced with this wide choice, a popular approach is to collect by colour, choosing only shades which harmonize with the furnishings of particular rooms. For example, ladies dressed in pastel shades might be suitable for a bedroom whilst richer colours might be more appropriate for the lounge or dining room. Displays could be changed to match the seasons, with all the ladies dressed in yellow and green featured in the spring and all the red outfits at Christmas time. There are many Doulton figures which celebrate the festive season, including **Noelle** (HN2179) with her ermine trimmed cloak and muff and **Santa Claus** himself (HN2725).

Figures can also be used effectively as table centres, whatever the season, or as feature displays with flower arrangements. Some of the figures are even portrayed arranging bowls of tiny hand-made flowers, whilst others carry baskets of blooms, lavish bouquets or a single red rose, so a fair ladies collection could be 'all a blooming'.

Swirling voluminous gowns have inspired many collections of dancing ladies, most of them the work of Peggy Davies who excelled at conveying movement in the folds of the fabric. Peggy's talent in this area can be seen in **Ninette** (HN2379) and **Elaine** (HN2791). **Minuet** (HN2019), one of her earliest figures (HN2019) was inspired by the stately minuet and over the years she added **Polka** (HN2156) **First Waltz** (HN2862) and the flamboyant **Gypsy Dance** (HN2230). She also studied many national dances and costumes for her **Dancers of the World** collection.

Many collectors are influenced by the names of the figures, whether it be the sentiment conveyed or the name of a loved one. In some cases it has been possible to put together a 'family' of figures representing children, grandchildren, and so on. 'Fair ladies', of course, can form part of much wider theme collections of the types suggested below.

Character Figures

As with the fair ladies there is a huge choice of character figures from all walks of life and most collectors look for a particular artist or theme. Art director Charles Noke specialized in character modelling and many of his personal interests can be seen in his range, including literature, history and the theatre. Leslie Harradine, renowned for his beautiful lady figures, was equally at home with characters, contributing country folk, such as **Lambing Time** (HN1890), and colourful street vendors selling balloons, silks and ribbons or fruit and flowers. One such example is **The Orange Seller** (HN1325).

Mary Nicoll dominated the character collection from the mid 1950s to the 1970s and she also launched the nautical figures, which are so popular with sea lovers today. She also developed a collection of figures featuring traditional crafts and professions, for example **The Clockmaker** (HN2279) and **The Judge** (HN2443) and she celebrated the twilight years in her studies of Old Dears, notably **Family Album** (HN2321) and **Teatime** (HN2255). All these successful sub-collections have been continued in recent years by Bill Harper, who has also recently expanded the London collection of characters with **The Lifeguard** (HN2781) and **The Guardsman** (HN2784). Former Art Director Eric Griffiths portrayed many members of the British Royal family before his retirement in 1991 and he was also responsible for the **Soldiers of the Revolution** collection of military figures.

Younger modellers are also making their mark. Robert Tabbenor is producing some fine sporting characters, such as **Teeing Off** (HN3276) and Alan Maslankowski

has excelled with his limited edition historical subjects, notably **Christopher Columbus** (HN3392).

Any one of these themes can form the basis of a fascinating collection, which can become even more rewarding by researching the characters behind the figures.

The World of Entertainment

Collecting Royal Doulton figures can literally be an 'entertaining' hobby as many of the stars of stage and screen have been portrayed by Doulton modellers. From the pierrots of pantomime and sea side concerts, to the great Shakespearean roles played by Henry Irving and Ellen Terry, many of the earliest figures reflect Charles Noke's fascination with the theatre. A taste for the exotic is particularly evident in his work, stemming from the fashionable oriental flavour of many operas, musicals and ballets of the time. Examples are the **Mandarin** (HN84) and the Eastern **Cobbler** (HN542).

(Fig. 6) A specialized collection of figurines from the performing arts would have to include these early and fine examples depicting 'Henry Irving as Cardinal Wolsey' from Shakespeare's 'Henry VIII,' and 'Doris Keane as Cavallini' from the 1915 play 'Romance.'

An interesting collection could include famous stage personalities of the past, such as the American actress **Doris Keane** (HN90), and more recent stars from the silver screen such as **Groucho Marx** (HN2777) and **Charlie Chaplin** (HN2771). As well as these classic clowns of the cinema, there are also lots of circus clowns by Mary Nicoll and Bill Harper to collect. Their ancestors of mirth, the court jesters, have also been popular characters in the figures collection since the earliest days, notably **Jack Point** (HN85) and **The Wandering Minstrel** (HN1224) from Gilbert and Sullivan's famous operettas.

The ballet has been a fertile source of inspiration for Doulton modellers from the great **Pavlova** (HN487) in her most famous role as 'The Dying Swan' to aspiring young dancers practising in frilly tutus, such as **Little Ballerina** (HN3395). Like many young girls, Peggy Davies had ambitions to be a ballerina and as a result she contributed many delightful studies of dancers, including **Coppelia** (HN2115) and **Giselle** (HN2140).

Music lovers can seek out figures playing instruments, whether they be an elegant orchestra of **Lady Musicians** or a precocious violinist such as **The Young Master** (HN2872). Even street performers, such as **The Organ Grinder** (HN2173) and **The Punch and Judy Man** (HN2765), could be included in this colourful revue of the world of entertainment.

Literature

Book lovers will enjoy all of the characters from literature that have been portrayed in the figure collection over the years. Classical myths, Eastern romances, European folklore and English classics have all provided inspiration for individual figures and series. Art Director Charles Noke was a great admirer of Shakespeare and he modelled the great bard himself for the Vellum range, as well as several of his characters. The novels of Charles Dickens were an even greater influence and there are several sets of his famous characters, including the very collectable miniatures. Children's books have also been a fertile source of ideas and, as well as the obvious collection of **Characters from Children's Literature**, there have been figures based on nursery rhymes, Kate Greenaway's picture books and Victorian classics, such as 'Treasure Island'. The figure of this name depicts a young boy poring over the pages of Stevenson's great adventure yarn and pages from the book can be enjoyed with the aid of a magnifying glass. There are many other 'readers' in the figures range, including several others with legible books and this has become a particularly popular collecting theme. A representative display might include the scholarly **Professor** (HN2281) with his nose in a book, **The Wizard** (HN2877) who is consulting his book of spells, or some of the daydreaming fair ladies who rest closed books on their laps.

History

The figures collection is like a historical pageant with famous people from all ages commemorated in clay. It is to be expected that an English company would pay homage to British national heroes and heroines such as **Florence Nightingale** (HN3144) and more recently **Winston Churchill** (HN3057), but there are also many historical personalities from other countries. It would be possible for patriotic Americans to form a 'Stars and Stripes' collection, which might include the **Soldiers of the Revolution** or the **Characters from Williamsburg**

series. Canadians can look for the unusual Mountie busts of **R.C.M.P. 1973** (HN2547) and **R.C.M.P. 1873** (HN2555) or the portrait figure of **Sir John A. MacDonald** (HN2860).

Those interested in military history could seek out the rare First World War soldiers, **Digger** (HN3221-2) and **Blighty** (HN323) or the **Drummer Boy** (HN2679) from the Napoleonic Wars whilst naval historians could add **Captain Cook** (HN2889) or **The Captain** (HN2260) to a general seafaring collection.

The current British royal family has proved to be a popular collection in recent years and many of the Queen's illustrious ancestors have also been portrayed as Doulton figures. **Henry VIII** (HN370, 1792 & 3350) and **King Charles I** (HN404) are good examples. As well as the reigning monarchs, there have also been portraits of their consorts, courtiers and even one of their courtesans, **Nell Gwynne** (HN1882)!

Collecting by Size

For collectors with limited display space miniature figures are particularly appealing. The M series was launched in 1932 but there had been miniature figures in the HN range before that, notably the tiny Dickens characters which were re-numbered in line with all the new introductions. By 1949, there were 24 Dickens characters in the M series and they continued in production with minor alterations until 1981-3.

The majority of the miniature fair ladies were scaled down versions of existing figures by Leslie Harradine. Although only 3 to 4 inches tall, the detailing of the costumes and accessories is exceptional, with tiny flower baskets 3/4 inch across and parasols less than an inch long. As in the standard range of the 1930s, there was also a wide range of colourways and **Polly Peachum** has been found in at least 15 different costumes. Unfortunately, rising labour costs led to the withdrawal of the miniature ladies by 1949 and, as many had only been made for about 10 years, they are very elusive for today's collector. Consequently, their prices do not match their diminutive size and they can cost as much, or more, than their standard size counterparts.

Miniature figures were revived in 1988 when the Royal Doulton International Collectors Club commissioned a tiny version of the ever popular **Top o' the Hill** (HN2126). More fair ladies followed in quick succession, with special rich colourways produced exclusively for Michael Doulton's signature collection. All have been allocated HN numbers and are reduced versions of popular figures in the current range. A selection of miniature character figures was introduced in 1989 but these were not well received. Several were quickly withdrawn so they will no doubt become hard to find in the future.

Also easily accommodated in a small display area are the figures of young girls dressed in fashions of the past. These range in size from 4 to 6 inches tall and some, such as **Dinky Do** (HN1678) and **Monica** (HN1467) have been in continuous production for over 50 years testifying to the appeal of this scale and subject matter.

Today, the average Doulton fair lady stands around 8 inches tall, whilst seated subjects in proportion measure around 6 inches. Limited editions and character figures tend to be a little larger, averaging 9 inches for standing subjects. Eric Griffiths, the former director of Sculpture, favoured larger scale figures, particularly for character portraits, as he believed a better likeness could be achieved. Consequently his figure of **Lord Olivier as Richard III** (HN2881) is above average size. He also introduced the **Haute Ensemble** series of tall, slender ladies and the attenuated **Images** and **Reflections** series.

In the past, there was much more variety of scale in the collection and figures of more than 12 inches in height were not unusual. **The Welsh Girl** (HN39) and **Lady With Shawl** (HN447) are good examples. Some large scale figures from the past now form the **Prestige** collection and **Princess Badoura** (HN2081), at 20 inches in height, is the largest in the range.

Collecting by Series

Numerous collectors subscribe to Royal Doulton's established series of figures, many of which are limited editions. In these cases the company has already chosen all the characters to fit a specific theme and has defined the limits of the collection so there are fewer decisions required than with the more general themes already discussed. This method also allows collectors to budget for forthcoming annual introductions in the more expensive limited edition series.

Some of the recently discontinued series are becoming increasingly difficult to find and it could take some time to find all 18 of the **Kate Greenaway** figures or all 24 **Dickens** miniatures. There always seems to be one or two figures in a series which are rarer than the others and prices rise accordingly. For example, **Tom Bombadil** (HN2924) is a particularly elusive model in the now desirable **Tolkien** series. Occasionally complete series come up for sale but for some collectors that spoils the fun of the chase.

Limited Editions Series

Age of Chivalry
Age of Innocence
Children of the Blitz
Dancers of the World
Gainsborough Ladies
Gentle Arts
King Henry VIII's Wives
Lady Musicians
Les Femmes Fatales
Les Saisons
Movie Comedians
Myths and Maidens
National Society for the Prevention
  of Cruelty to Children Centenary (NSPCC)
Queens of the Realm
Reynolds Ladies
Royal Family
Ships Figureheads
Soldiers of the Revolution
Sweet and Twenties

Other Series

Beggar's Opera
Characters from Children's Literature
Childhood Days
Dickens Characters
Enchantment
Figure of the Year
Flowers of the Month
Four Seasons
Gilbert and Sullivan
Haute Ensemble
Images
Kate Greenaway
Ladies of Covent Garden
Michael Doulton Exclusives
Nursery Rhymes
Period Figures in English History
Reflections
Royal Doulton International Collectors
  Club Exclusives
Vanity Fair
Williamsburg
Tolkien

MAKING DOULTON FIGURES

There are many people involved in the creation of each Royal Doulton figure, beginning with the artist who works with modelling clay to transform an image in his head, or on paper, into a three dimensional sculpture.

When the original model is complete it is taken to the mould maker, whose years of experience enable him to cut up the figure into separate parts so that a master mould, known as a block, can be produced. Complex figures are divided into many parts and a plaster of Paris mould is made from the original head, torso, arms, skirts and so on. Working moulds are made as required and care is taken to ensure that they are replaced regularly during production so that the crisp detail of the original is maintained.

Liquid clay, known as slip, is gently poured into each mould by the caster and once the body has set to the required thickness the excess slip is poured out. At this stage the parts of the figure are carefully removed from the mould and, as the clay is still very fragile, they are pieced together using slip as an adhesive.

Before the complete figure has been thoroughly dried, the seams are sponged away in a process known as fettling. The piece is then ready for its first firing. It is removed from the kiln, having shrunk to its 'biscuit' state and then, if it is a character figure, it is ready for painting. Painting takes place at this stage because pieces are coloured under-glaze to give the more rugged effect expected of these subjects.

Fair lady figures in their biscuit state are dipped into a vat of glaze and fired again before decorating begins. The dresses and accessories are painted with on-glaze colours and to achieve the rich colour effects, like the deep red, several applications of colour are needed. Each layer requires a separate firing. When the costume decoration is complete, the faces of the fair ladies are painted by the most experienced artists and a final firing ensures that the colours are permanently sealed under the glaze.

BODIES AND GLAZES

The fair lady figures are made from bone china which is a traditionally British body, composed of China clay, Cornish stone and bone ash. Most character figures are made from English Porcelain, a whiter coloured body formerly known as English Translucent China, which was pioneered by Royal Doulton chemists in 1959. Before the invention of English Porcelain, many Doulton figures were produced in an earthenware body, which is fired to a lower temperature than china and is more porous. There are slight differences in size between figures made of earthenware and those made of porcelain and colours often look different on the two bodies.

Most Royal Doulton figures have a brilliant glossy glaze. In the early 1970s, however, some matt figures were produced and this matt finish was also used for limited edition subjects as it enhanced the intricate modelling and gave a distinctive effect. A matt glazed black basalt body has been used more recently in the **Images** range of modern style sculptures.

There is obviously much more to a Royal Doulton figure than first meets the eye and collectors can enjoy watching the creative process during a tour of the Royal Doulton factory. For opening times and tour bookings contact: The Tours Organizer, Royal Doulton, Nile Street, Burslem, Stoke-on-Trent ST6 2AJ.

CARE AND REPAIR

A Royal Doulton figure collection can be enjoyed indefinitely as long as care is taken when handling and cleaning. When dusting in situ, a soft cosmetic brush or photographic lens brush is useful for getting into tight corners, particularly hand-modelled floral bouquets and baskets. When necessary, glazed figures should be washed in luke-warm water, using a mild liquid detergent, then rinsed thoroughly and dried naturally or buffed gently with a soft cloth. It is important that water does not get inside the figure so the hole in the bottom should be blocked up beforehand, perhaps with a cork or a rubber bung. Care should be taken not to knock figures against the tap or against each other as this may cause chips or imperceptible cracks in the glaze which could open up at a later date.

If the worst does happen, a professional restorer should be consulted as they can work 'miracles' with damaged figures. Whether it be a small chip or a shattered body, pieces can be mended so that the repair is invisible to all but the most experienced eye. It follows that when buying figures on the secondary market, it is advisable to check for restorations. The head, the arms and any projecting accessories are the most vulnerable parts, so look at these areas carefully in a good light. Repaired cracks can sometimes be detected by looking inside the figure through the hole in the bottom. There are special ultraviolet lamps which highlight some types of restoration but these are not widely used, except by professionals. Restored figures should be priced less than perfect examples, according to the amount of damage and the quality of the repair. Always enquire about the condition of a piece when buying, as a reputable dealer will stand by any guarantees they give regarding restorations.

CURRENT AND DISCONTINUED FIGURES

Figures which are produced at the Royal Doulton factories today are generally referred to as 'current' whilst models which are no longer made are variously described as 'withdrawn', 'retired' or 'discontinued'. A current figure might have been in the range for a long time and one or two have been in continuous production for over fifty years, for example **The Old Balloon Seller**. Because this figure is still generally available today, a 1930s version is unlikely to be worth more than the current model, even though it is older and probably differs slightly in appearance, due to changes in body and paint formulations over the years. It is worth remembering, however, that originally it would have been purchased for just a few pounds or dollars.

Figures are discontinued on an annual basis in order to make way for new introductions. There is a limit to the number of models the factory can produce, or the retailer can display, so eventually some have to go. In some cases the choice is easy as it is apparent that all the collectors who want a particular model have already purchased it and world-wide sales are decreasing. Occasionally figures disappear after only a couple of years in the range and these short-lived models often become very desirable on the secondary market.

The number of figures withdrawn each year varies enormously. Sometimes it is less than 12 a year and other times, after a major reassessment of the range, there might be 50 or so. The first withdrawals took place during the Second World War and it is unlikely that more than 2,000 of each of the early models were produced. This is less than many limited editions, so it is not surprising that these pieces are amongst the most desirable figures on the secondary market today. Older figures with short production runs are obviously less likely to appear in the market-place than those that were made for many years. However, this alone does not affect the price, which will probably also be governed by aesthetic considerations and market awareness.

Since 1990, Royal Doulton has given advance notice of the figures to be withdrawn so that collectors can purchase retiring pieces before they become more difficult to find. Such pieces are all marked on their bases 'final year of issue'.

LIMITED EDITIONS, PRESTIGE FIGURES AND SPECIAL EDITIONS

In 1933, discerning customers were offered a range of specially commissioned figures by Richard Garbe RA, a distinguished sculptor of the day. Inspired by his sculptures in other media, the new figures were larger than most others in the HN collection and many were embellished with gold. In order to emphasise their prestige status, it was announced that only a limited number of each model would be produced and the edition size was marked on the base. The editions ranged from 25 to 150 pieces and took several years to sell out. Not surprisingly, they are now very desirable on the secondary market. At the same time, Charles Noke introduced a limited edition figure of King Henry VIII, which is more typical of Doulton's later limited editions in terms of subject matter, scale and decoration.

During the 1950s, some of the largest and most impressive figures in the range were revamped to form the basis of a Prestige collection. Three of these subjects were originally modelled by Charles Noke, **The Moor** (HN2082), **Jack Point** (HN2080), and **King Charles** (HN2084), and they are still produced today, although in very limited quantities to special order. The most expensive prestige figure of all, **Princess Badoura** (HN2081), was introduced in 1952. The painting and gilding on this figure take about eight weeks to complete, hence the high cost. Repeated kiln firings and complex model assembly also add to the expense of producing prestige pieces, as with the spectacular **Matador and Bull** (HN2324), which was modelled by Peggy Davies in 1964. Two more of Peggy's ambitious large scale sculptures were produced in limited editions of 500 each, **The Indian Brave** (HN2376) produced in 1967 and **The Palio** (HN2428) of 1971. However, she is better known today for her limited edition collections of **Lady Musicians** (1970 - 76) and **Dancers of the World** (1977 - 82). These highly detailed and richly decorated models were each limited to 750 pieces and were introduced at the rate of one or two each year, complete with presentation boxes and certificates of authenticity. This has become the pattern for most of the company's limited editions today, although edition sizes have grown to reflect increased demand.

Special occasions have also inspired limited editions and there are portrait figures celebrating Royal weddings, birthdays and coronation anniversaries. The recent Expo'92 in Seville has prompted a limited edition colourway of **Mantilla** (HN3192) and a special edition of **Discovery** (HN3428), a reduced version of the symbolic sculpture in the British Pavilion. This piece was offered exclusively to members of the Royal Doulton International Collectors Club. The opportunity to purchase limited editions and special editions of figures is one of the benefits of joining the Club. Generally speaking, **special** editions are limited by the offer period, which in the case of the early Doulton Club commissions was six months. The term is also used more widely to describe special products commissioned by independent companies which are not individually numbered on their bases nor accompanied by a certificate of authenticity.

For the collector looking for something extra special, Royal Doulton limited and special editions are in great demand today and popular subjects are often quickly oversubscribed. It is important, therefore, to respond quickly to the announcements for new releases. Discontinued limited editions command premium prices in the secondary market, particularly if they are sold with their original literature and packaging and the first of a collection of six or twelve figures is usually the hardest to find.

COLOURWAYS AND VARIATIONS

From the earliest days of the figures collection, some of the most popular models have been produced in alternative colourways. The first fair lady figure, **The Crinoline**, was originally offered in a plain lilac dress or with a floral design. Each colourway was assigned a different HN number to distinguish the decorative treatment. Charles Noke's study of **A Jester** has been available in 12 different coloured suits as well as in Parian and Vellum finishes. Noke also experimented with different glaze effects on figures, including a lustrous red flambé, a mottled blue green Titanian, a glittering gold and a dark brown to simulate bronze. These were produced only in very limited numbers and were not given HN references.

During the 1920s, when more master painters joined the figure painting department, colour effects and patterns became more ambitious. The lady figures were dressed in all of the fashionable fabrics of the day with floral designs, polka dots, stripes, diapers and checks painted by hand. It was unusual to have a lady figure in just one colourway and in the case of **Victorian Lady**, there was a choice of 15 varied designs.

After the Second World War the collection was rationalized and alternative colourways became less common. However, the idea was revived during the 1980s, initially for special occasions such as Michael Doulton tours. A new colourway of **Wistful** (HN2472) was devised exclusively for his personal appearances in 1985. Since then, five figures have been given a new look for this purpose. Colourways have also been commissioned by independent retailers and in some cases the name has been changed as well as the colours. For example, a variation of **Adrienne** (HN2304) was commissioned to promote Joan's Gift Shop in Scotland and was renamed **Joan** (HN2217).

Alternative colourways now appear regularly in the general range, sometimes with a new name, and it is not just fair ladies which ring the changes. Character figures have also been given a fresh new look from time to time. **The Lobster Man**, for instance, is available with two different coloured sweaters (HN2317 and HN2323).

During the 1970s, former Art Director Eric Griffiths experimented with matt glazes but these were not a commercial success and most of the models were quickly withdrawn. An exception is **The Judge** (HN2443) which was changed from a matt to a glossy finish because it was so popular.

From time to time alterations have been made to models after they have been introduced, usually to decrease the risk of damage during production or in transit. In early models of **The Carpet Seller** (HN1464) for example, the character's hand is outstretched, whereas in later models the fingers are clasped around the carpet, making them less vulnerable to breakage. The figure of **Masque** (HN2554) also had to be modified as the long metal handle of the mask was easily broken. It was removed and the hand was remodelled. Eagle eyed collectors will also notice that early models of **Autumn Breezes** (HN1911) have two feet peeping out from under the dress whilst later models have only one.

There are some keen collectors who enjoy tracking down the different model and colour variations but the majority take advantage of the wide choice of shades and patterns to co-ordinate a new purchase with an existing display.

A GUIDE TO BACKSTAMPS AND DATING

There is a wealth of information on the base of a Royal Doulton figure and some of it will help date the piece.

Most prominent is the Royal Doulton factory mark which has featured a lion standing on a crown ever since the company was awarded the Royal Warrant in 1901. Before this honour was bestowed, the mark comprised a different style of crown and the words 'Doulton Burslem England'. This early mark is found on most of the Vellum figures modelled by Charles Noke in the 1890s.

The Royal Doulton lion and crown mark has been altered slightly over the years and this can help date the figure to a specific era. Collectors should note that the words 'Made in England' were added around 1920 so figures without this reference are usually very early models.

| 1927-1932 | 1932 -present |
| Printed or impressed | |

Often on miniature figures there was not enough room for the standard factory mark and so either part of it was used or just the words 'Doulton England'. Between 1932 and 1949 miniature figures were given M pattern numbers but earlier and later models have HN numbers.

| Miniature from 'M' Series | Miniature from 'HN' Series |

Some early figures have an impressed date on the base which gives the month, year and sometimes the day, when the mould was made (not when a particular finished piece was produced). For example, 12-10-23 represents October 12th, 1923. This practice ceased during the 1930s.

Printed numeral -
'1' stands for 1928, '2' for 1929, etc.

The precise year of manufacture, however, can be determined if the figure has a date code on the right side of the lion and crown symbol. A printed number 1 was used in 1928, when this dating system began. This system continued to number 27 in 1954. The year of manufacture can be easily calculated by adding the number on the figure to 1927. For example, a figure with the number 13 on it indicates that it was manufactured in 1940 (13+1927). Since 1990, new introductions have been marked 'first year of issue' and planned

| 1902-1922 | 1922-1927 |
| Printed or Impressed | Printed |

withdrawals 'final year of issue', which makes precise dating possible again for some figures.

Registration numbers, when they are present, indicate when the design was first registered, which could be up to a year before the figure was put into production. After the Second World War, it was usual to have several registration numbers which protected the design in Royal Doulton's main export markets but this has not been required since the early 1980s. Copyright dates have also been incorporated into the backstamp since the 1940s.

$$R^d N^o 791566$$

Registered mark

H.N.2041.
COPR.1948.
DOULTON & CO. LIMITED.
$R^d N^o$ 855287.
$R^d N^o$ 26360.
$R^d N^o$ 5772.
$R^d N^o$ 133/48.

Registered mark with copyright date

HN 2871
© ROYAL DOULTON
TABLEWARE LTD 1979

Copyright mark

Usually the design is copyrighted at least a year before production begins so, as with registration numbers, the copyright date does not necessarily indicate the year of introduction.

The HN number is particularly important as this catalogue and other reference works are designed to follow the HN sequence. Until the 1950s the HN number was written on the base by the painter so very occasionally it has been omitted. It is now incorporated in the printed backstamp along with the figure's name and copyright information. The initials stand for Harry Nixon who devised the colour schemes for the figures and recorded all the painting instructions in the pattern books. Each new decorative treatment was given an HN number, not necessarily in chronological order, and so a popular model such as **Victorian Lady** has several different numbers. Pattern number HN 1 was allocated to the figure **Darling** because of Queen Mary's interest, although it was not the first figure to be modelled.

Figures also have a model number impressed in the base but this does not normally concern collectors unless there are no other details recorded, which is sometimes the case with prototypes. Model numbers can be authenticated by referring to the shape books held in Royal Doulton's archive in Stoke-on-Trent.

Until around 1930 the figure's name was written by hand on the base and the modeller's name was

sometimes included. This practice lapsed in the general range for over 50 years but was revived in 1984 when the modeller's facsimile signature was incorporated in the backstamp.

Figure's name styles

Modeller's signature

The painters responsible for the decoration of the figures usually initial their work on the base and in recent years the individual craftsmanship of the piece has been further emphasised by the addition of the words "Hand made and hand decorated".

Backstamps on limited edition pieces have added information about the edition size and, decorative typefaces and motifs inspired by the subject are now often incorporated into the design. Special commissions, including new models, colourways and pre-releases, frequently have backstamps with details of the event being commemorated. Backstamps may also include the customer who has commissioned the piece. For example, all of the annual figures produced exclusively for Michael Doulton's tours have a special backstamp.

Although 'seconds' figures are not sold by Royal Doulton to the public, slightly faulty models can be bought by company employees at special sales and so they occasionally come on to the secondary market. They are now clearly marked with either a scored line through the backstamp or a drilled hole defacing the centre of the lion and crown symbol.

WHERE TO BUY

Discontinued Royal Doulton figures can be found in antique shops, markets and fairs as well as auction houses. Specialist dealers in Royal Doulton figures attend many of the venues and events below.

UNITED KINGDOM

Auction Houses

Phillips
101 New Bond Street
London W1

Christie's South Kensington
85 Old Brompton Road
London SW5

Bonhams
Montpelier Street
London SW7

Sotheby's
Summer's Place
Billingshurst, West Sussex

Louis Taylor
Percy Street
Hanley, Stoke-on-Trent

Peter Wilson
Victoria Gallery
Market Street
Nantwich, Cheshire

Antique Fairs

UK Doulton Collectors Fair
Park Lane Hotel
Piccadilly
London W1

Stafford International Doulton Fair
Stafford County Showground
Stafford

Antique Markets

Portobello Road Market
London W11
Saturday only

New Caledonian Market
Bermondsey Square
London SE1
Friday morning

Alfie's Antique Market
13-25 Church Street
London NW8
Tuesday - Saturday

Camden Passage Market
(off Upper Street)
London N1
Wednesday and Saturday

USA

Auction Houses

Phillips New York
406 East 79th Street
New York, NY 10021

Antique Fairs

Florida Doulton Convention
Sheraton Design Centre
Fort Lauderdale, Florida

Doulton Show
Sheraton Poste House
Cherry Hill, New Jersey

Doulton Show
Holiday Inn
Independence, Ohio

CANADA

Auction Houses

D & J Ritchies
429 Richmond Street
Toronto, Ontario, M5A 1R1

Antique Shows

The International Doulton Collectors Weekend
Sheraton Toronto East Hotel
2035 Kennedy Road
Scarborough, Ontario

Antique Markets

Harbourfront Antique Market
390 Queen's Quay West
Toronto, Ontario
(Tuesday - Sunday)

PLACES TO VISIT

Royal Doulton Factory Tour
and the Sir Henry Doulton Gallery
Nile Street
Burslem, Stoke-on-Trent
For opening times and tour information telephone
(0782) 744766

CLUBS AND SOCIETIES

The Royal Doulton International Collectors Club was founded in 1980 to provide an information service on all aspects of the company's products, past and present. The Club's magazine 'Gallery' is published four times a year and local branches also publish newsletters. There are also several regional groups in the USA, which meet for lectures and other events and some publish newsletters. Contact the USA branch for further information.

Headquarters and UK Branch

Royal Doulton
Minton House
London Road
Stoke-on-Trent, ST4 7QD

Australian Branch

Royal Doulton Australia Pty Ltd.
17-23 Merriwa Street, Gordon,
Australia NSW 2072

Canadian Branch

Royal Doulton Canada Inc.
850 Progress Avenue,
Scarborough, Ontario, M1H 3C4

New Zealand Branch

Royal Doulton
P.O. Box 2059
Auckland, New Zealand

USA Branch

Royal Doulton USA Inc.
P.O. Box 1815
Somerset, New Jersey 08873

FURTHER READING

Figures and Character Jugs

Royal Doulton Figures by Desmond Eyles, Richard Dennis and Louise Irvine
The Charlton Standard Catalogue of Royal Doulton Jugs by Jean Dale
The Character Jug Collectors Handbook by Kevin Pearson
Collecting Character and Toby Jugs by Jocelyn Lukins
The Doulton Figure Collectors Handbook by Kevin Pearson

General

The Doulton Story by Paul Atterbury and Louise Irvine
Royal Doulton Series Wares by Louise Irvine (Vols 1-4)
Royal Doulton Bunnykins Figures by Louise Irvine
Bunnykins Collectors Book by Louise Irvine
Limited Edition Loving Cups and Jugs by Louise Irvine and Richard Dennis
Doulton for the Collector by Jocelyn Lukins
Doulton Kingsware Flasks by Jocelyn Lukins
Collecting Doulton Animals by Jocelyn Lukins
Doulton Burslem Advertising Wares by Jocelyn Lukins
Doulton Lambeth Advertising Wares by Jocelyn Lukins
The Doulton Lambeth Wares by Desmond Eyles
The Doulton Burslem Wares by Desmond Eyles
Hannah Barlow by Peter Rose
George Tinworth by Peter Rose
Sir Henry Doulton Biography by Edmund Gosse
Phillips Collectors Guide by Catherine Braithwaite
Collecting Doulton Magazine Edited by Alan Blakeman, BBR Publishing

HN SERIES

HN 1
Darling
Style One
Designer: C. Vyse
Height: 7 3/4", 19.5 cm
Issued: 1913-1928
Colour: Light grey
Varieties: HN 1319, 1371,
           1372

U.S.:	**$2,200.00**
Can.:	**$1,500.00**
Ster.:	**£ 600.00**

HN 2
Elizabeth Fry
Designer: C. Vyse
Height: 17", 43.2 cm
Issued: 1913-1938
Colour: Light blue,
           green base
Varieties: HN 2A

U.S.:	**$6,000.00**
Can.:	**$5,000.00**
Ster.:	**£2,000.00**

Unpainted variety also known

HN 2A
Elizabeth Fry
Designer: C. Vyse
Height: 17", 43.2 cm
Issued: 1913-1938
Colour: Light blue,
           blue base
Varieties: HN 2

U.S.:	**$6,000.00**
Can.:	**$5,000.00**
Ster.:	**£2,000.00**

HN 3
Milking Time
Designer: P. Stabler
Height: 6 1/2", 16.5 cm
Colour: Blue dress,
           white apron
Issued: 1913-1938
Varieties: HN 306

U.S.:	**Extremely**
Can.:	**Rare**
Ster.:	

Only three known to exist

HN 4
Picardy Peasant (woman)
Designer: P. Stabler
Height: 9 1/4", 23.5 cm
Colour: Blue and white
Issued: 1913-1938
Varieties: HN 5, 17A, 351,
           513

U.S.:	**$2,700.00**
Can.:	**$2,500.00**
Ster.:	**£ 850.00**

HN 5
Picardy Peasant (woman)
Designer: P. Stabler
Height: 9 1/2", 24.0 cm
Colour: Grey
Issued: 1913-1938
Varieties: HN 4, 17A, 351,
           513

U.S.:	**Extremely**
Can.:	**Rare**
Ster.:	

Photograph
Not
Available

HN 6
Dunce
Designer: C.J. Noke
Height: 10 1/2", 26.7 cm
Colour: Light blue
Issued: 1913-1938
Varieties: HN 310, 357

U.S.:	**Extremely**
Can.:	**Rare**
Ster.:	

Only two known to exist

HN 7
Pedlar Wolf
Designer: C.J. Noke
Height: 5 1/2", 14.0 cm
Colour: Blue and black
Issued: 1913-1938

U.S.:	**Extremely**
Can.:	**Rare**
Ster.:	

Only two known to exist

HN 8
The Crinoline
Designer: G. Lambert
Height: 6 1/4", 15.8 cm
Colour: Lavender
Issued: 1913-1938
Varieties: HN 9, 9A, 21, 21A,
413, 566, 628

U.S.: $2,500.00
Can.: $2,500.00
Ster.: £ 800.00

HN 9
The Crinoline
Designer: G. Lambert
Height: 6 1/4", 15.8 cm
Colour: Light green,
flowers on skirt
Issued: 1913-1938
Varieties: HN 8, 9A, 21, 21A,
413, 566, 628

U.S.: $2,500.00
Can.: $2,500.00
Ster.: £ 800.00

HN 9A
The Crinoline
Designer: G. Lambert
Height: 6 1/4", 15.8 cm
Colour: Light green,
no flowers
Issued: 1913-1938
Varieties: HN 8, 9, 21, 21A,
413, 566, 628

U.S.: Extremely
Can.: Rare
Ster.:

HN 10
Madonna of the Square
Designer: P. Stabler
Height: 7", 17.8 cm
Colour: Lavender
Issued: 1913-1938
Varieties: HN 10A, 11, 14,
27, 326, 573, 576,
594, 613, 764,
1968, 1969, 2034

U.S.: $2,000.00
Can.: $2,000.00
Ster.: £ 650.00

HN 10A
Madonna of the Square
Designer: P. Stabler
Height: 7", 17.8 cm
Colour: Green & blue
Issued: 1913-1938
Varieties: HN 10, 11, 14, 27,
326, 573, 576, 594,
613, 764, 1968,
1969, 2034

U.S.: Extremely
Can.: Rare
Ster.:

HN 11
Madonna of the Square
Designer: P. Stabler
Height: 7", 17.8 cm
Colour: Grey
Issued: 1913-1938
Varieties: HN 10, 10A, 14, 27,
326, 573, 576, 594,
613, 764, 1968,
1969, 2034

U.S.: Extremely
Can.: Rare
Ster.:

HN 12
Baby
Designer: C.J. Noke
Height: 4 3/4", 12.0 cm
Colour: Light blue
Issued: 1913-1938

U.S.: Extremely
Can.: Rare
Ster.:

Only two known to exist

HN 13
Picardy Peasant (man)
Designer: P. Stabler
Height: 9", 22.9 cm
Colour: Blue costume
with white cap
Issued: 1913-1938
Varieties: HN 17, 19

U.S.: Extremely
Can.: Rare
Ster.:

HN 14
Madonna of the Square
Designer: P. Stabler
Height: 7", 17.8 cm
Colour: Blue
Issued: 1913-1938
Varieties: HN 10, 10A, 11, 27, 326, 573, 576, 594, 613, 764, 1968, 1969, 2034

U.S.: $2,000.00
Can.: $2,000.00
Ster.: £ 650.00

HN 15
The Sleepy Scholar
Designer: W. White
Height: 6 3/4", 17.2 cm
Colour: Blue
Issued: 1913-1938
Varieties: HN 16, 29

U.S.: $3,700.00
Can.: $3,000.00
Ster.: £1,200.00

HN 16
The Sleepy Scholar
Designer: W. White
Height: 6 3/4", 17.2 cm
Colour: Green
Issued: 1913-1938
Varieties: HN 15, 29

U.S.: $3,700.00
Can.: $3,000.00
Ster.: £1,200.00

HN 17
Picardy Peasant (man)
Designer: P. Stabler
Height: 9 1/2", 24.0 cm
Colour: Blue
Issued: 1913-1938
Varieties: HN 13, 19,

U.S.: Extremely
Can.: Rare
Ster.:

HN 17A
Picardy Peasant (woman)
Designer: P. Stabler
Height: 9 1/2", 24.0 cm
Colour: Green
Issued: 1913-1938
Varieties: HN 4, 5, 351, 513

U.S.: Extremely
Can.: Rare
Ster.:

HN 18
Pussy
Designer: F.C. Stone
Height: 7 3/4", 19.7 cm
Colour: Light blue
Issued: 1913-1938
Varieties: HN 325, 507; also called "The Black Cat"

U.S.: Extremely
Can.: Rare
Ster.:

Only five known to exist

HN 19
Picardy Peasant (man)
Designer: P. Stabler
Height: 9 1/2", 24.0 cm
Colour: Green
Issued: 1913-1938
Varieties: HN 13, 17

U.S.: Extremely
Can.: Rare
Ster.:

HN 20
The Coquette
Designer: W. White
Height: 9 1/4", 23.5 cm
Colour: Blue
Issued: 1913-1938
Varieties: HN 20A, 37

U.S.: $3,500.00
Can.: $3,000.00
Ster.: £1,300.00

HN 20A
The Coquette
Designer: W. White
Height: 9 1/4", 23.5 cm
Colour: Green
Issued: 1913-1938
Varieties: HN 20, 37

U.S.: $3,000.00
Can.: $3,000.00
Ster.: £1,200.00

HN 21
The Crinoline
Designer: G. Lambert
Height: 6 1/4", 15.8 cm
Colour: Yellow with rosebuds
Issued: 1913-1938
Varieties: HN 8, 9, 9A, 21A, 413, 566, 628

U.S.: $2,700.00
Can.: $2,700.00
Ster.: £ 900.00

HN 21A
The Crinoline
Designer: G. Lambert
Height: 6 1/4", 15.8 cm
Colour: Yellow, no rosebuds
Issued: 1913-1938
Varieties: HN 8, 9, 9A, 21, 413, 566, 628

U.S.: Extremely
Can.: Rare
Ster.:

HN 22
The Lavender Woman
Designer: P. Stabler
Height: 8 1/4", 21.0 cm
Colour: Light blue
Issued: 1913-1938
Varieties: HN 23, 23A, 342, 569, 744

U.S.: $5,000.00
Can.: $4,000.00
Ster.: £1,200.00

HN 23
The Lavender Woman
Designer: P. Stabler
Height: 8 1/4", 21.0 cm
Colour: Green
Issued: 1913-1938
Varieties: HN 22, 23A, 342, 569, 744

U.S.: Extremely
Can.: Rare
Ster.:

HN 23A
The Lavender Woman
Designer: P. Stabler
Height: 8 1/4", 21.0 cm
Colour: Blue and green
Issued: 1913-1938
Varieties: HN 22, 23, 342, 569, 744

U.S.: Extremely
Can.: Rare
Ster.:

HN 24
Sleep
Designer: P. Stabler
Height: 8 1/4", 21.0 cm
Colour: Light blue
Issued: 1913-1938
Varieties: HN 24A, 25, 25A, 424, 692, 710

U.S.: $2,400.00
Can.: $2,500.00
Ster.: £ 800.00

HN 24A
Sleep
Designer: P. Stabler
Height: 8 1/4", 21.0 cm
Colour: Dark blue
Issued: 1913-1938
Varieties: HN 24, 25, 25A, 424, 692, 710

U.S.: $2,400.00
Can.: $2,500.00
Ster.: £ 800.00

HN 25
Sleep
Designer:	P. Stabler
Height:	8 1/4", 21.0 cm
Colour:	Dark green
Issued:	1913-1938
Varieties:	HN 24, 24A, 25A, 424, 692, 710
U.S.:	**$2,400.00**
Can.:	**$2,500.00**
Ster.:	**£ 800.00**

HN 25A
Sleep
Designer:	P. Stabler
Height:	8 1/4", 21.0 cm
Colour:	Dark Green
Issued:	1913-1938
Varieties:	HN 24, 24A, 25, 424, 692, 710
U.S.:	**Extremely**
Can.:	**Rare**
Ster.:	

HN 26
The Diligent Scholar
Designer:	W. White
Height:	7", 17.8 cm
Colour:	Mottled brown and green
Issued:	1913-1938
Varieties:	Also called "The Attentive Scholar"
U.S.:	**$3,500.00**
Can.:	**$3,000.00**
Ster.:	**£1,200.00**

HN 27
Madonna of the Square
Designer:	P. Stabler
Height:	7", 17.8 cm
Colour:	Blue
Issued:	1913-1938
Varieties:	HN 10, 10A, 11, 14, 326, 573, 576, 594, 613, 764, 1968, 1969, 2034
U.S.:	**Extremely**
Can.:	**Rare**
Ster.:	

Photograph
Not
Available

HN 28
Motherhood
Designer:	P. Stabler
Height:	8", 20.3 cm
Colour:	Light blue
Issued:	1913-1938
Varieties:	HN 30, 303
U.S.:	**$5,000.00**
Can.:	**$5,000.00**
Ster.:	**£1,800.00**

HN 29
The Sleepy Scholar
Designer:	W. White
Height:	6 3/4", 17.2 cm
Colour:	Brown
Issued:	1913-1938
Varieties:	HN 15, 16
U.S.:	**$3,700.00**
Can.:	**$3,500.00**
Ster.:	**£1,400.00**

HN 30
Motherhood
Designer:	P. Stabler
Height:	8", 20.3 cm
Colour:	White and blue
Issued:	1913-1938
Varieties:	HN 28, 303
U.S.:	**$5,000.00**
Can.:	**$5,000.00**
Ster.:	**£1,800.00**

HN 31
The Return of Persephone
Designer:	C. Vyse
Height:	16", 40.6 cm
Colour:	Grey and grey-blue
Issued:	1913-1938
U.S.:	**Extremely**
Can.:	**Rare**
Ster.:	

Only one known to exist.

HN 32
Child on Crab
Designer: C.J. Noke
Height: 5 1/4", 13.3 cm
Colour: Pale blue, green and brown
Issued: 1913-1938
Varieties: Also known in flambé

U.S.:	$4,000.00
Can.:	$4,000.00
Ster.:	£1,500.00

HN 33
An Arab
Designer: C.J. Noke
Height: 15 3/4", 40.0 cm
Colour: Dark blue, green
Issued: 1913-1938
Varieties: HN 343, 378; also called "The Moor" HN 1308, 1366, 1425, 1657, 2082

U.S.:	$3,000.00
Can.:	$3,000.00
Ster.:	£1,000.00

HN 34
A Moorish Minstrel
Designer: C.J. Noke
Height: 13 1/2", 34.3 cm
Colour: Deep purple
Issued: 1913-1938
Varieties: HN 364, 415, 797

U.S.:	$2,500.00
Can.:	$2,500.00
Ster.:	£ 900.00

Derived from Burslem figure produced in 1890's.

HN 35
Charley's Aunt
Style One
Designer: A. Toft
Height: 6 3/4", 17.2 cm
Colour: Black and white
Issued: 1913-1938
Varieties: HN 640

U.S.:	$800.00
Can.:	$750.00
Ster.:	£350.00

HN 36
The Sentimental Pierrot
Designer: C.J. Noke
Height: 5 1/2", 14.0 cm
Colour: Grey
Issued: 1914-1938
Varieties: HN 307

U.S.:	$5,000.00
Can.:	$4,000.00
Ster.:	£2,000.00

HN 37
The Coquette
Designer: W. White
Height: 9 1/4", 23.5 cm
Colour: Green
Issued: 1914-1938
Varieties: HN 20, 20A

U.S.:	$5,000.00
Can.:	$5,000.00
Ster.:	£2,000.00

HN 38
The Carpet Vendor
Style One
Designer: C.J. Noke
Height: 5 1/2", 14.0 cm
Colour: Blue and yellow
Issued: 1914-1938
Varieties: HN 76, 350

U.S.:	Extremely
Can.:	Rare
Ster.:	

Photograph
Not
Available

HN 38A
The Carpet Vendor
Style Two
Designer: C.J. Noke
Height: 6 1/4", 15.9 cm
Colour: Blue and yellow, patterned long carpet
Issued: 1914-1938
Varieties: HN 348

U.S.:	Extremely
Can.:	Rare
Ster.:	

HN 39
Myfanwy Jones
Designer: E.W. Light
Height: 12", 30.5 cm
Colour: Red, black, purple
Issued: 1914-1938
Varieties: HN 92, 456, 514, 516, 519, 520, 660, 668, 669, 701, 792; "The Welsh Girl"

U.S.:	$5,000.00
Can.:	$4,500.00
Ster.:	£2.000.00

HN 40
A Lady of the Elizabethan Period
Style One
Designer: E.W. Light
Height: 9 1/2", 24.1 cm
Colour: Orange and brown with pattern
Issued: 1914-1938
Varieties: HN 40A, 73, 411; "Elizabethan Lady"

U.S.:	Extremely
Can.:	Rare
Ster.:	

HN 40A
A Lady of the Elizabethan Period
Style One
Designer: E.W. Light
Height: 9 1/2", 24.1 cm
Colour: Orange and brown
Issued: 1914-1938
Varieties: HN 40, 73, 411; "Elizabethan Lady"

U.S.:	Extremely
Can.:	Rare
Ster.:	

HN 41
A Lady of the Georgian Period
Designer: E.W. Light
Height: 10 1/4", 26.0 cm
Colour: Gold and blue
Issued: 1914-1938
Varieties: HN 331, 444, 690, 702

U.S.:	$3,000.00
Can.:	$3,000.00
Ster.:	£1,000.00

HN 42
Robert Burns
Designer: E.W. Light
Height: 18", 45.7 cm
Colour: Brown, green and yellow
Issued: 1914-1938

U.S.:	Extremely
Can.:	Rare
Ster.:	

Only one known to exist

HN 43
A Woman of the Time of Henry VI
Designer: E.W. Light
Height: 9 1/4", 23.5 cm
Colour: Green and yellow
Issued: 1914-1938

U.S.:	Extremely
Can.:	Rare
Ster.:	

Only three known to exist

HN 44
A Lilac Shawl
Designer: C.J. Noke
Height: 8 3/4", 22.2 cm
Colour: Cream and blue
Issued: 1915-1938
Varieties: HN 44A; "In Grandma's Days" HN 339, 340, 388, 442; "The Poke Bonnet" HN 362, 612, 765

U.S.:	$2,000.00
Can.:	$2,000.00
Ster.:	£ 750.00

HN 44A
A Lilac Shawl
Designer: C.J. Noke
Height: 8 3/4", 22.2 cm
Colour: White and lilac
Issued: 1915-1938
Varieties: HN 44; "In Grandma's Days" HN 339, 340, 388, 442; "The Poke Bonnet" HN 362, 612, 765

U.S.:	$2,000.00
Can.:	$2,000.00
Ster.:	£ 750.00

HN 45
A Jester
Style One
Designer: C.J. Noke
Height: 9 1/2", 24.1 cm
Black and white
Issued: 1915-1938
Varieties: HN 71, 71A, 320,
367, 412, 426, 446,
552, 616, 627,
1295, 1702, 201

U.S.: $2,500.00
Can.: $2,000.00
Ster.: £ 850.00

HN 45A
A Jester
Style Two
Designer: C.J. Noke
Height: 10 1/4", 26.0 cm
Green and white
Issued: 1915-1938
Varieties: HN 45B, 55,
308, 630, 1333

U.S.: $3,000.00
Can.: $2,000.00
Ster.: £1,000.00

HN 45B
A Jester
Style Two
Designer: C.J. Noke
Height: 10 1/4", 26.0 cm
Colour: Red and white
Issued: 1915-1938
Varieties: HN 45A, 55, 308,
630, 1333; also
known in black
and white

U.S.: $3,000.00
Can.: $2,000.00
Ster.: £1,300.00

HN 46
The Gainsborough Hat
Designer: H. Tittensor
Height: 8 3/4", 22.2 cm
Colour: Lavender
Issued: 1915-1938
Varieties: HN 46A, 47,
329, 352, 383,
453, 675, 705

U.S.: $3,000.00
Can.: $3,000.00
Ster.: £1,200.00

HN 46A
The Gainsborough Hat
Designer: H. Tittensor
Height: 8 3/4", 22.2 cm
Colour: Lavender with
black collar
Issued: 1915-1938
Varieties: HN 46, 47,
329, 352, 383,
453, 675, 705

U.S.: $3,500.00
Can.: $3,000.00
Ster.: £1,200.00

HN 47
The Gainsborough Hat
Designer: H. Tittensor
Height: 8 3/4", 22.2 cm
Colour: Green
Issued: 1915-1938
Varieties: HN 46, 46A,
329, 352, 383,
453, 675, 705

U.S.: $3,000.00
Can.: $2,500.00
Ster.: £ 900.00

HN 48
Lady of the Fan
Designer: E.W. Light
Height: 9 1/2", 24.1 cm
Colour: Lavender
Issued: 1916-1938
Varieties: HN 52, 53, 53A,
335, 509

U.S.: $4,000.00
Can.: $3,000.00
Ster.: £1,350.00

HN 48A
Lady with Rose
Designer: E.W. Light
Height: 9 1/2", 24.1 cm
Colour: Cream and orange
Issued: 1916-1938
Varieties: HN 52A, 68,
304, 336, 515,
517, 584, 624

U.S.: $2,800.00
Can.: $3,000.00
Ster.: £1,000.00

HN 49
Under the Gooseberry Bush
Designer: C.J. Noke
Height: 3 1/2", 8.9 cm
Colour: Green and brown
Issued: 1916-1938

U.S.: $2,200.00
Can.: $2,500.00
Ster.: £ 750.00

HN 50
A Spook
Designer: H. Tittensor
Height: 7", 17.8 cm
Colour: Green robe,
black cap
Issued: 1916-1938
Varieties: HN 51, 51A,
51B, 58, 512,
625, 1218

U.S.: $2,500.00
Can.: $1,750.00
Ster.: £ 800.00

HN 51
A Spook
Designer: H. Tittensor
Height: 7", 17.8 cm
Colour: Green robe,
red cap
Issued: 1916-1938
Varieties: HN 50, 51A,
51B, 58, 512,
625, 1218; Also
known in flambé

U.S.: $3,000.00
Can.: $2,000.00
Ster.: £1,150.00

HN 51A
A Spook
Designer: H. Tittensor
Height: 7", 17.8 cm
Colour: Green robe,
black cap
Issued: 1916-1938
Varieties: HN 50, 51,
51B, 58, 512,
625, 1218

U.S.: $3,300.00
Can.: $2,300.00
Ster.: £1,300.00

HN 51B
A Spook
Designer: H. Tittensor
Height: 7", 17.8 cm
Colour: Blue robe, red cap
Issued: 1916-1938
Varieties: HN 50, 51,
51A, 58, 512,
625, 1218

U.S.: $3,300.00
Can.: $2,300.00
Ster.: £1,300.00

HN 52
Lady of the Fan
Designer: E.W. Light
Height: 9 1/2", 24.1 cm
Colour: Yellow
Issued: 1916-1938
Varieties: HN 48, 53, 53A,
335, 509

U.S.: $4,200.00
Can.: $3,750.00
Ster.: £1,500.00

HN 52A
Lady with Rose
Designer: E.W. Light
Height: 9 1/2", 24.1 cm
Colour: Yellow
Issued: 1916-1938
Varieties: HN 48A, 68,
304, 336, 515,
517, 584, 624

U.S.: $3,300.00
Can.: $3,000.00
Ster.: £1,500.00

HN 53
Lady of the Fan
Designer: E.W. Light
Height: 9 1/2", 24.1 cm
Colour: Dark Purple
Issued: 1916-1938
Varieties: HN 48, 52, 53A,
335, 509

U.S.: $3,250.00
Can.: $3,000.00
Ster.: £1,100.00

HN 53A
Lady of the Fan
Designer: E.W. Light
Height: 9", 22.9 cm
Colour: Green
Issued: 1916-1938
Varieties: HN 48, 52, 53, 335, 509

U.S.: $4,200.00
Can.: $3,750.00
Ster.: £1,500.00

HN 54
The Ermine Muff
Designer: C.J. Noke
Height: 8 1/2", 21.6 cm
Colour: Grey coat, pale green dress
Issued: 1916-1938
Varieties: HN 332, 671; also called "Lady With Ermine Muff" and "Lady Ermine"

U.S.: $2,400.00
Can.: $2,500.00
Ster.: £ 800.00

HN 55
A Jester
Style Two
Designer: C.J. Noke
Height: 10 1/4", 26.0 cm
Colour: Black and lavender
Issued: 1916-1938
Varieties: HN 45A, 45B, 308, 630, 1333

U.S.: $2,500.00
Can.: $2,250.00
Ster.: £ 800.00

HN 56
The Land of Nod
Designer: H. Tittensor
Height: 9 1/2", 24.1 cm
Colour: Ivory , green candlestick
Issued: 1916-1938
Varieties: HN 56A, 56B

U.S.: $4,500.00
Can.: $4,500.00
Ster.: £1,600.00

The owl was produced as animal figure HN 169.

HN 56A
The Land of Nod
Designer: H. Tittensor
Height: 9 1/2", 24.1 cm
Colour: Light grey, green candlestick
Issued: 1916-1938
Varieties: HN 56, 56B

U.S.: $4,500.00
Can.: $4,500.00
Ster.: £1,600.00

HN 56B
The Land of Nod
Designer: H. Tittensor
Height: 9 1/2", 24.1 cm
Colour: Light grey, red candlestick
Issued: 1916-1938
Varieties: HN 56, 56A

U.S.: $4,500.00
Can.: $4,500.00
Ster.: £1,600.00

HN 57
The Curtsey
Designer: E.W. Light
Height: 11", 27.9 cm
Colour: Orange
Issued: 1916-1938
Varieties: HN 57B, 66A, 327, 334, 363, 371, 518, 547, 629, 670

U.S.: $3,000.00
Can.: $3,000.00
Ster.: £1,200.00

HN 57A
The Flounced Skirt
Designer: E.W. Light
Height: 9 3/4", 24.7 cm
Colour: Orange
Issued: 1916-1938
Varieties: HN 66, 77, 78, 333; also called "The Bow"

U.S.: $3,000.00
Can.: $3,000.00
Ster.: £1,200.00

HN 57B
The Curtsey
Designer: E.W. Light
Height: 11", 27.9 cm
Colour: Lavender
Issued: 1916-1938
Varieties: HN 57, 66A, 327,
334, 363, 371, 518,
547, 629, 670

U.S.: $2,800.00
Can.: $3,000.00
Ster.: £1,100.00

HN 58
A Spook
Designer: H. Tittensor
Height: 7", 17.8 cm
Colour: Unknown
Issued: 1916-1938
Varieties: HN 50, 51, 51A,
51B, 512, 625,
1218

U.S.: $3,000.00
Can.: $3,000.00
Ster.: £1,200.00

HN 59
Upon Her Cheeks She Wept
Designer: L. Perugini
Height: 9", 22.8 cm
Colour: Grey dress
Issued: 1916-1938
Varieties: HN 511, 522

U.S.: $4,200.00
Can.: $3,500.00
Ster.: £1,400.00

HN 60
Shy Anne
Designer: L. Perugini
Height: 7 3/4", 19.7 cm
Colour: Blue dress with
flowers, blue bow
in hair
Issued: 1916-1938
Varieties: HN 64, 65, 568

U.S.: **Extremely**
Can.: **Rare**
Ster.:

HN 61
Katharine
Designer: E.W. Light
Height: 5 3/4", 14.6 cm
Colour: Green
Issued: 1916-1938
Varieties: HN 74, 341,
471, 615, 793

U.S.: $2,600.00
Can.: $2,500.00
Ster.: £ 900.00

Photograph
Not
Available

HN 62
A Child's Grace
Designer: L. Perugini
Height: 6 3/4", 17.2 cm
Colour: Green and black
coat with yellow
dress
Issued: 1916-1938
Varieties: HN 62A, 510

U.S.: **Extremely**
Can.: **Rare**
Ster.:

Only one known to exist

Photograph
Not
Available

HN 62A
A Child's Grace
Designer: L. Perugini
Height: 6 3/4", 17.2 cm
Colour: Green coat,
yellow dress
Issued: 1916-1938
Varieties: HN 62, 510

U.S.: **Extremely**
Can.: **Rare**
Ster.:

HN 63
The Little Land
Designer: H. Tittensor
Height: 7 1/2", 19.1 cm
Colour: Green and yellow
Issued: 1916-1938
Varieties: HN 67

U.S.: **Extremely**
Can.: **Rare**
Ster.:

HN 64
Shy Anne
Designer: L. Perugini
Height: 7 3/4", 19.7 cm
Colour: Pale blue, white
bow in hair
Issued: 1916-1938
Varieties: HN 60, 65, 568

U.S.: $3,000.00
Can.: $2,700.00
Ster.: £ 900.00

HN 65
Shy Anne
Designer: L. Perugini
Height: 7 3/4", 19.7 cm
Colour: Pale blue, dark
blue stripe around
hem of skirt
Issued: 1916-1938
Varieties: HN 60, 64, 568

U.S.: $3,500.00
Can.: $3,500.00
Ster.: £1,200.00

HN 66
The Flounced Skirt
Designer: E.W. Light
Height: 9 3/4", 24.7 cm
Colour: Lavender
Issued: 1916-1938
Varieties: HN 57A, 77, 78,
333; also called
"The Bow"

U.S.: $3,000.00
Can.: $3,000.00
Ster.: £1,000.00

HN 66A
The Curtsey
Designer: E.W. Light
Height: 11", 27.9 cm
Colour: Lavender
Issued: 1916-1938
Varieties: HN 57, 57B, 327,
334, 363, 371,
518, 547, 629, 670

U.S.: $3,000.00
Can.: $3,000.00
Ster.: £1,100.00

HN 67
The Little Land
Designer: H. Tittensor
Height: 7 1/2", 19.1 cm
Colour: Grey and yellow
Issued: 1916-1938
Varieties: HN 63

U.S.: $3,000.00
Can.: $3,000.00
Ster.: £1,200.00

HN 68
Lady With Rose
Designer: E.W. Light
Height: 9 1/2", 24.1 cm
Colour: Green and yellow
Issued: 1916-1938
Varieties: HN 48A, 52A,
304, 336, 515,
517, 584, 624

U.S.: $2,800.00
Can.: $3,000.00
Ster.: £1,000.00

HN 69
Pretty Lady
Designer: H. Tittensor
Height: 9 1/2", 24.1 cm
Colour: Blue dress
with flowers
Issued: 1916-1938
Varieties: HN 70, 302, 330,
361, 384, 565,
700, 763, 783

U.S.: $1,750.00
Can.: $1,750.00
Ster.: £ 700.00

HN 70
Pretty Lady
Designer: H. Tittensor
Height: 9 1/2", 24.1 cm
Colour: Grey
Issued: 1916-1938
Varieties: HN 69, 302, 330,
361, 384, 565,
700, 763, 783

U.S.: $1,500.00
Can.: $1,500.00
Ster.: £ 450.00

HN 71
A Jester
Style One
Designer: C.J. Noke
Height: 9", 22.9 cm
Colour: Green checks
Issued: 1917-1938
Varieties: HN 45, 71A, 320,
367, 412, 426, 446,
552, 616, 627,
1295, 1702, 2016

U.S.: $1,700.00
Can.: $2,000.00
Ster.: £ 700.00

HN 71A
A Jester
Style One
Designer: C.J. Noke
Height: 91/2", 24.1 cm
Colour: Green checks
Issued: 1917-1938
Varieties: HN 45, 71, 320,
367, 412, 426, 446,
552, 616, 627,
1295, 1702, 2016

U.S.: $1,950.00
Can.: $2,000.00
Ster.: £ 900.00

HN 72
An Orange Vendor
Designer: C.J. Noke
Height: 6 1/4". 15.9 cm
Colour: Green, white
and orange
Issued: 1917-1938
Varieties: HN 508, 521,
1966

U.S.: $1,250.00
Can.: $1,250.00
Ster.: £ 450.00

HN 73
A Lady of the
Elizabethan Period
Style One
Designer: E.W. Light
Height: 9 1/2", 24.1 cm
Colour: Dark turquoise
Issued: 1917-1938
Varieties: HN 40, 40A, 411;
also called
"Elizabethan Lady"

U.S.: $4,000.00
Can.: $4,000.00
Ster.: £1,500.00

HN 74
Katharine
Designer: E.W. Light
Height: 5 3/4", 14.6 cm
Colour: Light blue dress
with green
Issued: 1917-1938
Varieties: HN 61, 341, 471,
615, 793

U.S.: $2,600.00
Can.: $2,500.00
Ster.: £1,000.00

HN 75
Blue Beard
(With Plume on Turban)
Style One
Designer: E.W. Light
Height: 11", 27.9 cm
Colour: Light blue
Issued: 1917-1938
Varieties: HN 410

U.S.: $6,500.00
Can.: $6,500.00
Ster.: £2,700.00

HN 76
The Carpet Vendor
Style One
Designer: C.J. Noke
Height: 5 1/2", 14.0 cm
Colour: Blue and orange
Issued: 1917-1938
Varieties: HN 38, 350; also
known in flambé

U.S.: $4,500.00
Can.: $3,750.00
Ster.: £1,200.00

HN 77
The Flounced Skirt
Designer: E.W. Light
Height: 9 3/4", 24.7 cm
Colour: Yellow dress
with black
Issued: 1917-1938
Varieties: HN 57A, 66, 78,
333; also called
"The Bow"

U.S.: $3,000.00
Can.: $3,000.00
Ster.: £1,000.00

HN 78
The Flounced Skirt
Designer: E.W. Light
Height: 9 3/4", 24.7 cm
Colour: Yellow dress with flowers
Issued: 1917-1938
Varieties: HN 57A, 66, 77, 333; also called "The Bow"

U.S.: $3,800.00
Can.: $3,500.00
Ster.: £1,300.00

Photograph
Not
Available

HN 79
Shylock
Designer: C.J. Noke
Height: Unknown
Colour: Multi-coloured robe, yellow sleeves
Issued: 1917-1938
Varieties: HN 317

U.S.: **Extremely**
Can.: **Rare**
Ster.: Only one known

Photograph
Not
Available

HN 80
Fisherwoman
Designer: Unknown
Height: 11 3/4", 29.8 cm
Colour: Lavender, pink and green
Issued: 1917-1938
Varieties: HN 349, 359, 631; "Waiting For The Boats" and "Looking For The Boats"

U.S.: **None**
Can.: **known**
Ster.: **to exist**

HN 81
A Shepherd
Style One
Designer: C.J. Noke
Height: 13 1/4", 33.6 cm
Colour: Brown
Issued: 1918-1938
Varieties: HN 617, 632

U.S.: **Extremely**
Can.: **Rare**
Ster.:

Earthenware

HN 82
Lady with an Ermine Muff
Designer: E.W. Light
Height: 6 3/4", 17.2 cm
Colour: Grey and cream grey hat
Issued: 1918-1938
Varieties: Also called "Making a Call" and "Afternoon Call"

U.S.: $3,800.00
Can.: $3,500.00
Ster.: £1,250.00

HN 83
The Lady Anne
Designer: E.W. Light
Height: Unknown
Colour: Yellow
Issued: 1918-1938
Varieties: HN 87, 93

U.S.: $5,000.00
Can.: $5,000.00
Ster.: £2,000.00

HN 84
A Mandarin
Style One
Designer: C.J. Noke
Height: 10 1/4", 26.0 cm
Colour: Mauve and green
Issued: 1918-1938
Varieties: HN 316, 318, 382, 611, 746, 787, 791; "Chinese Mandarin" and "The Mikado"

U.S.: $6,000.00
Can.: $6,000.00
Ster.: £2,500.00

HN 85
Jack Point
Designer: C.J. Noke
Height: 16 1/4", 41.2 cm
Colour: Red checks, green base
Issued: 1918-1938
Varieties: HN 91, 99, 2080

U.S.: **None**
Can.: **known**
Ster.: **to exist**

HN 86
Out For a Walk
Designer:	H. Tittensor
Height:	10", 25.4 cm
Colour:	Grey, white and black
Issued:	1918-1936
Varieties:	HN 443, 748
U.S.:	$4,500.00
Can.:	$4,500.00
Ster.:	£1,700.00

HN 87
The Lady Anne
Designer:	E.W. Light
Height:	Unknown
Colour:	Green
Issued:	1918-1938
Varieties:	HN 83, 93
U.S.:	$5,000.00
Can.:	$5,000.00
Ster.:	£2,000.00

HN 88
Spooks
Designer:	C.J. Noke
Height:	7 1/4", 18.4 cm
Colour:	Green robes, black caps
Issued:	1918-1936
Varieties:	HN 89, 372; also called "Double Spook"
U.S.:	$4,000.00
Can.:	$4,000.00
Ster.:	£1,600.00

HN 89
Spooks
Designer:	C.J. Noke
Height:	7 1/4", 18.4 cm
Colour:	Green robes, red caps
Issued:	1918-1936
Varieties:	HN 88, 372; also called "Double Spook"
U.S.:	$4,500.00
Can.:	$4,500.00
Ster.:	£1,800.00

HN 90
Doris Keene as Cavallini
Style One
Designer:	C.J. Noke
Height:	11", 27.9 cm
Colour:	Dark green
Issued:	1918-1936
Varieties:	HN 467
U.S.:	$2,000.00
Can.:	$2,000.00
Ster.:	£ 800.00

HN 91
Jack Point
Designer:	C.J. Noke
Height:	16 1/4", 41.2 cm
Colour:	Green and black checked suit
Issued:	1918-1938
Varieties:	HN 85, 99, 2080
U.S.:	$3,500.00
Can.:	$3,500.00
Ster.:	£2,000.00

HN 92
Myfanwy Jones
Designer:	E.W. Light
Height:	12", 30.5 cm
Colour:	White
Issued:	1918-1938
Varieties:	HN 39, 456, 514, 516, 519, 520, 660 668, 669, 701, 792; also called "The Welsh Girl"
U.S.:	Extremely
Can.:	Rare
Ster.:	Only one known

HN 93
The Lady Anne
Designer:	E.W. Light
Height:	Unknown
Colour:	Blue
Issued:	1918-1938
Varieties:	HN 83, 87
U.S.:	$5,000.00
Can.:	$5,000.00
Ster.:	£2,000.00

HN 94
The Young Knight
Designer: C.J. Noke
Height: 9 1/2", 24.1 cm
Colour: Purple, green
               and black
Issued: 1918-1936

U.S.:   **Extremely**
Can.:   **Rare**
Ster.:

Only one known to exist

HN 95
Europa and the Bull
Style One
Designer: H. Tittensor
Height: 9 3/4", 24.7 cm
Colour: Lavender with
               browns
Issued: 1918-1938

U.S.:   **$6,000.00**
Can.:   **$6,000.00**
Ster.:   **£2,000.00**

HN 96
Doris Keene as Cavallini
Style Two
Designer: C.J. Noke
Height: 10 3/4", 27.8 cm
Colour: Black and white
Issued: 1918-1938
Varieties: HN 345; also
               called "Romance"

U.S.:   **$3,000.00**
Can.:   **$3,000.00**
Ster.:   **£1,000.00**

HN 97
The Mermaid
Designer: H. Tittensor
Height: 7", 17.8 cm
Colour: Green and
               cream
Issued: 1918-1936
Varieties: HN 300

U.S.:   **$1,000.00**
Can.:   **$1,000.00**
Ster.:   **£ 400.00**

HN 98
Guy Fawkes
Designer: C.J. Noke
Height: 10 1/2". 26.7 cm
Colour: Red cloak, black
               hat and robes
Issued: 1918-1949
Varieties: HN 347, 445

U.S.:   **$1,800.00**
Can.:   **$1,200.00**
Ster.:   **£ 750.00**

HN 99
Jack Point
Designer: C.J. Noke
Height: 16 1/4", 41.2 cm
Colour: Purple and green
Issued   1918-1938
Varieties: HN 85, 91, 2080

U.S.:   **$3,500.00**
Can.:   **$3,500.00**
Ster.:   **£1,200.00**

*

HN 300
The Mermaid
Designer: H. Tittensor
Height: 7", 17.8 cm
Colour: Green and cream,
               red berries in hair
Issued: 1918-1936
Varieties: HN 97

U.S.:   **Extremely**
Can.:   **Rare**
Ster.:

Only two known to exist

HN 301
Moorish Piper Minstrel
Designer: C.J. Noke
Height: 13 1/2", 34.3 cm
Colour: Purple
Issued: 1918-1938
Varieties: HN 328, 416

U.S.:   **$2,500.00**
Can.:   **$2,500.00**
Ster.:   **£1,000.00**

HN 302
Pretty Lady
Designer: H. Tittensor
Height: 9 1/2", 24.1 cm
Colour: Green and
lavender dress
Issued: 1918-1938
Varieties: HN 69, 70, 330,
361, 384, 565,
700, 763, 783

U.S.: $1,500.00
Can.: $1,500.00
Ster.: £ 450.00

HN 303
Motherhood
Designer: P. Stabler
Height: 8", 20.3 cm
Colour: White dress
with black
Issued: 1918-1938
Varieties: HN 28, 30

U.S.: $5,000.00
Can.: $5,000.00
Ster.: £1,800.00

HN 304
Lady with Rose
Designer: E.W. Light
Height: 9 1/2", 24.1 cm
Colour: Patterned
lavender dress
Issued: 1918-1938
Varieties: HN 48A, 52A,
68, 336, 515,
517, 584, 624

U.S.: $3,500.00
Can.: $3,000.00
Ster.: £1,350.00

HN 305
A Scribe
Designer: C.J. Noke
Height: 6", 15.2 cm
Colour: Green, blue
and orange
Issued: 1918-1936
Varieties: HN 324, 1235

U.S.: $2,300.00
Can.: $2,000.00
Ster.: £ 700.00

HN 306
Milking Time
Designer: P. Stabler
Height: 6 1/2", 16.5 cm
Colour: Light blue dress
with black
Issued: 1913-1938
Varieties: HN 3

U.S.: **Extremely**
Can.: **Rare**
Ster.:

HN 307
The Sentimental Pierrot
Designer: C.J. Noke
Height: 5 1/2", 14.0 cm
Colour: Black, white
Issued: 1918-1938
Varieties: HN 36

U.S.: $4,500.00
Can.: $4,000.00
Ster.: £1,400.00

HN 308
A Jester
Style Two
Designer: C.J. Noke
Height: 10 1/4", 26.0 cm
Colour: Black and
lavender
Issued: 1918-1938
Varieties: HN 45A, 45B,
55, 630, 1333

U.S.: **None**
Can.: **known**
Ster.: **to exist**

Photograph
Not
Available

HN 309
A Lady of the
Elizabethan Period
Style Two
Designer: E.W. Light
Height: 9 1/2", 24.1 cm
Colour: Dark blue,
yellow-green
Issued: 1918-1938
Varieties: Also called
"Elizabethan Lady"

U.S.: $4,000.00
Can.: $4,000.00
Ster.: £1,250.00

Photograph Not Available	Photograph Not Available		

HN 310
Dunce
Designer: C.J. Noke
Height: 10 1/2", 26.7 cm
Colour: Black and white with green base
Issued: 1918-1938
Varieties: HN 6, 357

U.S.: **None**
Can.: **known**
Ster.: **to exist**

HN 311
Dancing Figure
Designer: Unknown
Height: 17 3/4", 45.0 cm
Colour: Pink
Issued: 1918-1938

U.S.: **None**
Can.: **known**
Ster.: **to exist**

HN 312
Spring
Style One
Designer: Unknown
Height: 7 1/2". 19.1 cm
Colour: Yellow
Issued: 1918-1938
Varieties: HN 472
Series: The Seasons (Style One)

U.S.: $1,800.00
Can.: $1,750.00
Ster.: £ 650.00

HN 313
Summer
Style One
Designer: Unknown
Height: 7 1/2". 19.1 cm
Colour: Pale green
Issued: 1918-1938
Varieties: HN 473
Series: The Seasons (Style One)

U.S.: $1,800.00
Can.: $1,750.00
Ster.: £ 650.00

			Photograph Not Available

HN 314
Autumn
Style One
Designer: Unknown
Height: 7 1/4", 18.4 cm
Colour: Lavender
Issued: 1918-1938
Varieties: HN 474
Series: The Seasons (Style One)

U.S.: $1,800.00
Can.: $1,750.00
Ster.: £ 650.00

HN 315
Winter
Style One
Designer: Unknown
Height: 7 1/2". 19.1 cm
Colour: Pale green
Issued: 1918-1938
Varieties: HN 475
Series: The Seasons (Style One)

U.S.: $1,800.00
Can.: $1,750.00
Ster.: £ 650.00

HN 316
A Mandarin
Style One
Designer: C.J. Noke
Height: 10 1/4", 26.0 cm
Colour: Black and yellow
Issued: 1918-1938
Varieties: HN 84, 318, 382, 611, 746, 787, 791: "Chinese Mandarin" and "The Mikado"

U.S.: $6,000.00
Can.: $6,000.00
Ster.: £2,500.00

HN 317
Shylock
Designer: C.J. Noke
Height: Unknown
Colour: Brown and green
Issued: 1918-1938
Varieties: HN 79

U.S.: **Extremely**
Can.: **Rare**
Ster.:

HN 318
A Mandarin
Style One
Designer: C.J. Noke
Height: 10 1/4", 26.0 cm
Colour: Gold
Issued: 1918-1938
Varieties: HN 84, 316, 382,
          611, 746, 787, 791;
          "Chinese Mandarin"
          and "The Mikado"

U.S.: $6,000.00
Can.: $6,000.00
Ster.:   £2,500.00

HN 319
A Gnome
Designer: H. Tittensor
Height: 6 1/4", 15.9 cm
Colour: Light blue
Issued: 1918-1938
Varieties: HN 380, 381

U.S.:   **Extremely**
Can.:   **Rare**
Ster.:

HN 320
A Jester
Style One
Designer: C.J. Noke
Height: 10", 25.4 cm
Colour: Green and black
Issued: 1918-1938
Varieties: HN 45, 71, 71A,
          367, 412, 426, 446,
          552, 616, 627,
          1295, 1702, 2016

U.S.: $3,200.00
Can.: $2,750.00
Ster.:   £1,000.00

HN 321
Digger(New Zealand)
Designer: E.W. Light
Height: 11 1/4", 28.5 cm
Colour: Mottled green
Issued: 1918-1938

U.S.: $2,400.00
Can.: $1,750.00
Ster.:   £ 800.00

HN 322
Digger(Australian)
Designer: E.W. Light
Height: 11 1/4", 28.5 cm
Colour: Brown
Issued: 1918-1938
Varieties: HN 353

U.S.: $2,400.00
Can.: $1,750.00
Ster.:   £ 800.00

HN 323
Blighty
Designer: E.W. Light
Height: 11 1/4", 28.5 cm
Colour: Green
Issued: 1918-1938
Varieties: Khaki version

U.S.: $1,800.00
Can.: $1,750.00
Ster.:   £ 800.00

HN 324
A Scribe
Designer: C.J. Noke
Height: 6", 15.2 cm
Colour: Brown, green
          and blue
Issued: 1918-1938
Varieties: HN 305, 1235

U.S.: $2,300.00
Can.: $2,000.00
Ster.:   £ 700.00

HN 325
Pussy
Designer: F.C. Stone
Height: 7 1/2", 19.1 cm
Colour: White dress
          with black
Issued: 1918-1938
Varieties: HN 18, 507;
          also called
          "The Black Cat"

U.S.:   **Extremely**
Can.:   **Rare**
Ster.:   **Only one known**

HN 326
Madonna of the Square
Designer: P. Stabler
Height: 7", 17.8 cm
Colour: Grey
Issued: 1918-1938
Varieties: HN 10, 10A, 11,
14, 27, 573, 576,
594, 613, 764,
1968, 1969, 2034

U.S.: $2,500.00
Can.: $2,400.00
Ster.: £ 900.00

HN 327
The Curtsey
Designer: E.W. Light
Height: 11", 27.9 cm
Colour: Blue
Issued: 1918-1938
Varieties: HN 57, 57B, 66A,
334, 363, 371,
518, 547, 629 670

U.S.: $3,000.00
Can.: $3,000.00
Ster.: £1,200.00

HN 328
Moorish Piper Minstrel
Designer: C.J. Noke
Height: 13 1/2", 34.3 cm
Colour: Green and
brown stripes
Issued: 1918-1938
Varieties: HN 301, 416

U.S.: $2,800.00
Can.: $2,800.00
Ster.: £1,000.00

HN 329
The Gainsborough Hat
Designer: H. Tittensor
Height: 8 3/4", 22.2 cm
Colour: Patterned
blue dress
Issued: 1918-1938
Varieties: HN 46, 46A,
47, 352, 383,
453, 675, 705

U.S.: $3,200.00
Can.: $3,000.00
Ster.: £1,000.00

HN 330
Pretty Lady
Designer: H. Tittensor
Height: 9 1/2", 24.1 cm
Colour: Patterned
blue dress
Issued: 1918-1938
Varieties: HN 69, 70, 302,
361, 384, 565,
700, 763, 783

U.S.: $1,750.00
Can.: $1,750.00
Ster.: £ 650.00

HN 331
A Lady of the
Georgian Period
Designer: E.W. Light
Height: 10 1/4", 26.0 cm
Colour: Mottled green
overskirt, yellow
underskirt
Issued: 1918-1938
Varieties: HN 41, 444, 690,
702

U.S.: $2,700.00
Can.: $2,700.00
Ster.: £ 900.00

HN 332
The Ermine Muff
Designer: C.J. Noke
Height: 8 1/2", 21.6 cm
Colour: Red coat, green
and yellow skirt
Issued: 1918-1938
Varieties: HN 54, 671; also
called "Lady with
Ermine Muff" and
"Lady Ermine"

U.S.: Extremely
Can.: Rare
Ster.: Only one known

HN 333
The Flounced Skirt
Designer: E.W. Light
Height: 9 3/4", 24.7 cm
Colour: Green and blue
Issued: 1918-1938
Varieties: HN 57A, 66, 77,
78; also called
"The Bow"

U.S.: $3,000.00
Can.: $3,000.00
Ster.: £1,000.00

HN 334
The Curtsey
Designer:	E.W. Light
Height:	11", 27.9 cm
Colour:	Lavender
Issued:	1918-1938
Varieties:	HN 57, 57B, 66A, 327, 363, 371, 518, 547, 629, 670
U.S.:	$3,000.00
Can.:	$3,000.00
Ster.:	£1,100.00

HN 335
Lady of the Fan
Designer:	E.W. Light
Height:	9 1/2", 24.1 cm
Colour:	Blue
Issued:	1919-1938
Varieties:	HN 48, 52, 53, 53A, 509
U.S.:	$4,000.00
Can.:	$4,000.00
Ster.:	£1,350.00

HN 336
Lady with Rose
Designer:	E.W. Light
Height:	9 1/2", 24.1 cm
Colour:	Multi-coloured
Issued:	1919-1938
Varieties:	HN 48A, 52A, 68, 304, 515, 517, 584, 624
U.S.:	$3,500.00
Can.:	$3,500.00
Ster.:	£1,400.00

HN 337
The Parson's Daughter
Designer:	H. Tittensor
Height:	10", 25.4 cm
Colour:	Lavender dress with flowers
Issued:	1919-1938
Varieties:	HN 338, 441, 564, 790, 1242, 1356, 2018
U.S.:	$2,200.00
Can.:	$2,200.00
Ster.:	£ 700.00

HN 338
The Parson's Daughter
Designer:	H. Tittensor
Height:	10", 25.4 cm
Colour:	Green and red
Issued:	1919-1938
Varieties:	HN 337, 441, 564, 790, 1242, 1356, 2018
U.S.:	$2,200.00
Can.:	$2,200.00
Ster.:	£ 700.00

HN 339
In Grandma's Days
Designer:	C.J. Noke
Height:	8 3/4", 22.2 cm
Colour:	Green and yellow
Issued:	1919-1938
Varieties:	HN 340, 388, 442; "The Poke Bonnet" HN 362, 612, 765; "A Lilac Shawl" HN 44, 44A
U.S.:	$2,500.00
Can.:	$2,500.00
Ster.:	£ 850.00

HN 340
In Grandma's Days
Designer:	C.J. Noke
Height:	8 3/4", 22.2 cm
Colour:	Yellow and lavender
Issued:	1919-1938
Varieties:	HN 339, 388, 442; "The Poke Bonnet" HN 362, 612, 765; "A Lilac Shawl" HN 44, 44A
U.S.:	$2,500.00
Can.:	$2,500.00
Ster.:	£ 850.00

HN 341
Katharine
Designer:	E.W. Light
Height:	5 3/4", 14.6 cm
Colour:	Red
Issued:	1919-1938
Varieties:	HN 61, 74, 471, 615, 793
U.S.:	$2,800.00
Can.:	$2,800.00
Ster.:	£ 900.00

HN 342
The Lavender Woman
Designer: P. Stabler
Height: 8 1/4", 21.0 cm
Colour: Multi-coloured dress, lavender shawl
Issued: 1919-1938
Varieties: HN 22, 23, 23A, 569, 744

U.S.: $5,000.00
Can.: $5,000.00
Ster.: £1,600.00

HN 343
An Arab
Designer: C.J. Noke
Height: 16 1/2", 41.9 cm
Colour: Yellow and purple
Issued: 1919-1938
Varieties: HN 33, 378; "The Moor" HN 1308, 1366, 1425, 1657, 2082

U.S.: $4,000.00
Can.: $3,000.00
Ster.: £1,200.00

HN 344
Henry Irving as Cardinal Wolsey
Designer: C.J. Noke
Height: 13 1/4", 33.7 cm
Colour: Red
Issued: 1919-1949

U.S.: $4,500.00
Can.: $3,800.00
Ster.: £1,350.00

HN 345
Doris Keene as Cavallini
Style Two
Designer: C.J. Noke
Height: 10 1/2", 26.6 cm
Colour: Black and white, dark collar and striped muff
Issued: 1919-1949
Varieties: HN 96

U.S.: $4,000.00
Can.: $4,000.00
Ster.: £1,350.00

HN 346
Tony Weller
Style One
Designer: C.J. Noke
Height: 10 1/2", 26.7 cm
Colour: Green, blue and brown
Issued: 1919-1938
Varieties: HN 368, 684

U.S.: $3,000.00
Can.: $2,700.00
Ster.: £ 950.00

HN 347
Guy Fawkes
Designer: C.J. Noke
Height: 10 1/2", 26.7 cm
Colour: Brown cloak
Issued: 1919-1938
Varieties: HN 98, 445

U.S.: $3,500.00
Can.: $3,000.00
Ster.: £1,100.00

Photograph
Not
Available

HN 348
The Carpet Vendor
Style Two
Designer: C.J. Noke
Height: 6 1/4", 15.9 cm
Colour: Turquoise, long carpet
Issued: 1919-1938
Varieties: HN 38A

U.S.: None
Can.: known
Ster.: to exist

Photograph
Not
Available

HN 349
Fisherwoman
Designer: Unknown
Height: 11 3/4", 29.8 cm
Colour: Lavender, yellow and green
Issued: 1919-1938
Varieties: HN 80, 359, 631; "Waiting For The Boats" and "Looking For The Boats"

U.S.: None
Can.: known
Ster.: to exist

HN 350
The Carpet Vendor
Style One
Designer: C.J. Noke
Height: 5 1/2", 14.0 cm
Colour: Blue
Issued: 1919-1938
Varieties: HN 38, 76

U.S.: $3,500.00
Can.: $3,500.00
Ster.: £1,000.00

HN 351
Picardy Peasant (woman)
Designer: P. Stabler
Height: 9 1/2", 24.0 cm
Colour: Blue striped skirt,
          spotted hat
Issued: 1919-1938
Varieties: HN 4, 5, 17A,
            513

U.S.: $3,000.00
Can.: $2,500.00
Ster.: £ 950.00

HN 352
The Gainsborough Hat
Designer: H. Tittensor
Height: 8 3/4", 22.2 cm
Colour: Yellow dress,
          purple hat
Issued: 1919-1938
Varieties: HN 46, 46A, 47,
            329, 383, 453,
            675, 705

U.S.: $3,500.00
Can.: $3,000.00
Ster.: £1,000.00

HN 353
Digger (Australian)
Designer: E.W. Light
Height: 11 1/4", 28.5 cm
Colour: Brown
Issued: 1919-1938
Varieties: HN 322

U.S.: $2,400.00
Can.: $1,750.00
Ster.: £ 800.00

HN 354
A Geisha
Style One
Designer: H. Tittensor
Height: 10 3/4", 27.3 cm
Colour: Yellow
Issued: 1919-1938
Varieties: HN 376, 376A,
            387, 634, 741,
            779, 1321, 1322;
            "Japanese Lady"

U.S.: $6,000.00
Can.: $6,000.00
Ster.: £2,000.00

HN 355
Dolly
Style One
Designer: C.J. Noke
Height: 7 1/4", 18.4 cm
Colour: Blue
Issued: 1919-1938

U.S.: $4,500.00
Can.: $4,500.00
Ster.: £1,500.00

HN 356
Sir Thomas Lovell
Designer: C.J. Noke
Height: 7 3/4", 19.7 cm
Colour: Brown and green
Issued: 1919-1938

U.S.: $3,000.00
Can.: $2,750.00
Ster.: £1,000.00

Photograph
Not
Available

HN 357
Dunce
Designer: C.J. Noke
Height: 10 1/2", 26.7 cm
Colour: Light brown
Issued: 1919-1938
Varieties: HN 6, 310

U.S.: **Extremely**
Can.: **Rare**
Ster.:

HN 358
An Old King
Designer: C.J. Noke
Height: 9 3/4", 24.7 cm
Colour: Green and purple
Issued: 1919-1938
Varieties: HN 623, 1801,
2134

U.S.: $2,500.00
Can.: $2,500.00
Ster.: £ 800.00

Photograph
Not
Available

HN 359
Fisherwoman
Designer: Unknown
Height: 11 3/4", 29.8 cm
Colour: Lavender, red
and green
Issued: 1919-1938
Varieties: HN 80, 349, 631;
"Waiting For The
Boats" or "Looking
For The Boats"

U.S.: **Extremely**
Can.: **Rare**
Ster.: *

HN 361
Pretty Lady
Designer: H. Tittensor
Height: 9 1/2", 24.1 cm
Colour: Turquoise
Issued: 1919-1938
Varieties: HN 69, 70, 302,
330, 384, 565,
700, 763, 783

U.S.: $1,750.00
Can.: $1,750.00
Ster.: £ 575.00

HN 362
The Poke Bonnet
Designer: C.J. Noke
Height: 8 3/4", 22.2 cm
Colour: Green, yellow, red
Issued: 1919-1938
Varieties: HN 612, 765; "In
Grandma's Days"
HN 339, 340, 388,
442; "A Lilac Shawl"
HN 44, 44A

U.S.: $2,800.00
Can.: $2,500.00
Ster.: £ 850.00

HN 363
The Curtsey
Designer: E.W. Light
Height: 11", 27.9 cm
Colour: Lavender
and peach
Issued: 1919-1938
Varieties: HN 57, 57B, 66A,
327, 334, 371, 518,
547, 629, 670

U.S.: $3,000.00
Can.: $3,000.00
Ster.: £1,000.00

HN 364
A Moorish Minstrel
Designer: C.J. Noke
Height: 13 1/2", 34.3 cm
Colour: Blue, green
and orange
Issued: 1920-1938
Varieties: HN 34, 415, 797

U.S.: $2,400.00
Can.: $2,500.00
Ster.: £ 800.00

Photograph
Not
Available

HN 365
Double Jester
Designer: C.J. Noke
Height: Unknown
Colour: Brown, green
and purple
Issued: 1920-1938

U.S.: **Extremely**
Can.: **Rare**
Ster.:

Only one known to exist

Photograph
Not
Available

HN 366
A Mandarin
Style Two
Designer: C.J. Noke
Height: 8 1/4", 21.0 cm
Colour: Yellow and blue
Issued: 1920-1938
Varieties: HN 455, 641

U.S.: **Extremely**
Can.: **Rare**
Ster.:

Only one known to exist

HN 367
A Jester
Style One
Designer: C.J. Noke
Height: 10", 25.4 cm
Colour: Green and red
Issued: 1920-1938
Varieties: HN 45, 71, 71A,
320, 412, 426, 446,
552, 616, 627,
1295, 1702, 2016

U.S.: $2,500.00
Can.: $2,000.00
Ster.: £ 800.00

HN 368
Tony Weller
Style One
Designer: C.J. Noke
Height: 10 1/2", 26.7 cm
Colour: Green and brown
Issued: 1920-1938
Varieties: HN 346, 684

U.S.: $2,000.00
Can.: $2,000.00
Ster.: £ 650.00

Photograph
Not
Available

HN 369
Cavalier
Style One
Designer: Unknown
Height: Unknown
Colour: Turquoise
Issued: 1920-1938

U.S.: None
Can.: known
Ster.: to exist

Photograph
Not
Available

HN 370
Henry VIII
Style One
Designer: C.J. Noke
Height: Unknown
Colour: Brown,green
and purple
Issued: 1920-1938
Varieties: HN 673

U.S.: None
Can.: known
Ster.: to exist

HN 371
The Curtsey
Designer: E.W. Light
Height: 11", 27.9 gm
Colour: Yellow
Issued: 1920-1938
Varieties: HN 57, 57B, 66A,
327, 334, 363, 518,
547, 629, 670

U.S.: $3,000.00
Can.: $3,000.00
Ster.: £1,000.00

HN 372
Spooks
Designer: C.J. Noke
Height: 7 1/4", 18.4 cm
Colour: Brown
Issued: 1920-1936
Varieties: HN 88, 89;
also called
"Double Spook"

U.S.: $5,000.00
Can.: $5,000.00
Ster.: £1,500.00

HN 373
Boy on Crocodile
Designer: C.J. Noke
Height: 5", 12.7 cm;
Length: 14 1/2", 36.8 cm
Colour: Green-brown
Issued: 1920-1938
Varieties: Also known in
flambé

U.S.: Extremely
Can.: Rare
Ster.: Only two known

Photograph
Not
Available

HN 374
Lady and Blackamoor
Style One
Designer: H. Tittensor
Height: Unknown
Colour: Blue and
green
Issued: 1920-1938
Varieties: HN 375, 377,
470

U.S.: Extremely
Can.: Rare
Ster.: Only one known

HN 375
Lady and Blackamoor
Style Two
Designer: H. Tittensor
Height: Unknown
Colour: Purple and yellow
Issued: 1920-1938
Varieties: HN 374, 377, 470

U.S.:	**Extremely**
Can.:	**Rare**
Ster.:	**Only one known**

HN 376
A Geisha
Style One
Designer: H. Tittensor
Height: 10 3/4", 27.3 cm
Colour: Blue and yellow
Issued: 1920-1938
Varieties: HN 354, 376A, 387, 634, 741, 779, 1321, 1322; "Japanese Lady"

U.S.:	**$6,000.00**
Can:	**$6,000.00**
Ster.:	**£2,000.00**

HN 376A
A Geisha
Style One
Designer: H. Tittensor
Height: 10 3/4", 27.3 cm
Colour: Blue
Issued: 1920-1938
Varieties: HN 354, 376, 387, 634, 741, 779, 1321, 1322; "The Japanese Lady"

U.S.:	**$6,000.00**
Can.:	**$6,000.00**
Ster.:	**£2,000.00**

HN 377
Lady and Blackamoor
Style Two
Designer: H. Tittensor
Height: Unknown
Colour: Pink and green
Issued: 1920-1938
Varieties: HN 375, 470

U.S.:	**None**
Can.:	**known**
Ster.:	**to exist**

HN 378
An Arab
Designer: C.J. Noke
Height: 16 1/2", 41.9 cm
Colour: Green, brown and yellow
Issued: 1920-1938
Varieties: HN 33, 343; also called "The Moor: HN 1308, 1366, 1425, 1657, 2082

U.S.:	**$4,000.00**
Can.:	**$3,000.00**
Ster.:	**£1,250.00**

HN 379
Ellen Terry as Queen Catharine
Designer: C.J. Noke
Height: 12 1/2", 31.7 cm
Colour: Purple and blue
Issued: 1920-1949

U.S.:	**$3,500.00**
Can.:	**$3,500.00**
Ster.:	**£1,200.00**

HN 380
A Gnome
Designer: H. Tittensor
Height: 6 1/4", 15.9 cm
Colour: Purple
Issued: 1920-1938
Varieties: HN 319, 381

U.S.:	**Extremely**
Can.:	**Rare**
Ster.:	

HN 381
A Gnome
Designer: H. Tittensor
Height: 6 1/4", 15.9 cm
Colour: Green
Issued: 1920-1938
Varieties: HN 319, 380

U.S.:	**Extremely**
Can.:	**Rare**
Ster.:	

Only one known to exist.

HN 382
A Mandarin
Style One
Designer: C.J. Noke
Height: 10 1/4", 26.0 cm
Colour: Green
Issued: 1920-1938
Varieties: HN 84, 316, 318,
           611, 746, 787, 791;
           "Chinese Mandarin"
           and "The Mikado"

U.S.:	$6,000.00
Can.:	$6,000.00
Ster.:	£2,000.00

HN 383
The Gainsborough Hat
Designer: H. Tittensor
Height: 8 3/4", 22.2 cm
Colour: Green stripes
Issued: 1920-1938
Varieties: HN 46, 46A, 47,
           329, 352, 453,
           675, 705

U.S.:	$3,500.00
Can.:	$3,000.00
Ster.:	£1,000.00

HN 384
Pretty Lady
Designer: H. Tittensor
Height: 9 1/2", 24.1 cm
Colour: Red
Issued: 1920-1938
Varieties: HN 69, 70, 302,
           330, 361, 565,
           700, 763, 783

U.S.:	$1,700.00
Can.:	$1,750.00
Ster.:	£ 550.00

HN 385
St. George
Style One
Designer: S. Thorogood
Height: 16", 40.6 cm
Colour: Multi-coloured
Issued: 1920-1938
Varieties: HN 386, 1800,
           2067

U.S.:	$4,000.00
Can.:	$3,500.00
Ster.:	£1,250.00

HN 386
St. George
Style One
Designer: S. Thorogood
Height: 16", 40.6 cm
Colour: Blue and white
Issued: 1920-1938
Varieties: HN 385, 1800,
           2067

U.S.:	$4,000.00
Can.:	$3,500.00
Ster.:	£1,250.00

HN 387
A Geisha
Style One
Designer: H. Tittensor
Height: 10 3/4", 27.3 cm
Colour: Blue and yellow
Issued: 1920-1938
Varieties: HN 354, 376,
           376A, 634, 741,
           779, 1321, 1322;
           "Japanese Lady"

U.S.:	$6,000.00
Can.:	$6,000.00
Ster.:	£2,000.00

HN 388
In Grandma's Days
Designer: C.J. Noke
Height: 8 3/4", 22.2 cm
Colour: Blue
Issued: 1920-1938
Varieties: HN 339, 340, 442;
           "The Poke Bonnet"
           HN 362, 612, 765;
           "A Lilac Shawl"
           HN 44, 44A

U.S.:	$3,000.00
Can.:	$2,750.00
Ster.:	£ 950.00

HN 389
The Little Mother
Style One
Designer: H. Tittensor
Height: 11", 27.9 cm
Colour: Pink dress,
           blond hair
Issued: 1920-1938
Varieties: HN 390; also
           called "Dolly"
           HN 469

U.S.:	Extremely
Can.:	Rare
Ster.:	Only one known

HN 390
The Little Mother
Style One
Designer: H. Tittensor
Height: 11", 27.9 cm
Colour: Pink dress,
brown hair
Issued: 1920-1938
Varieties: HN 389;
also called
"Dolly" HN 469

U.S.: **Extremely**
Can.: **Rare**
Ster.: **Only one known**

HN 391
A Princess
Designer: Unknown
Height: 9 1/4", 23.5 cm
Colour: Green
Issued: 1920-1938
Varieties: HN 392, 420,
430, 431, 633

U.S.: **Extremely**
Can.: **Rare**
Ster.:

Only one known to exist

HN 392
A Princess
Designer: Unknown
Height: 9 1/4", 23.5 cm
Colour: Multi-coloured
Issued: 1920-1938
Varieties: HN 391, 420,
430, 431, 633

U.S.: **Extremely**
Can.: **Rare**
Ster.:

Only one known to exist

Photograph
Not
Available

HN 393
Lady Without Bouquet
Designer: G. Lambert
Height: 9", 22.9 cm
Colour: Pink and lilac
Issued: 1920-1938
Varieties: HN 394

U.S.: **None**
Can.: **known**
Ster.: **to exist**

Photograph
Not
Available

HN 394
Lady Without Bouquet
Designer: G. Lambert
Height: 9", 22.9 cm
Colour: Blue and yellow
Issued: 1920-1938
Varieties: HN 393

U.S.: **None**
Can.: **known**
Ster.: **to exist**

HN 395
Contentment
Designer: L. Harradine
Height: 7 1/4". 18.4 cm
Colour: Yellow and blue
Issued: 1920-1938
Varieties: HN 396, 421,
468, 572, 685,
686, 1323

U.S.: **$2,700.00**
Can.: **$2,700.00**
Ster.: **£ 850.00**

HN 396
Contentment
Designer: L. Harradine
Height: 7 1/4". 18.4 cm
Colour: Blue, yellow
and pink
Issued: 1920-1938
Varieties: HN 395, 421,
468, 572, 685,
686, 1323

U.S.: **$3,000.00**
Can.: **$3,000.00**
Ster.: **£ 950.00**

HN 397
Puff and Powder
Designer: L. Harradine
Height: 6 1/2", 16.5 cm
Colour: Yellow skirt,
brown bodice
Issued: 1920-1938
Varieties: HN 398, 400,
432, 433

U.S.: **$4,500.00**
Can.: **$4,500.00**
Ster.: **£1,500.00**

HN 398
Puff and Powder
Designer: L. Harradine
Height: 6 1/2", 16.5 cm
Colour: Lavender
Issued: 1920-1938
Varieties: HN 397, 400, 432, 433

U.S.: **$4,500.00**
Can.: **$4,500.00**
Ster.: **£1,500.00**

HN 399
Japanese Fan
Designer: H. Tittensor
Height: 4 3/4", 12.1 cm
Colour: Blue and yellow
Issued: 1920-1938
Varieties: HN 405, 439, 440; also known in flambé

U.S.: **$4,500.00**
Can.: **$4,500.00**
Ster.: **£1,500.00**

HN 400
Puff and Powder
Designer: L. Harradine
Height: 6 1/2", 16.5 cm
Colour: Green, blue and yellow
Issued: 1920-1938
Varieties: HN 397, 398, 432, 433

U.S.: **$4,500.00**
Can.: **$4,500.00**
Ster.: **£1,500.00**

Photograph
Not
Available

HN 401
Marie
Style One
Designer: L. Harradine
Height: 7", 17.8 cm
Colour: Pink, cream and blue
Issued: 1920-1938
Varieties: HN 434, 502, 504, 505, 506

U.S.: **Extremely**
Can.: **Rare**
Ster.:

Photograph
Not
Available

HN 402
Betty
Style One
Designer: L. Harradine
Height: 7 1/2", 19.1 cm
Colour: Pink
Issued: 1920-1938
Varieties: HN 403, 435, 438, 477, 478

U.S.: **None**
Can.: **known**
Ster.: **to exist**

Photograph
Not
Available

HN 403
Betty
Style One
Designer: L. Harradine
Height: 7 1/2" 19.1 cm
Colour: Green
Issued: 1920-1938
Varieties: HN 402, 435, 438, 477, 478

U.S.: **Extremely**
Can.: **Rare**
Ster.:

HN 404
King Charles
Designer: C.J. Noke and H. Tittensor
Height: 16 3/4", 42.5 cm
Colour: Black, pink base
Issued: 1920-1951
Varieties: HN 2084, 3459

U.S.: **$4,000.00**
Can.: **$3,500.00**
Ster.: **£1,250.00**

HN 405
Japanese Fan
Designer: H. Tittensor
Height: 4 3/4", 12.1 cm
Colour: Light yellow
Issued: 1920-1938
Varieties: HN 399, 439, 440

U.S.: **$5,000.00**
Can.: **$5,000.00**
Ster.: **£1,600.00**

HN 406
The Bouquet
Designer: G. Lambert
Height: 9", 22.9 cm
Colour: Unknown
Issued: 1920-1938
Varieties: HN 414, 422, 428,
           429, 567, 794;
           also called
           "The Nosegay"

U.S.: $5,000.00
Can.: $3,000.00
Ster.: £ 800.00

HN 407
Omar Khayyam
and the Beloved
Designer: C.J. Noke
Height: 10", 25.4 cm
Colour: Unknown
Issued: 1920-1938
Varieties: HN 419, 459,
           598

U.S.:   None
Can.:   known
Ster.: to exist

HN 408
Omar Khayyam
Style One
Designer: C.J. Noke
Height: 6", 15.2 cm
Colour: Blue, green
           and brown
Issued: 1920-1938
Varieties: HN 409

U.S.:   Extremely
Can.:   Rare
Ster.:

Only one known to exist.

HN 409
Omar Khayyam
Style One
Designer: C.J. Noke
Height: 6", 15.2 cm
Colour: Black and
           yellow
Issued: 1920-1938
Varieties: HN 408

U.S.:   None
Can.:   known
Ster.: to exist

HN 410
Blue Beard
(Without plume on turban)
Style One
Designer: E.W. Light
Height: 11", 27.9 cm
Colour: Green and blue
Issued: 1920-1938
Varieties: HN 75

U.S.: $8,500.00
Can.: $8,500.00
Ster.: £2,700.00

HN 411
A Lady of the Elizabethan
Period
Style One
Designer: E.W. Light
Height: 9 3/4". 24.7 cm
Colour: Purple
Issued: 1920-1938
Varieties: HN 40, 40A, 73;
           "Elizabethan Lady"

U.S.: $4,000.00
Can.: $4,000.00
Ster.: £1,200.00

HN 412
A Jester
Style One
Designer: C.J. Noke
Height: 10", 25.4 cm
Colour: Green and red
Issued: 1920-1938
Varieties: HN 45, 71, 71A,
           320, 367, 426,
           446, 552, 616, 627,
           1295, 1702, 2016

U.S.: $3,000.00
Can.: $2,500.00
Ster.: £ 950.00

HN 413
The Crinoline
Designer: G. Lambert
Height: 6 1/4", 15.8 cm
Colour: Light blue
           and lemon
Issued: 1920-1938
Varieties: HN 8, 9, 9A, 21,
           21A, 566, 628

U.S.: $3,000.00
Can.: $2,700.00
Ster.: £ 900.00

HN 414
The Bouquet
Designer: G. Lambert
Height: 9", 22.9 cm
Colour: Pink and yellow
Issued: 1920-1938
Varieties: HN 406, 422, 428,
429, 567, 794;
also called
"The Nosegay"

U.S.: $4,500.00
Can.: $4,500.00
Ster.: £1,500.00

HN 415
A Moorish Minstrel
Designer: C.J. Noke
Height: 13 1/2", 34.3 cm
Colour: Green and yellow
Issued: 1920-1938
Varieties: HN 34, 364, 797

U.S.: $3,000.00
Can.: $3,000.00
Ster.: £ 900.00

HN 416
Moorish Piper Minstrel
Designer: C.J. Noke
Height: 13 1/2". 34.3 cm
Colour: Green and yellow
stripes
Issued: 1920-1938
Varieties: HN 301, 328

U.S.: $3,000.00
Can.: $3,000.00
Ster.: £1,000.00

HN 417
One of the Forty
Style One
Designer: H. Tittensor
Height: 8 1/4", 21.0 cm
Colour: Green and blue
Issued: 1920-1938
Varieties: HN 490, 495, 501,
528, 648, 677,
1351, 1352

U.S.: $2,500.00
Can.: $2,500.00
Ster.: £ 800.00

HN 418
One of the Forty
Style Two
Designer: H. Tittensor
Height: 7 1/4", 18.4 cm
Colour: Striped green
robes
Issued: 1920-1938
Varieties: HN 494, 498, 647,
666, 704, 1353

U.S.: $2,500.00
Can.: $2,500.00
Ster.: £ 800.00

HN 419
Omar Khayyam
and the Beloved
Designer: C.J. Noke
Height: 10", 25.4 cm
Colour: Green and blue
Issued: 1920-1938
Varieties: HN 407, 459, 598

U.S.: **Extremely**
Can.: **Rare**
Ster.:

Only one known to exist

HN 420
A Princess
Designer: Unknown
Height: 9 1/4", 23.5 cm
Colour: Pink and green
striped skirt,
blue cape
Issued: 1920-1938
Varieties: HN 391, 392,
430, 431, 633

U.S.: **Extremely**
Can.: **Rare**
Ster.: **Only one known**

HN 421
Contentment
Designer: L. Harradine
Height: 7 1/4", 18.4 cm
Colour: Light green
Issued: 1920-1938
Varieties: HN 395, 396,
468, 572, 685,
686, 1323

U.S.: $3,200.00
Can.: $3,000.00
Ster.: £1,000.00

HN 422
The Bouquet
Designer: G. Lambert
Height: 9", 22.9 cm
Colour: Yellow and pink
Issued: 1920-1938
Varieties: HN 406, 414, 428, 429, 567, 794; also called "The Nosegay"

U.S.: $4,500.00
Can.: $4,500.00
Ster.: £1,500.00

HN 423
One of the Forty
Style Three
Designer: H. Tittensor
Height: 3", 7.6 cm
Colour: Varied
Issued: 1921-1938

U.S.: $1,200.00
Can.: $1,000.00
Ster.: £ 350.00

Photograph
Not
Available

HN 423A
One of the Forty
Style Four
Designer: H. Tittensor
Height: Unknown
Colour: Varied
Issued: 1921-1938

U.S.: $1,200.00
Can.: $1,000.00
Ster.: £ 350.00

HN 423B
One of the Forty
Style Five
Designer: H. Tittensor
Height: 2 3/4", 6.9 cm
Colour: Varied
Issued: 1921-1938

U.S.: $1,200.00
Can.: $1,000.00
Ster.: £ 350.00

HN 423C
One of the Forty
Style Six
Designer: H. Tittensor
Height: 2 3/4", 6.9 cm
Colour: Varied
Issued: 1921-1938

U.S.: $1,200.00
Can.: $1,000.00
Ster.: £ 350.00

HN 423D
One of the Forty
Style Seven
Designer: H. Tittensor
Height: 2 3/4", 6.9 cm
Colour: Varied
Issued: 1921-1938

U.S.: $1,200.00
Can.: $1,000.00
Ster.: £ 350.00

Photograph
Not
Available

HN 423E
One of the Forty
Style Eight
Designer: H. Tittensor
Height: Unknown
Colour: Varied
Issued: 1921-1938

U.S.: $1,200.00
Can.: $1,000.00
Ster.: £ 350.00

HN 424
Sleep
Designer: P. Stabler
Height: 6", 15.2 cm
Colour: Blue
Issued: 1921-1938
Varieties: HN 24, 24A, 25, 25A, 692, 710

U.S.: $2,500.00
Can.: $2,500.00
Ster.: £ 800.00

HN 425
The Goosegirl
Style One
Designer: L. Harradine
Height: 8", 20.3 cm
Colour: Blue
Issued: 1921-1938
Varieties: HN 436, 437, 448, 559, 560

U.S.: $5,500.00
Can.: $5,000.00
Ster.: £1,700.00

HN 426
A Jester
Style One
Designer: C.J. Noke
Height: 10", 25.4 cm
Colour: Pink and black
Issued: 1921-1938
Varieties: HN 45, 71, 71A, 320, 367, 412, 446, 552, 616, 627, 1295, 1702, 2016

U.S. $3,000.00
Can.: $2,700.00
Ster.: £ 970.00

Photograph
Not
Available

HN 427
One of the Forty
Style Nine
Designer: H. Tittensor
Height: Unknown
Colour: Green
Issued: 1921-1938

U.S.: $2,500.00
Can.: $2,500.00
Ster.: £ 800.00

HN 428
The Bouquet
Designer: G. Lambert
Height: 9", 22.9 cm
Colour: Blue and green
Issued: 1921-1938
Varieties: HN 406, 414, 422, 429, 567, 794; also called "The Nosegay"

U.S.: $4,500.00
Can.: $4,500.00
Ster.: £1,500.00

HN 429
The Bouquet
Designer: G. Lambert
Height: 9", 22.9 cm
Colour: Green and red
Issued: 1921-1938
Varieties: HN 406, 414, 422, 428, 567, 794; also called "The Nosegay"

U.S.: $4,500.00
Can.: $4,500.00
Ster.: £1,500.00

HN 430
A Princess
Designer: Unknown
Height: 9 1/4", 23.5 cm
Colour: Green
Issued: 1921-1938
Varieties: HN 391, 392, 420, 431, 633

U.S.: Extremely
Can.: Rare
Ster.:

Only one known to exist

HN 431
A Princess
Designer: Unknown
Height: 9 1/4", 23.5 cm
Colour: Yellow and white
Issued: 1921-1938
Varieties: HN 391, 392, 420, 430, 633

U.S.: Extremely
Can.: Rare
Ster.:

Only one known to exist

HN 432
Puff and Powder
Designer: L. Harradine
Height: 6 1/2" 16.5 cm
Colour: Lavender and orange
Issued: 1921-1938
Varieties: HN 397, 398, 400, 433

U.S.: $4,500.00
Can.: $4,500.00
Ster.: £1,500.00

HN 433
Puff and Powder
Designer: L. Harradine
Height: 6 1/2", 16.5 cm
Colour: Lilac and green
Issued: 1921-1938
Varieties: HN 397, 398,
400, 432

U.S.: $4,500.00
Can.: $4,500.00
Ster.: £1,500.00

Photograph
Not
Available

HN 434
Marie
Style One
Designer: L. Harradine
Height: 7", 17.8 cm
Colour: Yellow and
orange
Issued: 1921-1938
Varieties: HN 401, 502,
504, 505, 506

U.S.: None
Can.: known
Ster.: to exist

Photograph
Not
Available

HN 435
Betty
Style One
Designer: L. Harradine
Height: 7 1/2" 19.1 cm
Colour: Blue and yellow
Issued: 1921-1938
Varieties: HN 402, 403,
438, 477, 478

U.S.: None
Can.: known
Ster.: to exist

HN 436
The Goosegirl
Style One
Designer: L. Harradine
Height: 8", 20.3 cm
Colour: Green and
blue
Issued: 1921-1938
Varieties: HN 425, 437,
448, 559, 560

U.S.: $5,500.00
Can.: $5,000.00
Ster.: £1,700.00

HN 437
The Goosegirl
Style One
Designer: L. Harradine
Height: 8", 20.3 cm
Colour: Brown and
blue
Issued: 1921-1938
Varieties: HN 425, 436,
448, 559, 560

U.S.: $5,500.00
Can.: $5,000.00
Ster.: £1,700.00

Photograph
Not
Available

HN 438
Betty
Style One
Designer: L. Harradine
Height: 7 1/2", 19.1 cm
Colour: Green
Issued: 1921-1938
Varieties: HN 402, 403,
435, 477, 478

U.S.: None
Can.: known
Ster.: to exist

HN 439
Japanese Fan
Designer: H. Tittensor
Height: 4 3/4", 12.1 cm
Colour: Blue
Issued: 1921-1938
Varieties: HN 399, 405, 440

U.S.: $5,000.00
Can.: $5,000.00
Ster.: £1,750.00

HN 440
Japanese Fan
Designer: H. Tittensor
Height: 4 3/4", 12.1 cm
Colour: Cream and
orange
Issued: 1921-1938
Varieties: HN 399, 405, 439

U.S.: $4,500.00
Can.: $4,500.00
Ster.: £1,500.00

HN 441
The Parson's Daughter
Designer: H. Tittensor
Height: 10", 25.4 cm
Colour: Yellow and
orange
Issued: 1921-1938
Varieties: HN 337, 338,
564, 790, 1242,
1356, 2018

U.S.: **$2,000.00**
Can.: **$2,000.00**
Ster.: **£ 650.00**

HN 442
In Grandma's Days
Designer: C.J. Noke
Height: 8 3/4", 22.2 cm
Colour: White and green
Issued: 1921-1938
Varieties: HN 339, 340, 388;
"The Poke Bonnet"
HN 362, 612, 765;
"A Lilac Shawl"
HN 44, 44A

U.S: **$3,000.00**
Can.: **$2,500.00**
Ster.: **£ 850.00**

HN 443
Out For a Walk
Designer: H. Tittensor
Height: 10", 25.4 cm
Colour: Brown
Issued: 1921-1936
Varieties: HN 86, 748

U.S.: **$5,000.00**
Can.: **$5,000.00**
Ster.: **£1,700.00**

HN 444
**A Lady of the
Georgian Period**
Designer: E.W. Light
Height: 10 1/4", 26.0 cm
Colour: Turquoise
Issued: 1921-1938
Varieties: HN 41, 331,
690, 702

U.S.: **$3,500.00**
Can.: **$3,500.00**
Ster.: **£1,200.00**

HN 445
Guy Fawkes
Designer: C.J. Noke
Height: 10 1/2", 26.7 cm
Colour: Green cloak
Issued: 1921-1938
Varieties: HN 98, 347

U.S.: **$4,000.00**
Can.: **$3,500.00**
Ster.: **£1,350.00**

HN 446
A Jester
Style One
Designer: C.J. Noke
Height: 10", 25.4 cm
Colour: Black, green, blue
Issued: 1921-1938
Varieties: HN 45, 71, 71A,
320, 367, 412, 426,
552, 616, 627,
1295, 1702, 2016

U.S: **$3,000.00**
Can.: **$2,500.00**
Ster.: **£ 900.00**

Photograph
Not
Available

HN 447
Lady with Shawl
Designer: L. Harradine
Height: 13 1/4", 33.7 cm
Colour: Green and white
striped dress
Issued: 1921-1938
Varieties: HN 458, 626,
678, 679

U.S.: **$4,500.00**
Can.: **$4,500.00**
Ster.: **£1,500.00**

HN 448
The Goosegirl
Style One
Designer: L. Harradine
Height: 8", 20.3 cm
Colour: Blue
Issued: 1921-1938
Varieties: HN 425, 436,
437, 559, 560

U.S.: **$5,500.00**
Can.: **$5,500.00**
Ster.: **£1,700.00**

HN 449
Fruit Gathering
Designer: L. Harradine
Height: 7 3/4", 19.7 cm
Colour: Blue
Issued: 1921-1938
Varieties: HN 476, 503, 561,
562, 706, 707

U.S.: $3,750.00
Can.: $3,750.00
Ster.:   £1,250.00

Photograph
Not
Available

HN 450
Chu Chin Chow
Designer: C.J. Noke
Height: 6 1/2", 16.5 cm
Colour: Red coat and
green cap
Issued: 1921-1938
Varieties: HN 460, 461

U.S.:   **Extremely**
Can.:   **Rare**
Ster.:

Photograph
Not
Available

HN 451
An Old Man
Designer: Unknown
Height: Unknown
Colour: Unknown
Issued: 1921-1938

U.S.:   **Extremely**
Can.:   **Rare**
Ster.:

Only one known to exist.

*

HN 453
The Gainsborough Hat
Designer: H. Tittensor
Height: 8 3/4", 22.2 cm
Colour: Red, blue and
green
Issued: 1921-1938
Varieties: HN 46, 46A, 47,
329, 352, 383,
675, 705

U.S.: $3,200.00
Can.: $3,000.00
Ster.:   £1,000.00

HN 454
The Smiling Buddha
Designer: C.J. Noke
Height: 6 1/4", 15.9 cm
Colour: Green-blue
Issued: 1921-1938
Varieties: Also known in
flambé and Sung

U.S.: $4,500.00
Can.: $4,500.00
Ster.:   £1,500.00

Photograph
Not
Available

HN 455
A Mandarin
Style Two
Designer: C.J. Noke
Height: 8 1/4", 21.0 cm
Colour: Green
Issued: 1921-1938
Varieties: HN 366, 641

U.S.:   **None**
Can.:   **known**
Ster.:   **to exist**

HN 456
Myfanwy Jones
Designer: E.W. Light
Height: 12", 30.5 cm
Colour: Green and brown
Issued: 1921-1938
Varieties: HN 39, 92, 514,
516, 519, 520, 660,
668, 669, 701, 792;
also called "The
Welsh Girl"

U.S: $6,000.00
Can.: $6,000.00
Ster.:   £2,000.00

HN 457
Crouching Nude
Designer: Unknown
Height: 5 1/2", 14.0 cm
Colour: Cream, green
base
Issued: 1921-1938

U.S.: $4,000.00
Can.: $3,500.00
Ster.:   £1,200.00

HN 458
Lady with Shawl
Designer: L. Harradine
Height: 13 1/4", 33.7 cm
Colour: Pink
Issued: 1921-1938
Varieties: HN 447, 626,
 678, 679

U.S.: **$6,000.00**
Can.: **$6,000.00**
Ster.: **£2,000.00**

HN 459
Omar Khayyam
and the Beloved
Designer: C.J. Noke
Height: 10", 25.4 cm
Colour: Multi-coloured
Issued: 1921-1938
Varieties: HN 407, 419,
 598

U.S.: **None**
Can.: **known**
Ster.: **to exist**

HN 460
Chu Chow Chin
Designer: C.J. Noke
Height: 6 1/2", 16.5 cm
Colour: Blue and green
Issued: 1921-1938
Varieties: HN 450, 461

U.S.: **None**
Can.: **known**
Ster.: **to exist**

HN 461
Chu Chow Chin
Designer: C.J. Noke
Height: 6 1/2", 16.5 cm
Colour: Blue
Issued: 1921-1938
Varieties: HN 450, 460

U.S.: **Extremely**
Can.: **Rare**
Ster.:

Only one known to exist.

HN 462
Woman Holding Child
Designer: Unknown
Height: 9 1/4", 23.5 cm
Colour: Green and white
Issued: 1921-1938
Varieties: HN 570, 703,
 743

U.S.: **$6,000.00**
Can.: **$6,000.00**
Ster.: **£2,000.00**

HN 463
Polly Peachum
Style One
Designer: L. Harradine
Height: 6 1/4", 15.9 cm
Colour: Pale blue
Issued: 1921-1949
Varieties: HN 465, 550, 589,
 614, 680, 693
Series: Beggar's Opera

U.S.: **$1,100.00**
Can.: **$1,200.00**
Ster.: **£ 450.00**

HN 464
Captain MacHeath
Designer: L. Harradine
Height: 7", 17.8 cm
Colour: Red, yellow
 and black
Issued: 1921-1949
Varieties: HN 590, 1256
Series: Beggar's Opera

U.S.: **$ 900.00**
Can.: **$1,000.00**
Ster.: **£ 450.00**

HN 465
Polly Peachum
Style One
Designer: L. Harradine
Height: 6 1/4", 15.9 cm
Colour: Red
Issued: 1921-1949
Varieties: HN 463, 550, 589,
 614, 680, 693
Series: Beggar's Opera

U.S.: **$ 900.00**
Can.: **$1,000.00**
Ster.: **£ 450.00**

HN 466
Tulips
Designer: Unknown
Height: 9 1/2", 24.1 cm
Colour: Green
Issued: 1921-1938
Varieties: HN 488, 672,
747, 1334

U.S.: **$3,800.00**
Can.: **$4,000.00**
Ster.: **£1,250.00**

HN 467
Doris Keene as Cavallini
Style One
Designer: C.J. Noke
Height: 11", 27.9 cm
Colour: Dark green with
gold jewellery
Issued: 1921-1936
Varieties: HN 90

U.S.: **$5,000.00**
Can.: **$5,000.00**
Ster.: **£1,600.00**

HN 468
Contentment
Designer: L. Harradine
Height: 7 1/4", 18.4 cm
Colour: Green spotted
dress
Issued: 1921-1938
Varieties: HN 395, 396,
421, 572, 685,
686, 1323

U.S.: **$3,500.00**
Can.: **$3,500.00**
Ster.: **£1,350.00**

HN 469
Dolly
Style Two
Designer: H. Tittensor
Height: 11", 27.9 cm
Colour: White
Issued: 1921-1938
Varieties: Also called "The
Little Mother"
HN 389, 390

U.S.: **Extremely**
Can.: **Rare**
Ster.: **Only one known**

Photograph
Not
Available

HN 470
Lady and Blackamoor
Style Two
Designer: H. Tittensor
Height: Unknown
Colour: Green and
lavender
Issued: 1921-1938
Varieties: HN 374, 375,
377

U.S.: **None**
Can.: **known**
Ster.: **to exist**

HN 471
Katharine
Designer: E.W. Light
Height: 5 3/4", 14.6 cm
Colour: Patterned green
dress
Issued: 1921-1938
Varieties: HN 61, 74,
341, 615, 793

U.S.: **$2,800.00**
Can.: **$2,800.00**
Ster.: **£ 900.00**

HN 472
Spring
Style One
Designer: Unknown
Colour: Patterned
yellow robe
Height: 7 1/2", 19.1 cm
Issued: 1921-1938
Varieties: HN 312
Series: The Seasons
(Style One)

U.S: **$3,000.00**
Can.: **$2,750.00**
Ster.: **£ 950.00**

HN 473
Summer
Style One
Designer: Unknown
Height: 7 1/2", 19.1 cm
Colour: Patterned light
green robes
Issued: 1921-1938
Varieties: HN 313
Series: The Seasons
(Style One)

U.S.: **$3,000.00**
Can.: **$2,750.00**
Ster.: **£ 950.00**

HN 474
Autumn
Style One
Designer: Unknown
Height: 7 1/2", 19.1 cm
Colour: Patterned pink
            robes
Issued: 1921-1938
Varieties: HN 314
Series: The Seasons
            (Style One)

U.S.: $3,000.00
Can.: $2,750.00
Ster.:   £ 900.00

HN 475
Winter
Style One
Designer: Unknown
Height: 7 1/2", 19.1 cm
Colour: Patterned pale
            green robes
Issued: 1921-1938
Varieties: HN 315
Series: The Seasons
            (Style One)

U.S.: $3,000.00
Can.: $2,750.00
Ster.:   £ 900.00

HN 476
Fruit Gathering
Designer: L. Harradine
Height: 7 3/4", 19.7 cm
Colour: Green and blue
Issued: 1921-1938
Varieties: HN 449, 503, 561,
            562, 706, 707

U.S.: $3,250.00
Can.: $3,250.00
Ster.:   £1,100.00

Photograph
Not
Available

HN 477
Betty
Style One
Designer: L. Harradine
Height: 7 1/2", 19.1 cm
Colour: Green
Issued: 1921-1938
Varieties: HN 402, 403,
            435, 438, 478

U.S.:   **None**
Can.:   **known**
Ster.:   **to exist**

Photograph
Not
Available

HN 478
Betty
Style One
Designer: L. Harradine
Height: 7 1/2", 19.1 cm
Colour: White
Issued: 1921-1938
Varieties: HN 402, 403,
            435, 438, 477

U.S.:   **Extremely**
Can.:   **Rare**
Ster.:

HN 479
The Balloon Seller
Designer: L. Harradine
Height: 9", 22.9 cm
Colour: Blue and white
Issued: 1921-1938
Varieties: HN 486, 548, 583,
            697; also called
            "The Balloon
            Woman"

U.S.: $3,500.00
Can.: $3,000.00
Ster.:   £1,000.00

HN 480
One of the Forty
Style Ten
Designer: H. Tittensor
Height: 7", 17.8 cm
Colour: Brown, yellow
            and blue
Issued: 1921-1938
Varieties: HN 493, 497, 499,
            664, 714

U.S.: $2,500.00
Can.: $2,500.00
Ster.:   £ 800.00

Photograph
Not
Available

HN 481
One of the Forty
Style Eleven
Designer: H. Tittensor
Height: Unknown
Colour: Dark colour
Issued: 1921-1938
Varieties: HN 483, 491,
            646, 667, 712,
            1336, 1350

U.S.: $2,500.00
Can.: $2,500.00
Ster.:   £ 800.00

Photograph Not Available	Photograph Not Available	Photograph Not Available	

HN 482
One of the Forty
Style Twelve
Designer:	H. Tittensor
Height:	6", 15.2 cm
Colour:	White
Issued:	1921-1938
Varieties:	HN 484, 492, 645, 663, 713

U.S.:	**$2,500.00**
Can.:	**$2,500.00**
Ster.:	**£ 800.00**

HN 483
One of the Forty
Style Eleven
Designer:	H. Tittensor
Height:	Unknown
Colour:	Brown and green
Issued:	1921-1938
Varieties:	HN 481, 491, 646, 667, 712, 1336, 1350

U.S.:	**$2,500.00**
Can.:	**$2,500.00**
Ster.:	**£ 800.00**

HN 484
One of the Forty
Style Twelve
Designer:	H. Tittensor
Height:	6", 15.2 cm
Colour:	Green
Issued:	1921-1938
Varieties:	HN 482, 492, 645, 663, 713

U.S.:	**$2,500.00**
Can.:	**$2,500.00**
Ster.:	**£ 800.00**

HN 485
Lucy Lockett
Style One
Designer:	L. Harradine
Height:	6", 15.2 cm
Colour:	Green
Issued:	1921-1949
Varieties:	HN 524
Series:	Beggar's Opera

U.S.:	**$1,000.00**
Can.:	**$1,000.00**
Ster.:	**£ 450.00**

HN 486
The Balloon Seller
Designer:	L. Harradine
Height:	9", 22.9 cm
Colour:	Blue dress, no hat
Issued:	1921-1938
Varieties:	HN 479, 548, 583, 697; also called "The Balloon Woman"

U.S.:	**$3,500.00**
Can.:	**$3,500.00**
Ster.:	**£1,200.00**

HN 487
Pavlova
Designer:	C.J. Noke
Height:	4 1/4", 10.8 cm
Colour:	White, black base
Issued:	1921-1938
Varieties:	HN 676; also called "Swan Song"

U.S.:	**Extremely**
Can.:	**Rare**
Ster.:	**Only two known**

HN 488
Tulips
Designer:	Unknown
Height:	9 1/2", 24.1 cm
Colour:	Cream
Issued:	1921-1938
Varieties:	HN 466, 672, 747, 1334

U.S.:	**$3,800.00**
Can.:	**$4,000.00**
Ster.:	**£1,250.00**

HN 489
Polly Peachum
Style Two
Designer:	L. Harradine
Height:	4 1/4", 10.8 cm
Colour:	Turquoise
Issued:	1921-1938
Varieties:	HN 549, 620, 694, 734
Series:	Beggar's Opera

U.S.:	**$ 950.00**
Can.:	**$1,000.00**
Ster.:	**£ 350.00**

HN 490
One of the Forty
Style One
Dsigner: H. Tittensor
Height: 8 1/4", 21.0 cm
Colour: Blue and brown
Issued: 1921-1938
Varieties: HN 417, 495, 501, 528, 648, 677, 1351, 1352

U.S.: $2,500.00
Can.: $2,500.00
Ster.: £ 800.00

Photograph
Not
Available

HN 491
One of the Forty
Style Eleven
Designer: H. Tittensor
Height: Unknown
Colour: Green and white
Issued: 1921-1938
Varieties: HN 481, 483, 646, 667, 712, 1336, 1350

U.S.: $2,500.00
Can.: $2,500.00
Ster.: £ 800.00

Photograph
Not
Available

HN 492
One of the Forty
Style Twelve
Designer: H. Tittensor
Height: 6", 15.2 cm
Colour: Yellow and white
Issued: 1921-1938
Varieties: HN 482, 484, 645, 663, 713

U.S.: $2,500.00
Can.: $2,500.00
Ster.: £ 800.00

HN 493
One of the Forty
Style Ten
Designer: H. Tittensor
Height: 6 3/4", 17.1 cm
Colour: Blue and black
Issued: 1921-1938
Varieties: HN 480, 497, 499, 664, 714

U.S.: $2,500.00
Can.: $2,500.00
Ster.: £ 800.00

HN 494
One of the Forty
Style Two
Designer: H. Tittensor
Height: 7 1/4", 18.4 cm
Colour: White
Issued: 1921-1938
Varieties: HN 418, 498, 647, 666, 704, 1353

U.S.: $2,500.00
Can.: $2,500.00
Ster.: £ 800.00

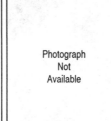

HN 495
One of the Forty
Style One
Designer: H. Tittensor
Height: 8 1/4", 21.0 cm
Colour: Brown and blue
Issued: 1921-1938
Varieties: HN 417, 490, 501, 528, 648, 677, 1351, 1352

U.S.: $3,500.00
Can.: $2,500.00
Ster.: £ 800.00

Photograph
Not
Available

HN 496
One of the Forty
Style Thirteen
Designer: H. Tittensor
Height: 7 3/4", 19.6 cm
Colour: Orange and yellow checks
Issued: 1921-1938
Varieties: HN 500, 649, 665, 1354

U.S.: $2,500.00
Can.: $2,500.00
Ster.: £ 800.00

HN 497
One of the Forty
Style Ten
Designer: H. Tittensor
Height: 6 3/4", 17.1 cm
Colour: Brown and green
Issued: 1921-1938
Varieties: HN 480, 493, 499, 664, 714

U.S.: $2,500.00
Can.: $2,500.00
Ster.: £ 800.00

HN 498
One of the Forty
Style Two
Designer: H. Tittensor
Height: 7 1/4", 18.4 cm
Colour: Dark colours
Issued: 1921-1938
Varieties: HN 418, 494, 647,
            666, 704, 1353

U.S.: $2,500.00
Can.: $2,500.00
Ster.:   £ 800.00

HN 499
One of the Forty
Style Ten
Designer: H. Tittensor
Height: 6 3/4", 17.1 cm
Colour: Cream and
            green
Issued: 1921-1938
Varieties: HN 480, 493,
            497, 664, 714

U.S.: $2,500.00
Can.: $2,500.00
Ster.:   £ 800.00

Photograph
Not
Available

HN 500
One of the Forty
Style Thirteen
Designer: H. Tittensor
Height: 7 3/4", 19.6 cm
Colour: Orange checks
            and red turban
Issued: 1921-1938
Varieties: HN 496, 649,
            665, 1354

U.S.: $2,500.00
Can.: $2,500.00
Ster.:   £ 800.00

HN 501
One of the Forty
Style One
Designer: H Tittensor
Height: 8 1/4", 21.0 cm
Colour: Green stripes
Issued: 1921-1938
Varieties: HN 417, 490,
            495, 528, 648,
            677, 1351, 1352

U.S.: $2,500.00
Can.: $2,500.00
Ster.:   £ 800.00

Photograph
Not
Available

HN 502
Marie
Style One
Designer: L. Harradine
Height: 7", 17.8 cm
Colour: White, red
            and blue
Issued: 1921-1938
Varieties: HN 401, 434,
            504, 505, 506

U.S.:   None
Can.:   known
Ster.:   to exist

HN 503
Fruit Gathering
Designer: L. Harradine
Height: 7 3/4", 19.7 cm
Colour: Brown and blue
Issued: 1921-1938
Varieties: HN 449, 476, 561,
            562, 706, 707

U.S.: $3,750.00
Can.: $3,750.00
Ster.:   £1,250.00

Photograph
Not
Available

HN 504
Marie
Style One
Designer: L. Harradine
Height: 7", 17.8 cm
Colour: Green and
            blue
Issued: 1921-1938
Varieties: HN 401, 434,
            502, 505, 506

U.S.:   None
Can.:   known
Ster.:   to exist

Photograph
Not
Available

HN 505
Marie
Style One
Designer: L. Harradine
Height: 7", 17.8 cm
Colour: Blue, green
            and lavender
Issued: 1921-1938
Varieties: HN 401, 434,
            502, 504, 506

U.S.:   None
Can.:   known
Ster.:   to exist

HN 506
Marie
Style One
Designer: L. Harradine
Height: 7", 17.8 cm
Colour: Blue, green
and lavender
Issued: 1921-1938
Varieties: HN 401, 434,
502, 504, 505

U.S.: **None**
Can.: **known**
Ster.: **to exist**

HN 507
Pussy
Designer: F.C. Stone
Height: 7 1/2", 19.1 cm
Colour: Spotted blue
dress
Issued: 1921-1938
Varieties: HN 18, 325;
also called
"TheBlack Cat"

U.S.: **None**
Can.: **known**
Ster.: **to exist**

HN 508
An Orange Vendor
Designer: C.J. Noke
Height: 6 1/4", 15.9 cm
Colour: Purple
Issued: 1921-1938
Varieties: HN 72, 521,
1966

U.S.: **$2,000.00**
Can.: **$2,000.00**
Ster.: **£ 650.00**

HN 509
Lady of the Fan
Designer: E.W. Light
Height: 9 1/2", 24.1 cm
Colour: Green and
lavender
Issued: 1921-1938
Varieties: HN 48, 52,
53, 53A, 335

U.S.: **$4,000.00**
Can.: **$4,000.00**
Ster.: **£1,350.00**

HN 510
A Child's Grace
Designer: L. Perugini
Height: 6 3/4", 17.2 cm
Colour: Green and
yellow
Issued: 1921-1938
Varieties: HN 62, 62A

U.S.: **None**
Can.: **known**
Ster.: **to exist**

HN 511
Upon Her Cheeks She Wept
Designer: L. Perugini
Height: 9", 22.8 cm
Colour: Lavender
Issued: 1921-1938
Varieties: HN 59, 522

U.S.: **None**
Can.: **known**
Ster.: **to exist**

HN 512
A Spook
Designer: H. Tittensor
Height: 7", 17.8 cm
Colour: Blue
Issued: 1921-1938
Varieties: HN 50, 51, 51A
51B, 58, 625
1218

U.S.: **None**
Can.: **known**
Ster.: **to exist**

HN 513
Picardy Peasant (woman)
Designer: P. Stabler
Height: 9 1/2", 24.0 cm
Colour: Blue
Issued: 1921-1938
Varieties: HN 4, 5, 17A,
351

U.S.: **None**
Can.: **known**
Ster.: **to exist**

HN 514
Myfanwy Jones
Designer: E.W. Light
Height: 12", 30.5 cm
Colour: Green and red
Issued: 1921-1938
Varieties: HN 39, 92, 456,
516, 519, 520, 660,
668, 669, 701, 792;
also called "The
Welsh Girl"

U.S.: None
Can.: known
Ster.: to exist

HN 515
Lady with Rose
Designer: E.W. Light
Height: 9 1/2", 24.1 cm
Colour: Lavender, green
Issued: 1921-1938
Varieties: HN 48A, 52A,
68, 304, 336,
517, 584, 624

U.S.: None
Can.: known
Ster.: to exist

HN 516
Myfanwy Jones
Designer: E.W. Light
Height: 12", 30.4 cm
Colour: Black and lavender
Issued: 1921-1938
Varieties: HN 39, 92, 456,
514, 519, 520, 660,
668, 669, 701, 792;
also called "The
Welsh Girl"

U.S.: None
Can.: known
Ster.: to exist

HN 517
Lady with Rose
Designer: E.W. Light
Height: 9 1/2", 24.1 cm
Colour: Lavender with
orange spots
Issued: 1921-1938
Varieties: HN 48A, 52A,
68, 304, 336,
515, 584, 624

U.S.: None
Can.: known
Ster.: to exist

HN 518
The Curtsey
Designer: E.W. Light
Height: 11", 27.9 cm
Colour: Lavender
Issued: 1921-1938
Varieties: HN 57, 57B, 66A,
327, 334, 363, 371,
547, 629, 670

U.S.: None
Can.: known
Ster.: to exist

HN 519
Myfanwy Jones
Designer: E.W. Light
Height: 12", 30.5 cm
Colour: Blue and lavender
Issued: 1921-1938
Varieties: HN 39, 92, 456,
514, 516, 520, 660,
668, 669, 701, 792;
also called "The
Welsh Girl"

U.S.: None
Can.: known
Ster.: to exist

HN 520
Myfanwy Jones
Designer: E.W. Light
Height: 12", 30.5 cm
Colour: Black and lavender
Issued: 1921-1938
Varieties: HN 39, 92, 456,
514, 516, 519, 660,
668, 669, 701, 792;
also called "The
Welsh Girl"

U.S.: None
Can.: known
Ster.: to exist

HN 521
An Orange Vendor
Designer: C.J. Noke
Height: 6 1/4", 15.9 cm
Colour: Light blue
Issued: 1921-1938
Varieties: HN 72, 508,
1966

U.S.: None
Can.: known
Ster.: to exist

HN 522
Upon Her Cheeks She Wept
Designer: L. Perugini
Height: 9", 22.8 cm
Colour: Lavender
Issued: 1921-1938
Varieties: HN 59, 511

U.S.: **None**
Can.: **known**
Ster.: **to exist**

HN 523
Sentinel
Designer: Unknown
Height: 17 1/2", 44.4 cm
Colour: Red, blue
and black
Issued: 1921-1938

U.S.: **Extremely**
Can.: **Rare**
Ster.:

Only two known to exist

HN 524
Lucy Lockett
Style One
Designer: L. Harradine
Height: 6", 15.2 cm
Colour: Orange
Issued: 1921-1949
Varieties: HN 485
Series: Beggar's Opera
Variaties: Earthenware
and China

U.S.: **$1,000.00**
Can.: **$1,000.00**
Ster.: **£ 350.00**

HN 525
The Flower Seller's Children
Designer: L. Harradine
Height: 8 1/4", 21.0 cm
Colour: Green and blue
Issued: 1921-1949
Varieties: HN 551, 1206,
1342, 1406

U.S.: **None**
Can.: **known**
Ster.: **to exist**

HN 526
The Beggar
Style One
Designer: L. Harradine
Height: 6 1/2", 16.5 cm
Colour: Green and blue
Issued: 1921-1949
Varieties: HN 591
Series: Beggar's Opera

U.S.: **$650.00**
Can.: **$650.00**
Ster.: **£350.00**

HN 527
The Highwayman
Designer: L. Harradine
Height: 6 1/2", 16.5 cm
Colour: Green and red
Issued: 1921-1949
Varieties: HN 592, 1257

U.S.: **$950.00**
Can.: **$950.00**
Ster.: **£350.00**

HN 528
One of the Forty
Style One
Designer: H. Tittensor
Height: 8 1/4", 21.0 cm
Colour: Brown
Issued: 1921-1938
Varieties: HN 417, 490,
495, 501, 648,
677, 1351, 1352

U.S.: **$2,500.00**
Can.: **$2,500.00**
Ster.: **£ 800.00**

HN 529
Mr Pickwick
Style One
Designer: L. Harradine
Height: 3 3/4", 9.5 cm
Colour: Black and tan
Issued: 1922-1932
Series: Dickens

U.S.: **$100.00**
Can.: **$125.00**
Ster.: **£ 40.00**

HN 530
The Fat Boy
Style One
Designer: L. Harradine
Height: 3 1/2", 8.9 cm
Colour: Blue and white
Issued: 1922-1932
Series: Dickens

U.S.: $100.00
Can.: $125.00
Ster.:   £ 40.00

HN 531
Sam Weller
Designer: L. Harradine
Height: 4", 10.1 cm
Colour: Yellow and
           brown
Issued: 1922-1932
Series: Dickens

U.S.: $100.00
Can.: $125.00
Ster.:   £ 40.00

HN 532
Mr Micawber
Style One
Designer: L. Harradine
Height: 3 1/2", 8.9 cm
Colour: Tan and black
Issued: 1922-1932
Series: Dickens

U.S.: $100.00
Can.: $125.00
Ster.:   £ 40.00

HN 533
Sairey Gamp
Style One
Designer: L. Harradine
Height: 4", 10.1 cm
Colour: Light and
           dark green
Issued: 1922-1932
Series: Dickens

U.S.: $100.00
Can.: $125.00
Ster.:   £ 40.00

HN 534
Fagin
Designer: L. Harradine
Height: 4", 10.1 cm
Colour: Dark brown
Issued: 1922-1932
Series: Dickens

U.S.: $100.00
Can.: $125.00
Ster.:   £ 40.00

HN 535
Pecksniff
Style One
Designer: L. Harradine
Height: 3 3/4", 9.5 cm
Colour: Brown
Issued: 1922-1932
Series: Dickens

U.S.: $100.00
Can.: $125.00
Ster.:   £ 40.00

HN 536
Stiggins
Designer: L. Harradine
Height: 3 3/4", 9.5 cm
Colour: Black
Issued: 1922-1932
Series: Dickens

U.S.: $100.00
Can.: $125.00
Ster.:   £ 40.00

HN 537
Bill Sykes
Designer: L. Harradine
Height: 3 3/4", 9.5 cm
Colour: Black and
           brown
Issued: 1922-1932
Series: Dickens

U.S.: $100.00
Can.: $125.00
Ster.:   £ 40.00

HN 538
Buz Fuz
Designer: L. Harradine
Height: 3 3/4", 9.5 cm
Colour: Black and
                 brown
Issued: 1922-1932
Series: Dickens

U.S.:   **$100.00**
Can.:   **$125.00**
Ster.:   **£ 40.00**

HN 539
Tiny Tim
Designer: L. Harradine
Height: 3 1/2", 8.9 cm
Colour: Black, brown
                 and blue
Issued: 1922-1932
Series: Dickens

U.S.:   **$100.00**
Can.:   **$125.00**
Ster.:   **£ 40.00**

HN 540
Little Nell
Designer: L. Harradine
Height: 4", 10.1 cm
Colour: Pink
Issued: 1922-1932
Series: Dickens

U.S.:   **$100.00**
Can.:   **$125.00**
Ster.:   **£ 40.00**

HN 541
Alfred Jingle
Designer: L. Harradine
Height: 3 3/4", 9.5 cm
Colour: Brown and black
Issued: 1922-1932
Series: Dickens

U.S.:   **$100.00**
Can.:   **$125.00**
Ster.:   **£ 40.00**

HN 542
The Cobbler
Style One
Designer: C.J. Noke
Height: 7 1/2", 19.1 cm
Colour: Green and
                 brown
Issued: 1922-1939
Varieties: HN 543, 682

U.S.:   **$1,100.00**
Can.:   **$1,200.00**
Ster.:   **£ 450.00**

HN 543
The Cobbler
Style One
Designer: C.J. Noke
Height: 7 1/2", 19.1 cm
Colour: Green and
                 brown
Issued: 1922-1938
Varieties: HN 542, 682

U.S.:   **Extremely**
Can.:   **Rare**
Ster.:   **Only two known**

HN 544
Tony Weller
Style Two
Designer: L. Harradine
Height: 3 1/2", 8.9 cm
Colour: Green and yellow
Issued: 1922-1932
Series: Dickens

U.S.:   **$100.00**
Can.:   **$125.00**
Ster.:   **£ 40.00**

HN 545
Uriah Heep
Style One
Designer: L. Harradine
Height: 4", 10.1 cm
Colour: Black
Issued: 1922-1932
Series: Dickens

U.S.:   **$100.00**
Can.:   **$125.00**
Ster.:   **£ 40.00**

HN 546
The Artful Dodger
Designer: L. Harradine
Height: 3 3/4", 9.5 cm
Colour: Black and
           brown
Issued: 1922-1932
Series: Dickens

U.S.:	$100.00
Can.:	$125.00
Ster.:	£ 40.00

HN 547
The Curtsey
Designer: E.W. Light
Height: 11", 27.9 cm
Colour: Blue, green
           and yellow
Issued: 1922-1938
Varieties: HN 57, 57B, 66A,
           327, 334, 363, 371,
           518, 629, 670

U.S.:	$3,000.00
Can.:	$3,000.00
Ster.:	£1,000.00

HN 548
The Balloon Seller
Designer: L. Harradine
Height: 9", 22.9 cm
Colour: Blue and black
Issued: 1922-1938
Varieties: HN 479, 486, 583,
           697; also called
           "The Balloon
           Woman"

U.S.:	$3,500.00
Can.:	$3,500.00
Ster.:	£1,000.00

HN 549
Polly Peachum
Style Two
Designer: L. Harradine
Height: 4 1/4", 10.8 cm
Colour: Rose pink
Issued: 1922-1949
Varieties: HN 489, 620,
           694, 734
Series: Beggar's Opera

U.S.:	$750.00
Can.:	$595.00
Ster.:	£350.00

HN 550
Polly Peachum
Style One
Designer: L. Harradine
Height: 6 1/2", 16/5 cm
Colour: Rose pink
Issued: 1922-1949
Varieties: HN 463, 465, 589,
           614, 680, 693
Series: Beggar's Opera

U.S.:	$900.00
Can.:	$900.00
Ster.:	£350.00

HN 551
The Flower Seller's Children
Designer: L. Harradine
Height: 8 1/4", 21.0 cm
Colour: Blue, orange
           and yellow
Issued: 1922-1949
Varieties: HN 525, 1206,
           1342, 1406

U.S.:	None
Can.:	known
Ster.:	to exist

HN 552
A Jester
Style One
Designer: C.J. Noke
Height: 10", 25.4 cm
Colour: Black and red
Issued: 1922-1938
Varieties: HN 45, 71, 71A,
           320, 367, 412, 426,
           446, 616, 627,
           1295, 1702, 2016

U.S.:	$3,000.00
Can.:	$2,500.00
Ster.:	£1,000.00

HN 553
Pecksniff
Style Two
Designer: L. Harradine
Height: 7", 17.8 cm
Colour: Black and
           brown
Issued: 1923-1939
Varieties: HN 1891
Series: Dickens

U.S.:	$475.00
Can.:	$450.00
Ster.:	£200.00

HN 554
Uriah Heep
Style Two
Designer: L. Harradine
Height: 7 1/4", 18.4 cm
Colour: Black
Issued: 1923-1939
Varieties: HN 1892
Series: Dickens

U.S.: **$475.00**
Can.: **$450.00**
Ster.: **£200.00**

HN 555
The Fat Boy
Style Two
Designer: L. Harradine
Height: 7", 17.8 cm
Colour: Blue and cream
Issued: 1923-1939
Varieties: HN 1893
Series: Dickens

U.S.: **$525.00**
Can.: **$450.00**
Ster.: **£200.00**

HN 556
Mr Pickwick
Style Two
Designer: L. Harradine
Height: 7", 17.8 cm
Colour: Blue, yellow and tan
Issued: 1923-1939
Varieties: HN 1894
Series: Dickens

U.S.: **$475.00**
Can.: **$450.00**
Ster.: **£200.00**

HN 557
Mr Micawber
Style Two
Designer: L. Harradine
Height: 7", 17.8 cm
Colour: Brown, black and tan
Issued: 1923-1939
Varieties: HN 1895
Series: Dickens

U.S. **$475.00**
Can.: **$450.00**
Ster.: **£200.00**

HN 558
Sairey Gamp
Style Two
Designer: L. Harradine
Height: 7", 17.8 cm
Colour: Black
Issued: 1923-1939
Varieties: HN1896
Series: Dickens

U.S.: **$575.00**
Can.: **$450.00**
Ster.: **£250.00**

HN 559
The Goosegirl
Style One
Designer: L. Harradine
Height: 8", 20.3 cm
Colour: Pink
Issued: 1923-1938
Varieties: HN 425, 436, 437, 448, 560

U.S.: **$5,500.00**
Can.: **$5,500.00**
Ster.: **£1,750.00**

Earthenware

HN 560
The Goosegirl
Style One
Designer: L. Harradine
Height: 8", 20.3 cm
Colour: Pink and white
Issued: 1923-1938
Varieties: HN 425, 436, 437, 448, 559

U.S.: **$5,500.00**
Can.: **$5,500.00**
Ster.: **£1,750.00**

NOTE ON PRICING

Prices are given for three separate and distinct market areas:

Prices are given in the currency of each of these different trading areas.

Prices are not exchange rate calculations but are based on supply and demand in that market.

Prices listed are guidelines to the most current retail values but actual selling prices may vary slightly.

Prices for current figurines are those suggested by Royal Doulton.

Extremely rare or unique figurines have inconsistent retail values and their prices must therefore be determined between buyer and seller.

HN 561
Fruit Gathering
Designer: L. Harradine
Height: 7 3/4", 19.7 cm
Colour: Green and white
Issued: 1923-1938
Varieties: HN 449, 476, 503,
562, 706, 707

U.S.: $3,750.00
Can.: $3,750.00
Ster.: £1,250.00

HN 562
Fruit Gathering
Designer: L. Harradine
Height: 7 3/4", 19.7 cm
Colour: Pink, white
and green
Issued: 1923-1938
Varieties: HN 449, 476, 503,
561, 706, 707

U.S.: $3,250.00
Can.: $3,250.00
Ster.: £1,100.00

HN 563
Man in Tudor Costume
Designer: Unknown
Height: 3 3/4", 9.5 cm
Colour: Orange striped
tunic, black
cloak
Issued: 1923-1938

U.S.: $2,700.00
Can.: $2,700.00
Ster.: £ 900.00

HN 564
The Parson's Daughter
Designer: H. Tittensor
Height: 9 1/2", 24.1 cm
Colour: Red, yellow
and green
Issued: 1923-1949
Varieties: HN 337, 338,
441, 790, 1242,
1356, 2018

U.S.: $500.00
Can.: $575.00
Ster.: £300.00

HN 565
Pretty Lady
Designer: H. Tittensor
Height: 10", 25.4 cm
Colour: Yellow and green
Issued: 1923-1938
Varieties: HN 69, 70, 302,
330, 361, 384, 700,
763, 783; appears
in two colours,
yellow and orange

U.S.: $1,500.00
Can.: $1,500.00
Ster.: £ 450.00

HN 566
The Crinoline
Designer: G. Lambert
Height: 6 1/4", 15.8 cm
Colour: Cream and
green
Issued: 1923-1938
Varieties: HN 8, 9, 9A, 21,
21A, 413, 628

U.S.: $3,000.00
Can.: $2,700.00
Ster.: £ 950.00

HN 567
The Bouquet
Designer: G. Lambert
Height: 9 1/2", 24.1 cm
Colour: Pink dress, beige
patterned shawl
Issued: 1923-1938
Varieties: HN 406, 414, 422,
428, 429, 794;
also called
"The Nosegay"

U.S.: $3,000.00
Can.: $3,000.00
Ster.: £1,000.00

HN 568
Shy Anne
Designer: L. Perugini
Height: 7 1/2", 19.1 cm
Colour: Green dress
with black spots
Issued: 1923-1938
Varieties: HN 60, 64, 65

U.S.: $2,800.00
Can.: $2,500.00
Ster.: £ 900.00

Earthenware and China

HN 569
The Lavender Woman
Designer: P. Stabler
Height: 8 1/4", 21.0 cm
Colour: Lavender
Issued: 1924-1938
Varieties: HN 22, 23,
            23A, 342, 744

U.S.: $5,000.00
Can.: $5,000.00
Ster.:   £1,600.00

HN 570
Woman Holding Child
Designer: Unknown
Height: 9 1/4", 23.5 cm
Colour: Pink and green
Issued: 1923-1938
Varieties: HN 462, 703,
            743

U.S.: $6,000.00
Can.: $6,000.00
Ster.:   £2,000.00

HN 571
Falstaff
Style One
Designer: C.J. Noke
Height: 7", 17.8 cm
Colour: Brown and
            green
Issued: 1923-1938
Varieties: HN 575, 608,
            609, 619, 638,
            1216, 1606

U.S.: $2,000.00
Can.: $2,000.00
Ster.:   £ 700.00

HN 572
Contentment
Designer: L. Harradine
Height: 7 1/4", 18.4 cm
Colour: Cream and
            orange
Issued: 1923-1938
Varieties: HN 395, 396,
            421, 468, 685,
            686, 1323

U.S.: $3,000.00
Can.: $3,000.00
Ster.:   £1,000.00

HN 573
Madonna of the Square
Designer: P. Stabler
Height: 7", 17.8 cm
Colour: Orange
Issued: 1923-1938
Varieties: HN 10, 10A, 11,
            14, 27, 326, 576,
            594, 613, 764,
            1968, 1969, 2034

U.S.: $2,700.00
Can.: $2,500.00
Ster.:   £ 900.00   *

HN 575
Falstaff
Style One
Designer: C.J. Noke
Height: 7", 17.8 cm
Colour: Brown and
            yellow
Issued: 1923-1938
Varieties: HN 571, 608,
            609, 619, 638,
            1216, 1606

U.S.: $2,000.00
Can.: $2,000.00
Ster.:   £ 700.00

HN 576
Madonna of the Square
Designer: P. Stabler
Height: 7", 17.8 cm
Colour: Green and black
Issued: 1923-1938
Varieties: HN 10, 10A, 11,
            14, 27, 326, 573,
            594, 613, 764,
            1968, 1969, 2034

U.S.: $2,600.00
Can.: $2,400.00
Ster.:   £ 850.00

HN 577
The Chelsea Pair (woman)
Designer: L. Harradine
Height: 6", 15.2 cm
Colour: White dress
            with blue flowers
Issued: 1923-1938
Varieties: HN 578

U.S.: $825.00
Can.: $750.00
Ster.:   £400.00

HN 578
The Chelsea Pair (woman)
Designer: L. Harradine
Height: 6", 15.2 cm
Colour: White dress with
          yellow flowers
Issued: 1923-1938
Varieties: HN 577

U.S.: $925.00
Can.: $900.00
Ster.: £400.00

HN 579
The Chelsea Pair (man)
Designer: L. Harradine
Height: 6", 15.2 cm
Colour: Red and black,
          yellow flowers
Issued: 1923-1938
Varieties: HN 580

U.S.: $825.00
Can.: $750.00
Ster.: £400.00

HN 580
The Chelsea Pair (man)
Designer: L. Harradine
Height: 6", 15.2 cm
Colour: Red and black,
          blue flowers
Issued: 1923-1938
Varieties: HN 579

U.S.: $925.00
Can.: $900.00
Ster.: £400.00

HN 581
The Perfect Pair
Designer: L. Harradine
Height: 6 3/4", 17.2 cm
Colour: Pink and red
Issued: 1923-1938

U.S.: $1,200.00
Can.: $1,400.00
Ster.: £ 500.00

HN 582
Grossmith's 'Tsang Ihang'
Perfume of Thibet
Designer: Unknown
Height: 11 1/2", 29.2 cm
Colour: Yellow, black
          and blue
Issued: 1923-?

U.S.: $750.00
Can.: $750.00
Ster.: £350.00

Earthenware

HN 583
The Balloon Seller
Designer: L. Harradine
Height: 9", 22.9 cm
Colour: Green and cream
Issued: 1923-1949
Varieties: HN 479, 486,
          548, 697; also
          called "The
          BalloonWoman"

U.S.: $800.00
Can.: $750.00
Ster.: £350.00

HN 584
Lady with Rose
Designer: E.W. Light
Height: 9 1/2", 24.1 cm
Colour: Green and pink
Issued: 1923-1938
Varieties: HN 48A, 52A,
          68, 304, 336,
          515, 517, 624

U.S.: $3,000.00
Can.: $3,000.00
Ster.: £1,000.00

HN 585
Harlequinade
Designer: L. Harradine
Height: 6 1/2", 16.5 cm
Colour: Purple, black
          and green
Issued: 1923-1938
Varieties: HN 635, 711, 780

U.S.: $1,000.00
Can.: $1,000.00
Ster.: £ 450.00

HN 586
Boy with Turban
Designer: L. Harradine
Height: 3 3/4", 9.5 cm
Colour: Blue and green
Issued: 1923-1938
Varieties: HN 587, 661,
662, 1210, 1212,
1213, 1214, 1225

U.S.: $ 950.00
Can.: $1,000.00
Ster.: £ 400.00

HN 587
Boy with Turban
Designer: L. Harradine
Height: 3 3/4", 9.5 cm
Colour: Green, red
and blue
Issued: 1923-1938
Varieties: HN 586, 661, 662,
1210, 1212, 1213,
1214, 1225

U.S.: $ 950.00
Can.: $1,000.00
Ster.: £ 400.00

HN 588
Girl with Yellow Frock
(Spring)
Designer: Unknown
Height: 6 1/4". 15.9 cm
Colour: Yellow
Issued: 1923-1938

U.S.: **Extremely**
Can.: **Rare**
Ster.:

HN 589
Polly Peachum
Style One
Designer: L. Harradine
Height: 6 1/2", 16.5 cm
Colour: Pink and yellow
Issued: 1924-1949
Varieties: HN 463, 465, 550,
614, 680, 693
Series: Beggar's Opera

U.S.: $1,000.00
Can.: $1,200.00
Ster.: £ 350.00

HN 590
Captain MacHeath
Designer: L. Harradine
Height: 7", 17.8 cm
Colour: Red and black
Issued: 1924-1949
Varieties: HN 464, 1256
Series: Beggar's Opera

U.S.: $1,100.00
Can.: $1,100.00
Ster. £ 350.00

HN 591
The Beggar
Style One
Designer: L. Harradine
Height: 6 3/4", 17.2 cm
Colour: Green and blue
Issued: 1924-1949
Varieties: HN 526
Series: Beggar's Opera

U.S.: $1,100.00
Can.: $1,100.00
Ster.: £ 350.00

Earthenware

HN 592
The Highwayman
Designer: L. Harradine
Height: 6 1/2", 16.5 cm
Colour: Green and red
Issued: 1924-1949
Varieties: HN 527, 1257
Series: Beggar's Opera

U.S.: $1,200.00
Can.: $1,200.00
Ster.: £ 400.00

Photograph
Not
Available

HN 593
Nude on Rock
Designer: Unknown
Height: 6 3/4", 17.1 cm
Colour: Blue
Issued: 1924-1938

U.S.: **Extremely**
Can.: **Rare**
Ster.:

Only one known to exist

HN 594
Madonna of the Square
Designer: P. Stabler
Height: 7", 17.8 cm
Colour: Green and brown
Issued: 1924-1938
Varieties: HN 10, 10A, 11,
           14, 27, 326, 573,
           576, 613, 764,
           1968, 1969, 2034

U.S.: $3,000.00
Can.: $2,500.00
Ster.: £ 900.00

HN 595
Grief
Designer: C.J. Noke
Height: 1 3/4", 4.5 cm
Colour: Blue
Issued: 1924-1938

U.S.:   Extremely
Can.:   Rare
Ster.:

Only two known to exist

HN 596
Despair
Designer: C.J. Noke
Height: 4 1/2", 11.4 cm
Colour: Mottled blue
Issued: Unknown
Varieties: Also known in
           flambé

U.S.:   Extremely
Can.:   Rare
Ster.:

Only one known to exist

HN 596
Despair
Designer: C.J. Noke
Height: 4 1/2", 11.4 cm
Colour: Green
Issued: 1924-1938

U.S.:   Extremely
Can.:   Rare
Ster.:

Only one known to exist

HN 597
The Bather
Style One
Designer: L. Harradine
Height: 7 3/4", 19.7 cm
Colour: Grey
Issued: 1924-1938
Varieties: HN 687, 781,
           782, 1238, 1708

U.S.: $3,000.00
Can.: $3,000.00
Ster.: £1,000.00

HN 598
Omar Khayyam
and the Beloved
Designer: C.J. Noke
Height: 10", 25.4 cm
Colour: Green, pink
           and blue
Issued: 1924-1938
Varieties: HN 407, 419, 459

U.S.:   None
Can.:   known
Ster.: to exist

HN 599
Masquerade (man)
Style One
Designer: L. Harradine
Height: 6 3/4", 17.2 cm
Colour: Red and black
Issued: 1924-1949
Varieties: HN 636, 683

U.S.: $950.00
Can.: $950.00
Ster.: £400.00

HN 600
Masquerade (woman)
Style One
Designer: L. Harradine
Height: 6 3/4", 17.2 cm
Colour: Pink
Issued: 1924-1949
Varieties: HN 600A, 637,
           674

U.S.: $950.00
Can.: $950.00
Ster.: £400.00

HN 600A
Masquerade (woman)
Designer: L. Harradine
Height: 6", 15.2cm
Colour: Pink
Issued: 1924-1949
Varieties: HN 600, 637, 674

U.S.: $950.00
Can.: $950.00
Ster.: £400.00

HN 601
A Mandarin
Style Three
Designer: C.J. Noke
Height: 10", 25.4 cm
Colour: Red
Issued: 1924-1938

U.S.: $6,000.00
Can.: $6,000.00
Ster.: £2,000.00

*

HN 603A
A Child Study
Style One
Designer: L. Harradine
Height: 4 3/4", 12.0 cm
Colour: White, primroses around base
Issued: 1924-1938
Varieties: HN 603B, 1441; also known in flambé

U.S.: $750.00
Can.: $600.00
Ster.: £200.00

HN 603B
A Child Study
Style One
Designer: L. Harradine
Height: 4 3/4", 12.0 cm
Colour: White, kingcups around base
Issued: 1924-1938
Varieties: HN 603A, 1441

U.S.: $750.00
Can.: $600.00
Ster.: £200.00

HN 604A
A Child Study
Style Two
Designer: L. Harradine
Height: 5 1/2", 14.0 cm
Colour: White, primroses around base
Issued: 1924-1938
Varieties: HN 604B, 1442, 1443

U.S.: $750.00
Can.: $600.00
Ster.: £200.00

HN 604B
A Child Study
Style Two
Designer: L. Harradine
Height: 5 1/2", 14.0 cm
Colour: White, kingcups around base
Issued: 1924-1938
Varieties: HN 604A, 1442, 1443

U.S.: $750.00
Can.: $600.00
Ster.: £200.00

Photograph Not Available

HN 605A
A Child Study
Style Three
Designer: L. Harradine
Height: Unknown
Colour: White, primroses around base
Issued: 1924-1938
Varieties: HN 605B

U.S.: $750.00
Can.: $600.00
Ster.: £200.00

Photograph Not Available

HN 605B
A Child Study
Style Three
Designer: L. Harradine
Height: Unknown
Colour: White, kingcups around base
Issued: 1924-1938
Varieties: HN 605A

U.S.: $750.00
Can.: $600.00
Ster.: £200.00

HN 606A
Nude Study
Designer: L. Harradine
Height: 5", 12.7 cm
Colour: White, primroses around base
Issued: 1924-1938
Varieties: HN 606B; also known in flambé

U.S.: $750.00
Can.: $600.00
Ster.: £200.00

HN 606B
Nude Study
Designer: L. Harradine
Height: 5", 12.7 cm
Colour: White, kingcups around base
Issued: 1924-1938
Varieties: HN 606A

U.S.: $750.00
Can.: $600.00
Ster.: £200.00

*

HN 608
Falstaff
Style One
Designer: C.J. Noke
Height: 7", 17.8 cm
Colour: Red
Issued: 1924-1938
Varieties: HN 571, 575, 609, 619, 638, 1216, 1606

U.S.: None
Can.: known
Ster.: to exist

HN 609
Falstaff
Style One
Designer: C.J. Noke
Height: 7", 17.8 cm
Colour: Green
Issued: 1924-1938
Varieties: HN 571, 575, 608, 619, 638, 1216, 1606

U.S.: None
Can.: known
Ster.: to exist

HN 610
Henry Lytton as Jack Point
Designer: C.J. Noke
Height: 6 1/2", 16.5 cm
Colour: Blue, black and brown
Issued: 1924-1949

U.S.: $ 950.00
Can.: $1,000.00
Ster.: £ 400.00

HN 611
A Mandarin
Style One
Designer: C.J. Noke
Height: 10 1/4", 26.0 cm
Colour: Gold and yellow
Issued: 1924-1938
Varieties: HN 84, 316, 318, 382, 746, 787, 791; "Chinese Mandarin" and "The Mikado"

U.S.: $6,000.00
Can.: $6,000.00
Ster.: £2,000.00

HN 612
The Poke Bonnet
Designer: C.J. Noke
Height: 9 1/2", 24.1 cm
Colour: Yellow and green
Issued: 1924-1938
Varieties: HN 362, 765; "A Lilac Shawl" HN 44, 44A; "In Grandma's Days" HN 339, 340, 388, 442

U.S.: $2,200.00
Can.: $2,000.00
Ster.: £ 700.00

HN 613
Madonna of the Square
Designer: P. Stabler
Height: 7", 17.8 cm
Colour: Pink and orange
Issued: 1924-1938
Varieties: HN 10, 10A, 11, 14, 27, 326, 573, 576, 594, 764, 1968, 1969, 2034

U.S.: $2,400.00
Can.: $2,200.00
Ster.: £ 750.00

HN 614
Polly Peachum
Style One
Designer: L. Harradine
Height: 6 1/2", 16.5 cm
Colour: Pink and blue
Issued: 1924-1949
Varieties: HN 463, 465, 550, 589, 680, 693
Series: Beggar's Opera

U.S.: $ 950.00
Can.: $1,000.00
Ster.: £ 300.00

HN 615
Katharine
Designer: E.W. Light
Height: 5 3/4", 14.6 cm
Colour: Pink and green
Issued: 1924-1938
Varieties: HN 61, 74, 341, 471, 793

U.S.: $2,800.00
Can.: $2,800.00
Ster.: £ 900.00

HN 616
A Jester
Style One
Designer: C.J. Noke
Height: 10", 25.4 cm
Colour: Black and white
Issued: 1924-1938
Varieties: HN 45, 71, 71A, 320, 367, 412, 426, 446, 552, 627, 1295, 1702, 2016

U.S.: $3,500.00
Can.: $2,750.00
Ster.: £ 800.00

HN 617
A Shepherd
Style One
Designer: C.J. Noke
Height: 13 1/4", 33.6cm
Colour: Dark blue
Issued: 1924-1938
Varieties: HN 81, 632

U.S.: **Extremely**
Can.: **Rare**
Ster.:

China

HN 618
Falstaff
Style Two
Designer: C.J. Noke
Height: 7", 17.8 cm
Colour: Black, lilac and green
Issued: 1924-1938
Varieties: HN 2054

U.S.: **Extremely**
Can.: **Rare**
Ster.:

HN 619
Falstaff
Style One
Designer: C.J. Noke
Height: 7", 17.8 cm
Colour: Brown, green and yellow
Issued: 1924-1938
Varieties: HN 571, 575, 608, 609, 638, 1216, 1606

U.S.: **Extremely**
Can.: **Rare**
Ster.:

HN 620
Polly Peachum
Style Two
Designer: L. Harradine
Height: 4 1/4", 10.8 cm
Colour: Pink
Issued: 1924-1938
Varieties: HN 489, 549, 694, 734
Series: Beggar's Opera

U.S.: $1,000.00
Can.: $ 950.00
Ster.: £ 300.00

HN 621
Pan on Rock
Designer: Unknown
Height: 5 1/4", 13.3 cm
Colour: Cream, green base
Issued: 1924-1938
Varieties: HN 622

U.S.: **Extremely**
Can.: **Rare**
Ster.:

HN 622
Pan on Rock
Designer: Unknown
Height: 5 1/4", 13.3 cm
Colour: Cream, black base
Issued: 1924-1938
Varieties: HN 621

U.S.:	**Extremely**
Can.:	**Rare**
Ster.:	

HN 623
An Old King
Designer: C.J. Noke
Height: 9 3/4", 24.7 cm
Colour: Grey, red and green
Issued: 1924-1938
Varieties: HN 358, 1801, 2134

U.S.:	$2,500.00
Can.:	$2,500.00
Ster.:	£ 800.00

HN 624
Lady with Rose
Designer: E.W Light
Height: 9 1/2", 24.1 cm
Colour: Turquoise
Issued: 1924-1938
Varieties: HN 48A, 52A, 68, 304, 336, 515, 517, 584

U.S.:	$3,500.00
Can.:	$3,500.00
Ster.:	£1,400.00

HN 625
A Spook
Designer: H. Tittensor
Height: 7", 17.8 cm
Colour: Yellow
Issued: 1924-1938
Varieties: HN 50, 51, 51A, 51B, 58, 512, 1218

U.S.:	$3,300.00
Can.:	$2,800.00
Ster.:	£1,000.00

Photograph
Not
Available

HN 626
Lady with Shawl
Designer: L. Harradine
Height: 13 1/4", 33.6 cm
Colour: Yellow and white
Issued: 1924-1938
Varieties: HN 447, 458, 678, 679

U.S.:	$6,000.00
Can.:	$6,000.00
Ster.:	£2,000.00

HN 627
A Jester
Style One
Designer: C.J. Noke
Height: 10", 25.4 cm
Colour: Brown checks
Issued: 1924-1938
Varieties: HN 45, 71, 71A, 320, 367, 412, 426, 446, 552, 616, 1295, 1702, 2016

U.S.:	$3,000.00
Can.:	$2,500.00
Ster.:	£1,000.00

HN 628
The Crinoline
Designer: G. Lambert
Height: 6 1/4", 15.8 cm
Colour: Yellow and blue
Issued: 1924-1938
Varieties: HN 8, 9, 9A, 21, 21A, 413, 566

U.S.:	$3,000.00
Can.:	$2,700.00
Ster.:	£ 900.00

HN 629
The Curtsey
Designer: E.W. Light
Height: 11", 27.9 cm
Colour: Green and black
Issued: 1924-1938
Varieties: HN 57, 57B, 66A, 327, 334, 363, 371, 518, 547, 670

U.S.:	$3,000.00
Can.:	$3,000.00
Ster.:	£1,000.00

HN 630
A Jester
Style Two
Designer: C.J. Noke
Height: 10 1/4", 26.0 cm
Colour: Brown
Issued: 1924-1938
Varieties: HN 45A, 45B,
55, 308, 1333

U.S.: $3,000.00
Can.: $2,500.00
Ster.: £1,000.00

Photograph
Not
Available

HN 631
Fisherwomen
Designer: Unknown
Height: 11 3/4", 29.8 cm
Colour: Mauve and green
Issued: 1924-1938
Varieties: HN 80, 349, 359;
"Waiting For The
Boats" or "Looking
For The Boats"

U.S.: Extremely
Can.: Rare
Ster.:

HN 632
A Shepherd
Style One
Designer: C.J. Noke
Height: 13 1/4", 33.6 cm
Colour: Blue and white
Issued: 1924-1938
Varieties: HN 81, 617

U.S.: None
Can.: known
Ster.: to exist

China

HN 633
A Princess
Designer: Unknown
Height: 9 1/4", 23.5 cm
Colour: Black and white
Issued: 1924-1938
Varieties: HN 391, 392,
420, 430, 431

U.S.: None
Can.: known
Ster.: to exist

HN 634
A Geisha
Style One
Designer: H. Tittensor
Height: 10 3/4", 27.3 cm
Colour: Black and white
Issued: 1924-1938
Varieties: HN 354, 376, 376A,
387, 741, 779,
1321, 1322; "The
Japanese Lady"

U.S.: $4,000.00
Can.: $4,000.00
Ster.: £2,000.00

HN 635
Harlequinade
Designer: L. Harradine
Height: 6 1/2", 16.5 cm
Colour: Gold
Issued: 1924-1938
Varieties: HN 585, 711,
780

U.S.: $1,000.00
Can.: $1,000.00
Ster.: £ 450.00

HN 636
Masquerade (man)
Style One
Designer: L. Harradine
Height: 6 3/4", 17.2 cm
Colour: Gold
Issued: 1924-1938
Varieties: HN 599, 683

U.S.: $1,100.00
Can.: $1,100.00
Ster.: £ 450.00

HN 637
Masquerade (woman)
Style One
Designer: L. Harradine
Height: 6 3/4", 17.2 cm
Colour: Gold
Issued: 1924-1938
Varieties: HN 600, 600A,
674

U.S.: $1,100.00
Can.: $1,100.00
Ster.: £ 450.00

HN 638
Falstaff
Style One
Designer: C.J. Noke
Height: 7", 17.8 cm
Colour: Red and cream
Issued: 1924-1938
Varieties: HN 571, 575,
608, 609, 619,
1216, 1606

U.S.: $2,000.00
Can.: $2,000.00
Ster.: £ 700.00

HN 639
Elsie Maynard
Style One
Designer: C.J. Noke
Height: 7", 17.8 cm
Colour: Mauve and pink
Issued: 1924-1949

U.S.: $ 950.00
Can.: $1,000.00
Ster.: £ 450.00

HN 640
Charley's Aunt
Style One
Designer: A. Taft
Height: 7", 17.8 cm
Colour: Green and
lavender
Issued: 1924-1938
Varieties: HN 35

U.S.: $2,200.00
Can.: $2,000.00
Ster.: £ 800.00

Photograph
Not
Available

HN 641
A Mandarin
Style Two
Designer: C.J. Noke
Height: 8 1/4", 21.0 cm
Colour: Yellow and blue
Issued: 1924-1938
Varieties: HN 366, 455

U.S.: **Extremely**
Can.: **Rare**
Ster.:

Only one known to exist

HN 642
Pierrette
Style One
Designer: L. Harradine
Height: 7 1/4", 18.4 cm
Colour: Red
Issued: 1924-1938
Varieties: HN 643, 644,
691, 721, 731,
732, 784

U.S.: $3,500.00
Can.: $3,000.00
Ster.: £1,100.00

HN 643
Pierrette
Style One
Designer: L. Harradine
Height: 7 1/4", 18.4 cm
Colour: Red, black
and white
Issued: 1924-1938
Varieties: HN 642, 644,
691, 721, 731,
732, 784

U.S.: $3,000.00
Can.: $2,700.00
Ster.: £ 900.00

HN 644
Pierrette
Style One
Designer: L. Harradine
Height: 7 1/4", 18.4 cm
Colour: White and black
Issued: 1924-1938
Varieties: HN 642, 643,
691, 721, 731,
732, 784

U.S.: $1,000.00
Can.: $1,100.00
Ster.: £ 600.00

Photograph
Not
Available

HN 645
One of the Forty
Style Twelve
Designer: H. Tittensor
Height: 6", 15.2 cm
Colour: Blue, black
and white
Issued: 1924-1938
Varieties: HN 482, 484,
492, 663, 713

U.S.: $2,500.00
Can.: $2,500.00
Ster.: £ 800.00

HN 646
One of the Forty
Style Eleven
Designer: H. Tittensor
Height: Unknown
Colour: Blue, black and white
Issued: 1924-1938
Varieties: HN 481, 483, 491, 667, 712, 1336, 1350
U.S.: $2,500.00
Can.: $2,500.00
Ster.: £ 800.00

HN 647
One of the Forty
Style Two
Designer: H. Tittensor
Height: 7 1/4", 18.4 cm
Colour: Blue, black and white
Issued: 1924-1938
Varieties: HN 418, 494, 498, 666, 704, 1353
U.S.: $2,500.00
Can.: $2,500.00
Ster.: £ 800.00

HN 648
One of the Forty
Style One
Designer: H. Tittensor
Height: 8 1/4", 21.0 cm
Colour: Blue, black and white
Issued: 1924-1938
Varieties: HN 417, 490, 495, 501, 528, 677, 1351, 1352
U.S.: $2,500.00
Can.: $2,500.00
Ster.: £ 800.00

HN 649
One of the Forty
Style Thirteen
Designer: H. Tittensor
Height: 7 3/4", 19.7 cm
Colour: Blue, black and white
Issued: 1924-1938
Varieties: HN 496, 500, 665, 1354
U.S.: $2,500.00
Can.: $2,500.00
Ster.: £ 800.00

HN 650
Crinoline Lady
Designer: Unknown
Height: 3", 7.6 cm
Colour: Green and white
Issued: 1924-1938
Varieties: HN 651, 652, 653, 654, 655
U.S.: $2,000.00
Can.: $1,750.00
Ster.: £ 650.00

HN 651
Crinoline Lady
Designer: Unknown
Height: 3", 7.6 cm
Colour: Orange and white
Issued: 1924-1938
Varieties: HN 650, 652, 653, 654, 655
U.S.: $2,000.00
Can.: $1,750.00
Ster.: £ 650.00

HN 652
Crinoline Lady
Designer: Unknown
Height: 3", 7.6 cm
Colour: Purple
Issued: 1924-1938
Varieties: HN 650, 651, 653, 654, 655
U.S.: $2,000.00
Can.: $1,750.00
Ster.: £ 650.00

HN 653
Crinoline Lady
Designer: Unknown
Height: 3", 7.6 cm
Colour: Black and white
Issued: 1924-1938
Varieties: HN 650, 651, 652, 654, 655
U.S.: $2,000.00
Can.: $1,750.00
Ster.: £ 650.00

HN 654
Crinoline Lady
Designer: Unknown
Height: 3", 7.6 cm
Colour: Red and
purple
Issued: 1924-1938
Varieties: HN 650, 651,
652, 653, 655

U.S.: $2,000.00
Can.: $1,750.00
Ster.: £ 650.00

HN 655
Crinoline Lady
Designer: Unknown
Height: 3", 7.6 cm
Colour: Blue and black
Issued: 1924-1938
Varieties: HN 650, 651,
652, 653, 654

U.S.: $2,000.00
Can.: $1,750.00
Ster.: £ 650.00

HN 656
The Mask
Designer: L. Harradine
Height: 6 3/4", 17.2 cm
Colour: Blue and purple
Issued: 1924-1938
Varieties: HN 657, 729,
733, 785, 1271

U.S.: $1,500.00
Can.: $1,750.00
Ster.: £ 800.00

HN 657
The Mask
Designer: L. Harradine
Height: 6 3/4", 17.2 cm
Colour: Black and white
Issued: 1924-1938
Varieties: HN 656, 729,
733, 785, 1271

U.S.: $1,800.00
Can.: $2,000.00
Ster.: £ 800.00

HN 658
Mam'selle
Designer: L. Harradine
Height: 7", 17.8 cm
Colour: Black and white
Issued: 1924-1938
Varieties: HN 659, 724, 786

U.S.: $1,800.00
Can.: $2,000.00
Ster.: £ 800.00

HN 659
Mam'selle
Designer: L. Harradine
Height: 7", 17.8 cm
Colour: Dark blue
Issued: 1924-1938
Varieties: HN 658, 724,
786

U.S.: $1,800.00
Can.: $2,000.00
Ster.: £ 800.00

HN 660
Myfanwy Jones
Designer: E.W. Light
Height: 12", 30.5 cm
Colour: White and blue
Issued: 1924-1938
Varieties: HN 39, 92, 456,
514, 516, 519, 520,
668, 669, 701, 792;
also called "The
Welsh Girl"

U.S.: $5,500.00
Can.: $4,750.00
Ster.: £1,500.00

HN 661
Boy with Turban
Designer: L. Harradine
Height: 3 3/4", 9.5 cm
Colour: Blue
Issued: 1924-1938
Varieties: HN 586, 587,
662, 1210, 1212,
1213, 1214, 1225

U.S.: $ 950.00
Can.: $1,000.00
Ster.: £ 400.00

HN 662
Boy with Turban
Designer: L. Harradine
Height: 3 3/4", 9.5 cm
Colour: Black and white
Issued: 1924-1938
Varieties: HN 586, 587,
661, 1210, 1212,
1213, 1214, 1225

U.S.:	$ 950.00
Can.:	$1,000.00
Ster.:	£ 400.00

Photograph
Not
Available

HN 663
One of the Forty
Style Twelve
Designer: H. Tittensor
Height: 6", 15.2 cm
Colour: Yellow
Issued: 1924-1938
Varieties: HN 482, 484,
492, 645, 713,

U.S.:	$1,800.00
Can.:	$2,000.00
Ster.:	£ 800.00

HN 664
One of the Forty
Style Ten
Designer: H. Tittensor
Height: 7 3/4", 19.7 cm
Colour: Yellow, green
and black
Issued: 1924-1938
Varieties: HN 480, 493,
497, 499, 714

U.S.:	$1,800.00
Can.:	$2,000.00
Ster.:	£ 800.00

Photograph
Not
Available

HN 665
One of the Forty
Style Thirteen
Designer: H. Tittensor
Height: 7 3/4", 19.7 cm
Colour: Yellow
Issued: 1924-1938
Varieties: HN 496, 500,
649, 1354

U.S.:	$1,800.00
Can.:	$2,000.00
Ster.:	£ 800.00

HN 666
One of the Forty
Style Two
Designer: H. Tittensor
Height: 7 1/4", 18.4 cm
Colour: Yellow
Issued: 1924-1938
Varieties: HN 418, 494,
498, 647, 704,
1353

U.S.:	$1,800.00
Can.:	$2,000.00
Ster.:	£ 800.00

Photograph
Not
Available

HN 667
One of the Forty
Style Eleven
Designer: H. Tittensor
Height: Unknown
Colour: Yellow and
black
Issued: 1924-1938
Varieties: HN 481, 483,
491, 646, 712,
1336, 1350

U.S.:	$1,800.00
Can.:	$2,000.00
Ster.:	£ 800.00

HN 668
Myfanwy Jones
Designer: E.W. Light
Height: 12", 30.5cm
Colour: Yellow and pink
Issued: 1924-1938
Varieties: HN 39, 92, 456,
514, 516, 519, 520,
660, 669, 701, 792;
also called "The
Welsh Girl"

U.S.:	$6,000.00
Can.:	$5,000.00
Ster.:	£1,700.00

HN 669
Myfanwy Jones
Designer: E.W. Light
Height: 8 1/2", 21.5cm
Colour: Yellow and green
Issued: 1924-1938
Varieties: HN 39, 92, 456,
514, 516, 519, 520,
660, 668, 701, 792;
also called "The
Welsh Girl"

U.S.:	$5,000.00
Can.:	$4,000.00
Ster.:	£1,500.00

HN 670
The Curtsey
Designer: E.W. Light
Height: 11", 27.9 cm
Colour: Pink and yellow
Issued: 1924-1938
Varieties: HN 57, 57B,
66A, 327, 334,
363, 371, 518,
547, 629
U.S.: **$3,000.00**
Can.: **$3,000.00**
Ster.: **£1,000.00**

HN 671
The Ermine Muff
Designer: C.J. Noke
Height: 8 1/2", 21.6 cm
Colour: Green and yellow
Issued: 1924-1938
Varieties: HN 54, 332; also
called "Lady with
the Ermine Muff"
and "Lady Ermine"
U.S.: **$2,700.00**
Can.: **$2,700.00**
Ster.: **£ 900.00**

HN 672
Tulips
Designer: Unknown
Height: 9 1/2", 24.1 cm
Colour: Green
Issued: 1924-1938
Varieties: HN 466, 488,
747, 1334
U.S.: **$4,000.00**
Can.: **$3,500.00**
Ster.: **£1,200.00**

Earthenware

> Photograph
> Not
> Available

HN 673
Henry VIII
Style One
Designer: C.J. Noke
Height: Unknown
Colour: Brown and
lavender
Issued: 1924-1938
Varieties: HN 370
U.S.: **None**
Can.: **known**
Ster.: **to exist**

HN 674
Masquerade (woman)
Style One
Designer: L. Harradine
Height: 6 3/4", 17.2 cm
Colour: Orange and
yellow
Issued: 1924-1938
Varieties: HN 600, 600A,
637
U.S.: **$1,200.00**
Can.: **$1,200.00**
Ster.: **£ 400.00**

HN 675
The Gainsborough Hat
Designer: H. Tittensor
Height: 8 3/4", 22.2 cm
Colour: Cream
Issued: 1924-1938
Varieties: HN 46, 46A,
47, 329, 352,
383, 453, 705
U.S.: **$3,200.00**
Can.: **$3,000.00**
Ster.: **£ 975.00**

HN 676
Pavlova
Designer: C.J. Noke
Height: 4 1/4", 10.8 cm
Colour: White and blue
tu'tu, black base
Issued: 1924-1938
Varieties: HN 487;
also called
"Swan Song"
U.S.: **$6,000.00**
Can.: **$6,000.00**
Ster.: **£2.000.00**

HN 677
One of the Forty
Style One
Designer: H. Tittensor
Height: 8 1/4", 21.0 cm
Colour: Orange, yellow
and red
Issued: 1924-1938
Varieties: HN 417, 490,
495, 501, 528,
648, 1351, 1352
U.S.: **$1,800.00**
Can.: **$2,000.00**
Ster.: **£ 800.00**

Photograph Not Available	Photograph Not Available		Photograph Not Available

HN 678
Lady with Shawl
Designer: L. Harradine
Height: 13 1/4", 33.7 cm
Colour: Black, yellow and white
Issued: 1924-1938
Varieties: HN 447, 458, 626, 679

U.S.: $6,000.00
Can.: $6,000.00
Ster.: £2,000.00

HN 679
Lady with Shawl
Designer: L. Harradine
Height: 13 1/4", 33.7 cm
Colour: Black, yellow, blue and white
Issued: 1924-1938
Varieties: HN 447, 458, 626, 678

U.S.: $6,000.00
Can.: $6,000.00
Ster.: £2,000.00

HN 680
Polly Peachum
Style One
Designer: L. Harradine
Height: 6 1/2", 16.5 cm
Colour: White
Issued: 1924-1949
Varieties: HN 463, 465, 550, 589, 614, 693
Series: Beggar's Opera

U.S.: $950.00
Can.: $950.00
Ster.: £350.00

HN 681
The Cobbler
Style Two
Designer: C.J. Noke
Height: 8 1/2", 21.6 cm
Colour: Green and red
Issued: 1924-1938
Varieties: HN 1251, 1283

U.S.: $2,500.00
Can.: $2,000.00
Ster.: £ 750.00

HN 682
The Cobbler
Style One
Designer: C.J. Noke
Height: 7 1/2", 19.1 cm
Colour: Red and green
Issued: 1924-1938
Varieties: HN 542, 543

U.S.: $2,200.00
Can.: $1,750.00
Ster.: £ 650.00

HN 683
Masquerade (man)
Style One
Designer: L. Harradine
Height: 7 1/4", 18.4 cm
Colour: Green
Issued: 1924-1938
Varieties: HN 599, 636

U.S.: $ 950.00
Can.: $1,000.00
Ster.: £ 450.00

Earthenware

HN 684
Tony Weller
Style One
Designer: C.J. Noke
Height: 10 1/4". 26.0 cm
Colour: Green and brown
Issued: 1924-1938
Varieties: HN 346, 368

U.S.: $2,000.00
Can.: $1,700.00
Ster.: £ 600.00

HN 685
Contentment
Designer: L. Harradine
Height: 7 1/4", 18.4 cm
Colour: Black and white
Issued: 1924-1938
Varieties: HN 395, 396, 421, 468, 572, 686, 1323

U.S.: $3,000.00
Can.: $3,000.00
Ster.: £1,000.00

HN 686
Contentment
Designer: L. Harradine
Height: 7 1/4", 18.4 cm
Colour: Black and white
Issued: 1924-1938
Varieties: HN 395, 396, 421, 468, 572, 685, 1323

U.S.: $3,000.00
Can.: $3,000.00
Ster.: £1,000.00

HN 687
The Bather
Style One
Designer: L. Harradine
Height: 7 3/4", 19.7 cm
Colour: Blue
Issued: 1924-1949
Varieties: HN 597, 781, 782, 1238, 1708

U.S.: $1,100.00
Can.: $1,100.00
Ster.: £ 600.00

HN 688
A Yeoman of the Guard
Designer: L. Harradine
Height: 5 3/4", 14.6 cm
Colour: Red, gold and brown
Issued: 1924-1938
Varieties: HN 2122

U.S.: $1,200.00
Can.: $1,000.00
Ster.: £ 600.00

Photograph
Not
Available

HN 689
A Chelsea Pensioner
Designer: L. Harradine
Height: 5 3/4", 14.6 cm
Colour: Red
Issued: 1924-1938

U.S.: $2,000.00
Can.: $1,500.00
Ster.: £ 600.00

Also produced as miniature figurine, but without "M" number

HN 690
A Lady of the Georgian Period
Designer: E.W. Light
Height: 10 1/4", 26.0 cm
Colour: Pink, white and yellow overdress
Issued: 1925-1938
Varieties: HN 41, 331, 444, 702

U.S.: $2,900.00
Can.: $3,000.00
Ster.: £ 950.00

HN 691
Pierrette
Style One
Designer: L. Harradine
Height: 7 1/4", 18.4 cm
Colour: Gold
Issued: 1925-1938
Varieties: HN 642, 643, 644, 721, 731, 732, 784

U.S.: $1,800.00
Can.: $1,800.00
Ster.: £ 600.00

HN 692
Sleep
Designer: P. Stabler
Height: 6", 15.2 cm
Colour: Gold
Issued: 1925-1938
Varieties: HN 24, 24A, 25, 25A, 424, 710

U.S.: $2,800.00
Can.: $2,800.00
Ster.: £ 850.00

HN 693
Polly Peachum
Style One
Designer: L. Harradine
Height: 6 1/2", 16.5 cm
Colour: Pink and green
Issued: 1925-1949
Varieties: HN 463, 465, 550, 589, 614, 680
Series: Beggar's Opera

U.S.: $ 950.00
Can.: $1,000.00
Ster.: £ 300.00

HN 694
Polly Peachum
Style Two
Designer: L. Harradine
Height: 4 1/4", 10.8 cm
Colour: Pink and green
Issued: 1925-1949
Varieties: HN 489, 549,
620, 734
Series: Beggar's Opera

U.S.: $1,400.00
Can.: $1,000.00
Ster.: £ 450.00

HN 695
Lucy Lockett
Style Two
Designer: L. Harradine
Height: 6", 15.2 cm
Colour: Orange
Issued: 1925-1949
Varieties: HN 696
Series: Beggar's Opera

U.S.: $ 950.00
Can.: $1,000.00
Ster.: £ 300.00

HN 696
Lucy Lockett
Style Two
Designer: L. Harradine
Height: 6", 15.2 cm
Colour: Pale blue
Issued: 1925-1949
Varieties: HN 695
Series: Beggar's Opera

U.S.: $ 950.00
Can.: $1,000.00
Ster.: £ 300.00

HN 697
The Balloon Seller
Designer: L. Harradine
Height: 9", 22.9 cm
Colour: Red and blue
Issued: 1925-1938
Varieties: HN 479, 486, 548,
583; also called
"The Balloon
Woman"

U.S.: $3,500.00
Can.: $3,000.00
Ster.: £1,000.00

HN 698
Polly Peachum
Style Three
Designer: L. Harradine
Height: 2 1/4", 5.7 cm
Colour: Rose pink
Issued: 1925-1949
Varieties: HN 699, 757,
758, 759, 760,
761, 762

U.S.: $950.00
Can.: $950.00
Ster.: £450.00

HN 699
Polly Peachum
Style Three
Designer: L. Harradine
Height: 2 1/4", 5.7 cm
Colour: Pale blue
Issued: 1925-1949
Varieties: HN 698, 757,
758, 759, 760,
761, 762

U.S.: $950.00
Can.: $950.00
Ster.: £450.00

HN 700
Pretty Lady
Designer: H. Tittensor
Height: 9 1/2", 24.1 cm
Colour: Yellow and green
Issued: 1925-1938
Varieties: HN 69, 70, 302,
330, 361, 384,
565, 763, 783

U.S.: $1,750.00
Can.: $1,750.00
Ster.: £ 600.00

HN 701
Myfanwy Jones
Designer: E.W. Light
Height: 12", 30.5 cm
Colour: Multi-coloured
Issued: 1925-1938
Varieties: HN 39, 92, 456,
514, 516, 519, 520,
660, 668, 669, 792;
also called
"The Welsh Girl"

U.S.: $5,500.00
Can.: $4,500.00
Ster.: £1,500.00

HN 702
A Lady of the
Georgian Period
Designer: E.W. Light
Height: 10 1/4", 26.0 cm
Colour: Pink and green
Issued: 1925-1938
Varieties: HN 41, 331,
444, 690

U.S.: **$3,000.00**
Can.: **$3,000.00**
Ster.: **£1,000.00**

HN 703
Woman Holding Child
Designer: Unknown
Height: 9 1/4", 23.5 cm
Colour: Purple, black
and red
Issued: 1925-1938
Varieties: HN 462, 570,
743

U.S.: **$6,000.00**
Can.: **$6,000.00**
Ster.: **£2,000.00**

HN 704
One of the Forty
Style Two
Designer: H. Tittensor
Height: 7 1/4", 18.4 cm
Colour: Red
Issued: 1925-1938
Varieties: HN 418, 494,
498, 647, 666,
1353

U.S.: **$2,000.00**
Can.: **$2,000.00**
Ster.: **£ 800.00**

HN 705
The Gainsborough Hat
Designer: H. Tittensor
Height: 9", 22.9 cm
Colour: Blue
Issued: 1925-1938
Varieties: HN 46, 46A,
47, 329, 352,
383, 453, 675

U.S.: **$3,000.00**
Can.: **$2,750.00**
Ster.: **£ 950.00**

Earthenware

HN 706
Fruit Gathering
Designer: L. Harradine
Height: 7 1/4", 18.4 cm
Colour: Purple and yellow
Issued: 1925-1938
Varieties: HN 449, 476,
503, 561, 562
707

U.S.: **$4,000.00**
Can.: **$4,000.00**
Ster.: **£1,300.00**

HN 707
Fruit Gathering
Designer: L. Harradine
Height: 7 1/4", 18.4 cm
Colour: Red
Issued: 1925-1938
Varieties: HN 449, 476,
503, 561, 562,
706

U.S.: **$4,000.00**
Can.: **$4,000.00**
Ster.: **£1,300.00**

Earthenware

HN 708
Shepherdess
Style One
Designer: Unknown
Height: 3 1/2", 8.8 cm
Colour: Red, yellow
and pink
Issued: 1925-1948

U.S.: **$2,200.00**
Can.: **$2,000.00**
Ster.: **£ 800.00**

HN 709
Shepherd
Style Two
Designer: Unknown
Height: 3 1/2", 8.8 cm
Colour: Green, red
and black
Issued: 1925-1938

U.S.: **$2,200.00**
Can.: **$2,000.00**
Ster.: **£ 800.00**

HN 710
Sleep
Designer: P. Stabler
Height: 6", 15.2 cm
Colour: Blue
Issued: 1925-1938
Varieties: HN 24, 24A,
          25, 25A, 424,
          692
U.S.: $2,500.00
Can.: $2,500.00
Ster.:   £ 800.00

HN 711
Harlequinade
Designer: L. Harradine
Height: 6 1/2", 16.5 cm
Colour: White and black
Issued: 1925-1938
Varieties: HN 585, 635,
          780
U.S.: $1,200.00
Can.: $1,200.00
Ster.:   £ 450.00

Photograph
Not
Available

HN 712
One of the Forty
Style Eleven
Designer: H. Tittensor
Height: Unknown
Colour: Red
Issued: 1925-1938
Varieties: HN 481, 483,
          491, 646, 667,
          1336, 1350
U.S.: $2,500.00
Can.: $2,500.00
Ster.:   £ 800.00

Photograph
Not
Available

HN 713
One of the Forty
Style Twelve
Designer: H. Tittensor
Height: 6", 15.2 cm
Colour: Red
Issued: 1925-1938
Varieties: HN 482, 484,
          492, 645, 663
U.S.: $2,500.00
Can.: $2,500.00
Ster.:   £ 800.00

HN 714
One of the Forty
Style Ten
Designer: H. Tittensor
Height: 6 3/4", 17.2 cm
Colour: Red and blue
Issued: 1925-1938
Varieties: HN 480, 493,
          497, 499, 664
U.S.: $2,500.00
Can.: $2,500.00
Ster.:   £ 800.00

HN 715
Proposal (woman)
Designer: Unknown
Height: 5 3/4", 14.6 cm
Colour: Burgundy
          and black
Issued: 1925-1938
Varieties: HN 716, 788
U.S.: $2,000.00
Can.: $2,250.00
Ster.:   £ 700.00

HN 716
Proposal (woman)
Designer: Unknown
Height: 5 3/4", 14.6 cm
Colour: White and black
Issued: 1925-1938
Varieties: HN 715, 788
U.S.: $2,000.00
Can.: $2,250.00
Ster.:   £ 700.00

HN 717
Lady Clown
Designer: L. Harradine
Height: 7 1/2", 19.1 cm
Colour: White, red
          and black
Issued: 1925-1938
Varieties: HN 718, 738, 770;
          also called
          "Clownette"
          HN1263
U.S.: $4,500.00
Can.: $4,500.00
Ster.:   £1,500.00

HN 718
Lady Clown
Designer:	L. Harradine
Height:	7 1/2", 19.1 cm
Colour:	White, red and black
Issued:	1925-1938
Varieties:	HN 717, 738, 770; also called "Clownette" HN1263
U.S.:	**$5,000.00**
Can.:	**$5,000.00**
Ster.:	**£1,700.00**

HN 719
Butterfly
Designer:	L. Harradine
Height:	6 1/2", 16.5 cm
Colour:	Pink, yellow and black
Issued:	1925-1938
Varieties:	HN 720, 730, 1203; also called "Butterfly Girl" HN 1456
U.S.:	**$1,800.00**
Can.:	**$2,000.00**
Ster.:	**£ 800.00**

HN 720
Butterfly
Designer:	L. Harradine
Height:	6 1/2", 16.5 cm
Colour:	Orange, white and black
Issued:	1925-1938
Varieties:	HN 719, 730, 1203; also called "Butterfly Girl" HN 1456
U.S.:	**$1,800.00**
Can.:	**$2,000.00**
Ster.:	**£ 800.00**

HN 721
Pierrette
Style One
Designer:	L. Harradine
Height:	7 1/4", 18.4 cm
Colour:	Black and white
Issued:	1925-1938
Varieties:	HN 642, 643, 644, 691, 731, 732, 784
U.S.:	**$3,000.00**
Can.:	**$2,700.00**
Ster.:	**£ 950.00**

HN 722
Mephisto
Designer:	L. Harradine
Height:	6 1/2", 16.5 cm
Colour:	Black
Issued:	1925-1938
Varieties:	HN 723
U.S.:	**$3,900.00**
Can.:	**$3,500.00**
Ster.:	**£1,250.00**

HN 723
Mephisto
Designer:	L. Harradine
Height:	6 1/2", 16.5 cm
Colour:	Red and black
Issued:	1925-1938
Varieties:	HN 722
U.S.:	**$3,500.00**
Can.:	**$3,000.00**
Ster.:	**£1,100.00**

HN 724
Mam'selle
Designer:	L. Harradine
Height:	7", 17.8 cm
Colour:	White, red and yellow
Issued:	1925-1938
Varieties:	HN 658, 659, 786
U.S.:	**$2,000.00**
Can.:	**$2,200.00**
Ster.:	**£ 800.00**

HN 725
The Proposal (man)
Designer:	Unknown
Height:	5 1/2", 14.0 cm
Colour:	Red and black
Issued:	1925-1938
Varieties:	HN 1209
U.S.:	**$2,000.00**
Can.:	**$2,000.00**
Ster.:	**£ 700.00**

HN 726
A Victorian Lady
Designer: L. Harradine
Height: 7 1/2", 19.1 cm
Colour: Purple and yellow
Issued: 1925-1938
Varieties: HN 727, 728,
736, 739, 740,
742, 745, 1208,
1258, 1276, 1277,
1345, 1452, 1529

U.S.: $900.00
Can.: $950.00
Ster.: £300.00

HN 727
A Victorian Lady
Designer: L. Harradine
Height: 7 1/2", 19.1 cm
Colour: Pink and green
Issued: 1925-1938
Varieties: HN 726, 728,
736, 739, 740,
742, 745, 1208,
1258, 1276, 1277,
1345, 1452, 1529

U.S.: $450.00
Can.: $550.00
Ster.: £300.00

HN 728
A Victorian Lady
Designer: L. Harradine
Height: 7 3/4", 19.7 cm
Colour: Pink and purple
Issued: 1925-1952
Varieties: HN 726, 727, 736,
739, 740, 742, 745,
1208, 1258, 1276,
1277, 1345, 1452,
1529

U.S.: $450.00
Can.: $550.00
Ster.: £300.00

HN 729
The Mask
Designer: L. Harradine
Height: 6 3/4", 17.2 cm
Colour: Red and black
Issued: 1925-1938
Varieties: HN 656, 657,
733, 785, 1271

U.S.: $2,500.00
Can.: $2,250.00
Ster.: £ 900.00

HN 730
Butterfly
Designer: L. Harradine
Height: 6 1/2", 16.5 cm
Colour: Yellow , blue
and black
Issued: 1925-1938
Varieties: HN 719, 720,
1203; also called
"Butterfly Girl"
HN 1456

U.S.: $1,800.00
Can.: $2,000.00
Ster.: £ 800.00

HN 731
Pierrette
Style One
Designer: L. Harradine
Height: 7 1/4", 18.4 cm
Colour: Black and white
Issued: 1925-1938
Varieties: HN 642, 643,
644, 691, 721,
732, 784

U.S.: $3,000.00
Can.: $2,700.00
Ster.: £ 950.00

HN 732
Pierrette
Style One
Designer: L. Harradine
Height: 7 1/4", 18.4 cm
Colour: Black and white
Issued: 1925-1938
Varieties: HN 642, 643,
644, 691, 721,
731, 784

U.S.: $3,000.00
Can.: $2,700.00
Ster.: £ 950.00

HN 733
The Mask
Designer: L. Harradine
Height: 6 3/4", 17.2 cm
Colour: White and black
Issued: 1925-1938
Varieties: HN 656, 657,
729, 785, 1271

U.S.: $2,500.00
Can.: $2,500.00
Ster.: £ 900.00

HN 734
Polly Peachum
Style Two
Designer: L. Harradine
Height: 4 1/4", 10.8 cm
Colour: Black and white
Issued: 1925-1949
Varieties: HN 489, 549, 620, 694
Series: Beggar's Opera

U.S.: $1,200.00
Can.: $1,000.00
Ster.: £ 450.00

HN 735
Shepherdess
Style Two
Designer: Unknown
Height: 7", 17.8 cm
Colour: Blue and black
Issued: 1925-1938
Varieties: HN 750; also called "Milkmaid"

U.S.: $2,500.00
Can.: $2,500.00
Ster.: £ 850.00

HN 736
A Victorian Lady
Designer: L. Harradine
Height: 7 3/4", 19.7 cm
Colour: Pink and purple
Issued: 1925-1938
Varieties: HN 726, 727, 728, 739, 740, 742, 745, 1208, 1258, 1276, 1277, 1345,1452, 1529

U.S.: $650.00
Can.: $750.00
Ster.: £300.00   *

HN 738
Lady Clown
Designer: L. Harradine
Height: 7 1/2", 19.1 cm
Colour: Black, white and red
Issued: 1925-1938
Varieties: HN 717, 718, 770, 1263

U.S.: $5,000.00
Can.: $5,000.00
Ster.: £1,750.00

HN 739
A Victorian Lady
Designer: L. Harradine
Height: 7 3/4", 19.7 cm
Colour: Red, blue, yellow
Issued: 1925-1938
Varieties: HN 726, 727, 728, 736, 740, 742, 745, 1208, 1258, 1276, 1277, 1345, 1452, 1529

U.S.: $1,300.00
Can.: $1,000.00
Ster.: £ 375.00

HN 740
A Victorian Lady
Designer: L. Harradine
Height: 7 3/4", 19.7 cm
Colour: Pink
Issued: 1925-1938
Varieties: HN 726, 727, 728, 736, 739, 742, 745, 1208, 1258, 1276, 1277, 1345, 1452, 1529

U.S.: $1,300.00
Can.: $ 875.00
Ster.: £ 300.00

HN 741
A Geisha
Style One
Designer: H. Tittensor
Height: 10 3/4", 27.3 cm
Colour: Multi-coloured
Issued: 1925-1938
Varieties: HN 354, 376, 376A, 387, 634, 779, 1321, 1322; "Japanese Lady"

U.S.: $6,000.00
Can.: $6,000.00
Ster.: £2,000.00

HN 742
A Victorian Lady
Designer: L. Harradine
Height: 7 3/4", 19.7 cm
Colour: Black and white
Issued: 1925-1938
Varieties: HN 726, 727, 728, 736, 739, 740, 745, 1208, 1258, 1276, 1277, 1345, 1452, 1529

U.S.: $1,500.00
Can.: $1,200.00
Ster.: £ 450.00

HN 743
Woman Holding Child
Designer: Unknown
Height: 9 1/4", 23.5 cm
Colour: Blue and yellow
Issued: 1925-1938
Varieties: HN 462, 570,
            703

U.S.: $6,000.00
Can.: $6,000.00
Ster.:   £2,000.00

HN 744
The Lavender Woman
Designer: P. Stabler
Height: 8 1/4", 21.0 cm
Colour: Blue
Issued: 1925-1938
Varieties: HN 22, 23, 23A,
            342, 569

U.S.: $5,000.00
Can.: $5,000.00
Ster.:   £1,600.00

HN 745
A Victorian Lady
Designer: L. Harradine
Height: 7 3/4", 19.7 cm
Colour: Pink and green
Issued: 1925-1938
Varieties: HN 726, 727, 728,
            736, 739, 740, 742,
            1208, 1258, 1276,
            1277, 1345, 1452,
            1529

U.S.: $1,300.00
Can.: $ 950.00
Ster.:   £ 350.00

HN 746
A Mandarin
Style One
Designer: C.J. Noke
Height: 10 1/4", 26.0 cm
Colour: Black and green
Issued: 1925-1938
Varieties: HN 84, 316, 318,
            382, 611, 787, 791;
            "Chinese Mandarin"
            and "The Mikado"

U.S.: $6,000.00
Can.: $6,000.00
Ster.:   £2,000.00

HN 747
Tulips
Designer: Unknown
Height: 9 1/2", 24.1 cm
Colour: Blue and green
Issued: 1925-1938
Varieties: HN 466, 488,
            672, 1334

U.S.: $4,000.00
Can.: $3,500.00
Ster.:   £1,200.00

HN 748
Out For a Walk
Designer: H. Tittensor
Height: 10", 25.4 cm
Colour: Black, red
            and white
Issued: 1925-1936
Varieties: HN 86, 443

U.S.: $5,000.00
Can.: $5,000.00
Ster.:   £1,800.00

HN 749
London Cry, Strawberries
Designer: L. Harradine
Height: 6 3/4", 17.2 cm
Colour: Red and cream
Issued: 1925-1938
Varieties: HN 772

U.S.: $2,300.00
Can.: $1,950.00
Ster.:   £ 700.00

HN 750
Shepherdess
Style Two
Designer: Unknown
Height: 7", 17.8 cm
Colour: Pink and yellow
Issued: 1925-1938
Varieties: HN 735; also
            called "Milkmaid"

U.S.: $2,900.00
Can.: $2,900.00
Ster.:   £ 950.00

HN 751
Shepherd
Style Three
Designer: Unknown
Height: 7", 17.8 cm
Colour: Green, black,
red and white
Issued: 1925-1938
U.S.: $2,900.00
Can.: $2,900.00
Ster.: £ 950.00

HN 752
London Cry,
Turnips and Carrots
Designer: L. Harradine
Height: 6 3/4". 17.2 cm
Colour: Purple, red,
black and green
Issued: 1925-1938
Varieties: HN 771
U.S.: $2,300.00
Can.: $1,950.00
Ster.: £ 700.00

HN 753
The Dandy
Designer: L. Harradine
Height: 6 3/4". 17.2 cm
Colour: Red, white,
black and green
Issued: 1925-1938
U.S.: $1,250.00
Can.: $1,500.00
Ster.: £ 700.00

HN 754
The Belle
Style One
Designer: L. Harradine
Height: 6 1/2", 16.5 cm
Colour: Multi-coloured
Issued: 1925-1938
Varieties: HN 776
U.S.: $1,250.00
Can.: $1,500.00
Ster.: £ 500.00

HN 755
Mephistopheles
and Marguerite
Designer: C.J. Noke
Height: 7 3/4", 19.7 cm
Colour: Orange and
purple
Issued: 1925-1949
Varieties: HN 775
U.S.: $2,500.00
Can.: $2,500.00
Ster.: £ 800.00

HN 756
The Modern Piper
Designer: L. Harradine
Height: 8 1/2", 21.6 cm
Colour: Lavender
and green
Issued: 1925-1938
U.S.: $3,000.00
Can.: $3,000.00
Ster.: £1,200.00

HN 757
Polly Peachum
Style Three
Designer: L. Harradine
Height: 2 1/4", 5.7 cm
Colour: Red
Issued: 1925-1949
Varieties: HN 698, 699, 758,
759, 760, 761, 762
Series: Beggar's Opera
U.S.: $1,100.00
Can.: $1,000.00
Ster.: £ 450.00

HN 758
Polly Peachum
Style Three
Designer: L. Harradine
Height: 2 1/4", 5.7 cm
Colour: Pink and orange
Issued: 1925-1949
Varieties: HN 698, 699, 757,
759, 760, 761, 762
Series: Beggar's Opera
U.S.: $1,100.00
Can.: $1,000.00
Ster.: £ 450.00

HN 759
Polly Peachum
Style Three
Designer: L. Harradine
Height: 2 1/4", 5.7 cm
Colour: Yellow, white and black
Issued: 1925-1949
Varieties: HN 698, 699, 757, 758, 760, 761, 762
Series: Beggar's Opera

U.S.: $1,100.00
Can.: $1,000.00
Ster.: £ 450.00

HN 760
Polly Peachum
Style Three
Designer: L. Harradine
Height: 2 1/4", 5.7 cm
Colour: Multi-coloured
Issued: 1925-1949
Varieties: HN 698, 699, 757, 758, 759, 761, 762
Series: Beggar's Opera

U.S.: $1,100.00
Can.: $1,000.00
Ster.: £ 450.00

HN 761
Polly Peachum
Style Three
Designer: L. Harradine
Height: 2 1/4", 5.7 cm
Colour: Blue and purple
Issued: 1925-1949
Varieties: HN 698, 699, 757, 758, 759, 760, 762
Series: Beggar's Opera

U.S.: $1,100.00
Can.: $1,000.00
Ster.: £ 450.00

HN 762
Polly Peachum
Style Three
Designer: L. Harradine
Height: 2 1/4", 5.7 cm
Colour: Red and white
Issued: 1925-1949
Varieties: HN 698, 699, 757, 758, 759, 760, 761
Series: Beggar's Opera

U.S.: $1,100.00
Can.: $1,000.00
Ster.: £ 450.00

HN 763
Pretty Lady
Designer: H. Tittensor
Height: 9 1/2", 24.1 cm
Colour: Orange, white and green
Issued: 1925-1938
Varieties: HN 69, 70, 302, 330, 361, 384, 565, 700, 783

U.S.: $1,500.00
Can.: $1,750.00
Ster.: £ 500.00

HN 764
Madonna of the Square
Designer: P. Stabler
Height: 7", 17.8 cm
Colour: Blue, purple and yellow
Issued: 1925-1938
Varieties: HN 10, 10A, 11, 14, 27, 326, 573, 576, 594, 613, 1968, 1969, 2034

U.S.: $2,900.00
Can.: $2,700.00
Ster.: £ 900.00

HN 765
The Poke Bonnet
Designer: C.J. Noke
Height: 8 3/4", 22.2 cm
Colour: Green, blue, purple
Issued: 1925-1938
Varieties: HN 362, 612; "A Lilac Shawl" HN 44, 44A, "In Grandma's Days" HN339, 340, 388, 442

U.S.: $2,400.00
Can.: $2,200.00
Ster.: £ 750.00

HN 766
Irish Colleen
Designer: L. Harradine
Height: 6 1/2", 16.5 cm
Colour: Red, black, white and grey
Issued: 1925-1938
Varieties: HN 767

U.S.: $3,000.00
Can.: $3,000.00
Ster.: £1,000.00

HN 767
Irish Collen
Designer: L. Harradine
Height: 6 1/2", 16.5 cm
Colour: Black, red
and green
Issued: 1925-1938
Varieties: HN 766

U.S.: $3,000.00
Can.: $3,000.00
Ster.: £1,000.00

HN 768
Harlequinade Masked
Designer: L. Harradine
Height: 6 1/2", 16.5 cm
Colour: Black, red
and green
Issued: 1925-1938
Varieties: HN 769, 1274,
1304

U.S.: $3,500.00
Can.: $3,500.00
Ster.: £1,200.00

HN 769
Harlequinade Masked
Designer: L. Harradine
Height: 6 1/2", 16.5 cm
Colour: Blue, red
and yellow
Issued: 1925-1938
Varieties: HN 768, 1274
1304

U.S.: $3,500.00
Can.: $3,500.00
Ster.: £1,200.00

HN 770
Lady Clown
Designer: L. Harradine
Height: 7 1/2", 19.1 cm
Colour: White and green
Issued: 1925-1938
Varieties: HN 717, 718,
738, 1263

U.S.: $5,000.00
Can.: $5,000.00
Ster.: £1,700.00

HN 771
London Cry,
Turnips and Carrots
Designer: L. Harradine
Height: 6 3/4", 17.2 cm
Colour: Lavender, cream
and brown
Issued: 1925-1938
Varieties: HN 752

U.S.: $2,300.00
Can.: $1,950.00
Ster.: £ 700.00

HN 772
London Cry, Strawberries
Designer: L. Harradine
Height: 6 3/4", 17.2 cm
Colour: Lavender and
cream
Issued: 1925-1938
Varieties: HN 749

U.S.: $2,500.00
Can.: $2,250.00
Ster.: £ 800.00

HN 773
The Bather
Style Two
Designer: L. Harradine
Height: 7 1/2", 19.1 cm
Colour: Red, purple
and black
Issued: 1925-1938
Varieties: HN 774, 1227

U.S.: $3,500.00
Can.: $3,500.00
Ster.: £1,200.00

HN 774
The Bather
Style Two
Designer: L. Harradine
Height: 7 3/4", 19.7 cm
Colour: Blue and red
Issued: 1925-1938
Varieties: HN 773, 1227

U.S.: $3,500.00
Can.: $3,500.00
Ster.: £1,200.00

HN 775
Mephistopheles
and Marguerite
Designer: C.J. Noke
Height: 7 3/4", 19.7 cm
Colour: Orange and
            cream
Issued: 1925-1949
Varieties: HN 755

U.S.: $2,500.00
Can.: $2,500.00
Ster.:   £ 800.00

HN 776
The Belle
Style One
Designer: L. Harradine
Height: 6 1/2", 16.5 cm
Colour: Unknown
Issued: 1925-1938
Varieties: HN 754

U.S.: $1,800.00
Can.: $2,000.00
Ster.:   £ 625.00

HN 777
Bo-Peep
Style One
Designer: L. Harradine
Height: 6 3/4", 17.2 cm
Colour: Dark blue
Issued: 1926-1938
Varieties: HN 1202, 1327,
            1328

U.S.: $1,750.00
Can.: $1,750.00
Ster.:   £ 600.00

HN 778
Captain
Style One
Designer: L. Harradine
Height: 7", 17.8 cm
Colour: Red and white
Issued: 1926-1938

U.S.: $3,300.00
Can.: $3,300.00
Ster.:   £1,100.00

HN 779
Geisha
Style One
Designer: H. Tittensor
Height: 10 3/4", 27.3 cm
Colour: Red and purple
Issued: 1926-1938
Varieties: HN 354, 376,
            376A, 387, 634,
            741, 1321, 1322;
            "Japanese Lady"

U.S.: $6,000.00
Can.: $6,000.00
Ster.:   £2,000.00

HN 780
Harlequinade
Designer: L. Harradine
Height: 6 1/2", 16.5 cm
Colour: Pink, blue
            and brown
Issued: 1926-1938
Varieties: HN 585, 635,
            711

U.S.: $1,100.00
Can.: $1,000.00
Ster.:   £ 450.00

HN 781
The Bather
Style One
Designer: L. Harradine
Height: 7 3/4", 19.7 cm
Colour: Blue and green
Issued: 1926-1938
Varieties: HN 597, 687,
            782, 1238, 1708

U.S.: $3,000.00
Can.: $3,000.00
Ster.:   £1,000.00

HN 782
The Bather
Style One
Designer: L. Harradine
Height: 7 3/4", 19.7 cm
Colour: Purple and black
Issued: 1926-1938
Varieties: HN 597, 687,
            781, 1238, 1708

U.S.: $3,000.00
Can.: $3,000.00
Ster.:   £1,000.00

HN 783
Pretty Lady
Designer: H. Tittensor
Height: 9 1/2", 24.1 cm
Colour: Blue
Issued: 1926-1938
Varieties: HN 69, 70, 302,
          330, 361, 384,
          565, 700, 763

U.S.: $1,600.00
Can.: $1,750.00
Ster.:   £ 550.00

HN 784
Pierrette
Style One
Designer: L. Harradine
Height: 7 1/4", 18.4 cm
Colour: Pink and black
Issued: 1926-1938
Varieties: HN 642, 643,
          644, 691, 721,
          731, 732

U.S.: $2,800.00
Can.: $2,500.00
Ster.:   £ 850.00

HN 785
The Mask
Designer: L. Harradine
Height: 6 3/4", 17.2 cm
Colour: Blue, black
          and pink
Issued: 1926-1938
Varieties: HN 656, 657,
          729, 733, 1271

U.S.: $2,000.00
Can.: $2,200.00
Ster.:   £ 800.00

HN 786
Mam'selle
Designer: L. Harradine
Height: 7", 17.8 cm
Colour: Pink and black
Issued: 1926-1938
Varieties: HN 658, 659,
          724

U.S.: $2,000.00
Can.: $2,200.00
Ster.:   £ 800.00

HN 787
A Mandarin
Style One
Designer: C.J. Noke
Height: 10 1/4", 26.0 cm
Colour: Pink and orange
Issued: 1926-1938
Varieties: HN 84, 316, 318,
          382, 611, 746, 791;
          "Chinese Mandarin"
          and "The Mikado"

U.S.: $7,500.00
Can.: $7,500.00
Ster.:   £2,500.00

HN 788
Proposal (woman)
Designer: Unknown
Height: 5 3/4", 14.6 cm
Colour: Pink
Issued: 1926-1938
Varieties: HN 715, 716

U.S.: $2,300.00
Can.: $2,500.00
Ster.:   £ 750.00

HN 789
The Flower Seller
Designer: L. Harradine
Height: 8 3/4", 22.2 cm
Colour: Green, cream
          and white
Issued: 1926-1938

U.S.: $1,000.00
Can.: $1,150.00
Ster.:   £ 350.00

Earthenware

HN 790
The Parson's Daughter
Designer: H. Tittensor
Height: 10", 25.4 cm
Colour: Multicoloured
Issued: 1926-1938
Varieties: HN 337, 338,
          441, 564, 1242,
          1356, 2018

U.S.: $1,600.00
Can.: $1,400.00
Ster.:   £ 500.00

HN 791
A Mandarin
Style One
Designer: C.J. Noke
Height: 10 1/4", 26.0 cm
Colour: Yellow, green, red
Issued: 1926-1938
Varieties: HN 84, 316, 318, 382, 611, 746, 787; "Chinese Mandarin" and "The Mikado"

U.S.: $7,500.00
Can.: $7,500.00
Ster.: £2,500.00

HN 792
Myfanwy Jones
Designer: E.W. Light
Height: 12", 30.5 cm
Colour: Pink and blue
Issued: 1926-1938
Varieties: HN 39, 92, 456, 514, 516, 519, 520, 660, 668, 669, 701; also called "The Welsh Girl"

U.S.: $5,500.00
Can.: $4,500.00
Ster.: £1,500.00

HN 793
Katharine
Designer: E.W. Light
Height: 5 3/4", 14.6 cm
Colour: Lavender and green
Issued: 1926-1938
Varieties: HN 61, 74, 341, 471, 615

U.S.: $2,600.00
Can.: $2,500.00
Ster.: £ 900.00

HN 794
The Bouquet
Designer: G. Lambert
Height: 9", 22.9 cm
Colour: Blue, red and green
Issued: 1926-1938
Varieties: HN 406, 414, 422, 428, 429, 567; also called "The Nosegay"

U.S.: $4,500.00
Can.: $4,500.00
Ster.: £1,500.00

HN 795
Pierrette
Style Two
Designer: L. Harradine
Height: 3 1/2", 8.9 cm
Colour: Pink
Issued: 1926-1938
Varieties: HN 796

U.S.: $2,500.00
Can.: $2,250.00
Ster.: £ 775.00

HN 796
Pierrette
Style Two
Designer: L. Harradine
Height: 3 1/2", 8.9 cm
Colour: White and silver
Issued: 1926-1938
Varieties: HN 795

U.S.: $2,500.00
Can.: $2,250.00
Ster.: £ 775.00

HN 797
Moorish Minstrel
Designer: C.J. Noke
Height: 13 1/2", 34.3 cm
Colour: Purple
Issued: 1926-1949
Varieties: HN 34, 364, 415

U.S.: $2,700.00
Can.: $2,700.00
Ster.: £ 900.00

HN 798
Tete-a-Tete
Style One
Designer: L. Harradine
Height: 5 3/4", 14.6 cm
Colour: Pink and red
Issued: 1926-1938
Varieties: HN 799

U.S.: $2,000.00
Can.: $2,000.00
Ster.: £ 700.00

HN 799
Tete-a-Tete
Style One
Designer: L. Harradine
Height: 5 3/4", 14.6 cm
Colour: Blue and red
Issued: 1926-1938
Varieties: HN 798

U.S.: $2,000.00
Can.: $2,000.00
Ster.: £ 700.00

*

HN 1201
Hunts Lady
Designer: L. Harradine
Height: 8 1/4", 21.0 cm
Colour: Grey and cream
Issued: 1926-1938

U.S.: $2,800.00
Can.: $2,800.00
Ster.: £ 950.00

HN 1202
Bo-Peep
Style One
Designer: L. Harradine
Height: 6 3/4", 17.2 cm
Colour: Purple, green
and pink
Issued: 1926-1938
Varieties: HN 777, 1327,
1328

U.S.: $2,000.00
Can.: $2,000.00
Ster.: £ 700.00

HN 1203
Butterfly
Designer: L. Harradine
Height: 6 1/2", 16.5 cm
Colour: Black and gold
Issued: 1926-1938
Varieties: HN 719, 720, 730;
also called
"Butterfly Girl"
HN 1456

U.S.: $2,000.00
Can.: $2,000.00
Ster.: £ 650.00

HN 1204
Angela
Style One
Designer: L. Harradine
Height: 7 1/4", 18.4 cm
Colour: Purple and pink
Issued: 1926-1938
Varieties: HN 1303;
also called
"Fanny"

U.S.: $1,350.00
Can.: $1,500.00
Ster.: £ 650.00

HN 1205
Miss 1926
Designer: L. Harradine
Height: 7 1/4", 18.4 cm
Colour: Black and white
Issued: 1926-1938
Varieties: HN 1207

U.S.: $3,000.00
Can.: $3,000.00
Ster.: £1,000.00

HN 1206
The Flower Seller's Children
Designer: L. Harradine
Height: 8 1/4", 21.0 cm
Colour: Blue and purple
Issued: 1926-1949
Varieties: HN 525, 551,
1342, 1406

U.S.: $1,500.00
Can.: $1,500.00
Ster.: £ 550.00

HN 1207
Miss 1926
Designer: L. Harradine
Height: 7 1/4", 18.4 cm
Colour: Black
Issued: Unknown
Varieties: HN 1205

U.S.: $3,500.00
Can.: $3,500.00
Ster.: £1,200.00

HN 1208
A Victoria Lady
Designer: L. Harradine
Height: 7 3/4", 19.7 cm
Colour: Green andpurple
Issued: 1926-1938
Varieties HN 726, 727,
728, 736, 739,
740, 742, 745,
1258, 1276, 1277,
1345, 1452, 1529

U.S.: $900.00
Can.: $875.00
Ster: £300.00

HN 1209
TheProposal (Man)
Designer: Unknown
Height: 5 1/2", 14.0 cm
Colour: Blue and pink
Issued: 1926-1938
Varieties: HN 725

U.S.: $2,300.00
Can.: $2,300.00
Ster.: £ 800.00

HN 1210
Boy with Turban
Designer: L. Harradine
Height: 3 3/4", 9.5 cm
Colour: Orange, black
and white
Issued: 1926-1938
Varieties: HN 586, 587, 661,
662, 1212, 1213,
1214, 1225

U.S.: $ 850.00
Can.: $1,000.00
Ster.: £ 400.00

HN 1211
Quality Street
Designer: Unknown
Height: 7 1/4", 18.4 cm
Colour: Red
Issued: 1926-1938
Varieties: HN 1211A

U.S.: $1,500.00
Can.: $1,750.00
Ster.: £ 600.00

HN 1211A
Quality Street
Designer: Unknown
Height: 7 1/4", 18.4 cm
Colour: Lavender
Issued: 1926-1938
Varieties: HN 1211

U.S.: $2,000.00
Can.: $2,200.00
Ster.: £ 700.00

HN 1212
Boy with Turban
Designer: L. Harradine
Height: 3 3/4", 9.5 cm
Colour: Purple and green
Issued: 1926-1938
Varieties: HN 586, 587, 661,
662, 1210, 1213,
1214, 1225

U.S.: $ 850.00
Can.: $1,000.00
Ster.: £ 400.00

HN 1213
Boy with Turban
Designer: L. Harradine
Height: 3 3/4", 9.5 cm
Colour: White and black
Issued: 1926-1938
Varieties: HN 586, 587, 661,
662, 1210, 1212,
1214, 1225

U.S.: $ 950.00
Can.: $1,000.00
Ster.: £ 400.00

HN 1214
Boy with Turban
Designer: L. Harradine
Height: 3 1/2", 8.9 cm
Colour: Black, white
and green
Issued: 1926-1938
Varieties: HN 586, 587, 661,
662, 1210, 1212,
1213, 1225

U.S.: $ 950.00
Can.: $1,000.00
Ster.: £ 400.00

HN 1215
The Pied Piper
Designer: L. Harradine
Height: 8 1/4", 21.0 cm
Colour: Red, black
 and yellow
Issued: 1926-1938
Varieties: HN 2102

U.S.: **$2,000.00**
Can.: **$2,000.00**
Ster.: £ 650.00

HN 1216
Falstaff
Style One
Designer: C.J. Noke
Height: 7", 17.8 cm
Colour: Multi-coloured
Issued: 1926-1949
Varieties: HN 571, 575,
 608, 609, 619,
 638, 1606

U.S.: **$2,000.00**
Can.: **$2,000.00**
Ster.: £ 700.00

HN 1217
The Prince of Wales
Designer: L. Harradine
Height: 7 1/2", 19.1 cm
Colour: Red and white
Issued: 1926-1938

U.S.: **$1,750.00**
Can.: **$1,750.00**
Ster.: £ 800.00

HN 1218
A Spook
Designer: H. Tittensor
Height: 7", 17.8 cm
Colour: Multi-coloured
Issued: 1926-1938
Varieties: HN 50, 51,
 51A, 51B, 58,
 512, 625

U.S.: **$2,500.00**
Can.: **$2,500.00**
Ster.: £ 800.00

HN 1219
Negligée
Designer: L. Harradine
Height: 5", 12.7 cm
Colour: Bluish-yellow,
 blue hair band
Issued: 1927-1938
Varieties: HN 1228, 1272,
 1273, 1454

U.S.: **$1,400.00**
Can.: **$1,500.00**
Ster.: £ 600.00

HN 1220
Lido Lady
Designer: L. Harradine
Height: 6 3/4", 17.2 cm
Colour: Pink
Issued: 1927-1938
Varieties: HN 1229

U.S.: **$1,200.00**
Can.: **$1,300.00**
Ster.: £ 600.00

HN 1221
Lady Jester
Style One
Designer: L. Harradine
Height: 7", 17.8 cm
Colour: Multi-coloured
Issued: 1927-1938
Varieties: HN 1222, 1332

U.S.: **$2,500.00**
Can.: **$2,500.00**
Ster.: £ 800.00

HN 1222
Lady Jester
Style One
Designer: L. Harradine
Height: 7", 17.8 cm
Colour: Black and white
Issued: 1927-1938
Varieties: HN 1221, 1332

U.S.: **$2,500.00**
Can.: **$2,500.00**
Ster.: £ 800.00

HN 1223
A Geisha
Style Two
Designer: C.J. Noke
Height: 6 3/4", 17.2 cm
Colour: Black and orange
Issued: 1927-1938
Varieties: HN 1234, 1292,
1310

U.S.: $1,400.00
Can.: $1,400.00
Ster.: £ 600.00

HN 1224
The Wandering Minstrel
Designer: L. Harradine
Height: 7", 17.8 cm
Colour: Purple and red
Issued: 1927-1938

U.S.: $2,750.00
Can.: $3,000.00
Ster.: £ 700.00

HN 1225
Boy with Turban
Designer: L. Harradine
Height: 3 3/4", 9.5 cm
Colour: Yellow and blue
Issued: 1927-1938
Varieties: HN 586, 587,
661, 662, 1210,
1212, 1213, 1214

U.S.: $ 950.00
Can.: $1,000.00
Ster.: £ 400.00

HN 1226
The Huntsman
Style One
Designer: L. Harradine
Height: 8 3/4", 22.2 cm
Colour: Red and white
Issued: 1927-1938

U.S.: $2,500.00
Can.: $2,500.00
Ster.: £ 800.00

HN 1227
The Bather
Style Two
Designer: L. Harradine
Height: 7 1/2", 19.1 cm
Colour: Pink
Issued: 1927-1938
Varieties: HN 773, 774

U.S.: $3,200.00
Can.: $3,200.00
Ster.: £1,100.00

HN 1228
Negligée
Designer: L. Harradine
Height: 5", 12.7 cm
Colour: Bluish-yellow,
red hair band
Issued: 1927-1938
Varieties: HN 1219, 1272,
1273, 1454

U.S.: $1,400.00
Can.: $1,500.00
Ster.: £ 600.00

HN 1229
Lido Lady
Designer: L. Harradine
Height: 6 3/4", 17.2 cm
Colour: Blue
Issued: 1927-1938
Varieties: HN 1220

U.S.: $2,500.00
Can.: $2,500.00
Ster.: £ 800.00

HN 1230
Baba
Designer: L. Harradine
Height: 3 1/4", 8.3 cm
Colour: Blue, yellow
and purple
Issued: 1927-1938
Varieties: HN 1243, 1244,
1245, 1246, 1247,
1248

U.S.: $700.00
Can.: $950.00
Ster.: £450.00

HN 1231
Cassim
Style One
Designer: L. Harradine
Height: 3", 7.6 cm
Colour: Blue, yellow and turquoise
Issued: 1927-1938
Varieties: HN 1232

U.S.: $700.00
Can.: $950.00
Ster.: £400.00

HN 1232
Cassim
Style One
Designer: L. Harradine
Height: 3", 7.6 cm
Colour: Orange and black
Issued: 1927-1938
Varieties: HN 1231

U.S.: $700.00
Can.: $950.00
Ster.: £400.00

HN 1233
Susanna
Designer: L. Harradine
Height: 6", 15.2 cm
Colour: Pink
Issued: 1927-1938
Varieties: HN 1288, 1299

U.S.: $1,100.00
Can.: $1,200.00
Ster.: £ 650.00

HN 1234
A Geisha
Style Two
Designer: C.J. Noke
Height: 6 3/4", 17.2 cm
Colour: Green and red
Issued: 1927-1938
Varieties: HN 1223, 1292, 1310

U.S.: $1,000.00
Can.: $1,000.00
Ster.: £ 600.00

HN 1235
A Scribe
Designer: C.J. Noke
Height: 6", 15.2 cm
Colour: Brown and blue
Issued: 1927-1938
Varieties: HN 305, 324

U.S.: $2,300.00
Can.: $2,000.00
Ster.: £ 700.00

HN 1236
Tete-a-Tete
Style Two
Designer: C.J. Noke
Height: 3", 7.6 cm
Colour: Purple and red
Issued: 1927-1938
Varieties: HN 1237

U.S.: $2,000.00
Can.: $2,000.00
Ster.: £ 675.00

HN 1237
Tete-a-Tete
Style Two
Designer: C.J. Noke
Height: 3", 7.6 cm
Colour: Pink
Issued: 1927-1938
Varieties: HN 1236

U.S.: $2,000.00
Can.: $2,000.00
Ster.: £ 675.00

HN 1238
The Bather
Style One
Designer: L. Harradine
Height: 7 3/4", 19.7 cm
Colour: Red and black
Issued: 1927-1938
Varieties: HN 597, 687, 781, 782, 1708

U.S.: $1,800.00
Can.: $2,000.00
Ster.: £ 650.00

*

HN 1242
The Parson's Daughter
Designer: H. Tittesnor
Height: 10", 25.4 cm
Colour: Lavender and yellow
Issued: 1927-1938
Varieties: HN 337, 338, 441, 564, 790, 1356, 2018

U.S.: $1,500.00
Can.: $1,200.00
Ster.: £ 600.00

HN 1243
Baba
Designer: L. Harradine
Height: 3 1/4", 8.3 cm
Colour: Orange
Issued: 1927-1938
Varieties: HN 1230, 1244, 1245, 1246, 1247, 1248

U.S.: $800.00
Can.: $950.00
Ster.: £450.00

HN 1244
Baba
Designer: L. Harradine
Height: 3 1/4", 8.3 cm
Colour: Yellow and green
Issued: 1927-1938
Varieties: HN 1230, 1243, 1245, 1246, 1247, 1248

U.S.: $800.00
Can.: $950.00
Ster.: £450.00

HN 1245
Baba
Designer: L. Harradine
Height: 3 1/4", 8.3 cm
Colour: White and black
Issued: 1927-1938
Varieties: HN 1230, 1243, 1244, 1246, 1247, 1248

U.S.: $800.00
Can.: $950.00
Ster.: £450.00

HN 1246
Baba
Designer: L. Harradine
Height: 3 1/4", 8.3 cm
Colour: Green
Issued: 1927-1938
Varieties: HN 1230, 1243, 1244, 1245, 1247, 1248

U.S.: $800.00
Can.: $950.00
Ster.: £450.00

HN 1247
Baba
Designer: L. Harradine
Height: 3 1/4", 8.3 cm
Colour: Black, white and orange
Issued: 1927-1938
Varieties: HN 1230, 1243, 1244, 1245, 1246, 1248

U.S.: $800.00
Can.: $950.00
Ster.: £450.00

HN 1248
Baba
Designer: L. Harradine
Height: 3 1/4", 8.3 cm
Colour: Green and orange
Issued: 1927-1938
Varieties: HN 1230, 1243, 1244, 1245, 1246, 1247

U.S.: $800.00
Can.: $950.00
Ster.: £450.00

HN 1249
Circe
Designer: L. Harradine
Height: 7 3/4", 17.1 cm
Colour: Green, orange and pink
Issued: 1927-1938
Varieties: HN 1250, 1254, 1255

U.S.: $2,800.00
Can.: $3,000.00
Ster.: £ 900.00

HN 1250
Circe
Designer: L. Harradine
Height: 7 1/2", 19.1 cm
Colour: Orange and black
Issued: 1927-1938
Varieties: HN 1249, 1254, 1255

U.S.: $2,800.00
Can.: $3,000.00
Ster.: £ 900.00

Photograph
Not
Available

HN 1251
The Cobbler
Style Two
Designer: C.J. Noke
Height: 8 1/2", 21.6 cm
Colour: Black and red
Issued: 1927-1938
Varieties: HN 681, 1283

U.S.: $2,500.00
Can.: $2,000.00
Ster.: £ 750.00

HN 1252
Kathleen
Style One
Designer: L. Harradine
Height: 7 3/4", 19.7 cm
Colour: Lavender, pink and purple
Issued: 1927-1938
Varieties: HN 1253,1275, 1279, 1291, 1357, 1512

U.S.: $1,150.00
Can.: $1,200.00
Ster.: £ 400.00

HN 1253
Kathleen
Style One
Designer: L. Harradine
Height: 7 1/2", 19.1 cm
Colour: Red and purple
Issued: 1927-1938
Varieties: HN 1252, 1275, 1279, 1291, 1357, 1512

U.S.: $1,150.00
Can.: $1,200.00
Ster.: £ 400.00

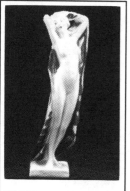

HN 1254
Circe
Designer: L. Harradine
Height: 7 1/2", 19.1 cm
Colour: Orange and red
Issued: 1927-1938
Varieties: HN 1249, 1250, 1255

U.S.: $2,800.00
Can.: $3,000.00
Ster.: £ 900.00

HN 1255
Circe
Designer: L. Harradine
Height: 7 1/2", 19.1 cm
Colour: Blue
Issued: 1927-1938
Varieties: HN 1249, 1250, 1254

U.S.: $2,800.00
Can.: $3,000.00
Ster.: £ 900.00

HN 1256
Captain MacHeath
Designer: L. Harradine
Height: 7", 17.8 cm
Colour: Red, yellow and black
Issued: 1927-1949
Varieties: HN 464, 590
Series: Beggar's Opera

U.S.: $1,100.00
Can.: $1,000.00
Ster.: £ 400.00

Earthenware

HN 1257
Highwayman
Designer: L. Harradine
Height: 6 1/2", 16.5 cm
Colour: Green and red
Issued: 1927-1949
Varieties: HN 527, 592
Series: Beggar's Opera

U.S.: $1,100.00
Can.: $ 950.00
Ster.: £ 400.00

Earthenware

HN 1258
A Victorian Lady
Designer: L. Harradine
Height: 7 3/4", 19.7 cm
Colour: Purple and blue
Issued: 1927-1938
Varieties: HN 726, 727, 728,
736, 739, 740, 742,
745, 1208, 1276,
1277, 1345, 1452,
1529

U.S.: $1,250.00
Can..: $1,100.00
Ster.: £ 350.00

HN 1259
The Alchemist
Designer: L. Harradine
Height: 11 1/2", 29.2 cm
Colour: Green and red
Issued: 1927-1938
Varieties: HN 1282

U.S.: $2,500.00
Can.: $2,750.00
Ster.: £ 800.00

HN 1260
Carnival
Designer: L. Harradine
Height: 8 1/4", 21.0 cm
Colour: Red, black
and purple
Issued: 1927-1938
Varieties: HN 1278

U.S.: $4,000.00
Can.: $4,000.00
Ster.: £1,300.00

HN 1261
Sea Sprite
Style One
Designer: L. Harradine
Height: 5", 12.7 cm
Colour: Red, purple
and black
Issued: 1927-1938

U.S.: $ 950.00
Can.: $1,000.00
Ster.: £ 400.00

HN 1262
Spanish Lady
Designer: L. Harradine
Height: 8 1/2", 21.6 cm
Colour: Black with red
flowers
Issued: 1927-1938
Varieties: HN 1290, 1293,
1294, 1309

U.S.: $1,400.00
Can.: $1,500.00
Ster.: £ 600.00

HN 1263
Clownette
Designer: L. Harradine
Height: 7 1/4", 18.4 cm
Colour: Mottled purple
Issued: 1927-1938
Varieties: Also called
"Lady Clown"
HN 717, 718,
738, 770

U.S.: $4,500.00
Can.: $4,500.00
Ster.: £1,500.00

HN 1264
Judge and Jury
Designer: J.G. Hughes
Height: 6", 15.2 cm
Colour: Red and white
Issued: 1927-1938

U.S.: **Extremely**
Can.: **Rare**
Ster.:

HN 1265
Lady Fayre
Designer: L. Harradine
Height: 5 1/4", 13.3 cm
Colour: Lavender
and red
Issued: 1928-1938
Varieties: HN 1557

U.S.: $950.00
Can.: $950.00
Ster.: £400.00

HN 1266
Ko-Ko
Style One
Designer: L. Harradine
Height: 5", 12.7 cm
Colour: Black, white
  and yellow
Issued: 1928-1949
Varieties: HN 1286

U.S.: $1,150.00
Can.: $1,000.00
Ster.: £ 400.00

HN 1267
Carmen
Style One
Designer: L. Harradine
Height: 7", 17.8 cm
Colour: Red and black
Issued: 1928-1938
Varieties: HN 1300

U.S.: $1,300.00
Can.: $1,500.00
Ster.: £ 600.00

HN 1268
Yum-Yum
Style One
Designer: L. Harradine
Height: 5", 12.7 cm
Colour: Pink and cream
Issued: 1928-1938
Varieties: HN 1287

U.S.: $ 950.00
Can.: $1,000.00
Ster.: £ 400.00

HN 1269
Scotch Girl
Designer: L. Harradine
Height: 7 1/2", 19.1 cm
Colour: Red and green
Issued: 1928-1938

U.S.: $3,500.00
Can.: $3,500.00
Ster.: £1,150.00

HN 1270
The Swimmer
Designer: L. Harradine
Height: 7 1/4", 18.4 cm
Colour: Multi-coloured
Issued: 1928-1938
Varieties: HN 1326, 1329

U.S.: $1,500.00
Can.: $1,600.00
Ster.: £ 800.00

HN 1271
The Mask
Designer: L. Harradine
Height: 6 3/4", 17.2 cm
Colour: Black, blue
  and red
Issued: 1928-1938
Varieties: HN 656, 657,
  729, 733, 785

U.S.: $2,500.00
Can.: $2,500.00
Ster.: £1,000.00

HN 1272
Negligée
Designer: L. Harradine
Height: 5", 12.7 cm
Colour: Red and black
Issued: 1928-1938
Varieties: HN 1219, 1228,
  1273, 1454,

U.S.: $1,600.00
Can.: $1,750.00
Ster.: £ 600.00

HN 1273
Negligée
Designer: L. Harradine
Height: 5", 12.7 cm
Colour: White and pink
Issued: 1928-1938
Varieties: HN 1219, 1228,
  1272, 1454

U.S.: $1,600.00
Can.: $1,750.00
Ster.: £ 600.00

HN 1274
Harlequinade Masked
Designer: L. Harradine
Height: 6 1/2", 16.5 cm
Colour: Orange and
black
Issued: 1928-1938
Varieties: HN 768, 769,
1304

U.S.: $3,o00.00
Can.: $3,000.00
Ster.: £1,000.00

HN 1275
Kathleen
Style One
Designer: L. Harradine
Height: 7 1/2", 19.1 cm
Colour: Pink and black
Issued: 1928-1938
Varieties: HN 1252, 1253,
1279, 1291,
1357, 1512

U.S.: $1,400.00
Can.: $1,300.00
Ster.: £ 400.00

HN 1276
A Victorian Lady
Designer: L. Harradine
Height: 7 1/2", 19.1 cm
Colour: Purple, red, yellow
Issued: 1928-1938
Varieties: HN 726, 727, 728,
736, 739, 740, 742,
745, 1208, 1258,
1277, 1345, 1452,
1529

U.S.: $1,250.00
Can.: $1,000.00
Ster.: £ 350.00

HN 1277
A Victorian Lady
Designer: L. Harradine
Height: 7 3/4", 19.7 cm
Colour: Red, yellow, blue
Issued: 1928-1938
Varieties: HN 726, 727, 728,
736, 739, 740, 742,
745, 1208, 1258,
1276, 1345, 1452,
1529

U.S.: $1,250.00
Can.: $1,000.00
Ster.: £ 350.00

HN 1278
Carnival
Designer: L. Harradine
Height: 8 1/2", 21.6 cm
Colour: Blue, orange
and purple
Issued: 1928-1938
Varieties: HN 1260

U.S.: $5,000.00
Can.: $5,000.00
Ster.: £1,600.00

HN 1279
Kathleen
Style One
Designer: L. Harradine
Height: 7 3/4", 19.7 cm
Colour: Red
Issued: 1928-1938
Varieties: HN 1252, 1253,
1275, 1291,
1357, 1512

U.S.: $1,200.00
Can.: $1,200.00
Ster.: £ 400.00

HN 1280
Blue Bird
Designer: L. Harradine
Height: 4 3/4", 12.0 cm
Colour: Pink base
Issued: 1928-1938

U.S.: $950.00
Can.: $950.00
Ster.: £350.00

HN 1281
Scotties
Designer: L. Harradine
Height: 5 1/2", 14.0 cm
Colour: Red and black
Issued: 1928-1938
Varieties: HN 1349

U.S.: $2,000.00
Can.: $2,000.00
Ster.: £ 600.00

HN 1282
The Alchemist
Designer: L. Harradine
Height: 11 1/4", 28.5 cm
Colour: Purple and red
Issued: 1928-1938
Varieties: HN 1259

U.S.:	**$1,500.00**
Can.:	**$1,500.00**
Ster.:	**£ 650.00**

Earthenware

Photograph
Not
Available

HN 1283
The Cobbler
Style Two
Designer: C.J. Noke
Height: 8 1/2", 21.6 cm
Colour: Light green
Issued: 1928-1949
Varieties: HN 681, 1251

U.S.:	**$1,400.00**
Can.:	**$1,500.00**
Ster.:	**£ 400.00**

HN 1284
Lady Jester
Style Two
Designer: L. Harradine
Height: 4 1/4", 10.8 cm
Colour: Purple and red
Issued: 1928-1938
Varieties: HN 1285

U.S.:	**$2,200.00**
Can.:	**$2,200.00**
Ster.:	**£ 800.00**

HN 1285
Lady Jester
Style Two
Designer: L. Harradine
Height: 4 1/4", 10.8 cm
Colour: Red, pink
and blue
Issued: 1928-1938
Varieties: HN 1284

U.S.:	**$2,200.00**
Can.:	**$2,200.00**
Ster.:	**£ 800.00**

HN 1286
Ko-Ko
Style One
Designer: L. Harradine
Height: 5", 12.7 cm
Colour: Red and
purple
Issued: 1938-1949
Varieties: HN 1266

U.S.:	**$1,200.00**
Can.:	**$1,150.00**
Ster.:	**£ 450.00**

HN 1287
Yum-Yum
Style One
Designer: L. Harradine
Height: 5", 12.7 cm
Colour: Purple and
cream
Issued: 1928-1939
Varieties: HN 1268

U.S.:	**$1,200.00**
Can.:	**$1,150.00**
Ster.:	**£ 450.00**

HN 1288
Susanna
Designer: L. Harradine
Height: 6", 15.2 cm
Colour: Red
Issued: 1928-1938
Varieties: HN 1233, 1299

U.S.:	**$1,500.00**
Can.:	**$1,500.00**
Ster.:	**£ 650.00**

HN 1289
Midinette
Style One
Designer: L. Harradine
Height: 9", 22.9 cm
Colour: Purple and pink
Issued: 1928-1938
Varieties: HN 1306

U.S.:	**$4,000.00**
Can.:	**$4,000.00**
Ster.:	**£1,000.00**

HN 1290
Spanish Lady
Designer: L. Harradine
Height: 8 1/4", 21.0 cm
Colour: Lavender, yellow and black
Issued: 1928-1938
Varieties: HN 1262, 1293, 1294, 1309

U.S.: $1,400.00
Can.: $1,500.00
Ster.: £ 600.00

HN 1291
Kathleen
Style One
Designer: L. Harradine
Height: 7 1/2", 19.1 cm
Colour: Red and yellow
Issued: 1928-1938
Varieties: HN 1252, 1253, 1275, 1279, 1357, 1512

U.S.: $1,500.00
Can.: $1,500.00
Ster.: £ 400.00

HN 1292
A Geisha
Style Two
Designer: C.J. Noke
Height: 6 3/4", 17.2 cm
Colour: Pink and lavender
Issued: 1928-1938
Varieties: HN 1223, 1234, 1310

U.S.: $1,100.00
Can.: $1,200.00
Ster.: £ 600.00

HN 1293
Spanish Lady
Designer: L. Harradine
Height: 8 1/4", 21.0 cm
Colour: Black with yellow flowers
Issued: 1928-1938
Varieties: HN 1262, 1290, 1294, 1309

U.S.: $1,800.00
Can.: $1,800.00
Ster.: £ 600.00

HN 1294
Spanish Lady
Designer: L. Harradine
Height: 8 1/4", 21.0 cm
Colour: Red and black
Issued: 1928-1938
Varieties: HN 1262, 1290, 1293, 1309

U.S.: $1,300.00
Can.: $1,300.00
Ster.: £ 600.00

HN 1295
A Jester
Style One
Designer: C.J. Noke
Height: 10", 25.4 cm
Colour: Brown and purple
Issued: 1928-1949
Varieties: HN 45, 71, 71A, 320, 367, 412, 426, 446, 552, 616, 627, 1702, 2016

U.S.: $1,400.00
Can.: $1,400.00
Ster.: £ 450.00

HN 1296
Columbine
Style One
Designer: L. Harradine
Height: 6", 15.2 cm
Colour: Orange and lavender
Issued: 1928-1938
Varieties: HN 1297, 1439

U.S.: $1,100.00
Can.: $1,250.00
Ster.: £ 600.00

HN 1297
Columbine
Style One
Designer: L. Harradine
Height: 6", 15.2 cm
Colour: Pink and purple
Issued: 1928-1938
Varieties: HN 1296, 1439

U.S.: $1,100.00
Can.: $1,250.00
Ster.: £ 600.00

HN 1298
Sweet and Twenty
Style One
Designer: L. Harradine
Height: 5 3/4", 14.6 cm
Colour: Red and blue-green
Issued: 1928-1969
Varieties: HN 1360, 1437,
1438, 1549,
1563, 1649

U.S.: $375.00
Can.: $450.00
Ster.: £250.00

HN 1299
Susanna
Designer: L. Harradine
Height: 6", 15.2 cm
Colour: Black, red
and blue
Issued: 1928-1938
Varieties: HN 1233, 1288

U.S.: $1,900.00
Can.: $2,000.00
Ster.: £ 650.00

HN 1300
Carmen
Style One
Designer: L. Harradine
Height: 7", 17.8 cm
Colour: Pale blue-
lavender
Issued: 1928-1938
Varieties: HN 1267

U.S.: $2,500.00
Can.: $2,000.00
Ster.: £ 750.00

HN 1301
Young Mother with Child
Designer: Unknown
Height: 14 1/2", 37.0 cm
Colour: Green and red
Issued: 1928-1938

U.S.: **Extremely**
Can.: **Rare**
Ster.:

Only one known to exist

HN 1302
The Gleaner
Designer: Unknown
Height: 14 1/2", 36.2 cm
Colour: Red, and cream
Issued: 1928-1938

U.S.: **Extremely**
Can.: **Rare**
Ster.:

Only one known to exist

HN 1303
Angela
Style One
Designer: L. Harradine
Height: 7 1/4", 18.4 cm
Colour: Blue
Issued: 1928-1938
Varieties: HN 1204; also
called "Fanny"

U.S.: $2,500.00
Can.: $2,700.00
Ster.: £ 850.00

HN 1304
Harlequinade Masked
Designer: L. Harradine
Height: 6 1/2", 16.5 cm
Colour: Mottled blue
Issued: 1928-1938
Varieties: HN 768, 769,
1274

U.S.: $3,500.00
Can.: $3,500.00
Ster.: £1,200.00

HN 1305
Siesta
Designer: L. Harradine
Height: 4 3/4", 12.0 cm
Colour: Red
Issued: 1928-1938

U.S.: $2,750.00
Can.: $2,750.00
Ster.: £ 950.00

HN 1306
Midinette
Style One
Designer: L. Harradine
Height: 9", 22.9 cm
Colour: Red and green
Issued: 1928-1938
Varieties: HN 1289

U.S.: $4,000.00
Can.: $4,000.00
Ster.: £1,300.00

HN 1307
An Irishman
Designer: H. Fenton
Height: 6 3/4", 17.2 cm
Colour: Green coat with
brown striped
trousers
Issued: 1928-1938

U.S.: $4,000.00
Can.: $4,000.00
Ster.: £1,300.00

HN 1308
The Moor
Designer: C.J. Noke
Height: 16 1/2", 41.9 cm
Colour: Blue and mottled
red
Issued: 1929-1938
Varieties: HN 1366, 1425,
1657, 2080; also
called "An Arab"
HN 33, 343, 378

U.S.: $3,000.00
Can.: $2,750.00
Ster.: £ 950.00

HN 1309
Spanish Lady
Designer: L. Harradine
Height: 8 1/4", 21.0 cm
Colour: Black and
multi-coloured
Issued: 1929-1938
Varieties: HN 1262, 1290,
1293, 1294

U.S.: $1,400.00
Can.: $1,500.00
Ster.: £ 600.00

HN 1310
A Geisha
Style Two
Designer: C.J. Noke
Height: 6 3/4", 17.2 cm
Colour: Green
Issued: 1929-1938
Varieties: HN 1223, 1234,
1292

U.S.: $1,100.00
Can.: $1,250.00
Ster.: £ 600.00

Photograph
Not
Available

HN 1311
Cassim
Style Two
Designer: L. Harradine
Height: 3 3/4", 9.5 cm
Colour: Unknown
Issued: 1929-1938
Varieties: HN 1312

U.S.: $1,300.00
Can.: $1,300.00
Ster.: £ 400.00

Photograph
Not
Available

HN 1312
Cassim
Style Two
Designer: L. Harradine
Height: 3 3/4", 9.5 cm
Colour: Unknown
Issued: 1929-1938
Varieties: HN 1311

U.S.: $1,300.00
Can.: $1,300.00
Ster.: £ 400.00

HN 1313
Sonny
Designer: L. Harradine
Height: 3 1/2", 8.9 cm
Colour: Pink
Issued: 1929-1938
Varieties: HN 1314

U.S.: $2,200.00
Can.: $2,200.00
Ster.: £ 700.00

HN 1314
Sonny
Designer: L. Harradine
Height: 3 1/2", 8.9 cm
Colour: Blue
Issued: 1928-1938
Varieties: HN 1313

U.S.: **$1,100.00**
Can.: **$1,100.00**
Ster.: £ **700.00**

HN 1315
Old Balloon Seller
Designer: L. Harradine
Height: 7 1/2", 19.1 cm
Colour: Green, purple, and white
Issued: 1929 to the present

U.S.: **$250.00**
Can.: **$415.00**
Ster.: £109.00

Earthenware and china

Photograph
Not
Available

HN 1316
Toys
Designer: L. Harradine
Height: Unknown
Colour: Green, red and yellow
Issued: 1929-1938

U.S.: **Extremely**
Can.: **Rare**
Ster.:

HN 1317
The Snake Charmer
Designer: Unknown
Height: 4", 10.1 cm
Colour: Green and black
Issued: 1929-1938

U.S.: **$1,900.00**
Can.: **$2,000.00**
Ster.: £ **800.00**

HN 1318
Sweet Anne
Designer: L. Harradine
Height: 7 1/2", 19.1 cm
Colour: Blue and green
Issued: 1929-1949
Varieties: HN 1330, 1331, 1453, 1496, 1631, 1701

U.S.: **$275.00**
Can.: **$450.00**
Ster.: £200.00

HN 1319
Darling
Style One
Designer: C. Vyse
Height: 7 1/2", 19.1 cm
Colour: White, black base
Issued: 1929-1959
Varieties: HN 1, 1371, 1372

U.S.: **$225.00**
Can.: **$350.00**
Ster.: £120.00

HN 1320
Rosamund
Style One
Designer: L. Harradine
Height: 7 1/4", 18.4 cm
Colour: Lavender
Issued: 1929-1938

U.S.: **$2,000.00**
Can.: **$2,250.00**
Ster.: £ **800.00**

HN 1321
A Geisha
Style One
Designer: H. Tittensor
Height: 10 3/4", 27.3 cm
Colour: Green
Issued: 1929-1938
Varieties: HN 354, 376, 376A, 387, 634, 741, 779, 1322; also called "Japanese Lady"

U.S.: **$6,000.00**
Can.: **$6,000.00**
Ster.: £2,000.00

HN 1322
A Geisha
Designer: H. Tittensor
Height: 10 3/4", 27.3 cm
Colour: Pink and blue
Issued: 1929-1938
Varieties: HN 354, 376, 376A,
387, 634, 741, 779,
1321; also called
"Japanese Lady"

U.S.: $6,000.00
Can.: $6,000.00
Ster.: £2,000.00

HN 1323
Contentment
Designer: L. Harradine
Height: 7 1/4", 18.4 cm
Colour: Red and blue
Issued: 1929-1938
Varieties: HN 395, 396,
421, 468, 572,
685, 686

U.S.: $2,000.00
Can.: $2,000.00
Ster.: £ 700.00

HN 1324
Fairy
Style One
Designer: L. Harradine
Height: 6 1/2", 16.5 cm
Colour: Multi-coloured
Issued: 1929-1938

U.S.: $1,200.00
Can.: $1,300.00
Ster.: £ 600.00

HN 1325
The Orange Seller
Designer: L. Harradine
Height: 7", 17.8 cm
Colour: Green and
lavender
Issued: 1929-1949

U.S.: $1,200.00
Can.: $1,200.00
Ster.: £ 600.00

HN 1326
The Swimmer
Designer: L. Harradine
Height: 7 1/2", 19.1 cm
Colour: Pink and purple
Issued: 1929-1938
Varieties: HN 1270, 1329

U.S.: $1,700.00
Can.: $1,800.00
Ster.: £ 800.00

HN 1327
Bo-Peep
Style One
Designer: L. Harradine
Height: 6 3/4", 17.2 cm
Colour: Multi-coloured
Issued: 1929-1938
Varieties: HN 777, 1202,
1328

U.S.: $2,500.00
Can.: $2,500.00
Ster.: £ 800.00

HN 1328
Bo-Peep
Style One
Designer: L. Harradine
Height: 6 3/4", 17.2 cm
Colour: Purple and cream
Issued: 1929-1938
Varieties: HN 777, 1202,
1327

U.S.: $2,500.00
Can.: $2,500.00
Ster.: £ 800.00

HN 1329
The Swimmer
Designer: L. Harradine
Height: 7 1/2", 19.1 cm
Colour: Pink
Issued: 1929-1938
Varieties: HN 1270, 1326

U.S.: $2,500.00
Can.: $2,500.00
Ster.: £ 800.00

HN 1330
Sweet Anne
Designer: L. Harradine
Height: 7 1/4", 18.4 cm
Colour: Blue, pink-yellow
Issued: 1929-1949
Varieties: HN 1318, 1331,
           1453, 1496,
           1631, 1701

U.S.: $500.00
Can.: $575.00
Ster.:   £200.00

HN 1331
Sweet Anne
Designer: L. Harradine
Height: 7 1/4", 18.4 cm
Colour: Red, blue-yellow
Issued: 1929-1949
Varieties: HN 1318, 1330,
           1453, 1496,
           1631, 1701

U.S.: $500.00
Can.: $575.00
Ster.:   £200.00

HN 1332
Lady Jester
Style One
Designer: L. Harradine
Height: 7", 17.8 cm
Colour: Red, blue
           and black
Issued: 1929-1938
Varieties: HN 1221, 1222

U.S.: $2,750.00
Can.: $2,750.00
Ster.:   £ 900.00

HN 1333
A Jester
Style Two
Designer: C.J. Noke
Height: 10 1/4", 26.0 cm
Colour: Blue, yellow
           and black
Issued: 1929-1949
Varieties: HN 45A, 45B,
           55, 308, 630

U.S.: $2,500.00
Can.: $2,250.00
Ster.:   £ 800.00

HN 1334
Tulips
Designer: Unknown
Height: 9 1/2", 24.1 cm
Colour: Lavender
           and pink
Issued: 1929-1938
Varieties: HN 466, 488,
           672, 747

U.S.: $2,500.00
Can.: $2,400.00
Ster.:   £ 800.00

HN 1335
Folly
Designer: L. Harradine
Height: 9", 22.9 cm
Colour: Lavender with
           orange and
           yellow balloons
Issued: 1929-1938
Varieties: HN 1750

U.S.: $1,700.00
Can.: $1,800.00
Ster.:   £ 800.00

China

Photograph
Not
Available

HN 1336
One of the Forty
Style Eleven
Designer: H. Tittensor
Height: Unknown
Colour: Red, orange
           and blue
Issued: 1929-1938
Varieties: HN 481, 483,
           491, 646, 667,
           712, 1350

U.S.: $2,500.00
Can.: $2,500.00
Ster.:   £ 800.00

HN 1337
Priscilla
Designer: L. Harradine
Height: 8", 20.3 cm
Colour: Lavender
           and yellow
Issued: 1929-1938
Varieties: HN 1340, 1495,
           1501, 1559

U.S.: $ 900.00
Can.: $1,000.00
Ster.:   £ 350.00

HN 1338
The Courtier
Designer: L. Harradine
Height: 4 1/2", 11.4 cm
Colour: Red and white
Issued: 1929-1938

U.S.: $3,500.00
Can.: $3,500.00
Ster.:   £1,200.00

HN 1339
Covent Garden
Style One
Designer: L. Harradine
Height: 9", 22.9 cm
Colour: Green and
           lavender
Issued: 1929-1938

U.S.: $2,000.00
Can.: $2,000.00
Ster.:   £ 700.00

HN 1340
Priscilla
Designer: L. Harradine
Height: 8", 20.3 cm
Colour: Red and purple
Issued: 1929-1949
Varieties: HN 1337, 1495,
           1501, 1559

U.S.: $475.00
Can.: $650.00
Ster.:   £250.00

HN 1341
Marietta
Desgner: L. Harradine
Height: 8", 20.3 cm
Colour: Red and black
Issued: 1929-1949
Varieties: HN 1446, 1699

U.S.: $1,350.00
Can.: $1,500.00
Ster.:   £ 600.00

HN 1342
The Flower Seller's Children
Designer: L. Harradine
Height: 8", 20.3 cm
Colour: Purple, red
           and yellow
Issued: 1929 to the
           present
Varieties: HN 525, 551,
           1206, 1406

U.S.: $695.00
Can.: $865.00
Ster.:   £265.00

HN 1343
Dulcinea
Designer: L. Harradine
Height: 5 1/2", 14.0 cm
Colour: Multi-coloured
Issued: 1929-1938
Varieties: HN 1419

U.S.: $2,000.00
Can.: $2,000.00
Ster.:   £ 800.00

HN 1344
Sunshine Girl
Designer: L. Harradine
Height: 5", 12.7 cm
Colour: Green, black
           and red
Issued: 1929-1938
Varieties: HN 1348

U.S.: $3,500.00
Can.: $3,500.00
Ster.:   £1,200.00

HN 1345
A Victorian Lady
Designer: L. Harradine
Height: 7 3/4", 19.7 cm
Colour: Green and purple
Issued: 1929-1949
Varieties: HN 726, 727, 728,
           736, 739, 740, 742,
           745, 1208, 1258,
           1276, 1277, 1452,
           1529

U.S.: $900.00
Can.: $950.00
Ster.:   £300.00

HN 1346
Iona
Designer: L. Harradine
Height: 7 1/2", 19.1 cm
Colour: Green, black
and lavender
Issued: 1929-1938

U.S.: $3,500.00
Can.: $3,500.00
Ster.: £1,200.00

HN 1347
Moira
Designer: L. Harradine
Height: 6 1/2", 16.5 cm
Colour: Lavender, pink
and green
Issued: 1929-1938

U.S.: $3,500.00
Can.: $3,500.00
Ster.: £1,200.00

HN 1348
Sunshine Girl
Designer: L. Harradine
Height: 5", 12.7 cm
Colour: Black and
orange
Issued: 1929-1938
Varieties: HN 1344

U.S.: $2,200.00
Can.: $2,500.00
Ster.: £1,000.00

HN 1349
Scotties
Designer: L. Harradine
Height: 5 1/4", 13.3 cm
Colour: Blue
Issued: 1929-1949
Varieties: HN 1281

U.S.: $4,000.00
Can.: $4,000.00
Ster.: £1,300.00

Photograph
Not
Available

HN 1350
One of the Forty
Style Eleven
Designer: H. Tittensor
Height: Unknown
Colour: Multi-coloured
Issued: 1929-1949
Varieties: HN 481, 483,
491, 646, 667,
712, 1336

U.S.: $2,500.00
Can.: $2,500.00
Ster.: £ 800.00

HN 1351
One of the Forty
Style One
Designer: H. Tittensor
Height: 8 1/4", 21.0 cm
Colour: Mottled red
and purple
Issued: 1929-1949
Varieties: HN 417, 490,
495, 501, 528,
648, 677, 1352

U.S.: $2,500.00
Can.: $2,500.00
Ster.: £ 800.00

HN 1352
One of the Forty
Style One
Designer: H. Tittensor
Height: 8 1/4", 21.0 cm
Colour: Multi-coloured
Issued: 1929-1949
Varieties: HN 417, 490,
495, 501, 528,
648, 677, 1351

U.S.: $2,500.00
Can.: $2,500.00
Ster.: £ 800.00

HN 1353
One of the Forty
Style Two
Designer: H. Tittensor
Height: 7 1/4", 18.4 cm
Colour: Orange and purple
Issued: 1929-1949
Varieties: HN 418, 494,
498, 647, 666,
704

U.S.: $2,500.00
Can.: $2,500.00
Ster.: £ 800.00

HN 1354
One of the Forty
Style Thirteen
Designer: H. Tittensor
Height: 7 3/4", 19.7 cm
Colour: Multi-coloured
Issued: 1929-1949
Varieties: HN 496, 500, 649, 665

U.S.: $2,500.00
Can.: $2,500.00
Ster.: £ 800.00

HN 1355
The Mendicant
Designer: L. Harradine
Height: 8 1/4", 21.0 cm
Issued: 1929-1938
Colour: Brown
Varieties: HN 1365 (Minor glaze difference)

U.S.: $350.00
Can.: $400.00
Ster.: £250.00

Earthenware

HN 1356
The Parson's Daughter
Designer: H. Tittensor
Height: 9 1/4", 23.5 cm
Colour: Multi-coloured
Issued: 1929-1938
Varieties: HN 337, 338, 441, 564, 790, 1242, 2018

U.S.: $1,000.00
Can.: $1,000.00
Ster.: £ 300.00

HN 1357
Kathleen
Style One
Designer: L. Harradine
Height: 7 1/2", 19.1 cm
Colour: Pink and lavender
Issued: 1929-1938
Varieties: HN 1252, 1253, 1275, 1279, 1291, 1512

U.S.: $1,400.00
Can.: $1,400.00
Ster.: £ 475.00

HN 1358
Rosina
Designer: L. Harradine
Height: 5 3/4", 14.6 cm
Colour: Red
Issued: 1929-1938
Varieties: HN 1364, 1556

U.S.: $1,200.00
Can.: $1,200.00
Ster.: £ 450.00

HN 1359
Two-A-Penny
Designer: L. Harradine
Height: 8 1/4", 21.0 cm
Colour: Red and green
Issued: 1929-1938

U.S.: $3,500.00
Can.: $3,500.00
Ster.: £1,200.00

Earthenware

HN 1360
Sweet and Twenty
Style One
Designer: L. Harradine
Height: 6", 15.2 cm
Colour: Blue and green
Issued: 1929-1938
Varieties: HN 1298, 1437, 1438, 1549, 1563, 1649

U.S.: $750.00
Can.: $850.00
Ster.: £300.00

HN 1361
Mask Seller
Designer: L. Harradine
Height: 8 1/2", 21.6 cm
Colour: Black, white and red
Issued: 1929-1938
Varieties: HN 2103

U.S.: $2,000.00
Can.: $2,000.00
Ster.: £ 650.00

HN 1362
Pantalettes
Designer: L. Harradine
Height: 7 3/4", 19.7 cm
Colour: Green and blue
Issued: 1929-1938
Varieties: HN 1412, 1507, 1709

U.S.: $500.00
Can.: $650.00
Ster.: £250.00

HN 1363
Doreen
Designer: L. Harradine
Height: 5 1/4", 13.3 cm
Colour: Red
Issued: 1929-1938
Varieties: HN 1389, 1390

U.S.: $1,300.00
Can.: $1,250.00
Ster.: £ 450.00

HN 1364
Rosina
Designer: L. Harradine
Height: 5 1/4", 13.3 cm
Colour: Purple and red
Issued: 1929-1938
Varieties: HN 1358, 1556

U.S.: $1,300.00
Can.: $1,300.00
Ster.: £ 450.00

HN 1365
The Mendicant
Designer: L. Harradine
Height: 8 1/4", 21.0 cm
Colour: Brown
Issued: 1929-1969
Varieties: HN 1355

U.S.: $325.00
Can.: $370.00
Ster.: £250.00

Earthenware

HN 1366
The Moor
Designer: C.J. Noke
Height: 16 1/2", 41.9 cm
Colour: Multi-coloured
Issued: 1930-1949
Varieties: HN 1308, 1425, 1657, 2082; also called "An Arab" HN 33, 343, 378

U.S.: $2,500.00
Can.: $2,500.00
Ster.: £ 800.00

Photograph
Not
Available

HN 1367
Kitty
Designer: Unknown
Height: 4", 10.1 cm
Colour: White, yellow and purple
Issued: 1930-1938

U.S.: **Extremely**
Can.: **Rare**
Ster.:

HN 1368
Rose
Designer: L. Harradine
Height: 4 1/2", 11.4 cm
Colour: Pink
Issued: 1930 to the present
Varieties: HN 1387, 1416, 1506, 1654, 2123

U.S.: $110.00
Can.: $150.00
Ster.: £ 43.00

Photograph Not Available	

HN 1369
Boy on Pig
Designer: C.J. Noke
Height: 4", 10.1 cm
Colour: Green and brown
Issued: 1930-1938
Varieties: Also known in flambé

U.S.:	**Extremely**
Can.:	**Rare**
Ster.:	

HN 1370
Marie
Style Two
Designer: L. Harradine
Height: 4 3/4", 12.0 cm
Colour: Purple
Issued: 1930-1988
Varieties: HN 1388, 1417, 1489, 1531, 1635, 1655

U.S.:	**$135.00**
Can.:	**$175.00**
Ster.:	**£ 80.00**

HN 1371
Darling
Style One
Designer: C. Vyse
Height: 7 1/2", 19.1 cm
Colour: Green
Issued: 1930-1938
Varieties: HN 1, 1319, 1372

U.S.:	**$1,000.00**
Can.:	**$1,250.00**
Ster.:	**£ 650.00**

HN 1372
Darling
Style One
Designer: C. Vyse
Height: 7 3/4", 19.7 cm
Colour: Pink
Issued: 1930-1938
Varieties: HN 1, 1319, 1371

U.S.:	**$800.00**
Can.:	**$900.00**
Ster.:	**£650.00**

HN 1373
Sweet Lavender
Designer: L. Harradine
Height: 9", 22.8 cm
Colour: Green, red and black
Issued: 1930-1949
Varieties: Also called "Any Old Lavender"

U.S.:	**$950.00**
Can.:	**$950.00**
Ster.:	**£450.00**

Earthenware

HN 1374
Fairy
Style Two
Designer: L. Harradine
Height: 4", 10.1 cm
Colour: Yellow flowers
Issued: 1930-1938
Varieties: HN 1380, 1532

U.S.:	**$1,500.00**
Can.:	**$1,500.00**
Ster.:	**£ 450.00**

HN 1375
Fairy
Style Three
Designer: L. Harradine
Height: 3", 7.6 cm
Colour: Yellow flowers
Issued: 1930-1938
Varieties: HN 1395, 1533

U.S.:	**$1,500.00**
Can.:	**$1,500.00**
Ster.:	**£ 450.00**

HN 1376
Fairy
Style Four
Designer: L. Harradine
Height: 2 1/2", 6.3 cm
Colour: Yellow flowers
Issued: 1930-1938
Varieties: HN 1536

U.S.:	**$1,000.00**
Can.:	**$1,000.00**
Ster.:	**£ 450.00**

<table>
<tr><td>

Photograph
Not
Available

HN 1377
Fairy
Style Five
Designer: L. Harradine
Height: 1 1/2", 3.8 cm
Colour: Lavender and yellow
Issued: 1930-1938

U.S.: $1,100.00
Can.: $1,200.00
Ster.: £ 450.00

</td><td>

HN 1378
Fairy
Style Six
Designer: L. Harradine
Height: 2 1/2", 6.3 cm
Colour: Orange flowers
Issued: 1930-1938
Varieties: HN 1396, 1535

U.S.: $1,000.00
Can.: $1,100.00
Ster.: £ 450.00

</td><td>

HN 1379
Fairy
Style Seven
Designer: L. Harradine
Height: 2 1/2", 6.3 cm
Colour: Blue flowers
Issued: 1930-1938
Varieties: HN 1394, 1534

U.S.: $1,000.00
Can.: $1,000.00
Ster.: £ 450.00

</td><td>

HN 1380
Fairy
Style Two
Designer: L. Harradine
Height: 4", 10.1 cm
Colour: Multi-coloured
Issued: 1930-1938
Varieties: HN 1374, 1532

U.S.: $1,500.00
Can.: $1,500.00
Ster.: £ 450.00

*

</td></tr>
<tr><td>

HN 1387
Rose
Designer: L. Harradine
Height: 4 1/2", 11.4 cm
Colour: Blue, pink and orange
Issued: 1930-1938
Varieties: HN 1368, 1416, 1506, 1654, 2123

U.S.: $325.00
Can.: $375.00
Ster.: £200.00

</td><td>

HN 1388
Marie
Style Two
Designer: L. Harradine
Height: 4 1/2", 11.4 cm
Colour: Pink
Issued: 1930-1938
Varieties: HN 1370, 1417, 1489, 1531, 1635, 1655

U.S.: $325.00
Can.: $375.00
Ster.: £200.00

</td><td>

HN 1389
Doreen
Designer: L. Harradine
Height: 5 1/4", 13.3 cm
Colour: Green
Issued: 1930-1038
Varieties: HN 1363, 1390

U.S.: $1,300.00
Can.: $1,250.00
Ster.: £ 450.00

</td><td>

HN 1390
Doreen
Designer: L. Harradine
Height: 5 3/4", 14.6 cm
Colour: Lavender
Issued: 1929-1938
Varieties: HN 1363, 1389

U.S.: $1,500.00
Can.: $1,250.00
Ster.: £ 450.00

</td></tr>
</table>

HN 1391
Pierrette
Style Three
Designer: L. Harradine
Height: 8 1/2", 21.6 cm
Colour: Red
Issued: 1930-1938
Varieties: HN 1749

U.S.: $2,000.00
Can.: $2,250.00
Ster.: £ 800.00

Earthenware

HN 1392
Paisley Shawl
Style One
Designer: L. Harradine
Height: 8 1/4", 21.0 cm
Colour: Red shawl,
flowered cream
dress
Issued: 1930-1949
Varieties: HN 1460, 1707,
1739, 1987

U.S.: $450.00
Can.: $600.00
Ster.: £250.00

HN 1393
Fairy
Style Eight
Designer: L. Harradine
Height: 2 1/2", 6.3 cm
Colour: Yellow flowers
Issued: 1930-1938

U.S.: $1,000.00
Can.: $1,000.00
Ster.: £ 450.00

HN 1394
Fairy
Style Seven
Designer: L. Harradine
Height: 2 1/2", 6.3 cm
Colour: Yellow flowers
Issued: 1930-1938
Varieties: HN 1379, 1534

U.S.: $1,000.00
Can.: $1,000.00
Ster.: £ 450.00

HN 1395
Fairy
Style Three
Designer: L. Harradine
Height: 3", 7.6 cm
Colour: Blue flowers
Issued: 1930-1938
Varieties: HN 1375, 1533

U.S.: $1,500.00
Can.: $1,500.00
Ster.: £ 450.00

HN 1396
Fairy
Style Six
Designer: L. Harradine
Height: 2 1/2", 6.3 cm
Colour: Blue flowers
Issued: 1930-1938
Varieties: HN 1378, 1535

U.S.: $1,300.00
Can.: $1,200.00
Ster.: £ 450.00

HN 1397
Gretchen
Designer: L. Harradine
Height: 7 3/4", 19.7 cm
Colour: Blue and white
Issued: 1930-1938
Varieties: HN 1562

U.S.: $1,000.00
Can.: $1,000.00
Ster.: £ 600.00

HN 1398
Derrick
Designer: L. Harradine
Height: 8", 20.3 cm
Colour: Blue and white
Issued: 1930-1938

U.S.: $1,000.00
Can.: $1,000.00
Ster.: £ 600.00

HN 1399
The Young Widow
Style One
Designer: L. Harradine
Height: 8", 20.3 cm
Issued: 1930-1930
Colour: Purple
Varieties: Also called "Little
             Mother" Style Two
             HN 1418, 1641

U.S.: $3,000.00
Can.: $3,000.00
Ster.:   £1,000.00

HN 1400
The Windmill Lady
Designer: L. Harradine
Height: 8 1/2", 21.6 cm
Colour: Green, yellow
             and orange
Issued: 1930-1938

U.S.: $4,000.00
Can.: $4,000.00
Ster.:   £1,300.00

HN 1401
Chorus Girl
Designer: L. Harradine
Height: 8 1/2", 21.6 cm
Colour: Red and orange
Issued: 1930-1938

U.S.: $2,000.00
Can.: $2,200.00
Ster.:   £   800.00

HN 1402
Miss Demure
Designer: L. Harradine
Height: 7 1/2", 19.1 cm
Colour: Lavender and
             pink
Issued: 1930-1975
Varieties: HN 1440, 1463,
             1499, 1560

U.S.: $250.00
Can.: $395.00
Ster.:   £200.00

*

HN 1404
Betty
Style Two
Designer: L. Harradine
Height: 4 1/2", 11.4 cm
Colour: Lavender
Issued: 1930-1938
Varieties: HN 1405, 1435,
             1436

U.S.: $3,000.00
Can.: $3,000.00
Ster.:   £1,000.00

HN 1405
Betty
Style Two
Designer: L. Harradine
Height: 4 1/2", 11.4 cm
Colour: Green
Issued: 1930-1938
Varieties: HN 1404, 1435,
             1436

U.S.: $3,000.00
Can.: $3,000.00
Ster.:   £1,000.00

HN 1406
The Flower Seller's
Children
Designer: L. Harradine
Height: 8 1/4", 21.0 cm
Colour: Yellow and blue
Issued: 1930-1938
Varieties: HN 525, 551,
             1206, 1342

U.S.: $1,750.00
Can.: $1,750.00
Ster.:   £   650.00

HN 1407
The Winner
Designer: Unknown
Height: 6 3/4", 17.2 cm
Colour: Red, blue and
             grey
Issued: 1930-1938

U.S.: $7,500.00
Can.: $7,500.00
Ster.:   £2,500.00

HN 1408
John Peel
Designer: Unknown
Height: 9 1/2", 24.1 cm
Colour: Red and brown
Issued: 1930-1937
Varieties: Also called
"The Huntsman"
Style Two
HN 1815

U.S.: $4,000.00
Can.: $4,000.00
Ster.: £1,300.00

HN 1409
Hunting Squire
Designer: Unknown
Height: 9 3/4", 24.7 cm
Colour: Red and grey
Issued: 1930-1938
Varieties: Also called
"The Squire"
HN 1814

U.S.: $4,000.00
Can.: $4,000.00
Ster.: £1,300.00

HN 1410
Abdullah
Designer: L. Harradine
Height: 5 3/4", 14.6 cm
Colour: Blue, lavender
and green
Issued: 1930-1938
Varieties: HN 2104

U.S.: $1,500.00
Can.: $1,500.00
Ster.: £ 650.00

HN 1411
Charley's Aunt
Style Two
Designer: H. Fenton
Height: 8", 20.3 cm
Colour: Black
Issued: 1930-1938
Varieties: HN 1554

U.S.: $1,500.00
Can.: $ 950.00
Ster.: £ 650.00

HN 1412
Pantalettes
Designer: L. Harradine
Height: 7 3/4", 19.7 cm
Colour: Blue and pink
Issued: 1930-1949
Varieties: HN 1362, 1507,
1709

U.S.: $850.00
Can.: $650.00
Ster.: £250.00

HN 1413
Margery
Designer: L. Harradine
Height: 11", 27.9 cm
Colour: Red and black
Issued: 1930-1949

U.S.: $700.00
Can.: $750.00
Ster.: £300.00

Earthenware

HN 1414
Patricia
Style One
Designer: L. Harradine
Height: 8 1/2", 21.6 cm
Colour: Yellow and green
Issued: 1930-1949
Varieties: HN 1431, 1462,
1567

U.S.: $ 950.00
Can.: $1,100.00
Ster.: £ 350.00

*

HN 1416
Rose
Designer: L. Harradine
Height: 4 1/2", 11.4 cm
Colour: Lavender
Issued: 1930-1949
Varieties: HN 1368, 1387,
1506, 1654,
2123

U.S.: $350.00
Can.: $400.00
Ster.: £200.00

HN 1417
Marie
Style Two
Designer: L. Harradine
Height: 4 3/4", 12.0 cm
Colour: Orange
Issued: 1930-1949
Varieties: HN 1370, 1388,
  1489, 1531,
  1635, 1655

U.S.: $350.00
Can.: $450.00
Ster.: £200.00

HN 1418
The Little Mother
Style Two
Designer: L. Harradine
Height: 8", 20.3 cm
Colour: Purple
Issued: 1930-1938
Varieties: HN 1641; also
  called "Young
  Widow" HN 1399

U.S.: $4,000.00
Can.: $4,000.00
Ster.: £1,300.00

HN 1419
Dulcinea
Designer: L. Harradine
Height: 5 1/2", 14.0 cm
Colour: Red
Issued: 1930-1938
Varieties: HN 1343

U.S.: $2,000.00
Can.: $2,000.00
Ster.: £ 800.00

HN 1420
Phyllis
Style One
Designer: L. Harradine
Height: 9", 22.9 cm
Colour: Purple and green
Issued: 1930-1949
Varieties: HN 1430, 1486,
  1698

U.S.: $1,100.00
Can.: $1,100.00
Ster.: £ 400.00

HN 1421
Barbara
Style One
Designer: L. Harradine
Height: 7 3/4", 19.7 cm
Colour: Cream and
  lavender
Issued: 1930-1938
Varieties: HN 1432, 1461

U.S.: $1,500.00
Can.: $1,500.00
Ster.: £ 600.00

HN 1422
Joan
Style One
Designer: L. Harradine
Height: 5 1/2", 14.0 cm
Colour: Blue
Issued: 1930-1949
Varieties: HN 2023 (minor
  glaze difference)

U.S.: $450.00
Can.: $575.00
Ster.: £250.00

HN 1423
Babette
Designer: L. Harradine
Height: 5", 12.7 cm
Colour: Yellow, green
  and red
Issued: 1930-1938
Varieties: HN 1424

U.S.: $1,200.00
Can.: $1,200.00
Ster.: £ 650.00

HN 1424
Babette
Designer: L. Harradine
Height: 5", 12.7 cm
Colour: Blue
Issued: 1930-1938
Varieties: HN 1423

U.S.: $ 900.00
Can.: $1,000.00
Ster.: £ 650.00

HN 1617 Primroses, HN 1549 Sweet and Twenty, HN 1492 Old Lavender Seller

HN 1496 Sweet Anne, HN 1558 Dorcas, HN 1412 Pantalettes, HN 1626 Bonnie Lassie

HN 1341 Marietta, HN 564 The Parson's Daughter, HN 612 The Poke Bonnet, HN 35 Charleys' Aunt (Style One)

M46 Sairey Gamp, M56 Tiny Tim

HN 1449 Little Mistress, HN 1589 Sweet and Twenty (Style Two), HN 1417 Marie

HN 1807 Spring Flowers, HN 1706 The Cobbler (Style Three), HN 1909 Honey, HN 1744 Mirabel

HN 1773 Delight, HN 1772 Delight, HN 1886 Nadine, HN 1662 Delicia

HN 1759 Orange Lady, HN 1771 Maureen, HN 1858A Dawn, HN 1712 Daffy-Down-Dilly
HN 1805 To Bed

HN 1729 Vera, HN 1897 Miss Fortune, HN 1798 Lily

HN 1911 Autumn Breezes, HN 1997 Belle o' the Ball, HN 1996 Prue, HN 1946 Marguerite

HN 1975 The Shepherd (Style Four), HN 2008 Philippa of Hainault, HN 2005 Henrietta Maria,
HN 1916 Janet (Style Two), HN 1998 Collinette, HN 1976 Easter Day

HN 1991 Market Day, HN 1979 Golliwog, HN 1937 Miss Muffet, HN 2004 A'Courting, HN 1953 Orange Lady

HN 2031 Granny's Heritage, HN 2025 Gossips, HN 2034 Madonna of the Square

HN 2011 Matilda, HN 2030 Memories, HN 2026 Suzette, HN 2039 Easter Day

HN 2041 Broken Lance, HN 2022 Janice, HN 2019 Minuet

HN 2010 Young Miss Nightingale, HN 2045 She Loves Me Not, HN 2046 She Loves Me,
HN 2036 Pearly Girl (Style Two), HN 2035 Pearly Boy (Style Two)

HN 1425
The Moor
Designer: C.J. Noke
Height: 16 1/2", 41.9 cm
Colour: Multi-coloured
Issued: 1930-1949
Varieties: HN 1308, 1366,
           1657, 2082; also
           called "An Arab"
           HN 33, 343, 378

U.S.: $3,000.00
Can.: $2,500.00
Ster.:   £ 950.00

HN 1426
The Gossips
Designer: L. Harradine
Height: 5 3/4", 14.6 cm
Colour: Turquoise and
           pink
Issued: 1930-1949
Varieties: HN 1429, 2025

U.S.: $1,800.00
Can.: $1,800.00
Ster.:   £ 600.00

HN 1427
Darby
Designer: L. Harradine
Height: 5 1/2", 14.0 cm
Colour: Pink and blue
Issued: 1930-1949
Varieties: HN 2024 (minor
           glaze difference)

U.S.: $450.00
Can.: $575.00
Ster.:   £250.00

HN 1428
Calumet
Designer: C.J. Noke
Height: 6", 15.2 cm
Colour: Brown, blue
           and yellow
Issued: 1930-1949
Varieties: HN 1689, 2068

U.S.: $1,250.00
Can.: $1,250.00
Ster.:   £ 450.00

HN 1429
The Gossips
Designer: L. Harradine
Height: 5 3/4", 14.6 cm
Colour: Red and cream
Issued: 1930-1949
Varieties: HN 1426, 2025

U.S.: $1,200.00
Can.: $1,200.00
Ster.:   £ 400.00

HN 1430
Phyllis
Style One
Designer: L. Harradine
Height: 9", 22.9 cm
Colour: Blue and pink
Issued: 1930-1938
Varieties: HN 1420, 1486,
           1698

U.S.: $1,750.00
Can.: $1,750.00
Ster.:   £ 550.00

HN 1431
Patricia
Style One
Designer: L. Harradine
Height: 8 1/2", 21.6 cm
Colour: Lavender
Issued: 1930-1949
Varieties: HN 1414, 1462,
           1567

U.S.: $1,000.00
Can.: $1,150.00
Ster.:   £ 350.00

HN 1432
Barbara
Style One
Designer: L. Harradine
Height: 7 3/4", 19.7 cm
Colour: Lavender
Issued: 1930-1938
Varieties: HN 1421, 1461

U.S.: $1,500.00
Can.: $1,500.00
Ster.:   £ 600.00

HN 1433
The Little Bridesmaid
Style One
Designer: L. Harradine
Height: 5 1/4", 13.3 cm
Colour: Lavender and
pink
Issued: 1930-1951
Varieties: HN 1434, 1530

U.S.:	$250.00
Can.:	$295.00
Ster.:	£100.00

HN 1434
The Little Bridesmaid
Style One
Designer: L. Harradine
Height: 5", 12.7 cm
Colour: Yellow-green
Issued: 1930-1949
Varieties: HN 1433, 1530

U.S.:	$400.00
Can.:	$425.00
Ster.:	£150.00

HN 1435
Betty
Style Two
Designer: L. Harradine
Height: 4 1/2", 11.4 cm
Colour: Multi-coloured
Issued: 1930-1938
Varieties: HN 1404, 1405,
1436

U.S.:	$3,000.00
Can.:	$3,000.00
Ster.:	£1,000.00

HN 1436
Betty
Style Two
Designer: L. Harradine
Height: 4 1/2", 11.4 cm
Colour: Green
Issued: 1930-1938
Varieties: HN 1404, 1405,
1435

U.S.:	$3,000.00
Can.:	$3,000.00
Ster.:	£1,000.00

HN 1437
Sweet and Twenty
Style One
Designer: L. Harradine
Height: 6", 15.2 cm
Colour: Red
Issued: 1930-1938
Varieties: HN 1298, 1360,
1438, 1549,
1563, 1649

U.S.:	$1,250.00
Can.:	$1,250.00
Ster.:	£ 400.00

HN 1438
Sweet and Twenty
Style One
Designer: L. Harradine
Height: 6", 15.2 cm
Colour: Multi-coloured
Issued: 1930-1938
Varieties: HN 1298, 1360,
1437, 1549,
1563, 1649

U.S.:	$1,250.00
Can.:	$1,250.00
Ster.:	£ 400.00

HN 1439
Columbine
Style One
Designer: L. Harradine
Height: 6", 15.2 cm
Colour: Mottled lavender
and cream
Issued: 1930-1938
Varieties: HN 1296, 1297

U.S.:	$1,100.00
Can.:	$1,250.00
Ster.:	£ 600.00

HN 1440
Miss Demure
Designer: L. Harradine
Height: 7", 17.8 cm
Colour: Blue
Issued: 1930-1949
Varieties: HN 1402, 1463,
1499, 1560

U.S.:	$950.00
Can.:	$950.00
Ster.:	£300.00

HN 1441
Child Study
Style One
Designer: L. Harradine
Height: 5", 12.7 cm
Colour: Cream, green flowered base
Issued: 1931-1938
Varieties: HN 603A, 603B

U.S.: $950.00
Can.: $800.00
Ster.: £275.00

HN 1442
Child Study
Style Two
Designer: L. Harradine
Height: 6 1/4", 15.9 cm
Colour: Cream, green flowered base
Issued: 1931-1938
Varieties: HN 604A, 604B 1443

U.S.: $950.00
Can.: $800.00
Ster.: £275.00

HN 1443
Child Study
Style Two
Designer: L. Harradine
Height: 5", 12.7 cm
Colour: Cream, green flowered base
Issued: 1931-1938
Varieties: HN 604A, 604B, 1442

U.S.: $950.00
Can.: $800.00
Ster.: £275.00

HN 1444
Pauline
Style One
Designer: L. Harradine
Height: 6", 15.2 cm
Colour: Blue
Issued: 1931-1938

U.S.: $600.00
Can.: $700.00
Ster.: £300.00

HN 1445
Biddy
Designer: L. Harradine
Height: 5 1/2", 14.0 cm
Colour: Yellow-green
Issued: 1931-1938
Varieties: HN 1500, 1513

U.S.: $425.00
Can.: $425.00
Ster.: £300.00

HN 1446
Marietta
Designer: L. Harradine
Height: 8", 20.3 cm
Colour: Green and lavender
Issued: 1931-1949
Varieties: HN 1341, 1699

U.S.: $1,700.00
Can.: $1,850.00
Ster.: £ 600.00

HN 1447
Marigold
Designer: L. Harradine
Height: 6", 15.2 cm
Colour: Lavender
Issued: 1931-1949
Varieties: HN 1451, 1555

U.S.: $550.00
Can.: $600.00
Ster.: £300.00

HN 1448
Rita
Designer: L. Harradine
Height: 7", 17.8 cm
Colour: Red dress with green shawl
Issued: 1931-1938
Varieties: HN 1450

U.S.: $1,250.00
Can.: $1,250.00
Ster.: £ 600.00

HN 1449
The Little Mistress
Designer: L. Harradine
Height: 5 3/4", 14.6 cm
Colour: Green and blue
Issued: 1931-1949

U.S.: $750.00
Can.: $850.00
Ster.: £300.00

HN 1450
Rita
Designer: L. Harradine
Height: 7", 17.8 cm
Colour: Blue dress
with red shawl
Issued: 1931-1938
Varieties: HN 1448

U.S.: $1,250.00
Can.: $1,250.00
Ster.: £ 600.00

HN 1451
Marigold
Designer: L. Harradine
Height: 6", 15.2 cm
Colour: Yellow
Issued: 1931-1938
Varieties: HN 1447, 1555

U.S.: $900.00
Can.: $900.00
Ster.: £400.00

HN 1452
A Victorian Lady
Designer: L. Harradine
Height: 7 3/4", 19.7 cm
Colour: Green
Issued: 1931-1949
Varieties: HN 726, 727, 728,
736, 739, 740, 742,
745, 1208, 1258,
1276, 1277, 1345,
1529

U.S.: $900.00
Can.: $900.00
Ster.: £275.00

HN 1453
Sweet Anne
Designer: L. Harradine
Height: 7", 17.8 cm
Colour: Green
Issued: 1931-1949
Varieties: HN 1318, 1330,
1331, 1496,
1631, 1701

U.S.: $950.00
Can.: $950.00
Ster.: £300.00

HN 1454
Negligée
Designer: L. Harradine
Height: 5", 12.7 cm
Colour: Pink
Issued: 1931-1938
Varieties: HN 1219, 1228,
1272, 1273

U.S.: $1,700.00
Can.: $1,800.00
Ster.: £ 600.00

HN 1455
Molly Malone
Designer: L. Harradine
Height: 7", 17.8 cm
Colour: Red and brown
Issued: 1931-1938

U.S.: $3,500.00
Can.: $3,500.00
Ster.: £1,200.00

HN 1456
The Butterfly Girl
Designer: L. Harradine
Height: 6 1/2", 16.5 cm
Colour: Lavender and
green
Issued: 1931-1938
Varieties: Also called
"Butterfly"
HN 719, 720,
730, 1203

U.S.: $2,000.00
Can.: $2,000.00
Ster.: £ 700.00

HN 1457
All-A-Bloooming
Designer: L. Harradine
Height: 6 1/2", 16.5 cm
Colour: Blue
Issued: 1931-?
Varieties: HN 1466

U.S.: $2,000.00
Can.: $2,000.00
Ster.: £ 700.00

HN 1458
Monica
Designer: L. Harradine
Height: 4", 10.1 cm
Colour: Flowered
cream dress
Issued: 1931-1949
Varieties: HN 1459, 1467

U.S.: $450.00
Can.: $500.00
Ster.: £250.00

HN 1459
Monica
Designer: L. Harradine
Height: 4", 10.1 cm
Colour: Lavender
Issued: 1931-?
Varieties: HN 1458, 1467

U.S.: $650.00
Can.: $700.00
Ster.: £250.00

HN 1460
Paisley Shawl
Style One
Designer: L. Harradine
Height: 8 1/4", 21.0 cm
Colour: Green
Issued: 1931-1949
Varieties: HN 1392, 1707,
1739, 1987

U.S.: $900.00
Can.: $975.00
Ster.: £350.00

HN 1461
Barbara
Style One
Designer: L. Harradine
Height: 7 3/4", 19.7 cm
Colour: Green
Issued: 1931-1938
Varieties: HN 1421, 1432

U.S.: $2,000.00
Can.: $2,000.00
Ster.: £ 700.00

HN 1462
Patricia
Style One
Designer: L. Harradine
Height: 8", 20.3 cm
Colour: Green
Issued: 1931-1938
Varieties: HN 1414, 1431,
1567

U.S.: $1,200.00
Can.: $1,200.00
Ster.: £ 375.00

Earthenware

HN 1463
Miss Demure
Designer: L. Harradine
Height: 7", 17.8 cm
Colour: Green
Issued: 1931-1949
Varieties: HN 1402, 1440,
1499, 1560

U.S.: $ 900.00
Can.: $1,000.00
Ster.: £ 300.00

HN 1464
The Carpet Seller
(Hand Open)
Style One
Designer: L. Harradine
Height: 9 1/4", 23.5 cm
Colour: Green and orange
Issued: 1929-?
Varieties: HN 1464A

U.S.: $1,000.00
Can.: $ 900.00
Ster.: £ 400.00

Earthenware

HN 1464A
The Carpet Seller
(Hand Closed)
Style Two
Designer: L. Harradine
Height: 9", 22.9 cm
Colour: Green and orange
Issued: ?-1969
Varieties: HN 1464

U.S.: $325.00
Can.: $485.00
Ster.:   £250.00

Porcelain

HN 1465
Lady Clare
Designer: L. Harradine
Height: 7 3/4", 19.7 cm
Colour: Red
Issued: 1931-1938

U.S.: $1,350.00
Can.: $1,200.00
Ster.:   £ 450.00

HN 1466
All-A-Blooming
Designer: L. Harradine
Height: 6 1/2", 16.5 cm
Colour: Purple, green
           and red
Issued: 1931-1938
Varieties: HN 1457

U.S.: $1,800.00
Can.: $1,800.00
Ster.:   £ 600.00

HN 1467
Monica
Designer: L. Harradine
Height: 4", 10.1 cm
Colour: Flowered
           purple dress
Issued: 1931 to the
           present
Varieties: HN 1458, 1459

U.S.: $175.00
Can.: $225.00
Ster.:   £ 65.00

HN 1468
Pamela
Style One
Designer: L. Harradine
Height: 7 1/2", 19.1 cm
Colour: Blue
Issued: 1931-1938
Varieties: HN 1469, 1564

U.S.: $1,250.00
Can.: $1,250.00
Ster.:   £ 600.00

HN 1469
Pamela
Style One
Designer: L. Harradine
Height: 7 1/2", 19.1 cm
Colour: Yellow
Issued: 1931-1938
Varieties: HN 1468, 1564

U.S.: $1,100.00
Can.: $1,100.00
Ster.:   £ 600.00

HN 1470
Chloe
Designer: L. Harradine
Height: 5 1/2", 14.0 cm
Colour: Yellow and purple
Issued: 1931-1949
Varieties: HN 1476, 1479,
           1498, 1765, 1956

U.S.: $600.00
Can.: $700.00
Ster.:   £300.00

HN 1471
Annette
Designer: L. Harradine
Height: 6 1/4", 15.9 cm
Colour: Blue and white
Issued: 1931-1938
Varieties: HN 1472, 1550

U.S.: $650.00
Can.: $675.00
Ster.:   £350.00

HN 1472
Annette
Designer: L. Harradine
Height: 6", 15.2 cm
Colour: Green
Issued: 1931-1949
Varieties: HN 1471, 1550

U.S.: $650.00
Can.: $725.00
Ster.: £350.00

HN 1473
Dreamland
Designer: L. Harradine
Height: 4 3/4", 12.0 cm
Colour: Lavender
Issued: 1931-1938
Varieties: HN 1481

U.S.: $4,000.00
Can.: $4,000.00
Ster.: £1,300.00

HN 1474
In the Stocks
Style One
Designer: L. Harradine
Height: 5", 12.7 cm
Colour: Red and brown
Issued: 1931-1938
Varieties: HN 1475; also
called "Love in
the Stocks" and
"Love Locked In"

U.S.: $2,500.00
Can.: $2,500.00
Ster.: £ 800.00

HN 1475
In the Stocks
Style One
Designer: L. Harradine
Height: 5 1/4", 13.3 cm
Colour: Green
Issued: 1931-1938
Varieties: HN 1474; also
called "Love in
the Stocks" and
"Love Locked In"

U.S.: $2,500.00
Can.: $2,500.00
Ster.: £ 800.00

HN 1476
Chloe
Designer: L. Harradine
Height: 5 1/2", 14.0 cm
Colour: Blue
Issued: 1931-1938
Varieties: HN 1470, 1479,
1498, 1765, 1956

U.S.: $450.00
Can.: $500.00
Ster.: £300.00

*

HN 1478
Sylvia
Designer: L. Harradine
Height: 10 1/2", 26.7 cm
Colour: Orange and blue
Issued: 1931-1938

U.S.: $850.00
Can.: $850.00
Ster.: £350.00

Earthenware

HN 1479
Chloe
Designer: L. Harradine
Height: 5 1/2", 14.0 cm
Colour: Lavender
Issued: 1931-1949
Varieties: HN 1470, 1476,
1498, 1765, 1956

U.S.: $900.00
Can.: $850.00
Ster.: £300.00

Photogaph
Not
Available

HN 1480
Newhaven Fishwife
Designer: H. Fenton
Height: 7 3/4", 19.7 cm
Colour: Red, white and
black
Issued: 1931-1938

U.S.: $4,000.00
Can.: $4,000.00
Ster.: £1,300.00

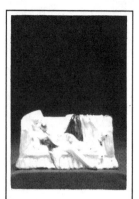

HN 1481
Dreamland
Designer: L. Harradine
Height: 4 3/4", 12.0 cm
Colour: Orange and purple
Issued: 1931-1938
Varieties: HN 1473

U.S.:	$4,000.00
Can.:	$4,000.00
Ster.:	£1,300.00

HN 1482
Pearly Boy
Style One
Designer: L. Harradine
Height: 5 1/2", 14.0 cm
Colour: Brown suit, red vest
Issued: 1931-1949
Varieties: HN 1547

U.S.:	$350.00
Can.:	$425.00
Ster.:	£180.00

HN 1483
Pearly Girl
Style One
Designer: L. Harradine
Height: 5 1/2", 14.0 cm
Colour: Orange and brown
Issued: 1931-1949
Varieties: HN 1548

U.S.:	$350.00
Can.:	$425.00
Ster.:	£180.00

HN 1484
Jennifer
Style One
Designer: L. Harradine
Height: 6 1/2", 16.5 cm
Colour: Yellow flowers on cream dress
Issued: 1931-1949

U.S.:	$750.00
Can.:	$800.00
Ster.:	£300.00

HN 1485
Greta
Designer: L. Harradine
Height: 5 1/2", 14.0 cm
Colour: Lavender
Issued: 1931-1953

U.S.:	$350.00
Can.:	$400.00
Ster.:	£250.00

HN 1486
Phyllis
Style One
Designer: L. Harradine
Height: 9", 22.9 cm
Colour: Lavender
Issued: 1931-1949
Varieties: HN 1420, 1430, 1698

U.S.:	$1,100.00
Can.:	$1,250.00
Ster.:	£ 400.00

HN 1487
Suzette
Designer: L. Harradine
Height: 7 1/2", 19.1 cm
Colour: Flowered pink dress
Issued: 1931-1950
Varieties: HN 1577, 1585, 1696, 2026

U.S.:	$450.00
Can.:	$525.00
Ster.:	£250.00

HN 1488
Gloria
Style One
Designer: L. Harradine
Height: 7 1/4", 18.4 cm
Colour: Green-blue
Issued: 1932-1938
Varieties: HN 1700

U.S.:	$2,500.00
Can.:	$2,500.00
Ster.:	£ 800.00

HN 1489
Marie
Style Two
Designer: L. Harradine
Height: 4 1/2", 11.4 cm
Colour: Pale green
Issued: 1932-1949
Varieties: HN 1370, 1388,
1417, 1531,
1635, 1655

U.S.: $650.00
Can.: $650.00
Ster.: £250.00

HN 1490
Dorcas
Designer: L. Harradine
Height: 7", 17.8 cm
Colour: Light blue
Issued: 1932-1938
Varieties: HN 1491, 1558

U.S.: $1,000.00
Can.: $1,100.00
Ster.: £ 400.00

HN 1491
Dorcas
Designer: L. Harradine
Height: 6 3/4", 17.2 cm
Colour: Pale green and
lavender
Issued: 1932-1938
Varieties: HN 1490, 1558

U.S.: $750.00
Can.: $800.00
Ster.: £300.00

HN 1492
Old Lavender Seller
Designer: L. Harradine
Height: 6", 15.2 cm
Colour: Green and
orange
Issued: 1932-1949
Varieties: HN 1571

U.S.: $850.00
Can.: $950.00
Ster.: £400.00

Earthenware

HN 1493
The Potter
Designer: C.J. Noke
Height: 7", 17.8 cm
Colour: Brown
Issued: 1932 to the
present
Varieties: HN 1518, 1522

U.S.: $600.00
Can.: $725.00
Ster.: £225.00

HN 1494
Gwendolen
Designer: L. Harradine
Height: 6", 15.2 cm
Colour: Green and pink
Issued: 1932-1938
Varieties: HN 1503, 1570

U.S.: $1,500.00
Can.: $1,500.00
Ster.: £ 600.00

HN 1495
Priscilla
Designer: L. Harradine
Height: 8", 20.3 cm
Colour: Blue
Issued: 1932-1949
Varieties: HN 1337, 1340,
1501, 1559

U.S.: $ 900.00
Can.: $1,000.00
Ster.: £ 350.00

HN 1496
Sweet Anne
Designer: L. Harradine
Height: 7", 17.8 cm
Colour: Purple
Issued: 1932-1967
Varieties: HN 1318, 1330,
1331, 1453,
1631, 1701

U.S.: $285.00
Can.: $450.00
Ster.: £225.00

HN 1497
Rosamund
Style Two
Designer: L. Harradine
Height: 8 1/2", 21.6 cm
Colour: Red
Issued: 1932-1938
Varieties: HN 1551

U.S.: $2,000.00
Can.: $2,000.00
Ster.: £ 700.00

HN 1498
Chloe
Designer: L. Harradine
Height: 6", 15.2 cm
Colour: Peach-yellow
Issued: 1932-1938
Varieties: HN 1470, 1476,
1479, 1765,
1956

U.S.: $900.00
Can.: $900.00
Ster.: £300.00

HN 1499
Miss Demure
Designer: L. Harradine
Height: 7", 17.8 cm
Colour: Pink and yellow
Issued: 1932-1938
Varieties: HN 1402, 1440,
1463, 1560

U.S.: $800.00
Can.: $900.00
Ster.: £300.00

HN 1500
Biddy
Designer: L. Harradine
Height: 5 1/2", 14.0 cm
Colour: Yellow
Issued: 1932-1938
Varieties: HN 1445, 1513

U.S.: $950.00
Can.: $750.00
Ster.: £300.00

HN 1501
Priscilla
Designer: L. Harradine
Height: 8", 20.3 cm
Colour: Orange
Issued: 1932-1938
Varieties: HN 1337, 1340,
1495, 1559

U.S.: $ 900.00
Can.: $1,000.00
Ster.: £ 300.00

HN 1502
Lucy Ann
Designer: L. Harradine
Height: 5 1/4", 13.3 cm
Colour: Lavender
Issued: 1932-1951
Varieties: HN 1565

U.S.: $375.00
Can.: $400.00
Ster.: £250.00

HN 1503
Gwendolen
Designer: L. Harradine
Height: 6", 15.2 cm
Colour: Orange and
yellow
Issued: 1932-1949
Varieties: HN 1494, 1570

U.S.: $1,300.00
Can.: $1,300.00
Ster.: £ 600.00

HN 1504
Sweet Maid
Style One
Designer: L. Harradine
Height: 8", 20.3 cm
Colour: Lavender
and blue
Issued: 1932-1938
Varieties: HN 1505

U.S.: $1,500.00
Can.: $1,700.00
Ster.: £ 600.00

HN 1505
Sweet Maid
Style One
Designer: L. Harradine
Height: 8", 20.3 cm
Colour: Red and green
Issued: 1932-1938
Varieties: HN 1504

U.S.: $1,500.00
Can.: $1,600.00
Ster.: £ 600.00

HN 1506
Rose
Designer: L. Harradine
Height: 4 1/2", 11.4 cm
Colour: Yellow
Issued: 1932-1938
Varieties: HN 1368, 1387,
1416, 1654,
2123

U.S.: $675.00
Can.: $675.00
Ster.: £250.00

HN 1507
Pantalettes
Designer: L. Harradine
Height: 7 3/4", 19.7 cm
Colour: Yellow
Issued: 1932-1949
Varieties: HN 1362, 1412,
1709

U.S.: $1,000.00
Can.: $1,000.00
Ster.: £ 350.00

HN 1508
Helen
Style One
Designer: L. Harradine
Height: 8", 20.3 cm
Colour: Flowered
green dress
Issued: 1932-1938
Varieties: HN 1509, 1572

U.S.: $1,250.00
Can.: $1,250.00
Ster.: £ 600.00

HN 1509
Helen
Style One
Designer: L. Harradine
Height: 8", 20.3 cm
Colour: Flowered blue-
yellow dress
Issued: 1932-1938
Varieties: HN 1508, 1572

U.S.: $1,250.00
Can.: $1,250.00
Ster.: £ 600.00

Photograph
Not
Available

HN 1510
Constance
Designer: L. Harradine
Height: 6 3/4", 17.1 cm
Colour: Yellow-purple
Issued: 1932-1938
Varieties: HN 1511

U.S.: $1,250.00
Can.: $1,250.00
Ster.: £ 600.00

Photograph
Not
Available

HN 1511
Constance
Designer: L. Harradine
Height: 6 3/4", 17.1 cm
Colour: Lavender
Issued: 1932-1938
Varieties: HN 1510

U.S.: $1,250.00
Can.: $1,250.00
Ster.: £ 600.00

HN 1512
Kathleen
Style One
Designer: L. Harradine
Height: 7 1/2", 19.1 cm
Colour: Lavender and blue
Issued: 1932-1938
Varieties: HN 1252, 1253,
1275, 1279,
1291, 1357

U.S.: $1,750.00
Can.: $1,750.00
Ster.: £ 550.00

117

HN 1513
Biddy
Designer: L. Harradine
Height: 5 1/2", 14.0 cm
Colour: Pink dress with mauve shawl
Issued: 1932-1951
Varieties: HN 1445, 1500

U.S.: $275.00
Can.: $375.00
Ster.: £180.00

HN 1514
Dolly Vardon
Designer: L. Harradine
Height: 8 1/2", 21.6 cm
Colour: Multi-coloured
Issued: 1932-1938
Varieties: HN 1515

U.S.: $1,100.00
Can.: $1,100.00
Ster.: £ 600.00

HN 1515
Dolly Vardon
Designer: L. Harradine
Height: 8 1/2", 21.6 cm
Colour: Red and lavender
Issued: 1932-1949
Varieties: HN 1514

U.S.: $1,250.00
Can.: $1,250.00
Ster.: £ 600.00

HN 1516
Cicely
Designer: L. Harradine
Height: 5 3/4", 14.6 cm
Colour: Purple and red
Issued: 1932-1949

U.S.: $1,400.00
Can.: $1,500.00
Ster.: £ 600.00

HN 1517
Veronica
Style One
Designer: L. Harradine
Height: 8", 20.3 cm
Colour: Red-cream
Issued: 1932-1951
Varieties: HN 1519, 1650, 1943

U.S.: $450.00
Can.: $485.00
Ster.: £250.00

HN 1518
The Potter
Designer: C.J. Noke
Height: 6 3/4", 17.2 cm
Colour: Green
Issued: 1932-1949
Varieties: HN 1493, 1522

U.S.: $1,250.00
Can.: $1,250.00
Ster.: £ 450.00

HN 1519
Veronica
Style One
Designer: L. Harradine
Height: 8", 20.3 cm
Colour: Blue-cream
Issued: 1932-1938
Varieties: HN 1517, 1650, 1943

U.S.: $900.00
Can.: $750.00
Ster.: £350.00

HN 1520
Eugene
Designer: L. Harradine
Height: 5 3/4", 14.6 cm
Colour: Green and pink
Issued: 1932-1938
Varieties: HN 1521

U.S.: $1,450.00
Can.: $1,450.00
Ster.: £ 600.00

HN 1521
Eugene
Designer: L. Harradine
Height: 5", 12.7 cm
Colour: Orange, yellow and white
Issued: 1932-1938
Varieties: HN 1520

U.S.: **$1,450.00**
Can.: **$1,450.00**
Ster.: £ 600.00

HN 1522
The Potter
Designer: L. Harradine
Height: 6 3/4", 17.2 cm
Colour: Green and purple
Issued: 1932-1949
Varieties: HN 1493, 1518

U.S.: **$1,800.00**
Can.: **$1,800.00**
Ster.: £ 575.00

HN 1523
Lisette
Designer: L. Harradine
Height: 5 1/4", 13.3 cm
Colour: Yellow and red
Issued: 1932-1938
Varieties: HN 1524, 1684

U.S.: **$1,600.00**
Can.: **$1,600.00**
Ster.: £ 600.00

HN 1524
Lisette
Designer: L. Harradine
Height: 5 1/4", 13.3 cm
Colour: Blue, pink and yellow
Issued: 1932-1938
Varieties: HN 1523, 1684

U.S.: **$1,900.00**
Can.: **$1,900.00**
Ster.: £ 650.00

HN 1525
Clarissa
Style One
Designer: L. Harradine
Height: 10", 25.4 cm
Colour: Green and red
Issued: 1932-1938
Varieties: HN 1687

U.S.: **$950.00**
Can.: **$950.00**
Ster.: £400.00

Earthenware

HN 1526
Anthea
Designer: L. Harradine
Height: 6 1/2", 16.5 cm
Colour: Green and blue
Issued: 1932-1938
Varieties: HN 1527, 1669

U.S.: **$1,400.00**
Can.: **$1,400.00**
Ster.: £ 600.00

HN 1527
Anthea
Designer: L. Harradine
Height: 6 1/2", 16.5 cm
Colour: Lavender
Issued: 1932-1949
Varieties: HN 1526, 1669

U.S.: **$1,200.00**
Can.: **$1,200.00**
Ster.: £ 600.00

HN 1528
Bluebeard
Style Two
Designer: L. Harradine
Height: 11 1/2", 29.2 cm
Colour: Red and purple
Issued: 1932-1949
Varieties: HN 2105

U.S.: **$1,000.00**
Can.: **$1,150.00**
Ster.: £ 450.00

Earthenware

HN 1529
A Victorian Lady
Designer: L. Harradine
Height: 7 3/4", 19.7 cm
Colour: Green and orange
Issued: 1932-1938
Varieties: HN 726, 727, 728, 736, 739, 740, 742, 745, 1208, 1258, 1276, 1277, 1345, 1452

U.S.: $900.00
Can.: $900.00
Ster.: £300.00

HN 1530
The Little Bridesmaid
Style One
Designer: L. Harradine
Height: 5", 12.7 cm
Colour: Yellow and green
Issued: 1932-1938
Varieties: HN 1433, 1434

U.S.: $750.00
Can.: $750.00
Ster.: £250.00

HN 1531
Marie
Style Two
Designer: L. Harradine
Height: 4 1/2", 11.4 cm
Colour: Yellow-green
Issued: 1932-1938
Varieties: HN 1370, 1388, 1417, 1489, 1635, 1655

U.S.: $600.00
Can.: $600.00
Ster.: £225.00

HN 1532
Fairy
Style Two
Designer: L. Harradine
Height: 4", 10.1 cm
Colour: Multi-coloured
Issued: 1932-1938
Varieties: HN 1374, 1380

U.S.: $1,500.00
Can.: $1,500.00
Ster.: £ 450.00

HN 1533
Fairy
Style Three
Designer: L. Harradine
Height: 3", 7.6 cm
Colour: Multi-coloured
Issued: 1932-1938
Varieties: HN 1375, 1395

U.S.: $1,500.00
Can.: $1,500.00
Ster.: £ 450.00

HN 1534
Fairy
Style Seven
Designer: L. Harradine
Height: 2 1/2", 6.3 cm
Colour: Yellow flowers
Issued: 1932-1938
Varieties: HN 1379, 1394

U.S.: $1,300.00
Can.: $1,300.00
Ster.: £ 450.00

HN 1535
Fairy
Style Six
Designer: L. Harradine
Height: 2 1/2", 6.3 cm
Colour: Yellow and blue flowers
Issued: 1932-1938
Varieties: HN 1378, 1396

U.S.: $1,000.00
Can.: $1,100.00
Ster.: £ 450.00

HN 1536
Fairy
Style Four
Designer: L. Harradine
Height: 2 1/2", 6.3 cm
Colour: Yellow and blue flowers
Issued: 1932-1938
Varieties: HN 1376

U.S.: $1,000.00
Can.: $1,000.00
Ster.: £ 450.00

HN 1537
Janet
Style One
Designer: L. Harradine
Height: 6 1/4", 15.9 cm
Colour: Red
Issued: 1932 to the present
Varieties: HN 1538, 1652, 1737

U.S.: **$225.00**
Can.: **$255.00**
Ster.: £ 75.00

HN 1538
Janet
Style One
Designer: L. Harradine
Height: 6 1/4", 15.9 cm
Colour: Purple
Issued: 1932-1949
Varieties: HN 1537, 1652, 1737

U.S.: **$700.00**
Can.: **$775.00**
Ster.: £300.00

HN 1539
A Saucy Nymph
Designer: Unknown
Height: 4 1/2", 11.4 cm
Colour: Green base
Issued: 1933-1949
Varieties: Also with pearl glaze and unpainted

U.S.: **$750.00**
Can.: **$750.00**
Ster.: £250.00

HN 1540
"Little Child so Rare and Sweet"
Style One
Designer: Unknown
Height: 5", 12.7 cm
Colour: Green base
Issued: 1933-1949

U.S.: **$900.00**
Can.: **$900.00**
Ster.: £300.00

HN 1541
"Happy Joy, Baby Boy"
Designer: Unknown
Height: 6 1/4", 15.9 cm
Colour: Green base
Issued: 1933-1949

U.S.: **$950.00**
Can.: **$950.00**
Ster.: £300.00

HN 1542
"Little Child so Rare and Sweet"
Style Two
Designer: Unknown
Height: 5", 12.7 cm
Colour: Blue base
Issued: 1933-1949

U.S.: **$800.00**
Can.: **$800.00**
Ster.: £300.00

HN 1543
"Dancing Eyes and Sunny Hair"
Designer: Unknown
Height: 5", 12.7 cm
Colour: Blue base
Issued: 1933-1949

U.S.: **$800.00**
Can.: **$800.00**
Ster.: £300.00

HN 1544
"Do You Wonder Where Fairies Are That Folk Declare Have Vanished"
Designer: Unknown
Height: 5", 12.7 cm
Colour: Lavender with yellow base
Issued: 1933-1949

U.S.: **$1,000.00**
Can.: **$1,000.00**
Ster.: £ 350.00

HN 1545
**"Called Love, A Little Boy,
Almost Naked, Wanton,
Blind, Cruel Now, and
Then as Kind"**
Designer: Unknown
Height: 3 1/2", 8.9 cm
Colour: Tan base
Issued: 1933-1949

U.S.: $1,000.00
Can.: $1,000.00
Ster.:   £ 350.00

HN 1546
"Here A Little Child I Stand"
Designer: Unknown
Height: 6 1/4", 15.9 cm
Colour: Lavender with
           green base
Issued: 1933-1949

U.S.: $1,000.00
Can.: $1,000.00
Ster.:   £ 350.00

HN 1547
Pearly Boy
Style One
Designer: L. Harradine
Height: 5 1/2", 14.0 cm
Colour: Green and purple
Issued: 1933-1949
Varieties: HN 1482

U.S.: $675.00
Can.: $725.00
Ster.:   £300.00

HN 1548
Pearly Girl
Style One
Designer: L. Harradine
Height: 5 1/2", 14.0 cm
Colour: Green and
           purple
Issued: 1933-1949
Varieties: HN 1483

U.S.: $675.00
Can.: $725.00
Ster.:   £300.00

HN 1549
Sweet and Twenty
Style One
Designer: L. Harradine
Height: 6", 15.2 cm
Colour: Multi-coloured
Issued: 1933-1949
Varieties: HN 1298, 1360,
           1437, 1438,
           1563, 1649

U.S.: $750.00
Can.: $850.00
Ster.:   £300.00

HN 1550
Annette
Designer: L. Harradine
Height: 6 1/4", 15.9 cm
Colour: Red and green
Issued: 1933-1949
Varieties: HN 1471, 1472

U.S.: $650.00
Can.: $675.00
Ster.:   £250.00

HN 1551
Rosamund
Style Two
Designer: L. Harradine
Height: 8 1/2", 21.6 cm
Colour: Blue
Issued: 1933-1938
Varieties: HN 1497

U.S.: $2,500.00
Can.: $2,500.00
Ster.:   £ 800.00

HN 1552
Pinkie
Designer: L. Harradine
Height: 5", 12.7 cm
Colour: Pink
Issued: 1933-1938
Varieties: HN 1553

U.S.: $ 975.00
Can.: $1,100.00
Ster.:   £ 600.00

HN 1553
Pinkie
Designer: L. Harradine
Height: 5", 12.7 cm
Colour: Yellow and
          blue
Issued: 1933-1938
Varieties: HN 1552

  U.S.: $1,300.00
  Can.: $1,450.00
  Ster.: £ 600.00

HN 1554
Charley's Aunt
Style Two
Designer: H. Fenton
Height: 7 1/2", 19.1 cm
Colour: Purple
Issued: 1933-1938
Varieties: HN 1411

  U.S.: $1,700.00
  Can.: $1,700.00
  Ster.: £ 650.00

HN 1555
Marigold
Designer: L. Harradine
Height: 6", 15.2 cm
Colour: Pink and blue
Issued: 1933-1949
Varieties: HN 1447, 1451

  U.S.: $700.00
  Can.: $750.00
  Ster.: £400.00

HN 1556
Rosina
Designer: L. Harradine
Height: 5 3/4", 14.6 cm
Colour: Lavender
Issued: 1933-1938
Varieties: HN 1358, 1364

  U.S.: $1,250.00
  Can.: $1,250.00
  Ster.: £ 400.00

HN 1557
Lady Fayre
Designer: L. Harradine
Height: 5 3/4", 14.6 cm
Colour: Red and purple
Issued: 1933-1938
Varieties: HN 1265

  U.S.: $975.00
  Can.: $975.00
  Ster.: £400.00

HN 1558
Dorcas
Designer: L. Harradine
Height: 6 3/4", 17.2 cm
Colour: Purple
Issued: 1933-1952
Varieties: HN 1490, 1491

  U.S.: $375.00
  Can.: $495.00
  Ster.: £250.00

HN 1559
Priscilla
Designer: L. Harradine
Height: 8", 20.3 cm
Colour: Purple
Issued: 1933-1949
Varieties: HN 1337, 1340,
           1495, 1501

  U.S.: $ 900.00
  Can.: $1,000.00
  Ster.: £ 300.00

HN 1560
Miss Demure
Designer: L. Harradine
Height: 7", 17.8 cm
Colour: Blue dress with
          red shawl
Issued: 1933-1949
Varieties: HN 1402, 1440,
           1463, 1499

  U.S.: $ 900.00
  Can.: $1,000.00
  Ster.: £ 300.00

HN 1561
Willy-Won't He
Designer: L. Harradine
Height: 6", 15.2 cm
Colour: Blue, pink and white
Issued: 1933-1949
Varieties: HN 1584, 2150

U.S.: $1,250.00
Can.: $1,250.00
Ster.: £ 400.00

HN 1562
Gretchen
Designer: L. Harradine
Height: 7 3/4", 19.7 cm
Colour: Purple and white
Issued: 1933-1938
Varieties: HN 1397

U.S.: $1,250.00
Can.: $1,250.00
Ster.: £ 600.00

HN 1563
Sweet and Twenty
Style One
Designer: L. Harradine
Height: 6", 15.2 cm
Colour: Black and light pink
Issued: 1933-1938
Varieties: HN 1298, 1360, 1437, 1438, 1549, 1649

U.S.: $ 950.00
Can.: $1,150.00
Ster.: £ 350.00

HN 1564
Pamela
Style One
Designer: L. Harradine
Height: 8", 20.3 cm
Colour: Pink
Issued: 1933-1938
Varieties: HN 1468, 1469

U.S.: $1,500.00
Can.: $1,700.00
Ster.: £ 600.00

HN 1565
Lucy Ann
Designer: L. Harradine
Height: 5 1/4", 13.3 cm
Colour: Light green
Issued: 1933-1938
Varieties: HN 1502

U.S.: $650.00
Can.: $750.00
Ster.: £300.00

HN 1566
Estelle
Designer: L. Harradine
Height: 8", 20.3 cm
Colour: Lavender
Issued: 1933-1938
Varieties: HN 1802

U.S.: $1,400.00
Can.: $1,500.00
Ster.: £ 600.00

HN 1567
Patricia
Style One
Designer: L. Harradine
Height: 8 1/2", 21.6 cm
Colour: Red
Issued: 1933-1949
Varieties: HN 1414, 1431, 1462

U.S.: $1,500.00
Can.: $1,500.00
Ster.: £ 350.00

HN 1568
Charmian
Designer: L. Harradine
Height: 6 1/2", 16.5 cm
Colour: Red and cream
Issued: 1933-1938
Varieties: HN 1569, 1651

U.S.: $ 950.00
Can.: $1,000.00
Ster.: £ 400.00

HN 1569
Charmian
Designer: L. Harradine
Height: 6 1/2", 16.5 cm
Colour: Cream and
lavender
Issued: 1933-1938
Varieties: HN 1568, 1651

U.S.: $ 950.00
Can.: $1,000.00
Ster.: £ 400.00

HN 1570
Gwendolen
Designer: L. Harradine
Height: 6", 15.2 cm
Colour: Pink
Issued: 1933-1949
Varieties: HN 1494, 1503

U.S.: $1,300.00
Can.: $1,300.00
Ster.: £ 600.00

HN 1571
Old Lavender Seller
Designer: L. Harradine
Height: 6 1/2", 16.5 cm
Colour: Orange and
black
Issued: 1933-1949
Varieties: HN 1492

U.S.: $ 950.00
Can.: $1,000.00
Ster.: £ 400.00

HN 1572
Helen
Style One
Designer: L. Harradine
Height: 8", 20.3 cm
Colour: Red
Issued: 1933-1938
Varieties: HN 1508, 1509

U.S.: $1,250.00
Can.: $1,250.00
Ster.: £ 600.00

HN 1573
Rhoda
Designer: L. Harradine
Height: 10 1/4", 26.7 cm
Colour: Green and orange
Issued: 1933-1949
Varieties: HN 1574, 1688

U.S.: $850.00
Can.: $850.00
Ster.: £350.00

Earthenware

HN 1574
Rhoda
Designer: L. Harradine
Height: 10 1/4", 26.7 cm
Colour: Burgundy and
orange
Issued: 1933-1938
Varieties: HN 1573, 1688

U.S.: $900.00
Can.: $900.00
Ster.: £350.00

HN 1575
Daisy
Designer: L. Harradine
Height: 3 3/4", 9.5 cm
Colour: Blue dress
with flowers
Issued: 1933-1949
Varieties: HN 1961

U.S.: $375.00
Can.: $475.00
Ster.: £300.00

HN 1576
Tildy
Designer: L. Harradine
Height: 5", 12.7 cm
Colour: Red and
pink-cream
Issued: 1933-1938
Varieties: HN 1859

U.S.: $1,100.00
Can.: $1,100.00
Ster.: £ 600.00

HN 1577
Suzette
Designer: L. Harradine
Height: 7 1/2", 19.1 cm
Colour: Flowered
lavender dress
Issued: 1933-1949
Varieties: HN 1487, 1585,
1696, 2026

U.S.: $650.00
Can.: $725.00
Ster.: £300.00

HN 1578
The Hinged Parasol
Designer: L. Harradine
Height: 6 1/2", 16.5 cm
Colour: Red and yellow
dress with spots
Issued: 1933-1949
Varieties: HN 1579

U.S.: $1,100.00
Can.: $1,100.00
Ster.: £ 400.00

HN 1579
The Hinged Parasol
Designer: L. Harradine
Height: 6 1/2", 16.5 cm
Colour: Red and purple
Issued: 1933-1949
Varieties: HN 1578

U.S.: $1,100.00
Can.: $1,000.00
Ster.: £ 400.00

HN 1580
Rosebud
Style One
Designer: L. Harradine
Height: 3", 7.6 cm
Colour: Pink
Issued: 1933-1938
Varieties: HN 1581

U.S.: $ 950.00
Can.: $1,150.00
Ster.: £ 400.00

HN 1581
Rosebud
Style One
Designer: L. Harradine
Height: 3", 7.6 cm
Colour: Blue dress
with flowers
Issued: 1933-1938
Varieties: HN 1580

U.S.: $ 750.00
Can.: $1,000.00
Ster.: £ 400.00

HN 1582
Marion
Designer: L. Harradine
Height: 6 1/2", 16.5 cm
Colour: Purple
Issued: 1933-1938
Varieties: HN 1583

U.S.: $1,750.00
Can.: $1,750.00
Ster.: £ 600.00

HN 1583
Marion
Designer: L. Harradine
Height: 6 1/2", 16.5 cm
Colour: Blue dress,
patterned shawl
Issued: 1933-1938
Varieties: HN 1582

U.S.: $1,750.00
Can.: $1,750.00
Ster.: £ 600.00

HN 1584
Willy-Won't He
Designer: L. Harradine
Height: 6", 15.2 cm
Colour: Red, green,
blue and white
Issued: 1933-1949
Varieties: HN 1561, 2150
(minor glaze
difference)

U.S.: $450.00
Can.: $600.00
Ster.: £250.00

HN 1585
Suzette
Designer: L. Harradine
Height: 7 1/2", 19.1 cm
Colour: Green and yellow
Issued: 1933-1938
Varieties: HN 1487, 1577,
           1696, 2026

U.S.: $750.00
Can.: $850.00
Ster.:   £300.00

HN 1586
Camille
Designer: L. Harradine
Height: 6 1/2", 16.5 cm
Colour: Red and pink
Issued: 1933-1949
Varieties: HN 1648, 1736

U.S.: $1,250.00
Can.: $1,250.00
Ster.:   £ 450.00

HN 1587
Fleurette
Designr: L. Harradine
Height: 6 1/2", 16.5 cm
Colour: Red and pink
Issued: 1933-1949

U.S.: $850.00
Can.: $850.00
Ster.:   £400.00

HN 1588
The Bride
Style One
Designer: L. Harradine
Height: 8 3/4", 22.2 cm
Colour: Cream
Issued: 1933-1938
Varieties: HN 1600, 1762,
           1841

U.S.: $1,100.00
Can.: $1,100.00
Ster.:   £ 400.00

HN 1589
Sweet and Twenty
Style Two
Designer: L. Harradine
Height: 3 1/2", 8.9 cm
Colour: Red dress,
           green sofa
Issued: 1933-1949
Varieties: HN 1610

U.S.: $375.00
Can.: $475.00
Ster.:   £225.00

*

HN 1598
Clothilde
Designer: L. Harradine
Height: 7 1/4", 18.4 cm
Colour: Yellow and red
Issued: 1933-1949
Varieties: HN 1599

U.S.: $900.00
Can.: $950.00
Ster.:   £450.00

HN 1599
Clothilde
Designer: L. Harradine
Height: 7 1/4", 18.4 cm
Colour: Purple and red
Issued: 1933-1949
Varieties: HN 1598

U.S.: $900.00
Can.: $950.00
Ster.:   £450.00

HN 1600
The Bride
Style One
Designer: L. Harradine
Height: 8 3/4", 22.2 cm
Colour: Pale pink
Issued: 1933-1949
Varieties: HN 1588, 1762,
           1841

U.S.: $1,200.00
Can.: $1,200.00
Ster.:   £ 600.00

*

HN 1604
The Emir
Designer: C.J. Noke
Height: 7 1/2", 19.1 cm
Colour: Yellow and red
Issued: 1933-1949
Varieties: HN 1605; also
called "Ibrahim"
HN 2095

U.S.: $1,100.00
Can.: $ 950.00
Ster.: £ 600.00

HN 1605
The Emir
Designer: C.J. Noke
Height: 7 1/4", 18.4 cm
Colour: Yellow and purple
Issued: 1933-1949
Varieties: HN 1604; also
called "Ibrahim"
HN 2095

U.S.: $1,100.00
Can.: $ 950.00
Ster.: £ 600.00

HN 1606
Falstaff
Style One
Designer: C.J. Noke
Height: 7", 17.8 cm
Colour: Red and brown
Issued: 1933-1949
Varieties: HN 571, 575,
608, 609, 619,
638, 1216

U.S.: $2,000.00
Can.: $2,000.00
Ster.: £ 700.00

HN 1607
Cerise
Designer: L. Harradine
Height: 5 1/4", 13.3 cm
Colour: Lavender dress
with flowers
Issued: 1933-1949

U.S.: $450.00
Can.: $475.00
Ster.: £250.00

*

HN 1610
Sweet and Twenty
Style Two
Designer: L. Harradine
Height: 3 1/2", 8.9 cm
Colour: Red dress,
green sofa
Issued: 1933-1938
Varieties: HN 1589

U.S.: $400.00
Can.: $425.00
Ster.: £250.00
*

HN 1617
Primroses
Designer: L. Harradine
Height: 6 1/2", 16.5 cm
Colour: Purple, red, white
and yellow
Issued: 1934-1949

U.S.: $900.00
Can.: $950.00
Ster.: £450.00

Earthenware

HN 1618
Maisie
Designer: L. Harradine
Height: 6 1/4", 15.9 cm
Colour: Yellow and blue
Issued: 1934-1949
Varieties: HN 1619

U.S.: $800.00
Can.: $900.00
Ster.: £400.00

HN 1619
Maisie
Designer: L. Harradine
Height: 6 1/4", 15.9 cm
Colour: Red and pink
Issued: 1934-1949
Varieties: HN 1618

U.S.: $400.00
Can.: $500.00
Ster.: £250.00

HN 1620
Rosabell
Designer: L. Harradine
Height: 6 3/4", 17.1 cm
Colour: Red and green
Issued: 1934-1938

U.S.: $1,500.00
Can.: $1,500.00
Ster.:   £ 600.00

HN 1621
Irene
Designer: L. Harradine
Height: 6 1/2", 16.5 cm
Colour: Yellow
Issued: 1934-1951
Varieties: HN 1697, 1952

U.S.: $500.00
Can.: $650.00
Ster.:   £250.00

HN 1622
Evelyn
Designer: L. Harradine
Height: 6 1/4", 15.9 cm
Colour: Red and cream
Issued: 1934-1949
Varieties: HN 1637

U.S.: $1,600.00
Can.: $1,600.00
Ster.:   £ 600.00

*

HN 1626
Bonnie Lassie
Designer: L. Harradine
Height: 5 1/4", 13.3 cm
Colour: Red
Issued: 1934-1953
Varieties: HN 1626A

U.S.: $500.00
Can.: $650.00
Ster.:   £250.00

HN 1627
Curly Knob
Designer: L. Harradine
Height: 6", 15.2 cm
Colour: Blue and red
Issued: 1934-1949

U.S.: $ 950.00
Can.: $1,000.00
Ster.:   £ 400.00

HN 1628
Margot
Designer: L. Harradine
Height: 5 1/2", 14.0 cm
Colour: Blue and yellow
Issued: 1934-1938
Varieties: HN 1636, 1653

U.S.: $1,200.00
Can.: $1,350.00
Ster.:   £ 600.00

HN 1629
Grizel
Designer: L. Harradine
Height: 6 3/4", 17.2 cm
Colour: Red and cream
Issued: 1934-1938

U.S.: $1,650.00
Can.: $1,650.00
Ster.:   £ 600.00

*

HN 1631
Sweet Anne
Designer: L. Harradine
Height: 7", 17.8 cm
Colour: Green, red, pink
           and yellow
Issued: 1934-1938
Varieties: HN 1318, 1330,
           1331, 1453,
           1496, 1701

U.S.: $1,300.00
Can.: $1,250.00
Ster.:   £ 400.00

HN 1632
A Gentlewoman
Designer: L. Harradine
Height: 7 1/2", 19.1 cm
Colour: Lavender dress, green hat
Issued: 1934-1949

U.S.: $950.00
Can.: $950.00
Ster.: £450.00

HN 1633
Clemency
Designer: L. Harradine
Height: 7", 17.8 cm
Colour: Lavender jacket, cream flowered dress
Issued: 1934-1938
Varieties: HN 1634, 1643

U.S.: $1,300.00
Can.: $1,300.00
Ster.: £ 600.00

HN 1634
Clemency
Designer: L. Harradine
Height: 7", 17.8 cm
Colour: Green and orange patterned jacket, green dress
Issued: 1934-1949
Varieties: HN 1633, 1643

U.S.: $1,500.00
Can.: $1,500.00
Ster.: £ 600.00

HN 1635
Marie
Style Two
Designer: L. Harradine
Height: 4 3/4", 12.0 cm
Colour: Blue, pink and white, pink flowers
Issued: 1934-1949
Varieties: HN 1370, 1388, 1417, 1489, 1531, 1655

U.S.: $600.00
Can.: $600.00
Ster.: £250.00

HN 1636
Margot
Designer: L. Harradine
Height: 5 3/4", 14.6 cm
Colour: Red, pink and yellow
Issued: 1934-1938
Varieties: HN 1628, 1653

U.S.: $1,200.00
Can.: $1,200.00
Ster.: £ 600.00

HN 1637
Evelyn
Designer: L. Harradine
Height: 6", 15.2 cm
Colour: White and blue
Issued: 1934-1938
Varieties: HN 1622

U.S.: $1,600.00
Can.: $1,600.00
Ster.: £ 600.00

HN 1638
Ladybird
Designer: L. Harradine
Height: 7 3/4", 19.7 cm
Colour: Pink
Issued: 1934-1949
Varieties: HN 1640

U.S.: $2,000.00
Can.: $2,250.00
Ster.: £ 800.00

HN 1639
Dainty May
Designer: L. Harradine
Height: 6", 15.2 cm
Colour: Red and green
Issued: 1934-1949
Varieties: HN 1656

U.S.: $475.00
Can.: $525.00
Ster.: £350.00

HN 1640
Ladybird
Designer:	L. Harradine
Height:	7 3/4", 19.7 cm
Colour:	Blue
Issued:	1934-1938
Varieties:	HN 1638
U.S.:	**$2,500.00**
Can.:	**$2,500.00**
Ster.:	**£ 850.00**

HN 1641
The Little Mother
Style Two
Designer:	L. Harradine
Height:	8", 20.3 cm
Colour:	Green
Issued:	1934-1949
Varieties:	HN 1418; also called "Young Widow" HN 1399
U.S.:	**$3,800.00**
Can.:	**$3,800.00**
Ster.:	**£1,300.00**

HN 1642
Granny's Shawl
Designer:	L. Harradine
Height:	5 3/4", 14.6 cm
Colour:	Cream dress, red shawl
Issued:	1934-1949
Varieties:	HN 1647
U.S.:	**$600.00**
Can.:	**$675.00**
Ster.:	**£300.00**

HN 1643
Clemency
Designer:	L. Harradine
Height:	7", 17.8 cm
Colour:	Red jacket, white and green dress
Issued:	1934-1938
Varieties:	HN 1633, 1634
U.S.:	**$1,300.00**
Can.:	**$1,300.00**
Ster.:	**£ 600.00**

HN 1644
Herminia
Designer:	L. Harradine
Height:	6 1/2", 16.5 cm
Colour:	Flowered cream dress
Issued:	1934-1938
Varieties:	HN 1646, 1704
U.S.:	**$1,600.00**
Can.:	**$1,600.00**
Ster.:	**£ 600.00**

HN 1645
Aileen
Designer:	L. Harradine
Height:	6", 15.2 cm
Colour:	Green dress, flowered shawl
Issued:	1934-1938
Varieties:	HN 1664, 1803
U.S.:	**$1,500.00**
Can.:	**$1,500.00**
Ster.:	**£ 600.00**

HN 1646
Herminia
Designer:	L. Harradine
Height:	6 1/2", 16.5 cm
Colour:	Red dress with cream stripe
Issued:	1934-1938
Varieties:	HN 1644, 1704
U.S.:	**$1,500.00**
Can.:	**$1,500.00**
Ster.:	**£ 600.00**

HN 1647
Granny's Shawl
Designer:	L. Harradine
Height:	5 3/4", 14.6 cm
Colour:	Cream dress with blue shawl
Issued:	1934-1949
Varieties:	HN 1642
U.S.:	**$475.00**
Can.:	**$525.00**
Ster.:	**£250.00**

HN 1648
Camille
Designer: L. Harradine
Height: 6 1/2", 16.5 cm
Colour: Pale green
flowered dress
Issued: 1934-1949
Varieties: HN 1586, 1736

U.S.: $1,750.00
Can.: $1,750.00
Ster.: £ 575.00

HN 1649
Sweet and Twenty
Style One
Designer: L. Harradine
Height: 6", 15.2 cm
Colour: Green and cream
dress, brown sofa
Issued: 1934-1949
Varieties: HN 1298, 1360,
1437, 1438,
1549, 1563

U.S.: $ 950.00
Can.: $1,000.00
Ster.: £ 400.00

HN 1650
Veronica
Style One
Designer: L. Harradine
Height: 8", 20.3 cm
Colour: Green
Issued: 1934-1949
Varieties: HN 1517, 1519,
1943

U.S.: $1,250.00
Can.: $1,350.00
Ster.: £ 400.00

HN 1651
Charmian
Designer: L. Harradine
Height: 6 1/2", 16.5 cm
Colour: Red and green
Issued: 1934-1938
Varieties: HN 1568, 1569

U.S.: $1,600.00
Can.: $1,600.00
Ster.: £ 500.00

HN 1652
Janet
Style One
Designer: L. Harradine
Height: 6 1/2", 16.5 cm
Colour: Red with pink
flowered skirt
Issued: 1934-1949
Varieties: HN 1537, 1538,
1737

U.S.: $ 900.00
Can.: $1,000.00
Ster.: £ 400.00

HN 1653
Margot
Designer: L. Harradine
Height: 5 3/4", 14.6 cm
Colour: White and red
Issued: 1934-1938
Varieties: HN 1628, 1636

U.S.: $1,400.00
Can.: $1,600.00
Ster.: £ 600.00

HN 1654
Rose
Designer: L. Harradine
Height: 4 1/2", 11.4 cm
Colour: Green
Issued: 1934-1938
Varieties: HN 1368, 1387,
1416, 1506,
2123

U.S.: $500.00
Can.: $575.00
Ster.: £250.00

HN 1655
Marie
Style Two
Designer: L. Harradine
Height: 4 1/2", 11.4 cm
Colour: Pink and white
Issued: 1934-1938
Varieties: HN 1370, 1388,
1417, 1489,
1531, 1635

U.S.: $600.00
Can.: $650.00
Ster.: £250.00

HN 1656
Dainty May
Designer: L. Harradine
Height: 6", 15.2 cm
Colour: Lavender
Issued: 1934-1949
Varieties: HN 1639

U.S.: $650.00
Can.: $725.00
Ster.: £300.00

HN 1657
The Moor
Designer: C.J. Noke
Height: 16 1/2", 41.9 cm
Colour: Red and black
Issued: 1934-1949
Varieties: HN 1308, 1366,
1425, 2082; "An
Arab" HN 33, 343, 378

U.S.: $2,750.00
Can.: $2,200.00
Ster.: £ 800.00

*

HN 1662
Delicia
Designer: L. Harradine
Height: 5 3/4", 14.6 cm
Colour: Pink and lavender
Issued: 1934-1938
Varieties: HN 1663, 1681

U.S.: $1,300.00
Can.: $1,300.00
Ster.: £ 500.00

HN 1663
Delicia
Designer: L. Harradine
Height: 5 3/4", 14.6 cm
Colour: Pink
Issued: 1934-1938
Varieties: HN 1662, 1681

U.S.: $1,300.00
Can.: $1,300.00
Ster.: £ 500.00

HN 1664
Aileen
Designer: L. Harradine
Height: 6", 15.2 cm
Colour: Pink dress,
patterned shawl
Issued: 1934-1938
Varieties: HN 1645, 1803

U.S.: $1,500.00
Can.: $1,500.00
Ster.: £ 600.00

HN 1665
Miss Winsome
Designer: L. Harradine
Height: 6 3/4", 17.2 cm
Colour: Lavender
Issued: 1934-1949
Varieties: HN 1666

U.S.: $1,000.00
Can.: $1,150.00
Ster.: £ 400.00

HN 1666
Miss Winsome
Designer: L. Harradine
Height: 6 3/4", 17.2 cm
Colour: Green dress,
patterned shawl
Issued: 1934-1938
Varieties: HN 1665

U.S.: $1,200.00
Can.: $1,275.00
Ster.: £ 400.00

NOTE ON PRICING

Prices are given for three separate and distinct market areas:

Prices are given in the currency of each of these different trading areas.

Prices are not exchange rate calculations but are based on supply and demand in that market.

Prices listed are guidelines to the most current retail values but actual selling prices may vary slightly.

Prices for current figurines are those suggested by Royal Doulton.

Extremely rare or unique figurines have inconsistent retail values and their prices must therefore be determined between buyer and seller.

HN 1667
Blossom
Designer: L. Harradine
Height: 6 3/4", 17.2 cm
Colour: Orange and blue
Issued: 1934-1949

U.S.: $2,000.00
Can.: $2,000.00
Ster.: £ 650.00

HN 1668
Sibell
Designer: L. Harradine
Height: 6 1/2", 16.5 cm
Colour: Red and green
Issued: 1934-1949
Varieties: HN 1695, 1735

U.S.: $1,000.00
Can.: $1,150.00
Ster.: £ 400.00

HN 1669
Anthea
Designer: L. Harradine
Height: 6 1/2", 16.5 cm
Colour: Pink dress,
green shawl
Issued: 1934-1938
Varieties: HN 1526, 1527

U.S.: $1,700.00
Can.: $1,700.00
Ster.: £ 600.00

HN 1670
Gillian
Style One
Designer: L. Harradine
Height: 7 3/4", 19.7 cm
Colour: Pink
Issued: 1934-1949
Varieties: HN 1670A

U.S.: $1,300.00
Can.: $1,300.00
Ster.: £ 600.00

HN 1670A
Gillian
Style One
Designer: L. Harradine
Height: 7 3/4", 19.7 cm
Colour: Green jacket, white
flowered shirt
Issued: Unknown
Varieties: HN 1670

U.S.: $1,400.00
Can.: $1,400.00
Ster.: £ 600.00

*

HN 1677
Tinkle Bell
Designer: L. Harradine
Height: 4 3/4", 12.0 cm
Colour: Pink
Issued: 1935-1988

U.S.: $125.00
Can.: $150.00
Ster: £ 60.00

HN 1678
Dinky Doo
Designer: L. Harradine
Height: 4 3/4", 12.0 cm
Colour: Lavender
Issued: 1934 to the
present
Varieties: HN 2120

U.S.: $110.00
Can.: $150.00
Ster.: £ 39.95

HN 1679
Babie
Designer: L. Harradine
Height: 4 3/4", 12.0 cm
Colour: Green
Issued: 1935-1992
Varieties: HN 1842, 2121

U.S.: $150.00
Can.: $150.00
Ster.: £ 49.95

HN 1680
Tootles
Designer: L. Harradine
Height: 4 3/4", 12.0 cm
Colour: Pink
Issued: 1935-1975

U.S.: $135.00
Can.: $150.00
Ster.: £ 80.00

HN 1681
Delicia
Designer: L. Harradine
Height: 5 3/4", 14.6 cm
Colour: Green and purple
Issued: 1935-1938
Varieties: HN 1662, 1663

U.S.: $1,500.00
Can.: $1,500.00
Ster.: £ 500.00

HN 1682
Teresa
Style One
Designer: L. Harradine
Height: 5 3/4", 14.6 cm
Colour: Red and brown
Issued: 1935-1949
Varieties: HN 1683

U.S.: $2,000.00
Can.: $2,000.00
Ster.: £ 700.00

HN 1683
Teresa
Style One
Designer: L. Harradine
Height: 5 3/4", 14.6 cm
Colour: Light blue
Issued: 1935-1938
Varieties: HN 1682

U.S.: $2,500.00
Can.: $2,500.00
Ster.: £ 800.00

HN 1684
Lisette
Designer: L. Harradine
Height: 5 1/4", 13.3 cm
Colour: Pink and green
Issued: 1935-1938
Varieties: HN 1523, 1524

U.S.: $1,800.00
Can.: $1,800.00
Ster.: £ 600.00

HN 1685
Cynthia
Style One
Designer: L. Harradine
Height: 5 3/4", 14.6 cm
Colour: Pink and
turquoise
Issued: 1935-1949
Varieties: HN 1686, 1686A

U.S.: $1,300.00
Can.: $1,100.00
Ster.: £ 600.00

HN 1686
Cynthia
Style One
Designer: L. Harradine
Height: 5 3/4", 14.6 cm
Colour: Blue and red
Issued: 1935-1949
Varieties: HN 1685, 1686A

U.S.: $1,300.00
Can.: $1,100.00
Ster.: £ 600.00

HN 1686A
Cynthia
Style One
Designer: L. Harradine
Height: 5 3/4", 14.6 cm
Colour: Red and purple
Issued: 1935-1949
Varieties: HN 1685, 1686

U.S.: $1,300.00
Can.: $1,100.00
Ster.: £ 600.00

HN 1687
Clarissa
Style One
Designer: L. Harradine
Height: 9 3/4", 24.8 cm
Colour: Blue, green
         and orange
Issued: 1935-1949
Varieties: HN 1525

U.S.:	**$1,000.00**
Can.:	**$1,000.00**
Ster.:	**£ 350.00**

Earthenware

HN 1688
Rhoda
Designer: L. Harradine
Height: 10 1/4", 26.7 cm
Colour: Orange and red
Issued: 1935-1949
Varieties: HN 1573, 1574

U.S.:	**$950.00**
Can.:	**$950.00**
Ster.:	**£350.00**

Earthenware

HN 1689
Calumet
Designer: C.J. Noke
Height: 6 1/2", 16.5 cm
Colour: Green and brown
Issued: 1935-1949
Varieties: HN 1428, 2068

U.S.:	**$950.00**
Can.:	**$800.00**
Ster.:	**£450.00**

Earthenware

HN 1690
June
Style One
Designer: L. Harradine
Height: 7 1/4", 18.4 cm
Colour: Pale green
         and pink
Issued: 1935-1949
Varieties: HN 1691, 1947,
            2027

U.S.:	**$1,000.00**
Can.:	**$1,000.00**
Ster.:	**£ 450.00**

HN 1691
June
Style One
Designer: L. Harradine
Height: 7 1/4", 18.4 cm
Colour: Yellow and pink
Issued: 1935-1949
Varieties: HN 1690, 1947,
            2027

U.S.:	**$900.00**
Can.:	**$750.00**
Ster.:	**£450.00**

HN 1692
Sonia
Designer: L. Harradine
Height: 6 1/4", 15.9 cm
Colour: Pink, white
         and green
Issued: 1935-1949
Varieties: HN 1738

U.S.:	**$1,300.00**
Can.:	**$1,300.00**
Ster.:	**£ 600.00**

HN 1693
Virginia
Designer: L. Harradine
Height: 7 1/2", 19.1 cm
Colour: Yellow and red
Issued: 1935-1949
Varieties: HN 1694

U.S.:	**$1,350.00**
Can.:	**$1,350.00**
Ster.:	**£ 600.00**

HN 1694
Virginia
Designer: L. Harradine
Height: 7 1/2", 19.1 cm
Colour: Green
Issued: 1935-1949
Varieties: HN 1693

U.S.:	**$1,500.00**
Can.:	**$1,500.00**
Ster.:	**£ 600.00**

HN 1695
Sibell
Designer: L. Harradine
Height: 6 1/2", 16.5 cm
Colour: Green and orange
Issued: 1935-1949
Varieties: HN 1668, 1735

U.S.: $ 900.00
Can.: $1,150.00
Ster.: £ 450.00

HN 1696
Suzette
Designer: L. Harradine
Height: 7 1/2", 19.1 cm
Colour: Flowered green dress
Issued: 1935-1949
Varieties: HN 1487, 1577, 1585, 2026

U.S.: $750.00
Can.: $850.00
Ster.: £300.00

HN 1697
Irene
Designer: L. Harradine
Height: 7", 17.8 cm
Colour: Pink
Issued: 1935-1949
Varieties: HN 1621, 1952

U.S.: $1,000.00
Can.: $1,100.00
Ster.: £ 350.00

HN 1698
Phyllis
Style One
Designer: L. Harradine
Height: 9", 22.9 cm
Colour: Green
Issued: 1935-1949
Varieties: HN 1420, 1430, 1486

U.S.: $1,300.00
Can.: $1,500.00
Ster.: £ 450.00

HN 1699
Marietta
Designer: L. Harradine
Height: 8", 20.3 cm
Colour: Green and red
Issued: 1935-1949
Varieties: HN 1341, 1446

U.S.: $1,850.00
Can.: $2,000.00
Ster.: £ 700.00

HN 1700
Gloria
Style One
Designer: L. Harradine
Height: 7", 17.8 cm
Colour: Green and black
Issued: 1935-1938
Varieties: HN 1488

U.S.: $2,750.00
Can.: $2,750.00
Ster.: £ 800.00

HN 1701
Sweet Anne
Designer: L. Harradine
Height: 7", 17.8 cm
Colour: Pink and blue
Issued: 1935-1938
Varieties: HN 1318, 1330, 1331, 1453, 1496, 1631

U.S.: $1,000.00
Can.: $1,150.00
Ster.: £ 300.00

HN 1702
A Jester
Style One
Designer: C.J. Noke
Height: 10", 25.4 cm
Colour: Brown and mauve
Issued: 1935-1949
Varieties: HN 45, 71, 71A, 320, 367, 412, 426, 446, 552, 616, 627, 1295, 2016

U.S.: $1,000.00
Can.: $ 750.00
Ster.: £ 400.00

Photograph
Not
Available

HN 1703
Charley's Aunt
Style Three
Designer: A. Toft
Height: 6", 15.2 cm
Colour: Lilac and white,
            no base
Issued: 1935-1938

U.S.:   **$1,800.00**
Can.:   **$2,000.00**
Ster.:   £ 600.00

HN 1704
Herminia
Designer: L. Harradine
Height: 6 3/4", 17.2 cm
Colour: Red
Issued: 1935-1938
Varieties: HN 1644, 1646

U.S.:   **$1,500.00**
Can.:   **$1,500.00**
Ster.:   £ 600.00

HN 1705
The Cobbler
Style Three
Designer: C.J. Noke
Height: 8". 20.3 cm
Colour: Purple and blue
Issued: 1935-1949
Varieties: HN 1706

U.S.:   **$1,000.00**
Can.:   **$1,150.00**
Ster.:   £ 350.00

Earthenware

HN 1706
The Cobbler
Style Three
Designer: C.J. Noke
Height: 8 1/4", 21.0 cm
Colour: Green and brown
Issued: 1935-1969
Varieties: HN 1705

U.S.:   **$350.00**
Can.:   **$450.00**
Ster.:   £200.00

Earthenware

HN 1707
Paisley Shawl
Style One
Designer: L. Harradine
Height: 8 1/4", 21.0 cm
Colour: Purple
Issued: 1935-1949
Varieties: HN 1392, 1460,
            1739, 1987

U.S.:   **$1,200.00**
Can.:   **$1,200.00**
Ster.:   £ 400.00

HN 1708
The Bather
Style One
Designer: L. Harradine
Height: 7 3/4", 19.7 cm
Colour: Black, red and
            turquoise
Issued: 1935-1938
Varieties: HN 597, 687,
            781, 782, 1238

U.S.:   **$2,200.00**
Can.:   **$2,500.00**
Ster.:   £ 800.00

HN 1709
Pantalettes
Designer: L. Harradine
Height: 8", 20.3 cm
Colour: Red
Issued: 1935-1938
Varieties: HN 1362, 1412,
            1507

U.S.:   **$1,200.00**
Can.:   **$1,100.00**
Ster.:   £ 350.00

HN 1710
Camilla
Designer: L. Harradine
Height: 7", 17.8 cm
Colour: Red and yellow
Issued: 1935-1949
Varieties: HN 1711

U.S.:   **$1,500.00**
Can.:   **$1,600.00**
Ster.:   £ 600.00

HN 1711
Camilla
Designer: L. Harradine
Height: 7", 17.8 cm
Colour: Green and yellow
Issued: 1935-1949
Varieties: HN 1710

U.S.: $1,500.00
Can.: $1,600.00
Ster.: £ 600.00

HN 1712
Daffy Down Dilly
Designer: L. Harradine
Height: 7 3/4", 19.7 cm
Colour: Green
Issued: 1935-1975
Varieties: HN 1713

U.S.: $450.00
Can.: $525.00
Ster.: £350.00

HN 1713
Daffy Down Dilly
Designer: L. Harradine
Height: 8 1/4", 21.0 cm
Colour: Turquoise
Issued: 1935-1949
Varieties: HN 1712

U.S.: $1,000.00
Can.: $1,000.00
Ster.: £ 400.00

HN 1714
Millicent
Designer: L. Harradine
Height: 8", 20.3 cm
Colour: Red
Issued: 1935-1949
Varieties: HN 1715, 1860

U.S.: $2,000.00
Can.: $2,200.00
Ster.: £ 700.00

HN 1715
Millicent
Designer: L. Harradine
Height: 8", 20.3 cm
Colour: Lavender
Issued: 1935-1949
Varieties: HN 1714, 1860

U.S.: $2,300.00
Can.: $2,500.00
Ster.: £ 750.00

HN 1716
Diana
Style One
Designer: L. Harradine
Height: 5 3/4", 14.6 cm
Colour: Pink and blue
Issued: 1935-1949
Varieties: HN 1717, 1986

U.S.: $500.00
Can.: $575.00
Ster.: £225.00

HN 1717
Diana
Style One
Designer: L. Harradine
Height: 5 3/4", 14.6 cm
Colour: Turquoise
Issued: 1935-1949
Varieties: HN 1716, 1986

U.S.: $650.00
Can.: $750.00
Ster.: £250.00

HN 1718
Kate Hardcastle
Designer: L. Harradine
Height: 8", 20.3 cm
Colour: Pink and green
Issued: 1935-1949
Varieties: HN 1719, 1734, 1861, 1919, 2028

U.S.: $1,350.00
Can.: $1,000.00
Ster.: £ 400.00

HN 1719
Kate Hardcastle
Designer: L. Harradine
Height: 8", 20.3 cm
Colour: Red and green
Issued: 1935-1949
Varieties: HN 1718, 1734,
1861, 1919, 2028

U.S.: $ 800.00
Can.: $1,000.00
Ster.: £ 400.00

HN 1720
Frangçon
Designer: L. Harradine
Height: 7 1/2", 19.1 cm
Colour: Lavender dress
with orange and
red flowers
Issued: 1935-1949
Varieties: HN 1721

U.S.: $1,500.00
Can.: $1,500.00
Ster.: £ 600.00

HN 1721
Frangçon
Designer: L. Harradine
Height: 7 1/4", 18.4 cm
Colour: Green
Issued: 1935-1949
Varieties: HN 1720

U.S.: $1,200.00
Can.: $1,200.00
Ster.: £ 600.00

HN 1722
The Coming of Spring
Designer: L. Harradine
Height: 12 1/2", 31.7 cm
Colour: Yellow-pink
Issued: 1935-1949
Varieties: HN 1723

U.S.: $2,500.00
Can.: $2,750.00
Ster.: £1,200.00

HN 1723
The Coming of Spring
Designer: L. Harradine
Height: 12 1/2", 31.7 cm
Colour: Pale green
Issued: 1935-1949
Varieties: HN 1722

U.S.: $2,500.00
Can.: $2,750.00
Ster.: £1,200.00

HN 1724
Ruby
Designer: L. Harradine
Height: 5 1/4", 13.3 cm
Colour: Red
Issued: 1935-1949
Varieties: HN 1725

U.S.: $500.00
Can.: $650.00
Ster.: £300.00

HN 1725
Ruby
Designer: L. Harradine
Height: 5 1/4", 13.3 cm
Colour: Blue
Issued: 1935-1949
Varieties: HN 1724

U.S.: $650.00
Can.: $775.00
Ster.: £300.00

HN 1726
Celia
Designer: L. Harradine
Height: 11 1/2", 29.2 cm
Colour: Pale lavender
Issued: 1935-1949
Varieties: HN 1727

U.S.: $2,000.00
Can.: $2,250.00
Ster.: £ 800.00

HN 1727
Celia
Designer: L. Harradine
Height: 11 1/2", 29.2 cm
Colour: Pale green
Issued: 1935-1949
Varieties: HN 1726

U.S.:	$1,400.00
Can.:	$1,600.00
Ster.:	£ 800.00

HN 1728
The New Bonnet
Designer: L. Harradine
Height: 7", 17.8 cm
Colour: Pink
Issued: 1935-1949
Varieties: HN 1957

U.S.:	$1,000.00
Can.:	$1,150.00
Ster.:	£ 500.00

HN 1729
Vera
Designer: L. Harradine
Height: 4 1/4", 10.8 cm
Colour: Pink
Issued: 1935-1938
Varieties: HN 1730

U.S.:	$1,000.00
Can.:	$1,000.00
Ster.:	£ 500.00

HN 1730
Vera
Designer: L. Harradine
Height: 4 1/4", 10.8 cm
Colour: Green
Issued: 1935-1938
Varieties: HN 1729

U.S.:	$900.00
Can.:	$900.00
Ster.:	£500.00

HN 1731
Daydreams
Designer: L. Harradine
Height: 5 3/4", 14.6 cm
Colour: Pink
Issued: 1935 to the present
Varieties: HN 1732, 1944

U.S.:	$275.00
Can.:	$335.00
Ster.:	£109.00

HN 1732
Daydreams
Designer: L. Harradine
Height: 5 1/2", 14.0 cm
Colour: Light blue and pink
Issued: 1935-1949
Varieties: HN 1731, 1944

U.S.:	$ 900.00
Can.:	$1,000.00
Ster.:	£ 300.00

*

HN 1734
Kate Hardcastle
Designer: L. Harradine
Height: 8 1/4", 21.0 cm
Colour: Green and white
Issued: 1935-1949
Varieties: HN 1718, 1719, 1861, 1919, 2028

U.S.:	$1,200.00
Can.:	$1,200.00
Ster.:	£ 400.00

HN 1735
Sibell
Designer: L. Harradine
Height: 6 1/2", 16.5 cm
Colour: White and blue
Issued: 1935-1949
Varieties: HN 1668, 1695

U.S.:	$1,200.00
Can.:	$1,350.00
Ster.:	£ 400.00

HN 1736
Camille
Designer: L. Harradine
Height: 6 1/2", 16.5 cm
Colour: Red and white
Issued: 1935-1949
Varieties: HN 1586, 1648

U.S.: $1,750.00
Can.: $1,750.00
Ster.: £ 575.00

HN 1737
Janet
Style One
Designer: L. Harradine
Height: 6 1/4", 15.9 cm
Colour: Green
Issued: 1935-1949
Varieties: HN 1537, 1538, 1652

U.S.: $700.00
Can.: $750.00
Ster.: £300.00

HN 1738
Sonia
Designer: L. Harradine
Height: 6 1/2", 16.5 cm
Colour: Green
Issued: 1935-1949
Varieties: HN 1692

U.S.: $1,350.00
Can.: $1,500.00
Ster.: £ 600.00

HN 1739
Paisley Shawl
Style One
Designer: L. Harradine
Height: 8 1/4", 21.0 cm
Colour: Green and red
Issued: 1935-1949
Varieties: HN 1392, 1460, 1707, 1987

U.S.: $800.00
Can.: $900.00
Ster.: £350.00

HN 1740
Gladys
Designer: L. Harradine
Height: 5 1/4", 13.3 cm
Colour: Green
Issued: 1935-1949
Varieties: HN 1741

U.S.: $1,000.00
Can.: $1,000.00
Ster.: £ 600.00

HN 1741
Gladys
Designer: L. Harradine
Height: 5", 12.7 cm
Colour: Pink
Issued: 1935-1938
Varieties: HN 1740

U.S.: $1,000.00
Can.: $1,000.00
Ster.: £ 600.00

HN 1742
Sir Walter Raleigh
Designer: L. Harradine
Height: 10 1/2", 26.7 cm
Colour: Green, purple and orange
Issued: 1935-1949
Varieties: HN 1751, 2015

U.S.: $4,200.00
Can.: $4,200.00
Ster.: £1,300.00

HN 1743
Mirabel
Designer: L. Harradine
Height: 7 3/4", 19.7 cm
Colour: Pale blue
Issued: 1935-1949
Varieties: HN 1744

U.S.: $1,750.00
Can.: $1,750.00
Ster.: £ 600.00

HN 1744
Mirabel
Designer: L. Harradine
Height: 7 3/4", 19.7 cm
Colour: Pink
Issued: 1935-1949
Varieties: HN 1743

U.S.:	$1,300.00
Can.:	$1,300.00
Ster.:	£ 600.00

HN 1745
The Rustic Swain
Designer: L. Harradine
Height: 5 1/4", 13.3 cm
Colour: Green, white
and brown
Issued: 1935-1949
Varieties: HN 1746

U.S.:	$2,200.00
Can.:	$2,400.00
Ster.:	£ 700.00

HN 1746
The Rustic Swain
Designer: L. Harradine
Height: 5 1/4", 13.3 cm
Colour: Green, blue
and pink
Issued: 1935-1949
Varieties: HN 1745

U.S.:	$2,600.00
Can.:	$2,750.00
Ster.:	£ 800.00

HN 1747
Afternoon Tea
Designer: P. Railston
Height: 5 3/4", 14.6 cm
Colour: Pink and blue
Issued: 1935-1982
Varieties: HN 1748

U.S.:	$450.00
Can.:	$550.00
Ster.:	£250.00

HN 1748
Afternoon Tea
Designer: P. Railston
Height: 5 1/4", 13.3 cm
Colour: Green
Issued: 1935-1949
Varieties: HN 1747

U.S.:	$1,850.00
Can.:	$1,850.00
Ster.:	£ 600.00

HN 1749
Pierrette
Style Three
Designer: L. Harradine
Height: 8 1/2", 21.6 cm
Colour: Purple
Issued: 1936-1949
Varieties: HN 1391

U.S.:	$2,000.00
Can.:	$2,250.00
Ster.:	£ 675.00

Earthenware

HN 1750
Folly
Designer: L. Harradine
Height: 9 1/2", 24.1 cm
Colour: Black-purple
Issued: 1936-1949
Varieties: HN 1335

U.S.:	$1,750.00
Can.:	$2,000.00
Ster.:	£ 600.00

Earthenware

HN 1751
Sir Walter Raleigh
Designer: L. Harradine
Height: 11 1/2", 29.2 cm
Colour: Orange and
purple
Issued: 1936-1949
Varieties: HN 1742, 2015

U.S.:	$1,400.00
Can.:	$1,250.00
Ster.:	£ 450.00

Earthenware

HN 1752
Regency
Designer: L. Harradine
Height: 8", 20.3 cm
Colour: Lavender and green
Issued: 1936-1949

U.S.: $1,400.00
Can.: $1,400.00
Ster.: £ 600.00

HN 1753
Eleanore
Designer: L. Harradine
Height: 7", 17.8 cm
Colour: Blue, green and pink
Issued: 1936-1949
Varieties: HN 1754

U.S.: $1,750.00
Can.: $1,750.00
Ster.: £ 600.00

HN 1754
Eleanore
Designer: L. Harradine
Height: 7", 17.8 cm
Colour: Orange and cream
Issued: 1936-1949
Varieties: HN 1753

U.S.: $1,500.00
Can.: $1,500.00
Ster.: £ 600.00

HN 1755
The Court Shoemaker
Designer: L. Harradine
Height: 6 3/4", 17.2 cm
Colour: Purple, brown and green
Issued: 1936-1949

U.S.: $2,750.00
Can.: $2,750.00
Ster.: £ 900.00

HN 1756
Lizana
Designer: L. Harradine
Height: 8 1/2", 21.6 cm
Colour: Green, pink and purple
Issued: 1936-1949
Varieties: HN 1761

U.S.: $1,400.00
Can.: $1,000.00
Ster.: £ 600.00

HN 1757
Romany Sue
Designer: L. Harradine
Height: 9 1/4", 23.5 cm
Colour: Green and red
Issued: 1936-1949
Varieties: HN 1758

U.S.: $1,000.00
Can.: $1,150.00
Ster.: £ 400.00

HN 1758
Romany Sue
Designer: L. Harradine
Height: 9 1/2", 24.1 cm
Colour: Lavender
Issued: 1936-1949
Varieties: HN 1757

U.S.: $1,350.00
Can.: $1,350.00
Ster.: £ 450.00

HN 1759
The Orange Lady
Designer: L. Harradine
Height: 8 3/4", 22.2 cm
Colour: Pink
Issued: 1936-1975
Varieties: HN 1953

U.S.: $325.00
Can.: $450.00
Ster.: £120.00

Earlier pieces have holes in the oranges.
Earthenware

HN 1760
4 O'Clock
Designer: L. Harradine
Height: 6", 15.2 cm
Colour: Lavender
Issued: 1936-1949

U.S.: $1,200.00
Can.: $1,300.00
Ster.: £ 600.00

HN 1761
Lizana
Designer: L. Harradine
Height: 8 1/2", 21.6 cm
Colour: Green
Issued: 1936-1938
Varieties: HN 1756

U.S.: $1,100.00
Can.: $1,150.00
Ster.: £ 400.00

HN 1762
The Bride
Style One
Designer: L. Harradine
Height: 8 3/4", 22.2 cm
Colour: Yellow
Issued: 1936-1949
Varieties: HN 1588, 1600,
1841

U.S.: $1,300.00
Can.: $1,300.00
Ster.: £ 600.00

HN 1763
Windflower
Style One
Designer: L. Harradine
Height: 7 1/4", 18.4 cm
Colour: Pink
Issued: 1936-1949
Varieties: HN 1764, 2029

U.S.: $550.00
Can.: $650.00
Ster.: £350.00

HN 1764
Windflower
Style One
Designer: L. Harradine
Height: 7 1/4", 18.4 cm
Colour: Blue
Issued: 1936-1949
Varieties: HN 1763, 2029

U.S.: $1,000.00
Can.: $1,000.00
Ster.: £ 400.00

HN 1765
Chloe
Designer: L. Harradine
Height: 6", 15.2 cm
Colour: Blue
Issued: 1936-1950
Varieties: HN 1470, 1476,
1479, 1498, 1956

U.S.: $375.00
Can.: $550.00
Ster.: £250.00

HN 1766
Nana
Designer: L. Harradine
Height: 4 3/4", 12.0 cm
Colour: Pink
Issued: 1936-1949
Varieties: HN 1767

U.S.: $400.00
Can.: $575.00
Ster.: £250.00

HN 1767
Nana
Designer: L. Harradine
Height: 4 3/4", 12.0 cm
Colour: Lavender
Issued: 1936-1949
Varieties: HN 1766

U.S.: $400.00
Can.: $575.00
Ster.: £200.00

HN 1768
Ivy
Designer: L. Harradine
Height: 4 3/4", 12.0 cm
Colour: Purple
Issued: 1936-1979
Varieties: HN 1769

U.S.: $125.00
Can.: $150.00
Ster.: £ 60.00

HN 1769
Ivy
Designer: L. Harradine
Height: 4 3/4", 12.0 cm
Colour: Unknown
Issued: 1936-1938
Varieties: HN 1768

U.S.: $450.00
Can.: $500.00
Ster.: £150.00

HN 1770
Maureen
Style One
Designer: L. Harradine
Height: 7 1/2", 19.1 cm
Colour: Pink
Issued: 1936-1959
Varieties: HN 1771

U.S.: $425.00
Can.: $550.00
Ster.: £250.00

HN 1771
Maureen
Style One
Designer: L. Harradine
Height: 7 1/2", 19.1 cm
Colour: Lavener
Issued: 1936-1949
Varieties: HN 1770

U.S.: $1,000.00
Can.: $ 950.00
Ster.: £ 400.00

HN 1772
Delight
Designer: L. Harradine
Height: 7", 17.8 cm
Colour: Red
Issued: 1936-1967
Varieties: HN 1773

U.S.: $250.00
Can.: $350.00
Ster.: £225.00

HN 1773
Delight
Designer: L. Harradine
Height: 6 3/4", 17.2 cm
Colour: Turquoise
Issued: 1936-1949
Varieties: HN 1772

U.S.: $900.00
Can.: $950.00
Ster.: £350.00

HN 1774
Spring (Matte)
Style Two
Designer: R. Garbe
Height: 21", 53.3 cm
Colour: Ivory
Issued: 1933 in a limited
            edition of 100
Varieties: HN 1827

U.S.:   Extremely
Can.:   Rare
Ster.:
Only five known to exist

HN 1775
Salome (Matte)
Style One
Designer: R. Garbe
Height: 8", 20.3 cm
Colour: Ivory
Issued: 1933 in a limited
            edition of 100
Varieties: HN 1828

U.S.:   Extremely
Can.:   Rare
Ster.:
Only two known to exist

HN 1776
West Wind (Matte)
Designer: R. Garbe
Height: 14 1/2", 36.8 cm
Colour: Ivory
Issued: 1933 in a limited
edition of 25
Varieties: HN 1826

U.S.:	**Extremely**
Can.:	**Rare**
Ster.:	

Only three known to exist

Photograph
Not
Available

HN 1777
Spirit of the Wind (Matte)
Designer: R. Garbe
Height: Unknown
Colour: Ivory
Issued: 1933 in a limited
edition of 50
Varieties: HN 1825

U.S.:	**None**
Can.:	**known**
Ster.:	**to exist**

Photograph
Not
Available

HN 1778
Beethoven (Matte)
Designer: R. Garbe
Height: 22", 55.8 cm
Colour: Ivory
Issued: 1933 in a limited
edition of 25

U.S.:	**Extremely**
Can.:	**Rare**
Ster.:	

Only one known to exist

Photograph
Not
Available

HN 1779
Macaw (Matte)
Designer: R. Garbe
Height: 14 1/2", 35.6 cm
Colour: Ivory
Issued: 1933-1949
Varieties: HN 1829

U.S.:	**Extremely**
Can.:	**Rare**
Ster.:	

Only one known to exist

HN 1780
Lady of the Snows
Designer: R. Garbe
Height: Unknown
Colour: Unknown
Issued: 1933 in a limited
edition of 50
Varieties: HN 1830

U.S.:	**Extremely**
Can.:	**Rare**
Ster.:	

Only one known to exist
*

HN 1791
**Old Balloon Seller and
Bulldog**
Designer: L. Harradine
Height: 7", 17.8 cm
Colour: Green, red
and white
Issued: 1932-1938
Varieties: HN 1912

U.S.:	**Extremely**
Can.:	**Rare**
Ster.:	

Only four known to exist

HN 1792
Henry VIII
Style Two
Designer: C. J. Noke
Height: 11 1/2", 29.2 cm
Colour: Multi-coloured
Issued: 1933 in a limited
edition of 200

U.S.:	**$6,000.00**
Can.:	**$6,000.00**
Ster.:	**£2,000.00**

HN 1793
This Little Pig
Designer: L. Harradine
Height: 4", 10.1 cm
Colour: Red
Issued: 1936 to the
present
Varieties: HN 1794, 2125

U.S.:	**$150.00**
Can.:	**$170.00**
Ster.:	**£ 49.95**

HN 1794
This Little Pig
Designer: L. Harradine
Height: 4", 10.1 cm
Colour: Blue
Issued: 1936-1949
Varieties: HN 1793, 2125

U.S.: $650.00
Can.: $550.00
Ster.: £350.00

HN 1795
M'Lady's Maid
Designer: L. Harradine
Height: 9", 22.9 cm
Colour: Red
Issued: 1936-1949
Varieties: HN 1822

U.S.: $2,200.00
Can.: $2,500.00
Ster.: £ 800.00

HN 1796
Hazel
Style One
Designer: L. Harradine
Height: 5 1/4", 13.3 cm
Colour: Green and red
Issued: 1936-1949
Varieties: HN 1797

U.S.: $600.00
Can.: $750.00
Ster.: £350.00

HN 1797
Hazel
Style One
Designer: L. Harradine
Height: 5 1/4", 13.3 cm
Colour: Pink and blue
Issued: 1936-1949
Varieties: HN 1796

U.S.: $500.00
Can.: $600.00
Ster.: £300.00

HN 1798
Lily
Designer: L. Harradine
Height: 5", 12.7 cm
Colour: Pink
Issued: 1936-1971
Varieties: HN 1799

U.S.: $175.00
Can.: $250.00
Ster.: £ 80.00

HN 1799
Lily
Designer: L. Harradine
Height: 5", 12.7 cm
Colour: Green and blue
Issued: 1936-1949
Varieties: HN 1798

U.S.: $450.00
Can.: $500.00
Ster.: £150.00

HN 1800
St. George
Style One
Designer: S. Thorogood
Height: 16", 40.6 cm
Colour: Purple, green
and grey
Issued: 1934-1950
Varieties: HN 385, 386, 2067

U.S.: $3,000.00
Can.: $3,000.00
Ster.: £1,000.00

Earthenware

HN 1801
An Old King
Designer: C.J. Noke
Height: 9 3/4", 24.7 cm
Colour: Unknown
Issued: 1937-1954
Varieties: HN 358, 623,
2134

U.S.: Extremely
Can.: Rare
Ster.:

HN 1802
Estelle
Designer: L. Harradine
Height: 8", 20.3 cm
Colour: Pink
Issued: 1937-1949
Varieties: HN 1566

U.S.: $1,650.00
Can.: $1,750.00
Ster.: £ 600.00

HN 1803
Aileen
Designer: L. Harradine
Height: 6", 15.2 cm
Colour: Cream dress
with blue shawl
Issued: 1937-1949
Varieties: HN 1645, 1664

U.S.: $2,000.00
Can.: $2,000.00
Ster.: £ 800.00

HN 1804
Granny
Designer: L. Harradine
Height: 7", 17.8 cm
Colour: Grey, purple
and brown
Issued: 1937-1949
Varieties: HN 1832

U.S.: Extremely
Can.: Rare
Ster.:

Only one known to exist

HN 1805
To Bed
Designer: L. Harradine
Height: 6", 15.2 cm
Colour: Green
Issued: 1937-1959
Varieties: HN 1806

U.S.: $200.00
Can.: $325.00
Ster.: £120.00

HN 1806
To Bed
Designer: L. Harradine
Height: 6", 15.2 cm
Colour: Lavender
Issued: 1937-1949
Varieties: HN 1805

U.S.: $500.00
Can.: $600.00
Ster.: £250.00

HN 1807
Spring Flowers
Designer: L. Harradine
Height: 7 1/4", 18.4 cm
Colour: Green and blue
Issued: 1937-1959
Varieties: HN 1945

U.S.: $450.00
Can.: $595.00
Ster.: £250.00

HN 1808
Cissie
Designer: L. Harradine
Height: 5", 12.7 cm
Colour: Green
Issued: 1937-1951
Varieties: HN 1809

U.S.: $500.00
Can.: $600.00
Ster.: £250.00

HN 1809
Cissie
Designer: L. Harradine
Height: 5", 12.7 cm
Colour: Pink
Issued: 1937 to the
present
Varieties: HN 1808

U.S.: $185.00
Can.: $225.00
Ster.: £ 65.00

HN 1810
Bo-Peep
Style Two
Designer: L. Harradine
Height: 5", 12.7 cm
Colour: Blue
Issued: 1937-1949
Varieties: HN 1811

U.S.:	$600.00
Can.:	$600.00
Ster.:	£250.00

HN 1811
Bo-Peep
Style Two
Designer: L. Harradine
Height: 5", 12.7 cm
Colour: Pink
Issued: 1937 to the present
Varieties: HN 1810

U.S.:	$175.00
Can.:	$225.00
Ster.:	£ 59.95

HN 1812
Forget-Me-Not
Style One
Designer: L. Harradine
Height: 6", 15.2 cm
Colour: Pink and green
Issued: 1937-1949
Varieties: HN 1813

U.S.:	$750.00
Can.:	$900.00
Ster.:	£450.00

HN 1813
Forget-Me-Not
Style One
Designer: L. Harradine
Height: 6", 15.2 cm
Colour: Pink and blue
Issued: 1937-1949
Varieties: HN 1812

U.S.:	$500.00
Can.:	$700.00
Ster.:	£400.00

HN 1814
The Squire
Designer: Unknown
Height: 9 3/4", 24.7 cm
Colour: Red and grey
Issued: 1937-1949
Varieties: Also called "Hunting Squire" HN 1409

U.S.:	$4,000.00
Can.:	$4,000.00
Ster.:	£1,250.00

Earthenware

HN 1815
The Huntsman
Style Two
Designer: Unknown
Height: 9 1/2", 24.1 cm
Colour: Red and brown
Issued: 1937-1949
Varieties: Also called "John Peel" HN 1408

U.S.:	$4,000.00
Can.:	$4,000.00
Ster.:	£1,250.00

Earthenware   *

HN 1818
Miranda
Style One
Designer: L. Harradine
Height: 8 1/2", 21.6 cm
Colour: Red and blue
Issued: 1937-1949
Varieties: HN 1819

U.S.:	$2,000.00
Can.:	$2,300.00
Ster.:	£ 700.00

HN 1819
Miranda
Style One
Designer: L. Harradine
Height: 8 1/2", 21.6 cm
Colour: Green
Issued: 1937-1949
Varieties: HN 1818

U.S.:	$2,000.00
Can.:	$2,300.00
Ster.:	£ 700.00

HN 1820
Reflections
Style One
Designer: L. Harradine
Height: 5", 12.7 cm
Colour: Red and green
Issued: 1937-1938
Varieties: HN 1821, 1847, 1848

U.S.: $2,400.00
Can.: $2,400.00
Ster.: £ 800.00

HN 1821
Reflections
Style One
Designer: L. Harradine
Height: 5", 12.7 cm
Colour: Green and red
Issued: 1937-1938
Varieties: HN 1820, 1847, 1848

U.S.: $2,900.00
Can.: $2,900.00
Ster.: £ 900.00

HN 1822
M'Lady's Maid
Designer: L. Harradine
Height: 9", 22.9 cm
Colour: Multi-coloured
Issued: 1937-1949
Varieties: HN 1795

U.S.: $2,200.00
Can.: $2,500.00
Ster.: £ 800.00

Photograph
Not
Available

HN 1825
Spirit of the Wind
Designer: R. Garbe
Height: Unknown
Colour: Green and ivory
Issued: 1937-1949
Varieties: HN 1777

U.S.: Extremely
Can.: Rare
Ster.:

Only four known to exist

HN 1826
West Wind
Designer: R. Garbe
Height: 14 1/2", 36.8 cm
Colour: Antique ivory
Issued: 1937-1949
Varieties: HN 1776

U.S.: Extremely
Can.: Rare
Ster.:

Only two known to exist

HN 1827
Spring
Style Two
Designer: R. Garbe
Height: 21", 53.3 cm
Colour: Green and ivory
Issued: 1937-1949
Varieties: HN 1774

U.S.: Extremely
Can.: Rare
Ster.:

Only four known to exist

HN 1828
Salome
Style One
Designer: R. Garbe
Height: 8", 20.3 cm
Colour: Pale blue
Issued: 1937-1949
Varieties: HN 1775

U.S.: Extremely
Can.: Rare
Ster.:

Only two known to exist

Photograph
Not
Available

HN 1829
Macaw
Designer: R. Garbe
Height: 14 1/2", 35.6 cm
Colour: Antique ivory
Issued: 1933-1949
Varieties: HN 1779

U.S.: Extremely
Can.: Rare
Ster.:

Only two known to exist

HN 1830
Lady of the Snows
Designer: R. Garbe
Height: Unknown
Colour: Antique ivory
Issued: 1937-1949
Varieties: HN 1780

U.S.: **Extremely**
Can.: **Rare**
Ster.:

Only two known to exist

Photograph
Not
Available

HN 1831
The Cloud
Designer: R. Garbe
Height: 23", 58.4 cm
Colour: Ivory and gold
Issued: 1937-1949

U.S.: **Extremely**
Can.: **Rare**
Ster.:

Only two known to exist

HN 1832
Granny
Designer: L. Harradine
Height: 6 3/4", 17.1 cm
Colour: Red and yellow
Issued: 1937-1949
Varieties: HN 1804

U.S.: $3,000.00
Can.: $2,500.00
Ster.: £1,200.00

HN 1833
Top o' the Hill
Designer: L. Harradine
Height: 7", 17.8 cm
Colour: Green and blue
Issued: 1937-1971
Varieties: HN 1834, 1849, 2127

U.S.: $275.00
Can.: $450.00
Ster.: £150.00

HN 1834
Top o' the Hill
Designer: L. Harradine
Height: 7", 17.8 cm
Colour: Red
Issued: 1937 to the present
Varieties: HN 1833, 1849, 2127

U.S.: $300.00
Can.: $390.00
Ster.: £119.00

HN 1835
Verena
Designer: L. Harradine
Height: 8 1/4", 21.0 cm
Colour: Green and peach
Issued: 1938-1949
Varieties: HN 1854

U.S.: $1,500.00
Can.: $1,600.00
Ster.: £ 600.00

HN 1836
Vanessa
Style One
Designer: L. Harradine
Height: 7 1/2", 19.1 cm
Colour: Green and blue
Issued: 1938-1949
Varieties: HN 1838

U.S.: $1,200.00
Can.: $1,350.00
Ster.: £ 600.00

HN 1837
Mariquita
Designer: L. Harradine
Height: 8", 20.3 cm
Colour: Red and purple
Issued: 1938-1949

U.S.: $2,750.00
Can.: $2,750.00
Ster.: £ 900.00

HN 1838
Vanessa
Style One
Designer: L. Harradine
Height: 7 1/2", 19.1 cm
Colour: Pink and green
Issued: 1938-1949
Varieties: HN 1836

U.S.:	$1,750.00
Can.:	$1,350.00
Ster.:	£ 600.00

HN 1839
Christine
Style One
Designer: L. Harradine
Height: 7 3/4", 19.6 cm
Colour: Lavender and blue
Issued: 1938-1949
Varieties: HN 1840

U.S.:	$1,400.00
Can.:	$1,400.00
Ster.:	£ 600.00

HN 1840
Christine
Style One
Designer: L. Harradine
Height: 7 3/4", 19.6 cm
Colour: Pink and blue
Issued: 1938-1949
Varieties: HN 1839

U.S.:	$1,100.00
Can.:	$1,200.00
Ster.:	£ 600.00

HN 1841
The Bride
Style One
Designer: L. Harradine
Height: 9 1/2", 24.1 cm
Colour: Blue
Issued: 1938-1949
Varieties: HN 1588, 1600, 1762

U.S.:	$1,700.00
Can.:	$1,700.00
Ster.:	£ 600.00

HN 1842
Babie
Designer: L. Harradine
Height: 4 3/4", 12.0 cm
Colour: Pink and green
Issued: 1938-1949
Varieties: HN 1679, 2121

U.S.:	$350.00
Can.:	$400.00
Ster.:	£150.00

HN 1843
Biddy Penny Farthing
Designer: L. Harradine
Height: 9", 22.9 cm
Colour: Green and lavender
Issued: 1938 to the present

U.S.:	$250.00
Can.:	$415.00
Ster.:	£109.00

Earthenware and China

HN 1844
Odds and Ends
Designer: L. Harradine
Height: 7 3/4", 19.6 cm
Colour: Orange and green
Issued: 1938-1949

U.S.:	$2,500.00
Can.:	$2,500.00
Ster.:	£ 800.00

Earthenware

HN 1845
Modena
Designer: L. Harradine
Height: 7 1/4", 18.4 cm
Colour: Blue and pink
Issued: 1938-1949
Varieties: HN 1846

U.S.:	$2,400.00
Can.:	$2,500.00
Ster.:	£ 800.00

HN 1846
Modena
Designer: L. Harradine
Height: 7 1/4", 18.4 cm
Colour: Red and green
Issued: 1938-1949
Varieties: HN 1845

U.S.: **$2,200.00**
Can.: **$2,200.00**
Ster.: **£ 800.00**

HN 1847
Reflections
Style One
Designer: L. Harradine
Height: 4 1/2", 11.4 cm
Colour: Red and green
Issued: 1938-1949
Varieties: HN 1820, 1821,
1848

U.S.: **$1,750.00**
Can.: **$1,750.00**
Ster.: **£ 800.00**

HN 1848
Reflections
Style One
Designer: L. Harradine
Height: 5", 12.7 cm
Colour: Green, blue
and pink
Issued: 1938-1949
Varieties: HN 1820, 1821,
1847

U.S.: **$2,000.00**
Can.: **$2,000.00**
Ster.: **£ 800.00**

HN 1849
Top o' the Hill
Designer: L. Harradine
Height: 7 1/4", 18.4 cm
Colour: Pink
Issued: 1938-1975
Varieties: HN 1833, 1834,
2127

U.S.: **$275.00**
Can.: **$400.00**
Ster.: **£120.00**

Photograph
Not
Available

HN 1850
Antoinette
Style One
Designer: L. Harradine
Height: 8 1/4", 21.0 cm
Colour: Red and pink
Issued: 1938-1949
Varieties: HN 1851

U.S.: **$1,800.00**
Can.: **$2,000.00**
Ster.: **£ 800.00**

Photograph
Not
Available

HN 1851
Antoinette
Style One
Designer: L. Harradine
Height: 8 1/4", 21.0 cm
Colour: Blue and
lavender
Issued: 1938-1949
Varieties: HN 1850

U.S.: **$2,000.00**
Can.: **$2,200.00**
Ster.: **£ 800.00**

HN 1852
The Mirror
Designer: L. Harradine
Height: 7 1/2", 18.4 cm
Colour: Pink
Issued: 1938-1949
Varieties: HN 1853

U.S.: **$2,750.00**
Can.: **$2,750.00**
Ster.: **£ 900.00**

HN 1853
The Mirror
Designer: L. Harradine
Height: 7 1/2", 18.4 cm
Colour: Blue
Issued: 1938-1949
Varieties: HN 1852

U.S.: **$4,000.00**
Can.: **$4,000.00**
Ster.: **£1,300.00**

HN 1854
Verena
Designer: L. Harradine
Height: 8 1/4", 21.0 cm
Colour: Blue and pink
Issued: 1938-1949
Varieties: HN 1835

U.S.: **$2,200.00**
Can.: **$2,200.00**
Ster.: **£ 800.00**

HN 1855
Memories
Designer: L. Harradine
Height: 6", 15.2 cm
Colour: Green and red
Issued: 1938-1949
Varieties: HN 1856, 1857, 2030

U.S.: **$ 950.00**
Can.: **$1,100.00**
Ster.: **£ 650.00**

HN 1856
Memories
Designer: L. Harradine
Height: 6", 15.2 cm
Colour: Blue and white
Issued: 1938-1949
Varieties: HN 1855, 1857, 2030

U.S.: **$1,000.00**
Can.: **$1,150.00**
Ster.: **£ 600.00**

HN 1857
Memories
Designer: L. Harradine
Height: 6", 15.2 cm
Colour: Red and lavender
Issued: 1938-1949
Varieties: HN 1855, 1856, 2030

U.S.: **$1,200.00**
Can.: **$1,300.00**
Ster.: **£ 600.00**

HN 1858
Dawn
(With head-dress)
Style One
Designer: L. Harradine
Height: 10", 25.4 cm
Colour: Green
Issued: 1938-?
Varieties: HN 1858A

U.S.: **$3,500.00**
Can.: **$3,500.00**
Ster.: **£1,200.00**

HN 1858A
Dawn
(Without head-dress)
Style One
Designer: L. Harradine
Height: 9 3/4", 24.7 cm
Colour: Green
Issued: ?-1949
Varieties: HN 1858

U.S.: **$2,000.00**
Can.: **$2,250.00**
Ster.: **£ 900.00**

HN 1859
Tildy
Designer: L. Harradine
Height: 5 1/2", 14.0 cm
Colour: Red and green
Issued: 1938-1949
Varieties: HN 1576

U.S.: **$1,600.00**
Can.: **$1,600.00**
Ster.: **£ 600.00**

HN 1860
Millicent
Designer: L. Harradine
Height: 8", 20.3 cm
Colour: Red and blue
Issued: 1938-1949
Varieties: HN 1714, 1715

U.S.: **$2,000.00**
Can.: **$2,200.00**
Ster.: **£ 650.00**

HN 1861
Kate Hardcastle
Designer: L. Harradine
Height: 8", 20.3 cm
Colour: Red and blue
Issued: 1938-1949
Varieties: HN 1718, 1719,
1734, 1919,
2028

U.S.: $1,600.00
Can.: $1,600.00
Ster.: £ 600.00

HN 1862
Jasmine
Designer: L. Harradine
Height: 7 1/4", 18.4 cm
Colour: Green , blue
and orange
Issued: 1938-1949
Varieties: HN 1863, 1876

U.S.: $1,100.00
Can.: $1,200.00
Ster.: £ 400.00

HN 1863
Jasmine
Designer: L. Harradine
Height: 7 1/2", 19.1 cm
Colour: Blue and green
Issued: 1938-1949
Varieties: HN 1862, 1876

U.S.: $1,500.00
Can.: $1,500.00
Ster.: £ 475.00

HN 1864
Sweet and Fair
Designer: L. Harradine
Height: 7 1/2", 19.1 cm
Colour: Pink
Issued: 1938-1949
Varieties: HN 1865

U.S.: $2,100.00
Can.: $1,750.00
Ster.: £ 800.00

HN 1865
Sweet and Fair
Designer: L. Harradine
Height: 7 1/4", 18.4 cm
Colour: Green
Issued: 1938-1949
Varieties: HN 1864

U.S.: $2,100.00
Can.: $1,750.00
Ster.: £ 800.00

HN 1866
Wedding Morn
Designer: L. Harradine
Height: 10 1/2", 26.7 cm
Colour: Cream
Issued: 1938-1949
Varieties: HN 1867

U.S.: $3,000.00
Can.: $3,000.00
Ster.: £1,000.00

HN 1867
Wedding Morn
Designer: L. Harradine
Height: 10 1/2", 26.7 cm
Colour: Red and cream
Issued: 1938-1949
Varieties: HN 1866

U.S.: $3,000.00
Can.: $3,000.00
Ster.: £1,000.00

HN 1868
Serena
Designer: L. Harradine
Height: 11", 27.9 cm
Colour: Red, pink
and blue
Issued: 1938-1949

U.S.: $1,400.00
Can.: $1,000.00
Ster.: £ 400.00

Earthenware

Photograph
Not
Available

HN 1869
Dryad of the Pines
Designer: R. Garbe
Height: 23", 58.4 cm
Colour: Ivory and gold
Issued: 1938-1949

U.S.:	**Extremely**
Can.:	**Rare**
Ster.:	

HN 1870
Little Lady Make Believe
Designer: L. Harradine
Height: 6 1/4", 15.9 cm
Colour: Red and blue
Issued: 1938-1949

U.S.:	**$550.00**
Can.:	**$675.00**
Ster.:	**£400.00**

HN 1871
Annabella
Designer: L. Harradine
Height: 5 1/4", 13.3 cm
Colour: Pink and green
Issued: 1938-1949
Varieties: HN 1872, 1875

U.S.:	**$1,100.00**
Can.:	**$1,200.00**
Ster.:	**£ 400.00**

HN 1872
Annabella
Designer: L. Harradine
Height: 5 1/4", 13.3 cm
Colour: Turquoise
and blue
Issued: 1938-1949
Varieties: HN 1871, 1875

U.S.:	**$1,000.00**
Can.:	**$1,100.00**
Ster.:	**£ 400.00**

HN 1873
Granny's Heritage
Designer: L. Harradine
Height: 6 3/4", 17.2 cm
Colour: Pink, blue and
grey
Issued: 1938-1949
Varieties: HN 1874, 2031

U.S.:	**$1,000.00**
Can.:	**$1,000.00**
Ster.:	**£ 400.00**

HN 1874
Granny's Heritage
Designer: L. Harradine
Height: 6 1/4", 15.9 cm
Colour: Blue and green
Issued: 1938-1949
Varieties: HN 1873, 2031

U.S.:	**$700.00**
Can.:	**$900.00**
Ster.:	**£300.00**

HN 1875
Annabella
Designer: L. Harradine
Height: 4 3/4", 12.0 cm
Colour: Red
Issued: 1938-1949
Varieties: HN 1871, 1872

U.S.:	**$1,000.00**
Can.:	**$1,100.00**
Ster.:	**£ 400.00**

HN 1876
Jasmine
Designer: L. Harradine
Height: 7 1/2", 19.1 cm
Colour: Green and blue
Issued: 1938-1949
Varieties: HN 1862, 1863

U.S.:	**$1,650.00**
Can.:	**$1,650.00**
Ster.:	**£ 500.00**

HN 1877
Jean
Style One
Designer: L. Harradine
Height: 7 1/2", 19.0 cm
Colour: Pink and purple
Issued: 1938-1949
Varieties: HN 1878, 2032

U.S.: $850.00
Can.: $950.00
Ster.: £350.00

HN 1878
Jean
Style One
Designer: L. Harradine
Height: 7 1/2", 19.0 cm
Colour: Green and red
Issued: 1938-1949
Varieties: HN 1877, 2032

U.S.: $550.00
Can.: $675.00
Ster.: £300.00

HN 1879
Bon Jour
Designer: L. Harradine
Height: 6 3/4", 17.2 cm
Colour: Green
Issued: 1938-1949
Varieties: HN 1888

U.S.: $1,300.00
Can.: $1,450.00
Ster.: £ 600.00

HN 1880
The Lambeth Walk
Designer: L. Harradine
Height: 10", 25.4 cm
Colour: Blue
Issued: 1938-1949
Varieties: HN 1881

U.S.: $3,000.00
Can.: $3,000.00
Ster.: £1,000.00

HN 1881
The Lambeth Walk
Designer: L. Harradine
Height: 10", 25.4 cm
Colour: Pink
Issued: 1938-1949
Varieties: HN 1880

U.S.: $2,400.00
Can.: $2,400.00
Ster.: £ 800.00

HN 1882
Nell Gwynn
Designer: L. Harradine
Height: 6 3/4", 17.2 cm
Colour: Green and pink
Issued: 1938-1949
Varieties: HN 1887

U.S.: $1,200.00
Can.: $1,200.00
Ster.: £ 650.00

HN 1883
Prudence
Designer: L. Harradine
Height: 6 3/4", 17.2 cm
Colour: Blue
Issued: 1938-1949
Varieties: HN 1884

U.S.: $1,000.00
Can.: $1,000.00
Ster.: £ 400.00

HN 1884
Prudence
Designer: L. Harradine
Height: 6 3/4", 17.2 cm
Colour: Pink
Issued: 1938-1949
Varieties: HN 1883

U.S.: $1,100.00
Can.: $1,000.00
Ster.: £ 400.00

HN 1885
Nadine
Designer: L. Harradine
Height: 7 3/4", 19.7 cm
Colour: Turquoise
Issued: 1938-1949
Varieties: HN 1886

U.S.:	$1,250.00
Can.:	$1,250.00
Ster.:	£ 400.00

HN 1886
Nadine
Designer: L. Harradine
Height: 7 3/4", 19.7 cm
Colour: Pink
Issued: 1938-1949
Varieties: HN 1885

U.S.:	$1,250.00
Can.:	$1,250.00
Ster.:	£ 400.00

HN 1887
Nell Gwynn
Designer: L. Harradine
Height: 6 3/4", 17.2 cm
Colour: Green and pink
Issued: 1938-1949
Varieties: HN 1882

U.S.:	$1,400.00
Can.:	$1,400.00
Ster.:	£ 650.00

HN 1888
Bon Jour
Designer: L. Harradine
Height: 6 3/4", 17.2 cm
Colour: Red
Issued: 1938-1949
Varieties: HN 1879

U.S.:	$1,000.00
Can.:	$1,200.00
Ster.:	£ 600.00

HN 1889
Goody Two Shoes
Designer: L. Harradine
Height: 4 3/4", 12.0 cm
Colour: Green and
purple
Issued: 1938-1949
Varieties: HN 1905, 2037

U.S.:	$450.00
Can.:	$575.00
Ster.:	£200.00

HN 1890
Lambing Time
Designer: L. Harradine
Height: 9 1/4", 23.5 cm
Colour: Light brown
Issued: 1938-1981

U.S.:	$250.00
Can.:	$375.00
Ster.:	£120.00

Earthenware

HN 1891
Pecksniff
Style Two
Designer: L. Harradine
Height: 7", 17.8 cm
Colour: Black and
brown
Issued: 1938-1952
Varieties: HN 553
Series: Dickens

U.S.:	$475.00
Can.:	$450.00
Ster.:	£200.00

HN 1892
Uriah Heep
Style Two
Designer: L. Harradine
Height: 7", 17.8 cm
Colour: Black
Issued: 1938-1952
Varieties: HN 554
Series: Dickens

U.S.:	$475.00
Can.:	$450.00
Ster.:	£200.00

HN 1893
The Fat Boy
Style Two
Designer: L. Harradine
Height: 7", 17.8 cm
Colour: Blue and cream
Issued: 1938-1952
Varieties: HN 555
Series: Dickens

U.S.:	**$475.00**
Can.:	**$450.00**
Ster.:	**£200.00**

HN 1894
Mr Pickwick
Style Two
Designer: L. Harradine
Height: 7", 17.8 cm
Colour: Blue, tan and cream
Issued: 1938-1952
Varieties: HN 556
Series: Dickens

U.S.:	**$475.00**
Can.:	**$450.00**
Ster.:	**£200.00**

Earthenware and porcelain

HN 1895
Mr Micawber
Style Two
Designer: L. Harradine
Height: 7", 17.8 cm
Colour: Brown, black and tan
Issued: 1938-1952
Varieties: HN 557
Series: Dickens

U.S.:	**$475.00**
Can.:	**$450.00**
Ster.:	**£200.00**

HN 1896
Sairey Gamp
Style Two
Designer: L. Harradine
Height: 7", 17.8 cm
Colour: Dark and light green
Issued: 1938-1952
Varieties: HN 558
Series: Dickens

U.S.:	**$500.00**
Can.:	**$450.00**
Ster.:	**£200.00**

HN 1897
Miss Fortune
Designer: L. Harradine
Height: 6", 15.2 cm
Colour: Pink and blue
Issued: 1938-1949
Varieties: HN 1898

U.S.:	**$ 875.00**
Can.:	**$1,000.00**
Ster.:	**£ 450.00**

HN 1898
Miss Fortune
Designer: L. Harradine
Height: 5 3/4", 14.6 cm
Colour: Blue
Issued: 1938-1949
Varieties: HN 1897

U.S.:	**$1,400.00**
Can.:	**$1,250.00**
Ster.:	**£ 600.00**

HN 1899
Midsummer Noon
Designer: L. Harradine
Height: 4 3/4", 12.0 cm
Colour: Pink
Issued: 1939-1949
Varieties: HN 1900, 2033

U.S.:	**$700.00**
Can.:	**$800.00**
Ster.:	**£350.00**

HN 1900
Midsummer Noon
Designer: L. Harradine
Height: 4 3/4", 12.0 cm
Colour: Blue
Issued: 1939-1949
Varieties: HN 1899, 2033

U.S.:	**$2,000.00**
Can.:	**$1,750.00**
Ster.:	**£ 600.00**

HN 1901
Penelope
Designer: L. Harradine
Height: 7", 17.8 cm
Colour: Red
Issued: 1939-1975
Varieties: HN 1902

U.S.: $400.00
Can.: $550.00
Ster.: £250.00

HN 1902
Penelope
Designer: L. Harradine
Height: 7", 17.8 cm
Colour: Lavender and green
Issued: 1939-1949
Varieties: HN 1901

U.S.: $1,800.00
Can.: $1,800.00
Ster.: £ 600.00

HN 1903
Rhythm
Designer: L. Harradine
Height: 6 3/4", 17.2 cm
Colour: Pink
Issued: 1939-1949
Varieties: HN 1904

U.S.: $3,000.00
Can.: $3,000.00
Ster.: £1,000.00

HN 1904
Rhythm
Designer: L. Harradine
Height: 6 3/4", 17.2 cm
Colour: Blue
Issued: 1939-1949
Varieties: HN 1903

U.S.: $3,750.00
Can.: $3,750.00
Ster.: £1,200.00

HN 1905
Goody Two Shoes
Designer: L. Harradine
Height: 4 3/4", 12.0 cm
Colour: Pink and red
Issued: 1939-1949
Varieties: HN 1889, 2037

U.S.: $350.00
Can.: $400.00
Ster.: £150.00

HN 1906
Lydia
Designer: L. Harradine
Height: 4 1/4", 10.8 cm
Colour: Orange and pink
Issued: 1939-1949
Varieties: HN 1907, 1908

U.S.: $850.00
Can.: $900.00
Ster.: £275.00

HN 1907
Lydia
Designer: L. Harradine
Height: 4 3/4", 12.0 cm
Colour: Green
Issued: 1939-1949
Varieties: HN 1906, 1908

U.S.: $650.00
Can.: $750.00
Ster.: £225.00

HN 1908
Lydia
Designer: L. Harradine
Height: 4 3/4", 12.0 cm
Colour: Red
Issued: 1939 to the present
Varieties: HN 1906, 1907

U.S.: $195.00
Can.: $255.00
Ster.: £ 75.00

HN 1909
Honey
Designer: L. Harradine
Height: 7", 17.8 cm
Colour: Pink
Issued: 1939-1949
Varieties: HN 1910, 1963

U.S.: $500.00
Can.: $575.00
Ster.: £300.00

HN 1910
Honey
Designer: L. Harradine
Height: 6 3/4", 17.2 cm
Colour: Blue
Issued: 1939-1949
Varieties: HN 1909, 1963

U.S.: $1,200.00
Can.: $ 950.00
Ster.: £ 400.00

HN 1911
Autumn Breezes
Designer: L. Harradine
Height: 7 1/2", 19.1 cm
Colour: Green and pink
Issued: 1939-1976
Varieties: HN 1913, 1934,
2131, 2147

U.S.: $250.00
Can.: $350.00
Ster.: £120.00

HN 1912
Old Balloon Seller
and Bulldog
Designer: L. Harradine
Height: 7", 17.8 cm
Colour: Unknown
Issued: 1939-1949
Varieties: HN 1791

U.S.: Extremely
Can.: Rare
Ster.:

Only one known to exist

HN 1913
Autumn Breezes
Designer: L. Harradine
Height: 7 1/2", 19.1 cm
Colour: Green and blue
Issued: 1939-1971
Varieties: HN 1911, 1934,
2131, 2147

U.S.: $300.00
Can.: $450.00
Ster.: £150.00

HN 1914
Paisley Shawl
Style Two
Designer: L. Harradine
Height: 6 1/2", 16.5 cm
Colour: Green and red
Issued: 1939-1949
Varieties: HN 1988

U.S.: $325.00
Can.: $450.00
Ster.: £150.00

HN 1915
Veronica
Style Two
Designer: L. Harradine
Height: 5 3/4", 14.6 cm
Colour: Red and green
Issued: 1939-1949

U.S.: $400.00
Can.: $450.00
Ster.: £250.00

HN 1916
Janet
Style Two
Designer: L. Harradine
Height: 5 1/4", 13.3 cm
Colour: Pink and blue
Issued: 1939-1949
Varieties: HN 1964

U.S.: $325.00
Can.: $495.00
Ster.: £200.00

HN 1917
Meryll
Designer:	L. Harradine
Height:	6 3/4", 17.2 cm
Colour:	Red and green
Issued:	1939-1940
Varieties:	Also called "Toinette" HN 1940
U.S.:	$3,000.00
Can.:	$3,000.00
Ster.:	£1,000.00

HN 1918
Sweet Suzy
Designer:	L. Harradine
Height:	6 1/2", 16.5 cm
Colour:	Pink and green
Issued:	1939-1949
U.S.:	$850.00
Can.:	$950.00
Ster.:	£450.00

HN 1919
Kate Hardcastle
Designer:	L. Harradine
Height:	8 1/4", 21.0 cm
Colour:	Red and green
Issued:	1939-1949
Varieties:	HN 1718, 1719, 1734, 1861, 2028
U.S.:	$1,500.00
Can.:	$1,600.00
Ster.:	£ 500.00

HN 1920
Windflower
Style Two
Designer:	L. Harradine
Height:	11", 27.9 cm
Colour:	Multi-coloured
Issued:	1939-1949
Varieties:	HN 1939
U.S.:	$3,000.00
Can.:	$3,000.00
Ster.:	£1,000.00

HN 1921
Roseanna
Designer:	L. Harradine
Height:	8", 20.3 cm
Colour:	Green
Issued:	1940-1949
Varieties:	HN 1926
U.S.:	$1,750.00
Can.:	$1,750.00
Ster.:	£ 550.00

HN 1922
Spring Morning
Designer:	L. Harradine
Height:	7 1/2", 19.1 cm
Colour:	Pink and blue
Issued:	1940-1973
Varieties:	HN 1923
U.S.:	$325.00
Can.:	$495.00
Ster.:	£150.00

HN 1923
Spring Morning
Designer:	L. Harradine
Height:	7 1/2", 19.1 cm
Colour:	Green and cream
Issued:	1940-1949
Varieties:	HN 1922
U.S.:	$950.00
Can.:	$950.00
Ster.:	£400.00

HN 1924
Fiona
Style One
Designer:	L. Harradine
Height:	5 3/4", 14.6 cm
Colour:	Pink and lavender
Issued:	1940-1949
Varieties:	HN 1925, 1933
U.S.:	$1,200.00
Can.:	$1,200.00
Ster.:	£ 600.00

HN 1925
Fiona
Style One
Designer: L. Harradine
Height: 5 3/4", 14.6 cm
Colour: Blue
Issued: 1940-1949
Varieties: HN 1924, 1933

U.S.:	$1,200.00
Can.:	$1,200.00
Ster.:	£ 600.00

HN 1926
Roseanna
Designer: L. Harradine
Height: 8", 20.3 cm
Colour: Pink
Issued: 1940-1959
Varieties: HN 1921

U.S.:	$450.00
Can.:	$675.00
Ster.:	£200.00

HN 1927
The Awakening
Style One
Designer: L. Harradine
Height: 10 1/4", 26.0 cm
Colour: Pale pink
Issued: 1940-1949

U.S.:	$3,000.00
Can.:	$3,000.00
Ster.:	£1,000.00

HN 1928
Marguerite
Designer: L. Harradine
Height: 8", 20.3 cm
Colour: Pink
Issued: 1940-1959
Varieties: HN 1929, 1930, 1946

U.S.:	$450.00
Can.:	$595.00
Ster.:	£250.00

HN 1929
Marguerite
Designer: L. Harradine
Height: 8", 20.3 cm
Colour: Pale pink and yellow
Issued: 1940-1949
Varieties: HN 1928, 1930, 1946

U.S.:	$850.00
Can.:	$975.00
Ster.:	£250.00

HN 1930
Marguerite
Designer: L. Harradine
Height: 8", 20.3 cm
Colour: Blue and purple
Issued: 1940-1949
Varieties: HN 1928, 1929, 1946

U.S.:	$1,600.00
Can.:	$1,750.00
Ster.:	£ 550.00

HN 1931
Meriel
Designer: L. Harradine
Height: 7 1/4", 18.4 cm
Colour: Pink
Issued: 1940-1949
Varieties: HN 1932

U.S.:	$1,750.00
Can.:	$1,850.00
Ster.:	£ 600.00

HN 1932
Meriel
Designer: L. Harradine
Height: 7 1/4", 18.4 cm
Colour: Green
Issued: 1940-1949
Varieties: HN 1931

U.S.:	$1,950.00
Can.:	$2,100.00
Ster.:	£ 650.00

HN 1933
Fiona
Style One
Designer: L. Harradine
Height: 5 3/4", 14.6 cm
Colour: Multi-coloured
Issued: 1940-1949
Varieties: HN 1924, 1925

  U.S.:   **$1,200.00**
  Can.:   **$1,350.00**
  Ster.:   **£ 600.00**

HN 1934
Autumn Breezes
Designer: L. Harradine
Height: 7 1/2", 19.1 cm
Colour: Red
Issued: 1940 to the
           present
Varieties: HN 1911, 1913,
           2131, 2147

  U.S.:   **$325.00**
  Can.:   **$390.00**
  Ster.:   **£109.00**

HN 1935
Sweeting
Designer: L. Harradine
Height: 6", 15.2 cm
Colour: Pink
Issued: 1940-1973
Varieties: HN 1938

  U.S.:   **$175.00**
  Can.:   **$285.00**
  Ster.:   **£ 80.00**

HN 1936
Miss Muffet
Designer: L. Harradine
Height: 5 1/2", 14.0 cm
Colour: Red
Issued: 1940-1967
Varieties: HN 1937

  U.S.:   **$200.00**
  Can.:   **$300.00**
  Ster.:   **£100.00**

HN 1937
Miss Muffet
Designer: L. Harradine
Height: 5 1/2", 14.0 cm
Colour: Green
Issued: 1940-1952
Varieties: HN 1936

  U.S.:   **$375.00**
  Can.:   **$385.00**
  Ster.:   **£150.00**

HN 1938
Sweeting
Designer: L. Harradine
Height: 6", 15.2 cm
Colour: Purple and red
Issued: 1940-1949
Varieties: HN 1935

  U.S.:   **$475.00**
  Can.:   **$600.00**
  Ster.:   **£150.00**

HN 1939
Windflower
Style Two
Designer: L. Harradine
Height: 11", 27.9 cm
Colour: Pink
Issued: 1940-1949
Varieties: HN 1920

  U.S.:   **$3,000.00**
  Can.:   **$3,000.00**
  Ster.:   **£1,000.00**

HN 1940
Toinette
Designer: L. Harradine
Height: 6 3/4", 17.1 cm
Colour: Red
Issued: 1940-1949
Varieties: Also called
           "Meryll" HN 1917

  U.S.:   **$1,900.00**
  Can.:   **$2,000.00**
  Ster.:   **£ 650.00**

HN 1941
Peggy
Designer: L. Harradine
Height: 5", 12.7 cm
Colour: Red and white
Issued: 1940-1949
Varieties: HN 2038

U.S.: $350.00
Can.: $400.00
Ster.: £100.00

HN 1942
Pyjams
Designer: L. Harradine
Height: 5 1/4", 13.3 cm
Colour: Pink
Issued: 1940-1949

U.S.: $700.00
Can.: $850.00
Ster.: £300.00

HN 1943
Veronica
Style One
Designer: L. Harradine
Height: 8", 20.3 cm
Colour: Pink and blue
Issued: 1940-1949
Varieties: HN 1517, 1519, 1650

U.S.: $1,000.00
Can.: $1,100.00
Ster.: £ 400.00

HN 1944
Daydreams
Designer: L. Harradine
Height: 5 1/2", 14.0 cm
Colour: Red
Issued: 1940-1949
Varieties: HN 1731, 1732

U.S.: $ 950.00
Can.: $1,000.00
Ster.: £ 350.00

HN 1945
Spring Flowers
Designer: L. Harradine
Height: 7 1/4", 18.4 cm
Colour: Red and green
Issued: 1940-1949
Varieties: HN 1807

U.S.: $1,500.00
Can.: $1,600.00
Ster.: £ 600.00

HN 1946
Marguerite
Designer: L. Harradine
Height: 8", 20.3 cm
Colour: Pink
Issued: 1940-1949
Varieties: HN 1928, 1929, 1930

U.S.: $900.00
Can.: $950.00
Ster.: £400.00

HN 1947
June
Style One
Designer: L. Harradine
Height: 7 1/4", 18.4 cm
Colour: Red
Issued: 1940-1949
Varieties: HN 1690, 1691, 2027

U.S.: $1,200.00
Can.: $1,200.00
Ster.: £ 400.00

HN 1948
Lady Charmian
Designer: L. Harradine
Height: 8", 20.3 cm
Colour: Green dress with red shawl
Issued: 1940-1973
Varieties: HN 1949

U.S.: $325.00
Can.: $485.00
Ster.: £250.00

HN 1949
Lady Charmian
Designer: L. Harradine
Height: 8", 20.3 cm
Colour: Red dress with green shawl
Issued: 1940-1975
Varieties: HN 1948

U.S.: $300.00
Can.: $425.00
Ster.: £220.00

HN 1950
Claribel
Designer: L. Harradine
Height: 4 3/4", 12.0 cm
Colour: Purple and pink
Issued: 1940-1949
Varieties: HN 1951

U.S.: $600.00
Can.: $750.00
Ster.: £300.00

HN 1951
Claribel
Designer: L. Harradine
Height: 4 3/4", 12.0 cm
Colour: Red
Issued: 1940-1949
Varieties: HN 1950

U.S.: $500.00
Can.: $650.00
Ster.: £300.00

HN 1952
Irene
Designer: L. Harradine
Height: 6 3/4", 17.2 cm
Colour: Blue and purple
Issued: 1940-1950
Varieties: HN 1621, 1697

U.S.: $1,250.00
Can.: $1,350.00
Ster.: £ 400.00

HN 1953
Orange Lady
Designer: L. Harradine
Height: 8 1/2", 21.6 cm
Colour: Light green dress, dark green shawl
Issued: 1940-1975
Varieties: HN 1759

U.S.: $300.00
Can.: $450.00
Ster.: £120.00

HN 1954
The Balloon Man
Designer: L. Harradine
Height: 7 1/4", 18.4 cm
Colour: Black and gray
Issued: 1940 to the present

U.S.: $250.00
Can.: $415.00
Ster.: £109.00

Earthenware and China

HN 1955
Lavinia
Designer: L. Harradine
Height: 5", 12.7 cm
Colour: Red
Issued: 1940-1979

U.S.: $135.00
Can.: $160.00
Ster.: £ 80.00

HN 1956
Chloe
Designer: L. Harradine
Height: 6", 15.2 cm
Colour: Red and green
Issued: 1940-1949
Varieties: HN 1470, 1476, 1479, 1498, 1765

U.S.: $ 950.00
Can.: $1,000.00
Ster.: £ 350.00

HN 1957
The New Bonnet
Designer: L. Harradine
Height: 7", 17.8 cm
Colour: Red
Issued: 1940-1949
Varieties: HN 1728

U.S.:	$1,400.00
Can.:	$1,500.00
Ster.:	£ 600.00

HN 1958
Lady April
Designer: L. Harradine
Height: 7", 17.8 cm
Colour: Red and purple
Issued: 1940-1959
Varieties: HN 1965

U.S.:	$375.00
Can.:	$495.00
Ster.:	£250.00

HN 1959
The Choice
Designer: L. Harradine
Height: 7 1/4", 18.4 cm
Colour: Red
Issued: 1941-1949
Varieties: HN 1960

U.S.:	$1,700.00
Can.:	$1,800.00
Ster.:	£ 600.00

HN 1960
The Choice
Designer: L. Harradine
Height: 7 1/4", 18.4 cm
Colour: Purple
Issued: 1941-1949
Varieties: HN 1959

U.S.:	$1,900.00
Can.:	$2,000.00
Ster.:	£ 650.00

HN 1961
Daisy
Designer: L. Harradine
Height: 3 1/2", 8.9 cm
Colour: Pink
Issued: 1941-1949
Varieties: HN 1575

U.S.:	$550.00
Can.:	$650.00
Ster.:	£250.00

HN 1962
Genevieve
Designer: L. Harradine
Height: 7", 17.8 cm
Colour: Red
Issued: 1941-1975

U.S.:	$350.00
Can.:	$495.00
Ster.:	£120.00

HN 1963
Honey
Designer: L. Harradine
Height: 6 3/4", 17.2 cm
Colour: Red and blue
Issued: 1941-1949
Varieties: HN 1909, 1910

U.S.:	$1,000.00
Can.:	$1,100.00
Ster.:	£ 300.00

HN 1964
Janet
Style Two
Designer: L. Harradine
Height: 5", 12.7 cm
Colour: Red
Issued: 1941-1949
Varieties: HN 1916

U.S.:	$850.00
Can.:	$850.00
Ster.:	£275.00

HN 1965
Lady April
Designer: L. Harradine
Height: 7", 17.8 cm
Colour: Green and
pink
Issued: 1941-1949
Varieties: HN 1958
U.S.: **$1,000.00**
Can.: **$1,200.00**
Ster.: **£ 400.00**

HN 1966
An Orange Vendor
Designer: C.J. Noke
Height: 6 1/4", 15.9 cm
Colour: Purple
Issued: 1941-1949
Varieties: HN 72, 508, 521
U.S.: **$1,100.00**
Can.: **$ 950.00**
Ster.: **£ 400.00**

Earthenware

HN 1967
Lady Betty
Designer: L. Harradine
Height: 6 1/2", 16.5 cm
Colour: Red
Issued: 1941-1951
U.S.: **$500.00**
Can.: **$550.00**
Ster.: **£300.00**

HN 1968
Madonna of the Square
Designer: P. Stabler
Height: 7", 17.8 cm
Colour: Light green
Issued: 1941-1949
Varieties: HN 10, 10A, 11,
14, 27, 326, 573,
576, 594, 613,
764, 1969, 2034
U.S.: **$2,300.00**
Can.: **$2,000.00**
Ster.: **£ 650.00**

HN 1969
Madonna of the Square
Designer: P. Stabler
Height: 7", 17.8 cm
Colour: Lavender
Issued: 1941-1949
Varieties: HN 10, 10A, 11,
14, 27, 326, 573,
576, 594, 613,
764, 1968, 2034
U.S.: **$2,300.00**
Can.: **$2,000.00**
Ster.: **£ 650.00**

HN 1970
Milady
Designer: L. Harradine
Height: 6 1/2", 16.5 cm
Colour: Pink
Issued: 1941-1949
U.S.: **$1,250.00**
Can.: **$1,250.00**
Ster.: **£ 400.00**

HN 1971
Springtime
Style One
Designer: L. Harradine
Height: 6", 15.2 cm
Colour: Pink and blue
Issued: 1941-1949
U.S.: **$ 950.00**
Can.: **$1,200.00**
Ster.: **£ 600.00**

HN 1972
Regency Beau
Designer: H. Fenton
Height: 8", 20.3 cm
Colour: Green and pink
Issued: 1941-1949
U.S.: **$ 950.00**
Can.: **$1,200.00**
Ster.: **£ 600.00**

HN 1973
The Corinthian
Designer: H. Fenton
Height: 7 3/4", 19.7 cm
Colour: Green, red and
cream
Issued: 1941-1949

U.S.: $1,000.00
Can.: $1,250.00
Ster.: £ 600.00

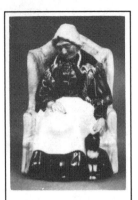

HN 1974
Forty Winks
Designer: H. Fenton
Height: 6 3/4", 17.2 cm
Colour: Green and tan
Issued: 1945-1973

U.S.: $300.00
Can.: $450.00
Ster.: £120.00

HN 1975
The Shepherd
Style Four
Designer: H. Fenton
Height: 8 1/2", 21.6 cm
Colour: Light brown
Issued: 1945-1975

U.S.: $275.00
Can.: $400.00
Ster.: £120.00

HN 1976
Easter Day
Designer: L. Harradine
Height: 7 1/4", 18.4 cm
Colour: White, lilac and
green
Issued: 1945-1951
Varieties: HN 2039

U.S.: $550.00
Can.: $700.00
Ster.: £250.00

HN 1977
Her Ladyship
Designer: L. Harradine
Height: 7 1/4", 18.4 cm
Colour: Red and cream
Issued: 1945-1959

U.S.: $400.00
Can.: $550.00
Ster.: £250.00

HN 1978
Bedtime
Style One
Designer: L. Harradine
Height: 5 3/4", 14.6 cm
Colour: White, black base
Issued: 1945 to the
present

U.S.: $ 95.00
Can.: $125.00
Ster.: £ 29.95

HN 1979
Gollywog
Designer: L. Harradine
Height: 5 1/4", 13.3 cm
Colour: Patterned white
dungarees
Issued: 1945-1959
Varieties: HN 2040

U.S.: $450.00
Can.: $600.00
Ster.: £250.00

HN 1980
Gwynneth
Designer: L. Harradine
Height: 7", 17.8 cm
Colour: Red
Issued: 1945-1952

U.S.: $450.00
Can.: $550.00
Ster.: £250.00

HN 1981
The Ermine Coat
Designer: L. Harradine
Height: 6 3/4", 17.2 cm
Colour: White and red
Issued: 1945-1967

U.S.: $350.00
Can.: $495.00
Ster.: £250.00

HN 1982
Sabbath Morn
Designer: L. Harradine
Height: 7 1/4", 18.4 cm
Colour: Red
Issued: 1945-1959

U.S.: $350.00
Can.: $495.00
Ster.: £250.00

HN 1983
Rosebud
Style Two
Designer: L. Harradine
Height: 7 1/2", 19.1 cm
Colour: Pink and red
Issued: 1945-1952

U.S.: $550.00
Can.: $625.00
Ster.: £300.00

HN 1984
The Patchwork Quilt
Designer: L. Harradine
Height: 6", 15.2 cm
Colour: Multi-coloured
Issued: 1945-1959

U.S.: $425.00
Can.: $575.00
Ster.: £300.00

HN 1985
Darling
Style Two
Designer: C. Vyse
Height: 5 1/4", 13.3 cm
Colour: White, black base
Issued: 1946 to the present

U.S.: $ 95.00
Can.: $125.00
Ster.: £ 29.95

HN 1986
Diana
Style One
Designer: L. Harradine
Height: 5 3/4", 14.6 cm
Colour: Red
Issued: 1946-1975
Varieties: HN 1716, 1717

U.S.: $200.00
Can.: $230.00
Ster.: £100.00

HN 1987
Paisley Shawl
Style One
Designer: L. Harradine
Height: 8 1/4", 21.0 cm
Colour: Red and cream
Issued: 1946-1959
Varieties: HN 1392, 1460, 1707, 1739

U.S.: $375.00
Can.: $500.00
Ster.: £180.00

HN 1988
Paisley Shawl
Style Two
Designer: L. Harradine
Height: 6 1/4", 15.9 cm
Colour: Red and pink
Issued: 1946-1975
Varieties: HN 1914

U.S.: $225.00
Can.: $325.00
Ster.: £180.00

HN 1989
Margaret
Style One
Designer: L. Harradine
Height: 7 1/4", 18.4 cm
Colour: Red and green
Issued: 1947-1959

U.S.:	$475.00
Can.:	$575.00
Ster.:	£200.00

HN 1990
Mary Jane
Designer: L. Harradine
Height: 7 1/2", 19.1 cm
Colour: Flowered pink dress
Issued: 1947-1952

U.S.:	$550.00
Can.:	$625.00
Ster.:	£300.00

HN 1991
Market Day
Designer: L. Harradine
Height: 7 1/4", 18.4 cm
Colour: Blue, pink and white
Issued: 1947-1955
Varieties: Also called "Country Lass" HN 1991A

U.S.:	$300.00
Can.:	$400.00
Ster.:	£120.00

HN 1991A
A Country Lass
Designer: L. Harradine
Height: 7 1/4", 18.4 cm
Colour: Blue, brown and white
Issued: 1975-1981
Varieties: Also called "Market Day" HN 1991

U.S.:	$175.00
Can.:	$295.00
Ster.:	£120.00

HN 1992
Christmas Morn
Designer: M. Davies
Height: 7", 17.8 cm
Colour: Red and white
Issued: 1947 to the present

U.S.:	$275.00
Can.:	$335.00
Ster.:	£109.00

HN 1993
Griselda
Designer: L. Harradine
Height: 5 3/4", 14.6 cm
Colour: Lavender and cream
Issued: 1947-1953

U.S.:	$475.00
Can.:	$550.00
Ster.:	£350.00

HN 1994
Karen
Style One
Designer: L. Harradine
Height: 8", 20.3 cm
Colour: Red
Issued: 1947-1955

U.S.:	$650.00
Can.:	$575.00
Ster.:	£350.00

HN 1995
Olivia
Style One
Designer: L. Harradine
Height: 7 1/2", 19.1 cm
Colour: Red and green
Issued: 1947-1951

U.S.:	$650.00
Can.:	$750.00
Ster.:	£400.00

HN 1996
Prue
Designer: L. Harradine
Height: 6 3/4", 17.2 cm
Colour: Red, white and black
Issued: 1947-1955

U.S.:	$500.00
Can.:	$550.00
Ster.:	£350.00

HN 1997
Belle o' the Ball
Designer: R. Asplin
Height: 6", 15.2 cm
Colour: Red and white
Issued: 1947-1979

U.S.:	$350.00
Can.:	$500.00
Ster.:	£250.00

HN 1998
Collinette
Designer: L. Harradine
Height: 7 1/4", 18.4 cm
Colour: Turquoise and cream
Issued: 1947-1949
Varieties: HN 1999

U.S.:	$850.00
Can.:	$975.00
Ster.:	£400.00

HN 1999
Collinette
Designer: L. Harradine
Height: 7 1/4", 18.4 cm
Colour: Red and cream
Issued: 1947-1949
Varieties: HN 1998

U.S.:	$750.00
Can.:	$775.00
Ster.:	£350.00

HN 2000
Jacqueline
Style One
Designer: L. Harradine
Height: 7 1/4", 18.4 cm
Colour: Lavender
Issued: 1947-1951
Varieties: HN 2001

U.S.:	$650.00
Can.:	$750.00
Ster.:	£300.00

HN 2001
Jacqueline
Style One
Designer: L. Harradine
Height: 7 1/4", 18.4 cm
Colour: Pink
Issued: 1947-1951
Varieties: HN 2000

U.S.:	$550.00
Can.:	$650.00
Ster.:	£250.00

HN 2002
Bess
Designer: L. Harradine
Height: 7 1/4", 18.4 cm
Colour: Red cloak, flowered cream dress
Issued: 1947-1969
Varieties: HN 2003

U.S.:	$350.00
Can.:	$525.00
Ster.:	£250.00

HN 2003
Bess
Designer: L. Harradine
Height: 7 1/4", 18.4 cm
Colour: Pink dress, purple cloak
Issued: 1947-1950
Varieties: HN 2002

U.S.:	$600.00
Can.:	$595.00
Ster.:	£300.00

HN 2004
A'Courting
Designer: L. Harradine
Height: 7 1/4", 18.4 cm
Colour: Red, black and grey
Issued: 1947-1953
U.S.: $500.00
Can.: $750.00
Ster.: £300.00

HN 2005
Henrietta Maria
Designer: M. Davies
Height: 9 1/2", 24.1 cm
Colour: Yellow and red
Issued: 1948-1953
Series: Period Figures in English History
U.S.: $700.00
Can.: $750.00
Ster.: £350.00

HN 2006
The Lady Anne Nevill
Designer: M. Davies
Height: 9 3/4", 24.7 cm
Colour: Purple and white
Issued: 1948-1953
Series: Period Figures in English History
U.S.: $950.00
Can.: $950.00
Ster.: £350.00

HN 2007
Mrs. Fitzherbert
Designer: M. Davies
Height: 9 1/4", 23.5 cm
Colour: Yellow and cream
Issued: 1948-1953
Series: Period Figures in English History
U.S.: $875.00
Can.: $750.00
Ster.: £350.00

HN 2008
Philippa of Hainault
Designer: M. Davies
Height: 9 3/4", 24.7 cm
Colour: Blue, brown and red
Issued: 1948-1953
Series: Period Figures in English History
U.S.: $775.00
Can.: $875.00
Ster.: £350.00

HN 2009
Eleanor of Provence
Designer: M. Davies
Height: 9 1/2", 24.1 cm
Colour: Purple and red
Issued: 1948-1953
Series: Period Figures in English History
U.S.: $775.00
Can.: $875.00
Ster.: £350.00

HN 2010
The Young Miss Nightingale
Designer: M. Davies
Height: 9 1/4", 23.5 cm
Colour: Red and green
Issued: 1948-1953
Series: Period Figures in English History
U.S.: $950.00
Can.: $950.00
Ster.: £350.00

HN 2011
Matilda
Designer: M. Davies
Height: 9 1/4", 23.5 cm
Colour: Red and purple
Issued: 1948-1953
Series: Period Figures in English History
U.S.: $700.00
Can.: $700.00
Ster.: £350.00

HN 2012
Margaret of Anjou
Designer: M. Davies
Height: 9 1/4", 23.5 cm
Colour: Green and yellow
Issued: 1948-1953
Series: Period Figures in
            English History

U.S.: $800.00
Can.: $900.00
Ster.:   £350.00

HN 2013
Angelina
Designer: L. Harradine
Height: 6 3/4", 17.1 cm
Colour: Red
Issued: 1948-1951

U.S.: $1,200.00
Can.: $1,200.00
Ster.:   £ 400.00

HN 2014
Jane
Style One
Designer: L. Harradine
Height: 6 1/4", 15.9 cm
Colour: Red and pink
Issued: 1948-1951

U.S.: $2,000.00
Can.: $2,000.00
Ster.:   £ 700.00

HN 2015
Sir Walter Raleigh
Designer: L. Harradine
Height: 11 1/2", 29.2 cm
Colour: Orange and
            purple
Issued: 1948-1955
Varieties: HN 1742, 1751

U.S.: $800.00
Can.: $900.00
Ster.:   £350.00

Earthenware

HN 2016
A Jester
Style One
Designer: C.J. Noke
Height: 10", 25.4 cm
Colour: Brown and mauve
Issued: 1949 to the present
Varieties: HN 45, 71, 71A,
            320, 367, 412, 426,
            446, 552, 616, 627,
            1295, 1702

U.S.: $395.00
Can.: $465.00
Ster.:   £149.00

HN 2017
Silks and Ribbons
Designer: L. Harradine
Height: 6", 15.2 cm
Colour: Green, red
            and white
Issued: 1949 to the
            present

U.S.: $225.00
Can.: $330.00
Ster.:   £ 99.95

HN 2018
The Parson's Daughter
Designer: H. Tittensor
Height: 9 3/4", 24.7 cm
Colour: Multi-coloured
Issued: 1949-1953
Varieties: HN 337, 338,
            441, 564, 790,
            1242, 1356

U.S.: $ 950.00
Can.: $1,000.00
Ster.:   £ 300.00

NOTE ON PRICING

Prices are given for three separate and distinct market areas:

Prices are given in the currency of each of these different trading areas.

Prices are not exchange rate calculations but are based on supply and demand in that market.

Prices listed are guidelines to the most current retail values but actual selling prices may vary slightly.

Prices for current figurines are those suggested by Royal Doulton.

Extremely rare or unique figurines have inconsistent retail values and their prices must therefore be determined between buyer and seller.

HN 2019
Minuet
Designer: M. Davies
Height: 7 1/4", 18.4 cm
Colour: Patterned
white dress
Issued: 1949-1971
Varieties: HN 2066

U.S.: $350.00
Can.: $450.00
Ster.: £250.00

HN 2020
Deidre
Designer: L. Harradine
Height: 7", 17.8 cm
Colour: Blue and pink
Issued: 1949-1955

U.S.: $550.00
Can.: $625.00
Ster.: £250.00

HN 2021
Blithe Morning
Designer: L. Harradine
Height: 7 1/4", 18.4 cm
Colour: Mauve and pink
Issued: 1949-1971
Varieties: HN 2065

U.S.: $275.00
Can.: $425.00
Ster.: £150.00

HN 2022
Janice
Designer: M. Davies
Height: 7 1/4", 18.4 cm
Colour: Green and
cream
Issued: 1949-1955
Varieties: HN 2165

U.S.: $650.00
Can.: $750.00
Ster.: £300.00

HN 2023
Joan
Style One
Designer: L. Harradine
Height: 5 3/4", 14.6 cm
Colour: Blue
Issued: 1949-1959
Varieties: HN 1422

U.S.: $300.00
Can.: $450.00
Ster.: £150.00

HN 2024
Darby
Designer: L. Harradine
Height: 5 3/4", 14.6 cm
Colour: Pink and blue
Issued: 1949-1959
Varieties: HN 1427

U.S.: $300.00
Can.: $450.00
Ster.: £150.00

HN 2025
Gossips
Designer: L. Harradine
Height: 5 1/2", 14.0 cm
Colour: Red and cream
Issued: 1949-1967
Varieties: HN 1426, 1429

U.S.: $500.00
Can.: $575.00
Ster.: £250.00

HN 2026
Suzette
Designer: L. Harradine
Height: 7 1/4", 18.4 cm
Colour: Flowered pink
dress
Issued: 1949-1959
Varieties: HN 1487, 1577,
1585, 1696

U.S.: $450.00
Can.: $500.00
Ster.: £250.00

HN 2027
June
Style One
Designer: L. Harradine
Height: 7 1/4", 18.4 cm
Colour: Yellow and pink
Issued: 1949-1952
Varieties: HN 1690, 1691,
             1947

U.S.:	$650.00
Can.:	$750.00
Ster.:	£350.00

HN 2028
Kate Hardcastle
Designer: L. Harradine
Height: 7 3/4", 19.7 cm
Colour: Green and red
Issued: 1949-1952
Varieties: HN 1718, 1719,
             1734, 1861, 1919

U.S.:	$700.00
Can.:	$900.00
Ster.:	£400.00

HN 2029
Windflower
Style One
Designer: L. Harradine
Height: 7 1/4", 18.4 cm
Colour: Pink
Issued: 1949-1952
Varieties: HN 1763, 1764

U.S.:	$600.00
Can.:	$750.00
Ster.:	£350.00

HN 2030
Memories
Designer: L. Harradine
Height: 6", 15.2 cm
Colour: Pink and green
Issued: 1949-1959
Varieties: HN 1855, 1856,
             1857

U.S.:	$575.00
Can.:	$600.00
Ster.:	£250.00

HN 2031
Granny's Heritage
Designer: L. Harradine
Height: 6 3/4", 17.2 cm
Colour: Lavender and
             green
Issued: 1949-1969
Varieties: HN 1873, 1874

U.S.:	$575.00
Can.:	$725.00
Ster.:	£300.00

HN 2032
Jean
Style One
Designer: L. Harradine
Height: 7 1/2", 19.1 cm
Colour: Green and red
Issued: 1949-1959
Varieties: HN 1877, 1878

U.S.:	$475.00
Can.:	$550.00
Ster.:	£250.00

HN 2033
Midsummer Noon
Designer: L. Harradine
Height: 4 3/4", 12.0 cm
Colour: Pink
Issued: 1949-1955
Varieties: HN 1899, 1900

U.S.:	$575.00
Can.:	$750.00
Ster.:	£300.00

HN 2034
Madonna of the Square
Designer: P. Stabler
Height: 7", 17.8 cm
Colour: Pale green
Issued: 1949-1951
Varieties: HN 10, 10A, 11,
             14, 27, 326, 573,
             576, 594, 613,
             764,1968, 1969

U.S.:	$ 950.00
Can.:	$1,100.00
Ster.:	£ 400.00

HN 2035
Pearly Boy
Style Two
Designer: L. Harradine
Height: 5 1/4", 13.3 cm
Colour: Reddish-brown
Issued: 1949-1959

U.S.: $200.00
Can.: $375.00
Ster.: £120.00

HN 2036
Pearly Girl
Style Two
Designer: L. Harradine
Height: 5 1/4", 13.3 cm
Colour: Reddish-brown
Issued: 1949-1959

U.S.: $200.00
Can.: $375.00
Ster.: £120.00

HN 2037
Goody Two Shoes
Designer: L. Harradine
Height: 5", 12.7 cm
Colour: Red and pink
Issued: 1949 to 1989
Varieties: HN 1889, 1905

U.S.: $140.00
Can.: $195.00
Ster.: £ 80.00

HN 2038
Peggy
Designer: L. Harradine
Height: 5", 12.7 cm
Colour: Red and white
Issued: 1949-1979
Varieties: HN 1941

U.S.: $140.00
Can.: $225.00
Ster.: £ 80.00

HN 2039
Easter Day
Designer: L. Harradine
Height: 7 1/4", 18.4 cm
Colour: Multi-coloured
Issued: 1949-1969
Varieties: HN 1976

U.S.: $400.00
Can.: $525.00
Ster.: £250.00

HN 2040
Gollywog
Designer: L. Harradine
Height: 5 1/4", 13.3 cm
Colour: Blue dungarees
Issued: 1949-1959
Varieties: HN 1979

U.S.: $350.00
Can.: $425.00
Ster.: £150.00

HN 2041
The Broken Lance
Designer: M. Davies
Height: 8 3/4", 22.2 cm
Colour: Blue, red and
yellow
Issued: 1949-1975

U.S.: $575.00
Can.: $850.00
Ster.: £300.00

HN 2042
Owd Willum
Designer: L. Harradine
Height: 6 3/4", 17.2 cm
Colour: Green and brown
Issued: 1949-1973

U.S.: $350.00
Can.: $495.00
Ster.: £180.00

"Harradine" incised on figurine.

HN 2043
The Poacher
Designer:	L. Harradine
Height:	6", 15.2 cm
Colour:	Black and brown
Issued:	1949-1959

U.S.:	**$400.00**
Can.:	**$495.00**
Ster.:	**£180.00**

HN 2044
Mary, Mary
Designer:	L. Harradine
Height:	5", 12.7 cm
Colour:	Pink
Issued:	1949-1973
Series:	Nursery Rhymes

U.S.:	**$250.00**
Can.:	**$250.00**
Ster.:	**£120.00**

HN 2045
She Loves Me Not
Designer:	L. Harradine
Height:	5 1/2", 14.0 cm
Colour:	Blue
Issued:	1949-1962
Series:	Nursery Rhymes

U.S.:	**$300.00**
Can.:	**$375.00**
Ster.:	**£120.00**

HN 2046
He Loves Me
Designer:	L. Harradine
Height:	5 1/2", 14.0 cm
Colour:	Flowered pink dress
Issued:	1949-1962
Series:	Nursery Rhymes

U.S.:	**$300.00**
Can.:	**$375.00**
Ster.:	**£120.00**

HN 2047
Once Upon a Time
Designer:	L. Harradine
Height:	4 1/4", 10.8 cm
Colour:	Pink dress with white spots
Issued:	1949-1955
Series:	Nursery Rhymes

U.S.:	**$450.00**
Can.:	**$450.00**
Ster.:	**£300.00**

HN 2048
Mary Had a Little Lamb
Designer:	M. Davies
Height:	3 1/2", 8.9 cm
Colour:	Lavender
Issued:	1949-1988
Series:	Nursery Rhymes

U.S.:	**$175.00**
Can.:	**$225.00**
Ster.:	**£120.00**

HN 2049
Curly Locks
Designer:	M. Davies
Height:	4 1/2", 11.4 cm
Colour:	Pink flowered dress
Issued:	1949-1953
Series:	Nursery Rhymes

U.S.:	**$450.00**
Can.:	**$525.00**
Ster.:	**£300.00**

HN 2050
Wee Willie Winkie
Style One
Designer:	M. Davies
Height:	5 1/4", 13.3 cm
Colour:	Blue
Issued:	1949-1953
Series:	Nursery Rhymes

U.S.:	**$350.00**
Can.:	**$350.00**
Ster.:	**£200.00**

HN 2051
St. George
Style Two
Designer: M. Davies
Height: 7 1/2", 19.1 cm
Colour: Green and white
Issued: 1950-1985

U.S.: $550.00
Can.: $725.00
Ster.: £300.00

HN 2052
Grandma
Designer: L. Harradine
Height: 6 3/4", 17.2 cm
Colour: Blue shawl with red and cream dress
Issued: 1950-1959
Varieties: HN 2052A

U.S.: $425.00
Can.: $550.00
Ster.: £200.00

Earthenware

HN 2052A
Grandma
Designer: L. Harradine
Height: 6 3/4", 17.2 cm
Colour: Brown shawl with red and cream dress
Issued: Unknown
Varieties: HN 2052

U.S.: $475.00
Can.: $550.00
Ster.: £200.00

Earthenware

HN 2053
The Gaffer
Designer: L. Harradine
Height: 7 3/4", 19.7 cm
Colour: Green and brown
Issued: 1950-1959

U.S.: $450.00
Can.: $650.00
Ster.: £200.00

Earthenware

HN 2054
Falstaff
Style Two
Designer: C.J. Noke
Height: 7", 17.8 cm
Colour: Brown
Issued: 1950 to the present
Varieties: HN 618

U.S.: $275.00
Can.: $335.00
Ster.: £ 95.95

Earthenware and China

HN 2055
The Leisure Hour
Designer: M. Davies
Height: 7", 17.8 cm
Colour: Green, yellow and brown
Issued: 1950-1965

U.S.: $500.00
Can.: $650.00
Ster.: £300.00

HN 2056
Susan
Style One
Designer: L. Harradine
Height: 7", 17.8 cm
Colour: Lavender dress with flowered apron
Issued: 1950-1959

U.S.: $500.00
Can.: $550.00
Ster.: £300.00

HN 2057
The Jersey Milkmaid
Designer: L. Harradine
Height: 6 1/2", 16.5 cm
Colour: Blue, white and red
Issued: 1950-1959
Varieties: Also called "The Milkmaid" HN 2057A

U.S.: $300.00
Can.: $375.00
Ster.: £200.00

HN 2057A
The Milkmaid
Designer: L. Harradine
Height: 6 1/2", 16.5 cm
Colour: Green, white
and brown
Issued: 1975-1981
Varieties: Also called
"Jersey Milkmaid"
HN 2057

U.S.: $200.00
Can.: $295.00
Ster.: £120.00

HN 2058
Hermione
Designer: M. Davies
Height: 7 3/4", 19.7 cm
Colour: Cream and
lavender
Issued: 1950-1952

U.S.: $1,850.00
Can.: $2,000.00
Ster.: £ 700.00

HN 2059
The Bedtime Story
Designer: L. Harradine
Height: 4 3/4", 12.0 cm
Colour: Pink, white,
yellow and blue
Issued: 1950 to the
present

U.S.: $395.00
Can.: $490.00
Ster.: £149.00

HN 2060
Jack
Designer: L. Harradine
Height: 5 1/2", 14.0 cm
Colour: Green, white
and black
Issued: 1950-1971
Series: Nursery Rhymes

U.S.: $225.00
Can.: $275.00
Ster.: £120.00

HN 2061
Jill
Designer: L. Harradine
Height: 5 1/2", 14.0 cm
Colour: Pink and white
Issued: 1950-1971
Series: Nursery Rhymes

U.S.: $225.00
Can.: $275.00
Ster.: £120.00

HN 2062
Little Boy Blue
Style One
Designer: L. Harradine
Height: 5 1/2", 14.0 cm
Colour: Blue
Issued: 1950-1973
Series: Nursery Rhymes

U.S.: $225.00
Can.: $250.00
Ster.: £120.00

HN 2063
Little Jack Horner
Style One
Designer: L. Harradine
Height: 4 1/2", 11.4 cm
Colour: Red and white
Issued: 1950-1953
Series: Nursery Rhymes

U.S.: $450.00
Can.: $525.00
Ster.: £300.00

HN 2064
My Pretty Maid
Designer: L. Harradine
Height: 5 1/2", 14.0 cm
Colour: Turquoise
Issued: 1950-1954
Series: Nursery Rhymes

U.S.: $450.00
Can.: $450.00
Ster.: £300.00

HN 2065
Blithe Morning
Designer: L. Harradine
Height: 7 1/4", 18.4 cm
Colour: Red
Issued: 1950-1973
Varieties: HN 2021

U.S.: $325.00
Can.: $395.00
Ster.: £120.00

HN 2066
Minuet
Designer: M. Davies
Height: 7 1/4", 18.4 cm
Colour: Red
Issued: 1950-1955
Varieties: HN 2019

U.S.: $950.00
Can.: $950.00
Ster.: £300.00

HN 2067
St. George
Style One
Designer: S. Thorogood
Height: 15 3/4", 40.0 cm
Colour: Multi-coloured
Issued: 1950-1979
Varieties: HN 385, 386,
1800; Fair and
dark hair

U.S.: $2,500.00
Can.: $2,500.00
Ster.: £ 700.00

HN 2068
Calumet
Designer: C.J. Noke
Height: 6 1/4", 15.9 cm
Colour: Green and brown
Issued: 1950-1953
Varieties: HN 1428, 1689

U.S.: $750.00
Can.: $850.00
Ster.: £450.00

Earthenware

HN 2069
Farmer's Wife
Style One
Designer: L. Harradine
Height: 9", 22.9 cm
Colour: Red, green
and brown
Issued: 1951-1955

U.S.: $600.00
Can.: $750.00
Ster.: £400.00

Earthenware

HN 2070
Bridget
Designer: L. Harradine
Height: 7 3/4", 19.7 cm
Colour: Green, brown
and lavender
Issued: 1951-197

U.S.: $350.00
Can.: $550.00
Ster.: £120.00

Earthenware

HN 2071
Bernice
Designer: M. Davies
Height: 7 3/4", 19.7 cm
Colour: Pink and red
Issued: 1951-1953

U.S.: $1,300.00
Can.: $1,300.00
Ster.: £ 600.00

HN 2072
The Rocking Horse
Designer: L. Harradine
Height: 7", 17.8 cm
Colour: Red, white, blue
and yellow
Issued: 1951-1953

U.S.: $2,500.00
Can.: $2,500.00
Ster.: £ 800.00

HN 2073
Vivienne
Designer: L. Harradine
Height: 7 3/4", 19.7 cm
Colour: Red
Issued: 1951-1967

U.S.: $350.00
Can.: $485.00
Ster.: £150.00

HN 2074
Marianne
Designer: L. Harradine
Height: 7 1/4", 18.4 cm
Colour: Red
Issued: 1951-1953

U.S.: $1,350.00
Can.: $1,350.00
Ster.: £ 600.00

HN 2075
French Peasant
Designer: L. Harradine
Height: 9 1/4", 23.5 cm
Colour: Brown and green
Issued: 1951-1955

U.S.: $600.00
Can.: $775.00
Ster.: £400.00

Earthenware

HN 2076
Promenade
Style One
Designer: M. Davies
Height: 8", 20.3 cm
Colour: Blue and
        orange
Issued: 1951-1953

U.S.: $2,000.00
Can.: $2,250.00
Ster.: £ 800.00

HN 2077
Rowena
Designer: L. Harradine
Height: 7 1/4", 18.4 cm
Colour: Red
Issued: 1951-1955

U.S.: $750.00
Can.: $850.00
Ster.: £400.00

HN 2078
Elfreda
Designer: L. Harradine
Height: 7 1/4", 18.4 cm
Colour: Red and purple
Issued: 1951-1955

U.S.: $900.00
Can.: $995.00
Ster.: £400.00

HN 2079
Damaris
Designer: M. Davies
Height: 7 1/4", 18.4 cm
Colour: Green, white
        and purple
Issued: 1951-1952

U.S.: $1,850.00
Can.: $1,850.00
Ster.: £ 650.00

HN 2080
Jack Point
Designer: C.J. Noke
Height: 16", 40.6 cm
Colour: Purple, green
        and lavender
Issued: 1952 to the
        present
Varieties: HN 85, 91, 99

U.S.: $2,900.00
Can.: $3,350.00
Ster.: £1.050.00

HN 2081
Princess Badoura
Designer: H. Tittensor, Harry
E. Stanton and F.
Van Allen Phillips
Height: 20", 50.8 cm
Colour: Multi-coloured
Issued: 1952 to the
present
U.S.: **$28,000.00**
Can.: **$33,000.00**
Ster.: **£10,750.00**

HN 2082
The Moor
Designer: C.J. Noke
Height: 16 1/4", 41.2 cm
Colour: Red and black
Issued: 1952 to the present
Varieties: HN 1308, 1366,
1425, 1657; also
called "An Arab"
HN 33, 343, 378
U.S.: **$2,500.00**
Can.: **$2,895.00**
Ster.: **£ 900.00**
*

HN 2084
King Charles
Designer: C.J. Noke
Height: 16", 40.6 cm
Colour: Black
Issued: 1952-1992
Varieties: HN 404
U.S.: **$2,500.00**
Can.: **$2,895.00**
Ster.: **£ 900.00**

HN 2085
Spring
Style Three
Designer: M. Davies
Height: 7 3/4", 19.6 cm
Colour: Lavender and
cream
Issued: 1952-1959
Series: The Seasons
(Style Two)
U.S.: **$575.00**
Can.: **$650.00**
Ster.: **£300.00**

HN 2086
Summer
Style Two
Designer: M. Davies
Height: 7 1/4", 18.4 cm
Colour: Red flowered
dress
Issued: 1952-1959
Series: The Seasons
(Style Two)
U.S.: **$575.00**
Can.: **$650.00**
Ster.: **£300.00**

HN 2087
Autumn
Style Two
Designer: M. Davies
Height: 7 1/4", 18.4 cm
Colour: Red and lavender
Issued: 1952-1959
Series: The Seasons
(Style Two)
U.S.: **$650.00**
Can.: **$725.00**
Ster.: **£300.00**

HN 2088
Winter
Style Two
Designer: M. Davies
Height: 6 1/4", 15.9 cm
Colour: Lavender, green
and red
Issued: 1952-1959
Series: The Seasons
(Style Two)
U.S.: **$575.00**
Can.: **$675.00**
Ster.: **£300.00**

HN 2089
Judith
Style One
Designer: L. Harradine
Height: 7", 17.8 cm
Colour: Red and blue
Issued: 1952-1959
U.S.: **$400.00**
Can.: **$650.00**
Ster.: **£200.00**

HN 2090
Midinette
Style Two
Designer: L. Harradine
Height: 7 1/4", 18.4 cm
Colour: Blue
Issued: 1952-1965

U.S.: $375.00
Can.: $495.00
Ster.: £200.00

HN 2091
Rosemary
Designer: L. Harradine
Height: 7", 17.8 cm
Colour: Red and blue
Issued: 1952-1959

U.S.: $550.00
Can.: $675.00
Ster.: £200.00

HN 2092
Sweet Maid
Style Two
Designer: L. Harradine
Height: 7", 17.8 cm
Colour: Lavender
Issued: 1952-1955

U.S.: $550.00
Can.: $625.00
Ster.: £300.00

HN 2093
Georgiana
Designer: M. Davies
Height: 8 1/4", 21.0 cm
Colour: Orange and blue
Issued: 1952-1955

U.S.: $1,500.00
Can.: $1,600.00
Ster.: £ 600.00

HN 2094
Uncle Ned
Designer: H. Fenton
Height: 6 3/4", 17.2 cm
Colour: Brown
Issued: 1952-1965

U.S.: $550.00
Can.: $650.00
Ster.: £180.00

Earthenware

HN 2095
Ibrahim
Designer: C.J. Noke
Height: 7 3/4", 19.7 cm
Colour: Brown and yellow
Issued: 1952-1955
Varieties: Also called
"The Emir"
HN 1604, 1605

U.S.: $700.00
Can.: $750.00
Ster.: £350.00

Earthenware

HN 2096
The Fat Boy
Style Three
Designer: L. Harradine
Height: 7 1/4", 18.4 cm
Colour: Blue and cream
Issued: 1952-1967
Series: Dickens

U.S.: $500.00
Can.: $450.00
Ster.: £200.00

Earthenware

HN 2097
Mr Micawber
Style Three
Designer: L. Harradine
Height: 7 1/2", 19.1 cm
Colour: Black and brown
Issued: 1952-1967
Series: Dickens

U.S.: $450.00
Can.: $450.00
Ster.: £200.00

Earthenware

HN 2098
Pecksniff
Style Three
Designer: L. Harradine
Height: 7 1/4", 18.4 cm
Colour: Black and brown
Issued: 1952-1967
Series: Dickens

U.S.:	$450.00
Can.:	$450.00
Ster.:	£200.00

Earthenware

HN 2099
Mr Pickwick
Style Three
Designer: L. Harradine
Height: 7 1/2", 19.1 cm
Colour: Blue and brown
Issued: 1952-1967
Series: Dickens

U.S.:	$500.00
Can.:	$450.00
Ster.:	£200.00

Earthenwae

HN 2100
Sairey Gamp
Style Three
Designer: L. Harradine
Height: 7 1/4", 18.4 cm
Colour: Green
Issued: 1952-1967
Series: Dickens

U.S.:	$550.00
Can.:	$450.00
Ster.:	£200.00

Earthenware

HN 2101
Uriah Heep
Style Three
Designer: L. Harradine
Height: 7 1/2", 19.1 cm
Colour: Black
Issued: 1952-1967
Series: Dickens

U.S.:	$450.00
Can.:	$450.00
Ster.:	£200.00

Earthenware

HN 2102
Pied Piper
Designer: L. Harradine
Height: 8 1/2", 21.6 cm
Colour: Black, red and yellow
Issued: 1953-1976
Varieties: HN 1215

U.S.:	$325.00
Can.:	$450.00
Ster.:	£150.00

HN 2103
Mask Seller
Designer: L. Harradine
Height: 8 1/2", 21.6 cm
Colour: Green and yellow
Issued: 1953 to the present
Varieties: HN 1361

U.S.:	$325.00
Can.:	$415.00
Ster.:	£119.00

Earthenware

HN 2104
Abdullah
Designer: L. Harradine
Height: 6", 15.2 cm
Colour: Multi-coloured
Issued: 1953-1962
Varieties: HN 1410

U.S.:	$575.00
Can.:	$775.00
Ster.:	£250.00

HN 2105
Bluebeard
Style Two
Designer: L. Harradine
Height: 11", 27.9 cm
Colour: Purple, green and brown
Issued: 1953-1992
Varieties: HN 1528

U.S.:	$695.00
Can.:	$835.00
Ster.:	£225.00

HN 2106
Linda
Style One
Designer: L. Harradine
Height: 4 3/4", 12.0 cm
Colour: Red
Issued: 1953-1976

U.S.:   **$175.00**
Can.:   **$250.00**
Ster.:   **£120.00**

HN 2107
Valerie
Designer: M. Davies
Height: 4 3/4", 12.0 cm
Colour: Red, pink
                 and white
Issued: 1953 to the
                 present

U.S.:   **$185.00**
Can.:   **$220.00**
Ster.:   **£ 65.00**

HN 2108
Baby Bunting
Designer: M. Davies
Height: 5 1/4", 13.3 cm
Colour: Brown and
                 cream
Issued: 1953-1959

U.S.:   **$325.00**
Can.:   **$395.00**
Ster.:   **£180.00**

HN 2109
Wendy
Designer: L. Harradine
Height: 5", 12.7 cm
Colour: Blue
Issued: 1953 to the
                 present

U.S.:   **$125.00**
Can.:   **$165.00**
Ster.:   **£ 49.95**

HN 2110
Christmas Time
Designer: M. Davies
Height: 6 1/2", 16.5 cm
Colour: Red with white
                 frills
Issued: 1953-1967

U.S.:   **$600.00**
Can.:   **$675.00**
Ster.:   **£250.00**

HN 2111
Betsy
Designer: L. Harradine
Height: 7", 17.8 cm
Colour: Lavender with
                 flowered apron
Issued: 1953-1959

U.S.:   **$450.00**
Can.:   **$595.00**
Ster.:   **£250.00**

HN 2112
Carolyn
Style One
Designer: L. Harradine
Height: 7", 17.8 cm
Colour: White and green
                 flowered dress
Issued: 1953-1965

U.S.:   **$400.00**
Can.:   **$535.00**
Ster.:   **£225.00**

HN 2113
Maytime
Designer: L. Harradine
Height: 7", 17.8 cm
Colour: Pink dress
                 with blue scarf
Issued: 1953-1967

U.S.:   **$400.00**
Can.:   **$550.00**
Ster.:   **£250.00**

HN 2114
Sleepyhead
Designer: M. Davies
Height: 5", 12.7 cm
Colour: Orange, blue
and white
Issued: 1953-1955

U.S.: $1,200.00
Can.: $1,350.00
Ster.: £ 500.00

HN 2115
Coppelia
Designer: M. Davies
Height: 7 1/4", 18.4 cm
Colour: Blue, red
and white
Issued: 1953-1959

U.S.: $700.00
Can.: $825.00
Ster.: £450.00

HN 2116
Ballerina
Style One
Designer: M. Davies
Height: 7 1/4", 18.4 cm
Colour: Lavender
Issued: 1953-1973

U.S.: $425.00
Can.: $500.00
Ster.: £250.00

HN 2117
The Skater
Style One
Designer: M. Davies
Height: 7 1/4", 18.4 cm
Colour: Red, white
and brown
Issued: 1953-1971

U.S.: $475.00
Can.: $550.00
Ster.: £250.00

HN 2118
Good King Wenceslas
Designer: M. Davies
Height: 8 1/2", 21.6 cm
Colour: Brown and purple
Issued: 1953-1976

U.S.: $450.00
Can.: $575.00
Ster.: £180.00

Earthenware

HN 2119
Town Crier
Designer: M. Davies
Height: 8 1/2", 21.6 cm
Colour: Purple, green
and yellow
Issued: 1953-1976

U.S.: $375.00
Can.: $485.00
Ster.: £180.00

Earthenware

HN 2120
Dinky Doo
Designer: L. Harradine
Height: 4 3/4" 12.0 cm
Colour: Red
Issued: 1983 to the
present
Varieties: HN 1678

U.S.: $110.00
Can.: $150.00
Ster.: £ 39.95

HN 2121
Babie
Designer: L. Harradine
Height: 4 3/4", 12.0 cm
Colour: Pink
Issued: 1983-1992
Varieties: HN 1679, 1842

U.S.: $150.00
Can.: $175.00
Ster.: £ 49.95

HN 2122
Yeoman of the Guard
Designer: L. Harradine
Height: 5 3/4", 14.6 cm
Colour: Red, gold
and brown
Issued: 1954-1959
Varieties: HN 688

U.S.:	**$900.00**
Can.:	**$900.00**
Ster.:	**£450.00**

HN 2123
Rose
Designer: L. Harradine
Height: 4 1/2", 11.4 cm
Colour: Lavender
Issued: 1983 to the
present
Varieties: HN 1368, 1387,
1416, 1506, 1654

U.S.:	**$110.00**
Can.:	**$150.00**
Ster.:	**£ 43.00**

*

HN 2125
This Little Pig
Designer: L. Harradine
Height: 4", 10.1 cm
Colour: White
Issued: 1984 to the
present
Varieties: HN 1793, 1794

U.S.:	**$ 95.00**
Can.:	**$110.00**
Ster.:	**£ 29.95**

HN 2126
Top o' The Hill
Designer: P. Gee
Height: 4", 10.1 cm
Colour: Green and
mauve
Issued: 1988-1988
Series: RDICC and
Miniatures

U.S.:	**$140.00**
Can.:	**$225.00**
Ster.:	**£150.00**

Issued for Australian Bicentary

HN 2127
Top o' The Hill
Designer: L. Harradine
Height: 7", 17.8 cm
Colour: Gold
Issued: 1986-1986
Series: RDICC
Varieties: HN 1833, 1834,
1849

U.S.:	**$325.00**
Can.:	**$375.00**
Ster.:	**£150.00**

HN 2128
River Boy
Designer: M. Davies
Height: 4", 10.1 cm
Colour: Blue and green
Issued: 1962-1975

U.S.:	**$225.00**
Can.:	**$250.00**
Ster.:	**£150.00**

HN2129
The Old Balloon Seller
Designer: L. Harradine
Height: 3 1/2", 8.9 cm
Colour: Green and white
Issued: 1989-1992
Series: Miniatures

U.S.:	**$150.00**
Can.:	**$210.00**
Ster.:	**£ 65.00**

HN2130
The Balloon Seller
Designer: L. Harradine
Height: 3 3/4", 8.9 cm
Colour: Green and
cream
Issued: 1989-1992
Series: Miniatures

U.S.:	**$140.00**
Can.:	**$210.00**
Ster.:	**£ 49.95**

HN 2131
Autumn Breezes
Designer: L. Harradine
Height: 7 1/2", 19.1 cm
Colour: Orange, yellow and black
Issued: 1990 to the present
Varieties: HN1911, 1913, 1934, 2147

U.S.: $275.00
Can.: $360.00
Ster.: £109.00

HN 2132
The Suitor
Designer: M. Davies
Height: 7 1/4", 18.4 cm
Colour: Green, yellow and blue
Issued: 1962-1971

U.S.: $400.00
Can.: $650.00
Ster.: £250.00

HN 2133
Faraway
Designer: M. Davies
Height: 2 1/2", 6.3 cm
Colour: Blue and white
Issued: 1958-1962
Series: Teenagers

U.S.: $450.00
Can.: $575.00
Ster.: £200.00

HN 2134
An Old King
Designer: C.J. Noke
Height: 10 3/4", 27.3 cm
Colour: Purple, red, green and brown
Issued: 1954 to the present
Varieties: HN 358, 623, 1801

U.S.: $ 675.00
Can.: $1,050.00
Ster.: £ 315.00

HN 2135
Gay Morning
Designer: M. Davies
Height: 7", 17.8 cm
Colour: Pink
Issued: 1954-1967

U.S.: $400.00
Can.: $450.00
Ster.: £150.00

HN 2136
Delphine
Designer: M. Davies
Height: 7 1/4", 18.4 cm
Colour: Blue and lavender
Issued: 1954-1967

U.S.: $350.00
Can.: $495.00
Ster.: £150.00

HN 2137
Lilac Time
Designer: M. Davies
Height: 7 1/4", 18.4 cm
Colour: Red
Issued: 1954-1969

U.S.: $400.00
Can.: $485.00
Ster.: £150.00

HN 2138
La Sylphide
Designer: M. Davies
Height: 7", 17.8 cm
Colour: White
Issued: 1954-1965

U.S.: $550.00
Can.: $625.00
Ster.: £300.00

HN 2139
Giselle
Designer: M. Davies
Height: 6", 15.2 cm
Colour: Blue and white
Issued: 1954-1969

U.S.: $525.00
Can.: $600.00
Ster.: £300.00

HN 2140
Giselle, The Forest Glade
Designer: M. Davies
Height: 7", 17.8 cm
Colour: White and blue
Issued: 1954-1965

U.S.: $525.00
Can.: $600.00
Ster.: £300.00

HN 2141
Choir Boy
Designer: M. Davies
Height: 4 3/4", 12.0 cm
Colour: White and red
Issued: 1954-1975

U.S.: $175.00
Can.: $225.00
Ster.: £ 80.00

HN 2142
Rag Doll
Designer: M. Davies
Height: 4 3/4", 12.0 cm
Colour: White, blue
         and red
Issued: 1954-1986

U.S.: $125.00
Can.: $175.00
Ster.: £ 60.00

HN 2143
Friar Tuck
Designer: M. Davies
Height: 7 1/2", 19.1 cm
Colour: Brown
Issued: 1954-1965

U.S.: $550.00
Can.: $695.00
Ster.: £450.00

Earthenware

HN 2144
The Jovial Monk
Designer: M. Davies
Height: 7 3/4", 19.7 cm
Colour: Brown
Issued: 1954-1976

U.S.: $275.00
Can.: $400.00
Ster.: £120.00

Earthenware

HN 2145
Wardrobe Mistress
Designer: M. Davies
Height: 5 3/4", 14.6 cm
Colour: Green, red,
         white and blue
Issued: 1954-1967

U.S.: $625.00
Can.: $750.00
Ster.: £350.00

Earthenware

HN 2146
The Tinsmith
Designer: M. Nicoll
Height: 6 1/2", 16.5 cm
Colour: Green and brown
Issued: 1962-1967

U.S.: $525.00
Can.: $750.00
Ster.: £350.00

HN 2147
Autumn Breezes
Designer: L. Harradine
Height: 7 1/2", 19.1 cm
Colour: Black and white
Issued: 1955-1971
Varieties: HN 1911, 1913,
1934, 2131

U.S.: $425.00
Can.: $525.00
Ster.: £250.00

HN 2148
The Bridesmaid
Style Two
Designer: M. Davies
Height: 5 1/2", 14.0 cm
Colour: Yellow
Issued: 1955-1959

U.S.: $225.00
Can.: $275.00
Ster.: £250.00

HN 2149
Love Letter
Style One
Designer: M. Davies
Height: 5 1/2", 14.0 cm
Colour: Pink and blue
Issued: 1958-1976

U.S.: $500.00
Can.: $575.00
Ster.: £250.00

HN 2150
Willy-Won't-He
Designer: L. Harradine
Height: 5 1/2", 14.0 cm
Colour: Red, green,
blue and white
Issued: 1955-1959
Varieties: HN 1561, 1584

U.S.: $400.00
Can.: $600.00
Ster.: £200.00

HN 2151
Mother's Help
Designer: M. Davies
Height: 5", 12.7 cm
Colour: Black and white
Issued: 1962-1969

U.S.: $225.00
Can.: $350.00
Ster.: £120.00

HN 2152
Adrienne
Designer: M. Davies
Height: 7 1/2", 19.1 cm
Colour: Purple
Issued: 1964-1976
Varieties: HN 2304, also
called "Joan"
HN 3217

U.S.: $200.00
Can.: $325.00
Ster.: £120.00

HN 2153
The One That Got Away
Designer: M. Davies
Height: 6 1/4", 15.9 cm
Colour: Brown
Issued: 1955-1959

U.S.: $400.00
Can.: $450.00
Ster.: £300.00

HN 2154
A Child From Williamsburg
Designer: M. Davies
Height: 5 1/2", 14.0 cm
Colour: Blur
Issued: 1964-1983
Series: Figures of
Williamsburg

U.S.: $200.00
Can.: $245.00
Ster.: £100.00

HN 2155
Kay
Designer:	M. Davies
Height:	8", 20.3 cm
Colour:	Dark blue and white
Issued:	1991-1991
Variations:	Also called "Fair Lady"
U.S.:	$225.00
Can.:	$275.00
Ster.:	£125.00

Issued by American Express

HN 2156
The Polka
Designer:	M. Davies
Height:	7 1/2", 19.1 cm
Colour:	Pink
Issued:	1955-1969
U.S.:	$425.00
Can.:	$485.00
Ster.:	£200.00

HN 2157
A Gypsy Dance
Style One
Designer:	M. Davies
Height:	7", 17.8 cm
Colour:	Lavender
Issued:	1955-1957
U.S.:	$1,000.00
Can.:	$ 750.00
Ster.:	£ 350.00

HN 2158
Alice
Style One
Designer:	M. Davies
Height:	5", 12.7 cm
Colour:	Blue
Issued:	1960-1981
U.S.:	$185.00
Can.:	$250.00
Ster.:	£100.00

HN 2159
Fortune Teller
Designer:	L. Harradine
Height:	6 1/2", 16.5 cm
Colour:	Green and brown
Issued:	1955-1967
U.S.:	$550.00
Can.:	$650.00
Ster.:	£300.00

Earthenware

HN 2160
The Apple Maid
Designer:	L. Harradine
Height:	6 1/2", 16.5 cm
Colour:	Blue, black and white
Issued:	1957-1962
U.S.:	$500.00
Can.:	$650.00
Ster.:	£300.00

HN 2161
The Hornpipe
Designer:	M. Nicoll
Height:	9 1/4", 23.5 cm
Colour:	Blue and white
Issued:	1955-1962
U.S.:	$800.00
Can.:	$950.00
Ster.:	£400.00

Earthenware

HN 2162
The Foaming Quart
Designer:	M. Davies
Height:	6", 15.2 cm
Colour:	Brown
Issued:	1955-1992
U.S.:	$300.00
Can.:	$395.00
Ster.:	£109.00

HN 2163
In The Stocks
Style Two
Designer: M. Nicoll
Height: 5 3/4", 14.6 cm
Colour: Red, brown
and black
Issued: 1955-1959

U.S.:	$800.00
Can.:	$850.00
Ster.:	£400.00

*

HN 2165
Janice
Designer: M. Davies
Height: 7 1/4", 18.4 cm
Colour: Black and pale
blue
Issued: 1955-1965
Varieties: HN 2022

U.S.:	$600.00
Can.:	$795.00
Ster.:	£300.00

HN 2166
The Bride
Style Two
Designer: M. Davies
Height: 8", 20.3 cm
Colour: Pink
Issued: 1956-1976

U.S.:	$225.00
Can.:	$450.00
Ster.:	£150.00

HN 2167
Home Again
Designer: M. Davies
Height: 3 1/4", 8.3 cm
Colour: Red and white
Issued: 1956 to the
present

U.S.:	$195.00
Can.:	$255.00
Ster.:	£ 69.95

HN 2168
Esmeralda
Designer: M. Davies
Height: 5 1/2", 14.0 cm
Colour: Yellow and red
Issued: 1956-1959

U.S.:	$500.00
Can.:	$575.00
Ster.:	£180.00

HN 2169
Dimity
Designer: L. Harradine
Height: 5 3/4", 14.6 cm
Colour: Green, lavender
and cream
Issued: 1956-1959

U.S.:	$450.00
Can.:	$475.00
Ster.:	£180.00

HN 2170
Invitation
Designer: M. Davies
Height: 5 1/2", 14.0 cm
Colour: Pink
Issued: 1956-1975

U.S.:	$200.00
Can.:	$350.00
Ster.:	£120.00

HN 2171
The Fiddler
Designer: M. Nicoll
Height: 8 3/4", 22.2 cm
Colour: Green, cream
and red
Issued: 1956-1962

U.S.:	$1,000.00
Can.:	$1,150.00
Ster.:	£ 400.00

Earthenware

HN 2172
Jolly Sailor
Designer: M. Nicoll
Height: 6 1/2", 16.5 cm
Colour: Black, brown,
blue and white
Issued: 1956-1965

U.S.: $700.00
Can.: $850.00
Ster.: £400.00

Earthenware

HN 2173
The Organ Grinder
Designer: M. Nicoll
Height: 8 3/4", 22.2 cm
Colour: Green, cream
and brown
Issued: 1956-1965

U.S.: $ 900.00
Can.: $1,000.00
Ster.: £ 400.00

Earthenware

HN 2174
The Tailor
Designer: M. Nicoll
Height: 5", 12.7 cm
Colour: Blue, cream
and Orange
Issued: 1956-1959

U.S.: $ 900.00
Can.: $1,000.00
Ster.: £ 400.00

Earthenware

HN 2175
The Beggar
Style Two
Designer: L. Harradine
Height: 6 3/4", 17.2 cm
Colour: Green
Issued: 1956-1962
Series: Beggar's Opera

U.S.: $500.00
Can.: $600.00
Ster.: £300.00

Earthenware

HN 2176
Autumn Breezes
Designer: L. Harradine
Height: 3 1/2", 8.9 cm
Colour: Red
Issued: 1991 to the
present
Series: Miniatures
Variations: HN2180

U.S.: $125.00
Can.: $175.00
Ster.: £ 49.95

HN 2177
My Teddy
Designer: M. Davies
Height: 3 1/4", 8.3 cm
Colour: Turquoise
and brown
Issued: 1962-1967

U.S.: $500.00
Can.: $550.00
Ster.: £300.00

HN 2178
Enchantment
Designer: M. Davies
Height: 7 1/2", 19.1 cm
Colour: Blue
Issued: 1957-1982

U.S.: $225.00
Can.: $300.00
Ster.: £100.00

HN 2179
Noelle
Designer: M. Davies
Height: 6 3/4", 17.2 cm
Colour: Orange, white
and black
Issued: 1957-1967

U.S.: $525.00
Can.: $750.00
Ster.: £200.00

HN 2180
Autumn Breezes
Designer: L. Harradine
Height: 3 1/2", 8.9 cm
Colour: Red, lavender, 22kt gold trim
Issued: 1991
Series: M. Doulton Signature Collection

U.S.: $125.00
Can.: $150.00
Ster.: £ 65.00

HN 2181
Summer's Day
Style One
Designer: M. Davies
Height: 5 3/4", 14.6 cm
Colour: White
Issued: 1957-1962

U.S.: $400.00
Can.: $500.00
Ster.: £200.00

*

HN 2183
Boy from Williamsburg
Designer: M. Davies
Height: 5 1/2", 14.0 cm
Colour: Blue and pink
Issued: 1969-1983
Series: Figures of Williamsburg

U.S.: $185.00
Can.: $250.00
Ster.: £100.00

HN 2184
Sunday Morning
Designer: M. Davies
Height: 7 1/2", 19.1 cm
Colour: Red and brown
Issued: 1963-1969

U.S.: $385.00
Can.: $425.00
Ster.: £200.00

HN 2185
Columbine
Style Two
Designer: M. Davies
Height: 7", 17.8 cm
Colour: Pink
Issued: 1957-1969
Series: Teenagers

U.S.: $300.00
Can.: $375.00
Ster.: £200.00

HN 2186
Harlequin
Style One
Designer: M. Davies
Height: 7 1/4", 18.4 cm
Colour: Blue
Issued: 1957-1969
Series: Teenagers

U.S.: $300.00
Can.: $375.00
Ster.: £200.00

*

HN 2191
Sea Sprite
Style Two
Designer: M. Davies
Height: 7", 17.8 cm
Colour: Pink and blue
Issued: 1958-1962
Series: Teenagers

U.S.: $325.00
Can.: $475.00
Ster.: £200.00

HN 2192
Wood Nymph
Designer: M. Davies
Height: 7 1/4", 18.4 cm
Colour: Blue and white
Issued: 1958-1962
Series: Teenagers

U.S.: $325.00
Can.: $450.00
Ster.: £200.00

HN 2193
Fair Lady
Designer: M. Davies
Height: 7 1/4", 18.4 cm
Colour: Green
Issued: 1963 to the
present
Varieties: HN 2832, 2835

U.S.: $275.00
Can.: $335.00
Ster.: £ 99.95

*

HN 2196
The Bridesmaid
Style Three
Designer: M. Davies
Height: 5 1/4", 13.3 cm
Colour: Pale blue
Issued: 1960-1976

U.S.: $135.00
Can.: $200.00
Ster.: £ 80.00

HN 2197
Olivia
Style Two
Designer: M. Davies
Height: 8", 20.3 cm
Colour: Rose and white
Issued: 1991-1991
Varieties: Also called
"Ninette" HN 2379,
3417

U.S.: $275.00
Can.: $360.00
Ster.: £130.00

*

HN 2202
Melody
Designer: M. Davies
Height: 6 1/4", 15.9 cm
Colour: Blue and peach
Issued: 1957-1962
Series: Teenagers

U.S.: $350.00
Can.: $450.00
Ster.: £180.00

HN 2203
Teenager
Designer: M. Davies
Height: 7 1/4", 18.4 cm
Colour: Orange and
white
Issued: 1957-1962
Series: Teenagers

U.S.: $300.00
Can.: $450.00
Ster.: £200.00

HN 2204
Long John Silver
Designer: M. Nicoll
Height: 9", 22.9 cm
Colour: Green, black
and white
Issued: 1957-1965

U.S.: $575.00
Can.: $750.00
Ster.: £400.00

Earthenware

HN 2205
Master Sweep
Designer: M. Nicoll
Height: 8 1/2", 21.6 cm
Colour: Green, black
and brown
Issued: 1957-1962

U.S.: $750.00
Can.: $850.00
Ster.: £400.00

Earthenware

HN 2206
Sunday Best
Designer: M. Davies
Height: 7 1/2", 19.1 cm
Colour: Yellow
Issued: 1979-1984
Varieties: HN 2698

U.S.: $250.00
Can.: $350.00
Ster.: £100.00

HN 2207
Stayed at Home
Designer: M. Davies
Height: 5", 12.7 cm
Colour: Green and white
Issued: 1958-1969

U.S.: $225.00
Can.: $350.00
Ster.: £100.00

HN 2208
Silversmith of Williamsburg
Designer: M. Davies
Height: 6 1/4", 15.9 cm
Colour: Blue, white and brown
Issued: 1960-1983
Series: Figures of Williamsburg

U.S.: $200.00
Can.: $295.00
Ster.: £100.00

HN 2209
Hostess of Williamsburg
Designer: M. Davies
Height: 7 1/4", 18.4 cm
Colour: Pink
Issued: 1960-1983
Series: Figures of Williamsburg

U.S.: $250.00
Can.: $295.00
Ster.: £100.00

HN 2210
Debutante
Style One
Designer: M. Davies
Height: 5", 12.7 cm
Colour: Blue
Issued: 1963-1967

U.S.: $375.00
Can.: $550.00
Ster.: £180.00

HN 2211
Fair Maiden
Designer: M. Davies
Height: 5 1/4", 13.3 cm
Colour: Green
Issued: 1967 to the present
Varieties: HN 2434

U.S.: $195.00
Can.: $225.00
Ster.: £ 65.00

HN 2212
Rendezvous
Designer: M. Davies
Height: 7 1/4", 18.4 cm
Colour: Red and white
Issued: 1962-1971

U.S.: $450.00
Can.: $575.00
Ster.: £250.00

HN 2213
Contemplation
Designer: M. Davies
Height: 12", 30.5 cm
Colour: White
Issued: 1982-1986
Varieties: HN 2241
Series: Images

U.S.: $225.00
Can.: $250.00
Ster.: £100.00

HN 2214
Bunny
Designer: M. Davies
Height: 5", 12.7 cm
Colour: Turquoise
Issued: 1960-1975

U.S.: $225.00
Can.: $250.00
Ster.: £100.00

HN 2215
Sweet April
Designer: M. Davies
Height: 7 1/4", 18.4 cm
Colour: Pink
Issued: 1965-1967

U.S.: $525.00
Can.: $525.00
Ster.: £200.00

HN 2216
Pirouette
Designer: M. Davies
Height: 5 3/4", 14.6 cm
Colour: Pale blue
Issued: 1959-1967

U.S.: $225.00
Can.: $450.00
Ster.: £180.00

HN 2217
Old King Cole
Designer: M. Davies
Height: 6 1/2", 16.5 cm
Colour: Brown, yellow
           and white
Issued: 1963-1967

U.S.: $700.00
Can.: $800.00
Ster.: £450.00

HN 2218
Cookie
Designer: M. Davies
Height: 4 3/4", 12.0 cm
Colour: Pink and white
Issued: 1958-1975

U.S.: $235.00
Can.: $285.00
Ster.: £120.00

*

HN 2220
Winsome
Designer: M. Davies
Height: 8", 20.3 cm
Colour: Red
Issued: 1960-1985

U.S.: $235.00
Can.: $325.00
Ster.: £100.00

HN 2221
Nanny
Designer: M. Nicoll
Height: 6", 15.2 cm
Colour: Blue and white
Issued: 1958-1991

U.S.: $275.00
Can.: $350.00
Ster.: £100.00

Earthenware

HN 2222
Camellia
Designer: M. Davies
Height: 7 3/4", 19.7 cm
Colour: Pink
Issued: 1960-1971

U.S.: $275.00
Can.: $450.00
Ster.: £120.00

HN 2223
Schoolmarm
Designer: M. Davies
Height: 6 3/4", 17.2 cm
Colour: Purple, grey
           and brown
Issued: 1958-1981

U.S.: $275.00
Can.: $395.00
Ster.: £120.00

HN 2224
Make Believe
Designer: M. Nicoll
Height: 5 3/4", 14.6 cm
Colour: White
Issued: 1984-1988
Varieties: HN 2225

U.S.:	$160.00
Can.:	$200.00
Ster.:	£ 80.00

HN 2225
Make Believe
Designer: M. Nicoll
Height: 5 3/4", 14.6 cm
Colour: Blue
Issued: 1962-1988
Varieties: HN 2224

U.S.:	$140.00
Can.:	$250.00
Ster.:	£ 80.00

HN 2226
The Cellist
Designer: M. Nicoll
Height: 8", 20.3 cm
Colour: Black and brown
Issued: 1960-1967

U.S.:	$500.00
Can.:	$750.00
Ster.:	£400.00

HN 2227
Gentleman from Williamsburg
Designer: M. Davies
Height: 6 1/4", 15.9 cm
Colour: Green and white
Issued: 1960-1983
Series: Figures of Williamsburg

U.S.:	$225.00
Can.:	$350.00
Ster.:	£100.00

HN 2228
Lady from Williamsburg
Designer: M. Davies
Height: 6", 15.2 cm
Colour: Green
Issued: 1960-1983
Series: Figures of Williamsburg

U.S.:	$225.00
Can.:	$375.00
Ster.:	£100.00

HN 2229
Southern Belle
Designer: M. Davies
Height: 7 1/2", 19.1 cm
Colour: Red and cream
Issued: 1958 to the present
Varieties: HN 2425

U.S.:	$375.00
Can.:	$445.00
Ster.:	£109.00

HN 2230
A Gypsy Dance
Style Two
Designer: M. Davies
Height: 7", 17.8 cm
Colour: Lavender
Issued: 1959-1971

U.S.:	$375.00
Can.:	$550.00
Ster.:	£180.00

HN 2231
Sweet Sixteen
Designer: M. Davies
Height: 7 1/4", 18.4 cm
Colour: Blue and white
Issued: 1958-1965
Series: Teenagers

U.S.:	$300.00
Can.:	$400.00
Ster.:	£200.00

*

HN 2233
Royal Governor's Cook
Designer: M. Davies
Height: 6", 15.2 cm
Colour: Dark blue, white and brown
Issued: 1960-1983
Series: Figures of Williamsburg

U.S.: $500.00
Can.: $650.00
Ster.: £180.00

HN 2234
Michele
Designer: M. Davies
Height: 7", 17.8 cm
Colour: Green
Issued: 1967 to the present

U.S.: $275.00
Can.: $335.00
Ster.: £ 99.95

HN 2235
Dancing Years
Designer: M. Davies
Height: 6 3/4", 17.2 cm
Colour: Lavender
Issued: 1965-1971

U.S.: $400.00
Can.: $550.00
Ster.: £250.00

HN 2236
Affection
Designer: M. Davies
Height: 4 1/2", 11.4 cm
Colour: Purple
Issued: 1962 to the present

U.S.: $185.00
Can.: $245.00
Ster.: £ 69.95

HN 2237
Celeste
Style One
Designer: M. Davies
Colour: Pale blue
Height: 6 3/4", 17.2 cm
Issued: 1959-1971

U.S.: $250.00
Can.: $395.00
Ster.: £120.00

HN 2238
My Pet
Designer: M. Davies
Height: 2 3/4", 7.0 cm
Colour: Blue and white
Issued: 1962-1975

U.S.: $200.00
Can.: $250.00
Ster.: £100.00

HN 2239
Wigmaker of Williamsburg
Designer: M. Davies
Height: 7 1/2", 19.1 cm
Colour: White and brown
Issued: 1960-1983
Series: Figures of Williamsburg

U.S.: $200.00
Can.: $375.00
Ster.: £100.00

HN 2240
Blacksmith of Willliamsburg
Designer: M. Davies
Height: 6 3/4", 17.2 cm
Colour: Grey and white
Issued: 1960-1983
Series: Figures of Williamsburg

U.S.: $200.00
Can.: $295.00
Ster.: £100.00

HN 2241
Contemplation
Designer: M. Davies
Height: 12", 30.5 cm
Colour: Black
Issued: 1982-1986
Varieties: HN 2213
Series: Images

U.S.: $225.00
Can.: $250.00
Ster.: £100.00

HN 2242
First Steps
Style One
Designer: M. Davies
Height: 6 1/2", 16.5 cm
Colour: Blue and yellow
Issued: 1959-1965

U.S.: $600.00
Can.: $725.00
Ster.: £300.00

HN 2243
Treasure Island
Designer: M. Davies
Height: 4 3/4", 12.0 cm
Colour: Blue and yellow
Issued: 1962-1975

U.S.: $275.00
Can.: $275.00
Ster.: £120.00

HN 2244
Newsboy
Designer: M. Nicoll
Height: 8 1/2, 21.6 cm
Colour: Green, brown and blue
Issued: 1959-1965
Varieties: Limited edition of 250 for Evening Sentinel

U.S.: $650.00
Can.: $750.00
Ster.: £300.00

HN 2245
The Basket Weaver
Designer: M. Nicoll
Height: 5 3/4", 14.6 cm
Colour: Pale blue and yellow
Issued: 1959-1962

U.S.: $500.00
Can.: $625.00
Ster.: £300.00

HN 2246
Cradle Song
Designer: M. Davies
Height: 5 1/2", 14.0 cm
Colour: Green and brown
Issued: 1959-1962

U.S.: $550.00
Can.: $700.00
Ster.: £300.00

HN 2247
Omar Khayyam
Style Two
Designer: M. Nicoll
Height: 6 1/4", 15.9 cm
Colour: Brown
Issued: 1965-1983

U.S.: $175.00
Can.: $300.00
Ster.: £100.00

Earthenware

HN 2248
Tall Story
Designer: M. Nicoll
Height: 6 1/2", 16.5 cm
Colour: Blue and grey
Issued: 1968-1975
Series: Sea Characters

U.S.: $275.00
Can.: $375.00
Ster.: £150.00

HN 2249
The Favourite
Designer: M. Nicoll
Height: 7 3/4", 19.7 cm
Colour: Blue and white
Issued: 1960-1990

U.S.: $200.00
Can.: $350.00
Ster.: £100.00

HN 2250
The Toymaker
Designer: M. Nicoll
Height: 6", 15.2 cm
Colour: Brown and red
Issued: 1959-1973

U.S.: $500.00
Can.: $575.00
Ster.: £250.00

HN 2251
Masquerade
Style Two
Designer: M. Davies
Height: 8 1/2", 21.6 cm
Colour: Blue and white
Issued: 1960-1965
Varieties: HN 2259

U.S.: $375.00
Can.: $500.00
Ster.: £200.00

HN 2252
The Joker
Style Two
Designer: M.Nicoll
Height: 8 1/2", 21.6 cm
Colour: White
Issued: 1990-1992
Series: Clowns

U.S.: $225.00
Can.: $295.00
Ster.: £ 85.00

HN 2253
The Puppetmaker
Designer: M. Nicoll
Height: 8", 20.3 cm
Colour: Green, brown
and red
Issued: 1962-1973

U.S.: $550.00
Can.: $700.00
Ster.: £300.00

HN 2254
Shore Leave
Designer: M. Nicoll
Height: 7 1/2", 19.1 cm
Colour: Black
Issued: 1965-1979
Series: Sea Characters

U.S.: $275.00
Can.: $375.00
Ster.: £150.00

HN 2255
Teatime
Designer: M. Nicoll
Height: 7 1/4", 18.4 cm
Colour: Brown
Issued: 1972 to the
present

U.S.: $300.00
Can.: $390.00
Ster.: £ 99.95

HN 2256
Twilight
Designer: M. Nicoll
Height: 5", 12.7 cm
Colour: Green and
black
Issued: 1971-1976

U.S.: $225.00
Can. $435.00
Ster.: £120.00

HN 2257
Sea Harvest
Designer: M. Nicoll
Height: 7 1/2", 19.1 cm
Colour: Blue and brown
Issued: 1969-1976
Series: Sea Characters

U.S.:	$275.00
Can.:	$425.00
Ster.:	£150.00

HN 2258
A Good Catch
Designer: M. Nicoll
Height: 7 1/4", 18.4 cm
Colour: Green and grey
Issued: 1966-1986
Series: Sea Characters

U.S.:	$200.00
Can.:	$350.00
Ster.:	£150.00

HN 2259
Masquerade
Style Two
Designer: M. Davies
Height: 8 1/2", 21.6 cm
Colour: Red and cream
Issued: 1960-1965
Varieties: HN 2251

U.S.:	$375.00
Can.:	$500.00
Ster.:	£180.00

HN 2260
The Captain
Style Two
Designer: M. Nicoll
Height: 9 1/2", 24.1 cm
Colour: Black and white
Issued: 1965-1982
Series: Sea Characters

U.S.:	$250.00
Can.:	$375.00
Ster.:	£120.00

HN 2261
Marriage of Art and Industry
Designer: M. Davies
Height: 19", 48.3 cm
Colour: Green
Issued: 1958 in a limited edition of 12

U.S.:	$10,000.00
Can.:	$10,000.00
Ster.:	£ 4,000.00

HN 2262
Lights Out
Designer: M. Davies
Height: 5", 12.7 cm
Colour: Blue trousers with yellow spotted shirt
Issued: 1965-1969

U.S.:	$325.00
Can.:	$375.00
Ster.:	£150.00

HN 2263
Seashore
Designer: M. Davies
Height: 3 1/2", 8.9 cm
Colour: Yellow, red and cream
Issued: 1961-1965

U.S.:	$350.00
Can.:	$425.00
Ster.:	£150.00

HN 2264
Elegance
Designer: M. Davies
Height: 7 1/4", 18.4 cm
Colour: Green
Issued: 1961-1985

U.S.:	$235.00
Can.:	$300.00
Ster.:	£100.00

HN 2265
Sara
Designer: M. Davies
Height: 7 1/2", 19.1 cm
Colour: Red and white
Issued: 1981 to the present
Varieties HN 3308

U.S.: **$375.00**
Can.: **$485.00**
Ster.: **£149.00**

HN 2266
Ballad Seller
Designer: M. Davies
Height: 7 1/2", 19.1 cm
Colour: Pink
Issued: 1968-1973

U.S.: **$350.00**
Can.: **$475.00**
Ster.: **£120.00**

HN 2267
Rhapsody
Designer: M. Davies
Height: 6 3/4", 17.2 cm
Colour: Green
Issued: 1961-1973

U.S.: **$300.00**
Can.: **$395.00**
Ster.: **£150.00**

HN 2268
Daphne
Designer: M. Davies
Height: 8 1/4", 21.0 cm
Colour: Pink
Issued: 1963-1975

U.S.: **$250.00**
Can.: **$375.00**
Ster.: **£150.00**

HN 2269
Leading Lady
Designer: M. Davies
Height: 7 3/4", 19.7 cm
Colour: Blue and yellow
Issued: 1965-1976

U.S.: **$250.00**
Can.: **$350.00**
Ster.: **£120.00**

HN 2270
Pillow Fight
Designer: M. Davies
Height: 5", 12.7 cm
Colour: Patterned pink nightdress
Issued: 1965-1969

U.S.: **$325.00**
Can.: **$385.00**
Ster.: **£120.00**

HN 2271
Melanie
Designer: M. Davies
Height: 7 3/4", 19.7 cm
Colour: Blue
Issued: 1965-1981

U.S.: **$200.00**
Can.: **$325.00**
Ster.: **£120.00**

HN 2272
Repose
Designer: M. Davies
Height: 5 1/4", 13.3 cm
Colour: Pink and green
Issued: 1972-1979

U.S.: **$250.00**
Can.: **$400.00**
Ster.: **£120.00**

HN 2273
Denise
Style One
Designer: M. Davies
Height: 7", 17.8 cm
Colour: Red
Issued: 1964-1971

U.S.:	$325.00
Can.:	$525.00
Ster.:	£150.00

HN 2274
Golden Days
Designer: M. Davies
Height: 3 3/4", 9.5 cm
Colour: Yellow , white and blue
Issued: 1964-1973

U.S.:	$225.00
Can.:	$285.00
Ster.:	£120.00

HN 2275
Sandra
Designer: M. Davies
Height: 7 3/4", 19.7 cm
Colour: Gold
Issued: 1969 to the present
Varieties: HN 2401

U.S.:	$250.00
Can.:	$335.00
Ster.:	£ 99.95

HN 2276
Heart to Heart
Designer: M. Davies
Height: 5 1/2", 14.0 cm
Colour: Lavender, green and yellow
Issued: 1961-1971

U.S.:	$600.00
Can.:	$600.00
Ster.:	£200.00

HN 2277
Slapdash
Designer: M.Nicoll
Height: 10", 25.4 cm
Colour: Green, white and blue
Issued: 1990 to the present
Series: Clowns

U.S.:	$250.00
Can.:	$350.00
Ster.:	£119.00

HN 2278
Judith
Style Two
Designer: M. Nicoll
Height: 6 3/4", 17.2 cm
Colour: Yellow
Issued: 1986 N.America 1987 Worldwide - 1989
Varieties: HN 2313

U.S.:	$235.00
Can.:	$250.00
Ster.:	£120.00

HN 2279
The Clockmaker
Designer: M. Nicoll
Height: 7", 17.8 cm
Colour: Green and brown
Issued: 1961-1975

U.S.:	$350.00
Can.:	$495.00
Ster.:	£300.00

HN 2280
The Mayor
Designer: M. Nicoll
Height: 8 1/4", 21.0 cm
Colour: Red and white
Issued: 1963-1971
Varieties: Two sizes 7 1/2" and 8 1/4"

U.S.:	$475.00
Can.:	$595.00
Ster.:	£300.00

HN 2281
The Professor
Designer: M. Nicoll
Height: 7 1/4", 18.4 cm
Colour: Brown and black
Issued: 1965-1981

U.S.: $230.00
Can.: $325.00
Ster.: £120.00

HN 2282
The Coachman
Designer: M. Nicoll
Height: 7 1/4", 18.4 cm
Colour: Purple, grey
and blue
Issued: 1963-1971

U.S.: $550.00
Can.: $625.00
Ster.: £300.00

HN 2283
Dreamweaver (matte)
Designer: M. Nicoll
Height: 8 1/4", 21.0 cm
Colour: Blue, grey and
brown
Issued: 1972-1976

U.S.: $300.00
Can.: $395.00
Ster.: £180.00

HN 2284
The Craftsman
Designer: M. Nicoll
Height: 6", 15.2 cm
Colour: Blue, tan
and brown
Issued: 1961-1965

U.S.: $650.00
Can.: $700.00
Ster.: £400.00

*

HN 2287
Symphony
Designer: D.B. Lovegrove
Height: 5 1/4", 13.3 cm
Colour: Brown
Issued: 1961-1965

U.S.: $300.00
Can.: $500.00
Ster.: £180.00

*

HN 2304
Adrienne
Designer: M. Davies
Height: 7 1/2", 19.1 cm
Colour: Blue
Issued: 1964-1991
Varieties: HN 2152, also
called "Joan"
HN 3217

U.S.: $175.00
Can.: $250.00
Ster.: £ 85.00

HN 2305
Dulcie
Designer: M. Davies
Height: 7 1/4", 18.4 cm
Colour: Blue
Issued: 1981-1984

U.S.: $250.00
Can.: $335.00
Ster.: £120.00

HN 2306
Reverie
Designer: M. Davies
Height: 6 1/2", 16.5 cm
Colour: Peach
Issued: 1964-1981

U.S.: $325.00
Can.: $395.00
Ster.: £120.00

HN 2307
Coralie
Designer: M. Davies
Height: 7 1/4", 18.4 cm
Colour: Yellow
Issued: 1964-1988

U.S.: $175.00
Can.: $295.00
Ster.: £100.00

HN 2308
Picnic
Designer: M. Davies
Height: 3 3/4", 9.5 cm
Colour: Yellow
Issued: 1965-1988

U.S.: $185.00
Can.: $225.00
Ster.: £ 80.00

HN 2309
Buttercup
Designer: M. Davies
Height: 7", 17.8 cm
Colour: Green dress with yellow sleeves
Issued: 1964 to the present
Varieties: HN 2399

U.S.: $250.00
Can.: $325.00
Ster.: £ 99.95

HN 2310
Lisa (matte)
Designer: M. Davies
Height: 7 1/4", 18.4 cm
Colour: Blue and white
Issued: 1969-1982
Varieties: HN 2394, 3265

U.S.: $175.00
Can.: $325.00
Ster.: £120.00

HN 2311
Lorna
Designer: M. Davies
Height: 8 1/4", 21.0 cm
Colour: Green dress, yellow shawl
Issued: 1965-1985

U.S.: $200.00
Can.: $295.00
Ster.: £120.00

HN 2312
Soiree
Designer: M. Davies
Height: 7 1/2", 19.1 cm
Colour: Green and cream
Issued: 1967-1984

U.S.: $175.00
Can.: $335.00
Ster.: £100.00

HN2313
Judith
Style Two
Designer: M. Nicoll
Height: 6 1/4", 15.9 cm
Colour: Red and cream
Issued: 1988 in a limited edition of 1,000
Varieties: HN 2278

U.S.: $250.00
Can.: $375.00
Ster.: £120.00

HN 2314
Old Mother Hubbard
Designer: M. Nicoll
Height: 8", 20.3 cm
Colour: Green and white
Issued: 1964-1975

U.S.: $425.00
Can.: $550.00
Ster.: £150.00

HN 2315
Last Waltz
Designer: M. Nicoll
Height: 7 3/4", 19.7 cm
Colour: Yellow and white
Issued: 1967 to the
present
Varieties: HN2316

U.S.: $325.00
Can.: $410.00
Ster.: £119.00

HN2316
Last Waltz
Designer: M. Nicoll
Height: 7 3/4", 19.7 cm
Colour: Pink and cream
Issued: 1987 in a limited
edition of 2000
Varieties: HN2316

U.S.: $225.00
Can.: $275.00
Ster.: £125.00

HN 2317
The Lobster Man
Designer: M. Nicoll
Height: 7 1/4", 18.4 cm
Colour: Blue, grey and
brown
Issued: 1964 to the
present
Varieties: HN 2323
Series: Sea Characters

U.S.: $300.00
Can.: $395.00
Ster.: £150.00

HN 2318
Grace
Designer: M. Nicoll
Height: 7 3/4", 19.7 cm
Colour: Green
Issued: 1966-1981

U.S.: $250.00
Can.: $350.00
Ster.: £150.00

HN 2319
The Bachelor
Designer: M. Nicoll
Height: 7", 17.8 cm
Colour: Green and
brown
Issued: 1964-1975

U.S.: $350.00
Can.: $400.00
Ster.: £250.00

HN 2320
Tuppence a Bag
Designer: M. Nicoll
Height: 5 1/2", 14.0 cm
Colour: Blue and green
Issued: 1968 to the
present

U.S.: $300.00
Can.: $395.00
Ster.: £ 99.95

HN 2321
Family Album
Designer: M. Nicholl
Height: 6 1/4", 15.9 cm
Colour: Lavender and
green
Issued: 1966-1973

U.S.: $475.00
Can.: $595.00
Ster.: £250.00

NOTE ON PRICING

Prices are given for three separate and distinct market areas:

Prices are given in the currency of each of these different trading areas.

Prices are not exchange rate calculations but are based on supply and demand in that market.

Prices listed are guidelines to the most current retail values but actual selling prices may vary slightly.

Prices for current figurines are those suggested by Royal Doulton.

Extremely rare or unique figurines have inconsistent retail values and their prices must therefore be determined between buyer and seller.

HN 2322
The Cup of Tea
Designer: M. Nicoll
Height: 7", 17.8 cm
Colour: Dark blue and grey
Issued: 1964-1983
U.S.: **$230.00**
Can.: **$295.00**
Ster.: **£120.00**

HN 2323
The Lobster Man
Designer: M. Nicoll
Height: 7 1/4", 18.4 cm
Colour: Cream, blue, gold and grey
Issued: 1987 to the present
Varieties: HN 2317
Series: Sea Characters
U.S.: **$300.00**
Can.: **$395.00**
Ster.: **£ 99.95**

HN 2324
Matador and the Bull
Designer: M. Davies
Height: 16", 40.6 cm
Colour: Black and yellow
Issued: 1964 to the present
U.S.: **$21,500.00**
Can.: **$25,000.00**
Ster.: **£ 7,900.00**

HN 2325
The Master
Designer: M. Davies
Height: 6 1/4", 15.9 cm
Colour: Green and brown
Issued: 1967-1992
U.S.: **$300.00**
Can.: **$395.00**
Ster.: **£109.00**

HN 2326
Antoinette
Style Two
Designer: M. Davies
Height: 6 1/4", 15.9 cm
Colour: White, white rose
Issued: 1967-1979
U.S.: **$175.00**
Can.: **$295.00**
Ster.: **£100.00**

HN 2327
Katrina
Designer: M. Davies
Height: 7 1/2", 19.1 cm
Colour: Red
Issued: 1965-1969
U.S.: **$375.00**
Can.: **$425.00**
Ster.: **£180.00**

HN 2328
Queen of Sheba
Designer: M. Davies
Height: 9", 22.9 cm
Colour: Purple and brown with green base
Issued: 1982 in a limited edition of 750
Series: Les Femmes Fatales
U.S.: **$1,300.00**
Can.: **$1,400.00**
Ster.: **£ 800.00**

HN 2329
Lynne
Designer: M. Davies
Height: 7", 17.8 cm
Colour: Green
Issued: 1971 to the present
Varieties: Also called "Kathy" HN 3305
U.S.: **$325.00**
Can.: **$385.00**
Ster.: **£ 99.95**

HN 2330
Meditation
Designer: M. Davies
Height: 5 3/4", 14.6 cm
Colour: Peach and cream
Issued: 1971-1983
U.S.: $325.00
Can.: $450.00
Ster.: £120.00

HN 2331
Cello
Designer: M. Davies
Height: 6", 15.2 cm
Colour: Yellow and brown
Issued: 1970 in a limited edition of 750
Series: Lady Musicians
U.S.: $1,500.00
Can.: $1,500.00
Ster.: £ 650.00

HN 2332
Monte Carlo
Designer: M. Davies
Height: 8 1/4", 21.0 cm
Colour: Green
Issued: 1982 in a limited edition of 1500
Series: Sweet and Twenties
U.S.: $300.00
Can.: $395.00
Ster.: £120.00

HN 2333
Jacqueline
Style Two
Designer: M. Davies
Height: 7 1/2", 19.1 cm
Colour: Purple
Issued: 1982 Canada, 1983 Worldwide - 1991
U.S.: $200.00
Can.: $275.00
Ster.: £ 90.00

HN 2334
Fragrance
Designer: M. Davies
Height: 7 1/4", 18.4 cm
Colour: Blue
Issued: 1966 to the present
Varieties: HN3311
U.S.: $300.00
Can.: $385.00
Ster.: £ 99.95

HN 2335
Hilary
Designer: M. Davies
Height: 7 1/4", 18.4 cm
Colour: Blue
Issued: 1967-1981
U.S.: $200.00
Can.: $350.00
Ster.: £120.00

HN 2336
Alison
Designer: M. Davies
Height: 7 1/2", 19.1 cm
Colour: Blue and white
Issued: 1966-1992
Varieties: HN 3264
U.S.: $250.00
Can.: $335.00
Ster.: £ 99.95

HN 2337
Loretta
Designer: M. Davies
Height: 7 3/4", 19.7 cm
Colour: Purple dress, yellow shawl
Issued: 1966-1981
U.S.: $200.00
Can.: $325.00
Ster.: £120.00

HN 2338
Penny
Designer: M. Davies
Height: 4 3/4", 12.0 cm
Colour: Green and white
Issued: 1968 to the
           present
Varieties: HN 2424

U.S.:   **$110.00**
Can.:   **$150.00**
Ster.: **£ 43.00**

HN 2339
My Love
Designer: M. Davies
Height: 6 1/4", 15.9 cm
Colour: White, red rose
Issued: 1969 to the
           present

U.S.:   **$325.00**
Can.:   **$410.00**
Ster.: **£119.00**

HN 2340
Belle
Style Two
Designer: M. Davies
Height: 4 1/2", 11.4 cm
Colour: Green
Issued: 1968-1988

U.S.:   **$ 95.00**
Can.:   **$135.00**
Ster.: **£ 60.00**

HN 2341
Cherie
Designer: M. Davies
Height: 5 1/2", 14.0 cm
Colour: Blue
Issued: 1966-1992

U.S.:   **$195.00**
Can.:   **$225.00**
Ster.: **£ 65.00**

HN 2342
Lucrezia Borgia
Designer: M. Davies
Height: 8", 20.3 cm
Colour: Yellow
Issued: 1985 in a limited
           edition of 750
Series: Les Femmes
           Fatales

U.S.:   **$1,300.00**
Can.:   **$1,000.00**
Ster.: **£ 800.00**

HN 2343
Premiere
(Hand holds cloak)
Designer: M. Davies
Height: 7 1/2", 19.1 cm
Colour: Green
Issued: 1969-?
Varieties: HN 2343A

U.S.:   **$200.00**
Can.:   **$375.00**
Ster.: **£120.00**

HN 2343A
Premiere
(Hand rests on cloak)
Designer: M. Davies
Height: 7 1/2", 19.1 cm
Colour: Green
Issued: ?-1979
Varieties: HN 2343

U.S.:   **$200.00**
Can.:   **$250.00**
Ster.: **£120.00**

HN 2344
Deauville
Designer: M. Davies
Height: 8 1/4", 21.0 cm
Colour: Yellow and white
Issued: 1982 in a limited
           edition of 1500
Series: Sweet and
           Twenties

U.S.:   **$300.00**
Can.:   **$395.00**
Ster.: **£120.00**

HN 2345
Clarissa
Style Two
Designer: M. Davies
Height: 7 1/2", 19.1 cm
Colour: Green
Issued: 1968-1981

  U.S.:   **$200.00**
  Can.:   **$275.00**
  Ster.:   **£120.00**

HN 2346
Kathy
Designer: M. Davies
Height: 4 3/4", 12.0 cm
Colour: Cream flowered
            dress
Issued: 1981-1987
Series: Kate Greenaway

  U.S.:   **$150.00**
  Can.:   **$225.00**
  Ster.:   **£120.00**

HN 2347
Nina (matte)
Designer: M. Davies
Height: 7 1/2", 19.1 cm
Colour: Blue
Issued: 1969-1976

  U.S.:   **$165.00**
  Can.:   **$295.00**
  Ster.:   **£100.00**

HN 2348
Geraldine (matte)
Designer: M. Davies
Height: 7 1/4", 18.4 cm
Colour: Green
Issued: 1972-1976

  U.S.:   **$175.00**
  Can.:   **$325.00**
  Ster.:   **£100.00**

HN 2349
Flora
Designer: M. Nicoll
Height: 7 3/4", 19.7 cm
Colour: Brown and white
Issued: 1966-1973

  U.S.:   **$375.00**
  Can.:   **$400.00**
  Ster.:   **£180.00**

HN 2352
A Stitch in Time
Designer: M. Nicoll
Height: 6 1/4", 15.9 cm
Colour: Purple, brown
            and turquoise
Issued: 1966-1981

  U.S.:   **$200.00**
  Can.:   **$225.00**
  Ster.:   **£150.00**

HN 2356
Ascot
Designer: M. Davies
Height: 5 3/4", 14.6 cm
Colour: Green dress with
            yellow shawl
Issued: 1968 to the
            present

  U.S.:   **$325.00**
  Can.:   **$410.00**
  Ster.:   **£109.00**

HN 2359
The Detective
Designer: E.J. Griffiths
Height: 9 1/4", 23.5 cm
Colour: Brown
Issued: 1977-1983

  U.S.:   **$300.00**
  Can.:   **$450.00**
  Ster.:   **£120.00**

HN 2361
The Laird
Designer: M. Nicoll
Height: 8", 20.3 cm
Colour: Green and brown
Issued: 1969 to the present

U.S.: $325.00
Can.: $415.00
Ster.: £109.00

HN 2362
The Wayfarer
Designer: M. Nicoll
Height: 5 1/2", 14.0 cm
Colour: Green, grey and brown
Issued: 1970-1976

U.S.: $250.00
Can.: $325.00
Ster.: £150.00

*

HN 2368
Fleur
Designer: J. Bromley
Height: 7 1/4", 18.4 cm
Colour: Green
Issued: 1968 to the present
Varieties: HN 2369; also called "Flower of Love" HN 2460

U.S.: $325.00
Can.: $410.00
Ster.: £109.00

HN 2369
Fleur
Designer: J. Bromley
Height: 7 1/4", 18.4 cm
Colour: Orange and blue
Issued: 1983-1986
Varieties: HN 2368; also called "Flower of Love" HN 2460

U.S.: $250.00
Can.: $325.00
Ster.: £120.00

HN 2370
Sir Edward
Designer: J. Bromley
Height: 11", 27.9 cm
Colour: Red and grey
Issued: 1979 in a limited edition of 500
Series: Age of Chivalry

U.S.: $675.00
Can.: $700.00
Ster.: £200.00

HN 2371
Sir Ralph
Designer: J. Bromley
Height: 10 3/4", 27.3cm
Colour: Turquoise and grey
Issued: 1979 in a limited edition of 500
Series: Age of Chivalry

U.S.: $675.00
Can.: $700.00
Ster.: £200.00

HN 2372
Sir Thomas
Designer: J. Bromley
Height: 11", 27.9 cm
Colour: Black
Issued: 1979 in a limited edition of 500
Series: Age of Chivalry

U.S.: $675.00
Can.: $700.00
Ster.: £200.00

HN 2373
Joanne
Designer: J. Bromley
Height: 5 1/4", 13.3 cm
Colour: White
Issued: 1982-1988
Series: Vanity Fair Ladies

U.S.: $225.00
Can.: $295.00
Ster.: £100.00

HN 2374
Mary
Designer: J. Bromley
Height: 7 3/4", 19.7 cm
Colour: White
Issued: 1984-1986
Series: Vanity Fair Ladies

U.S.: $375.00
Can.: $350.00
Ster.: £100.00

HN 2375
The Viking (matte)
Designer: J. Bromley
Height: 8 3/4", 22.2 cm
Colour: Blue and brown
Issued: 1973-1976

U.S.: $325.00
Can.: $475.00
Ster.: £200.00

HN 2376
Indian Brave
Designer: M. Davies
Height: 16", 40.6 cm
Colour: Multi-coloured
Issued: 1967 in a limited edition of 500

U.S.: $6,000.00
Can.: $6,000.00
Ster.: £1,200.00

HN 2377
Georgina
Designer: M. Davies
Height: 5 3/4", 14.6 cm
Colour: Red and yellow
Issued: 1981-1986
Series: Kate Greenaway

U.S.: $150.00
Can.: $225.00
Ster.: £120.00

HN 2378
Simone
Designer: M. Davies
Height: 7 1/4", 18.4 cm
Colour: Green
Issued: 1971-1981

U.S.: $200.00
Can.: $375.00
Ster.: £100.00

HN 2379
Ninette
Designer: M. Davies
Height: 7 1/2", 19.1 cm
Colour: Yellow and cream
Issued: 1971 to the present

U.S.: $325.00
Can.: $410.00
Ster.: £119.00

HN 2380
Sweet Dreams
Style One
Designer: M. Davies
Height: 5", 12.7 cm
Colour: Multi-coloured
Issued: 1971-1990

U.S.: $185.00
Can.: $275.00
Ster.: £100.00

HN 2381
Kirsty
Designer: M. Davies
Height: 7 1/2", 19.1 cm
Colour: Orange
Issued: 1971 to the present
Varieties: Also called "Janette" HN 3415

U.S.: $300.00
Can.: $410.00
Ster.: £119.00

HN 2382
Secret Thoughts
Designer: M. Davies
Height: 6 1/4", 15.9 cm
Colour: Green
Issued: 1971-1988

U.S.: $275.00
Can.: $425.00
Ster.: £100.00

HN 2383
Breton Dancer
Designer: M. Davies
Height: 8 1/2", 21.6 cm
Colour: Blue and white
Issued: 1981 in a limited
edition of 750
Series: Dancers of the
World

U.S.: $ 950.00
Can.: $1,050.00
Ster.: £ 450.00

HN 2384
West Indian Dancer
Designer: M. Davies
Height: 8 3/4", 22.2 cm
Colour: Yellow and white
Issued: 1981 in a limited
edition of 750
Series: Dancers of the
World

U.S.: $ 950.00
Can.: $1,050.00
Ster.: £ 450.00

HN 2385
Debbie
Designer: M. Davies
Height: 5 1/2", 14.0 cm
Colour: Blue and white
Issued: 1969-1982
Varieties: HN 2400

U.S.: $150.00
Can.: $250.00
Ster.: £ 80.00

HN 2386
HRH Prince Philip
Duke of Edinburgh
Designer: M. Davies
Height: 8 1/4", 21.0 cm
Colour: Black and gold
Issued: 1981 in a limited
edition of 1500

U.S.: $600.00
Can.: $750.00
Ster.: £200.00

HN 2387
Helen of Troy
Designer: M. Davies
Height: 9 1/4", 23.5 cm
Colour: Green and pink
Issued: 1981 in a limited
edition of 750
Series: Les Femmes
Fatales

U.S.: $1,500.00
Can.: $1,400.00
Ster.: £ 800.00

HN 2388
Karen
Style Two
Designer: M. Davies
Height: 8", 20.3 cm
Colour: Red and white
Issued: 1982 to the
present

U.S.: $375.00
Can.: $450.00
Ster.: £159.00

HN 2389
Angela
Style Two
Designer: M. Davies
Height: 7 1/2", 19.1 cm
Colour: White
Issued: 1983-1986
Series: Vanity Fair Ladies

U.S.: $200.00
Can.: $225.00
Ster.: £100.00

HN 2390
Spinning
Designer: M. Davies
Height: 7 1/4", 18.4 cm
Colour: Yellow, pink, blue and white
Issued: 1984 in a limited edition of 750
Series: Gentle Arts

U.S.: $1,300.00
Can.: $1,300.00
Ster.: £ 800.00

HN 2391
T'zu-hsi, Empress Dowager
Designer: M. Davis
Height: 8", 20.3 cm
Colour: Red, white and blue
Issued: 1983 in a limited edition of 750
Series: Les Femmes Fatales

US.:. $ 950.00
Can.: $1,300.00
Ster.: £ 800.00

HN 2392
Jennifer
Style Two
Designer: M. Davies
Height: 7", 17.8 cm
Colour: Blue
Issued: 1982-1992

U.S.: $275.00
Can.: $360.00
Ster.: £119.00

HN 2393
Rosalind
Designer: M. Davies
Height: 5 1/2", 14.0 cm
Colour: Blue
Issued: 1970-1975

U.S.: $225.00
Can.: $325.00
Ster.: £100.00

HN 2394
Lisa
Designer: M. Davies
Height: 7 1/4", 18.4 cm
Colour: Purple-yellow
Issued: 1983 -1990
Varieties: HN 2310, 3265

U.S.: $200.00
Can.: $300.00
Ster.: £100.00

HN 2395
Catherine
Style One
Designer: M. Davies
Height: 7 1/2", 19.1 cm
Colour: Red and yellow
Issued: 1983-1984
Series: Ladies of Covent Garden

U.S.: $450.00
Can.: $500.00
Ster.: £100.00

Commissioned by Amex.

HN 2396
Wistful
Designer: M. Davies
Height: 6 1/2", 16.5 cm
Colour: Peach and cream
Issued: 1979-1990
Varieties: HN 2472

U.S.: $325.00
Can.: $395.00
Ster.: £100.00

HN 2397
Margaret
Style Two
Designer: M. Davies
Height: 7 1/2", 19.1 cm
Colour: White dress, blue sash
Issued: 1982 to the present
Series: Vanity Fair Ladies

U.S.: $185.00
Can.: $220.00
Ster.: £ 69.95

HN 2398
Alexandra
Style One
Designer: M. Davies
Height: 7 3/4", 19.7 cm
Colour: Patterned
green dress,
yellow cape
Issued: 1970-1976

U.S.: **$235.00**
Can.: **$350.00**
Ster.: **£100.00**

HN 2399
Buttercup
Designer: M. Davies
Height: 7", 17.8 cm
Colour: Red dress with
yellow sleeves
Issued: 1983 to the
present
Varieties: HN 2309

U.S.: **$250.00**
Can.: **$325.00**
Ster.: **£ 99.95**

HN 2400
Debbie
Designer: M. Davies
Height: 5 1/2", 14.0 cm
Colour: Peach
Issued: 1983 to the
present
Varieties: HN 2385

U.S.: **$150.00**
Can.: **$215.00**
Ster.: **£ 55.00**

HN 2401
Sandra
Designer: M. Davies
Height: 7 3/4", 19.7 cm
Colour: Green
Issued: 1983-1992
Varieties: HN 2275

U.S.: **$250.00**
Can.: **$335.00**
Ster.: **£ 99.95**

*

HN 2408
A Penny's Worth
Designer: M. Nicoll
Height: 7", 17.8 cm
Colour: Pale blue, yellow
and white
Issued: 1986-1990

U.S.: **$150.00**
Can.: **$300.00**
Ster.: **£100.00**

*

HN 2410
Lesley
Designer: M. Nicoll
Height: 8", 20.3 cm
Colour: Orange and
yellow
Issued: 1986-1990

U.S.: **$225.00**
Can.: **$375.00**
Ster.: **£100.00**

*

HN 2417
The Boatman
Designer: M. Nicoll
Height: 6 1/2", 16.5 cm
Colour: Yellow
Issued: 1971-1987
Series: Sea Characters

U.S.: **$215.00**
Can.: **$325.00**
Ster.: **£150.00**

HN 2418
Country Love
Designer: J. Bromley
Height: 8", 20.3 cm
Colour: Pink flowered
dress
Issued: 1990 in a limited
edition of 12,500

U.S.: **$250.00**
Can.: **$350.00**
Ster.: **£145.00**

HN 2419
The Goose Girl
Style Two
Designer: J. Bromley
Height: 8", 20.3 cm
Colour: Blue and white
Issued: 1990 in a limited
edition of 12,500

U.S.: $450.00
Can.: $525.00
Ster.: £145.00

HN 2420
The Shepherdess
Style Four
Designer: J. Bromley
Height: 9", 22.9 cm
Colour: Peach, blue
and white
Issued: 1991 in a limited
edition of 12,500

U.S.: $270.00 *
Can.: $330.00 *
Ster.: £147.50

HN 2421
Charlotte
Designer: J. Bromley
Height: 6 1/2", 16.5 cm
Colour: Purple
Issued: 1972-1986
Varieties: HN 2423

U.S.: $225.00
Can.: $350.00
Ster.: £100.00

HN 2422
Francine
Designer: J. Bromley
Height: 5", 12.7 cm
Colour: Green and
white
Issued: 1972-1981

U.S.: $135.00
Can.: $175.00
Ster.: £100.00

HN 2423
Charlotte
Designer: J. Bromley
Height: 6 1/2", 16.5 cm
Colour: Pale blue
and pink
Issued: 1986-1992
Varieties: HN 2421

U.S.: $325.00
Can.: $390.00
Ster.: £109.00

HN 2424
Penny
Designer: M. Davies
Height: 4 3/4", 12.0 cm
Colour: Yellow and
white
Issued: 1983-1992
Varieties: HN 2338

U.S.: $110.00
Can.: $150.00
Ster.: £ 43.00

HN 2425
Southern Belle
Designer: M. Davies
Height: 7 1/2", 19.1 cm
Colour: Pale blue
and pink
Issued: 1983 to the
present
Varieties: HN 2229

U.S.: $275.00
Can.: $385.00
Ster.: £109.00

HN 2426
Tranquility
Designer: M. Davies
Height: 12", 30.5 cm
Colour: Black
Issued: 1981-1986
Varieties: HN 2469
Series: Images

U.S.: $200.00
Can.: $225.00
Ster.: £100.00

HN 2427
Virginals
Designer: M. Davies
Height: 6 1/4", 15.9 cm
Colour: Green, gold and brown
Issued: 1971 in a limited edition of 750
Series: Lady Musicians

U.S.: $2,000.00
Can.: $2,000.00
Ster.: £ 750.00

HN 2428
The Palio
Designer: M. Davies
Height: 17 1/2", 44.5 cm
Colour: Blue, yellow and brown
Issued: 1971 in a limited edition of 500

U.S.: $10,000.00
Can.: $10,000.00
Ster.: £ 4,000.00

HN 2429
Elyse
Designer: M. Davies
Height: 5 3/4", 14.6 cm
Colour: Blue
Issued: 1972 to the present
Varieties: HN 2474

U.S.: $300.00
Can.: $410.00
Ster.: £119.00

HN 2430
Romance
Designer: M. Davies
Height: 5 1/4", 13.3 cm
Colour: Gold and green
Issued: 1972-1981

U.S.: $200.00
Can.: $325.00
Ster.: £100.00

HN 2431
Lute
Designer: M. Davies
Height: 6 1/4", 15.9 cm
Colour: Blue, white and brown
Issued: 1972 in a limited edition of 750
Series: Lady Musicians

U.S.: $ 950.00
Can.: $1,000.00
Ster.: £ 650.00

HN 2432
Violin
Designer: M. Davies
Height: 6 1/4", 15.9 cm
Colour: Brown and gold
Issued: 1972 in a limited edition of 750
Series: Lady Musicians

U.S.: $ 950.00
Can.: $1,000.00
Ster.: £ 650.00

HN 2433
Peace
Designer: M. Davies
Height: 8", 20.3 cm
Colour: Black
Issued: 1981 to the present
Varieties: HN 2470
Series: Images

U.S.: $ 95.00
Can.: $115.00
Ster.: £ 39.95

HN 2434
Fair Maiden
Designer: M. Davies
Height: 5 1/4", 13.3 cm
Colour: Red and white
Issued: 1983 to the present
Varieties: HN 2211

U.S.: $195.00
Can.: $225.00
Ster.: £ 65.00

HN 2435
Queen of the Ice
Designer: M. Davies
Height: 8", 20.3 cm
Colour: Cream
Issued: 1983-1986
Series: Enchantment

U.S.: $275.00
Can.: $250.00
Ster.: £100.00

HN 2436
Scottish Highland Dancer
Designer: M. Davies
Height: 9 1/2", 24.1 cm
Colour: Red, black
and white
Issued: 1978 in a limited
edition of 750
Series: Dancers of the
World

U.S.: $1,200.00
Can.: $1,400.00
Ster.: £ 450.00

HN 2437
Queen of the Dawn
Designer: M. Davies
Height: 8 1/2", 21.6 cm
Colour: Cream
Issued: 1983-1986
Series: Enchantment

U.S.: $275.00
Can.: $300.00
Ster.: £100.00

HN 2438
Sonata
Designer: M. Davies
Height: 6 1/2", 16.5 cm
Colour: Cream
Issued: 1983-1985
Series: Enchantment

U.S.: $225.00
Can.: $250.00
Ster.: £100.00

HN 2439
Philippine Dancer
Designer: M. Davies
Height: 9 1/2", 24.1 cm
Colour: Green and cream
Issued: 1978 in a limited
edition of 750
Series: Dancers of the
World

U.S.: $900.00
Can.: $900.00
Ster.: £450.00

HN 2440
Cynthia
Style Two
Designer: M. Davies
Height: 7 1/4", 18.4 cm
Colour: Green and yellow
Issued: 1984-1992

U.S.: $225.00
Can.: $285.00
Ster.: £ 89.95

HN 2441
Pauline
Style Two
Designer: M. Davies
Height: 5", 12.7 cm
Colour: Peach
Issued: 1983 Canada,
1984 Worldwide
to 1989

U.S.: $235.00
Can.: $350.00
Ster.: £100.00

HN 2442
Sailor's Holiday
Designer: M. Nicoll
Height: 6 1/4", 15.9 cm
Colour: Gold, brown
and white
Issued: 1972-1979
Series: Sea Characters

U.S.: $275.00
Can.: $450.00
Ster.: £180.00

HN 2443
The Judge (matte)
Designer: M. Nicoll
Height: 6 1/2", 16.5 cm
Colour: Red and white
Issued: 1972-1976
Varieties: HN 2443A

U.S.:	$175.00
Can.:	$350.00
Ster.:	£100.00

HN 2443A
The Judge (gloss)
Designer: M. Nicoll
Height: 6 1/2", 16.5 cm
Colour: Red and white
Issued: 1976-1992
Varieties: HN 2443

U.S.:	$325.00
Can.:	$415.00
Ster.:	£119.00

HN 2444
Bon Appetit (matte)
Designer: M. Nicoll
Height: 6", 15.2 cm
Colour: Grey and brown
Issued: 1972-1976

U.S.:	$275.00
Can.:	$360.00
Ster.:	£120.00

HN 2445
Parisian (matte)
Designer: M. Nicoll
Height: 8", 20.3 cm
Colour: Blue and grey
Issued: 1972-1975

U.S.:	$225.00
Can.:	$335.00
Ster.:	£120.00

HN 2446
Thanksgiving (matte)
Designer: M. Nicoll
Height: 8", 20.3 cm
Colour: Blue, pink and grey
Issued: 1972-1976

U.S.:	$275.00
Can.:	$400.00
Ster.:	£120.00

*

HN 2455
The Seafarer (matte)
Designer: M. Nicoll
Height: 8 1/2", 21.6 cm
Colour: Gold, blue and grey
Issued: 1972-1976
Series: Sea Characters

U.S.:	$275.00
Can.:	$450.00
Ster.:	£180.00

*

HN2460
Flower of Lover
Designer: John Bromley
Height: 7 1/2" 19.1 cm
Colour: White and yellow
Issued: 1991 Canada
1992 Worldwide to the present
Series: Vantity Fair Ladies

U.S.:	$175.00
Can.:	$220.00
Ster.:	£ 59.95

HN2461
Janine
Designer: J. Bromley
Height: 7 1/2", 19.1 cm
Colour: Turquoise and white
Issued: 1971 to the present

U.S.:	$300.00
Can.:	$385.00
Ster.:	£109.00

*

HN 2463
Olga
Designer: J. Bromley
Height: 8 1/4", 21.0 cm
Colour: Turquoise and gold
Issued: 1972-1975
U.S.: $275.00
Can.: $350.00
Ster.: £120.00

*

HN 2465
Elizabeth
Style Two
Designer: J. Bromley
Height: 8 1/2", 21.6 cm
Colour: Blue
Issued: 1990 to the present
U.S.: $250.00
Can.: $360.00
Ster.: £109.00

HN 2466
Eve
Designer: M. Davies
Height: 9 1/4", 23.5 cm
Colour: Green and brown
Issued: 1984 in a limited edition of 750
Series: Les Femmes Fatales
U.S.: $1,100.00
Can.: $1,100.00
Ster.: £ 650.00

HN 2467
Melissa
Designer: M. Davies
Height: 6 3/4", 17.2 cm
Colour: Purple and cream
Issued: 1981 to the present
U.S.: $300.00
Can.: $385.00
Ster.: £109.00

HN 2468
Diana
Style Two
Designer: M. Davies
Height: 8", 20.3 cm
Colour: Flowered white dress
Issued: 1986 N.America, 1987 Worldwide to the present
Varieties: HN 3266
U.S.: $225.00
Can.: $280.00
Ster.: £ 95.00

HN 2469
Tranquility
Designer: M. Davies
Height: 12", 30.5 cm
Colour: White
Issued: 1981-1986
Varieties: HN 2426
Series: Images
U.S.: $200.00
Can.: $225.00
Ster.: £100.00

HN 2470
Peace
Designer: M. Davies
Height: 8", 20.3 cm
Colour: White
Issued: 1981 to the present
Varieties: HN 2433
Series: Images
U.S.: $ 95.00
Can.: $115.00
Ster.: £ 39.95

HN 2471
Victoria
Designer: M. Davies
Height: 6 1/2", 16.5 cm
Colour: Patterned pink dress
Issued: 1973 to the present
U.S.: $300.00
Can.: $385.00
Ster.: £109.00

HN 2472
Wistful
Designer: M. Davies
Height: 6 1/2", 16.5 cm
Colour: Blue and white
Issued: 1985-1985
Varieties: HN 2396

U.S.: $325.00
Can.: $370.00
Ster.: £100.00

HN 2473
At Ease
Designer: M. Davies
Height: 6", 15.2 cm
Colour: Yellow
Issued: 1973-1979

U.S.: $275.00
Can.: $375.00
Ster.: £100.00

HN 2474
Elyse
Designer: M. Davies
Height: 5 3/4", 14.6 cm
Colour: Patterned green
 dress
Issued: 1986 N.America,
 1987 Worldwide
 to the present
Varieties: HN 2429

U.S.: $250.00
Can.: $375.00
Ster.: £109.00

HN 2475
Vanity
Designer: M. Davies
Height: 5 1/4", 13.3 cm
Colour: Red
Issued: 1973-1992

U.S.: $185.00
Can.: $225.00
Ster.: £ 59.95

HN 2476
Mandy
Designer: M. Davies
Height: 4 1/2", 11.4 cm
Colour: White
Issued: 1982-1992

U.S.: $110.00
Can.: $155.00
Ster.: £ 49.95

HN 2477
Denise
Style Two
Designer: M. Davies
Height: 7 1/2", 19.1 cm
Colour: White
Issued: 1987 to the present
Series: Vanity Fair Ladies
Varieties: Also called
 "Summer Rose"
 HN 3309

U.S.: $185.00
Can.: $220.00
Ster.: £ 69.95

HN 2478
Kelly
Designer: M. Davies
Height: 7 1/2", 19.1 cm
Colour: White with blue
 flowers
Issued: 1985-1992

U.S.: $225.00
Can.: $270.00
Ster.: £ 79.95

HN 2479
Pamela
Style Two
Designer: M. Davies
Height: 7", 17.8 cm
Colour: White
Issued: 1986 to the
 present
Varieties: HN 3223
Series: Vanity Fair Ladies

U.S.: $185.00
Can.: $220.00
Ster.: £ 69.95

HN 2480
Adele
Designer: M. Davies
Height: 8", 20.3 cm
Colour: Flowered white dress
Issued: 1987-1992

U.S.: $225.00
Can.: $280.00
Ster.: £ 89.95

HN 2481
Maureen
Style Two
Designer: M. Davies
Height: 7 1/2", 19.1 cm
Colour: White dress, purple flowers
Issued: 1987-1992
Series: Vanity Fair Ladies

U.S.: $225.00
Can.: $280.00
Ster.: £ 89.95

HN 2482
Harp
Designer: M. Davies
Height: 8 3/4", 22.2 cm
Colour: Purple, green and gold
Issued: 1973 in a limited edition of 750
Series: Lady Musicians

U.S.: $1,750.00
Can.: $1,750.00
Ster.: £ 750.00

HN 2483
Flute
Designer: M. Davies
Height: 6", 15.2 cm
Colour: Red and white
Issued: 1973 in a limited edition of 750
Series: Lady Musicians

U.S.: $ 950.00
Can.: $1,000.00
Ster.: £ 650.00

HN 2484
Past Glory
Designer: M. Nicoll
Height: 7 1/2", 19.1 cm
Colour: Red and black
Issued: 1973-1979

U.S.: $265.00
Can.: $425.00
Ster.: £200.00

HN 2485
Lunchtime
Designer: M. Nicoll
Height: 8", 20.3 cm
Colour: Brown
Issued: 1973-1981

U.S.: $250.00
Can.: $375.00
Ster.: £120.00

*

HN 2487
Beachcomber (matte)
Designer: M. Nicoll
Height: 6 1/2", 15.9 cm
Colour: Purple and grey
Issued: 1973-1976

U.S.: $275.00
Can.: $375.00
Ster.: £120.00

*

HN 2492
Huntsman
Style Three
Designer: M. Nicoll
Height: 7 1/2", 19.1 cm
Colour: Grey and cream
Issued: 1974-1979

U.S.: $260.00
Can.: $350.00
Ster.: £150.00

*

HN 2494
Old Meg (matte)
Designer: M. Nicoll
Height: 8 1/4", 21.0 cm
Colour: Blue and grey
Issued: 1974-1976

U.S.: $250.00
Can.: $375.00
Ster.:   £150.00

*

HN 2499
Helmsman
Designer: M. Nicoll
Height: 9", 22.9 cm
Colour: Brown
Issued: 1974-1986
Series: Sea Characters

U.S.: $250.00
Can.: $275.00
Ster.:   £150.00

*

HN 2502
Queen Elizabeth II
Style One
Designer: M. Davies
Height: 7 3/4", 19.7 cm
Colour: Pale blue
Issued: 1973 in a limited
              edition of 750

U.S.: $2,000.00
Can.: $2,000.00
Ster.:   £ 800.00

*

HN 2520
The Farmer's Boy
Designer: W.M. Chance
Height: 8 1/2", 21.6 cm
Colour: White, brown
              and green
Issued: 1938-1960

U.S.: $1,600.00
Can.: $1,150.00
Ster.:   £ 450.00

HN 2521
Dapple Grey
Designer: W.M. Chance
Height: 7 1/4", 18.4 cm
Colour: White, red and
              brown
Issued: 1938-1960

U.S.: $3,000.00
Can.: $3,000.00
Ster.:   £1,000.00

HN 2542
Boudoir
Designer: E.J. Griffiths
Height: 12 1/4", 31.1 cm
Colour: Pale blue
Issued: 1974-1979
Series: Haute Ensemble

U.S.: $450.00
Can.: $550.00
Ster.:   £200.00

HN 2543
Eliza
(Handmade flowers)
Style One
Designer: E. J. Griffiths
Height: 11 3/4", 29.8 cm
Colour: Gold
Issued: 1975-1979
Series: Haute Ensemble
Varieties: HN 2543

U.S.: $325.00
Can.: $400.00
Ster.:   £200.00

HN 2543A
Eliza
(Painted flowers)
Style One
Designer: E. J. Griffiths
Height: 11 3/4", 29.8 cm
Colour: Gold
Issued: 1975-1979
Series: Haute Ensemble
Varieties: HN 2543

U.S.: $300.00
Can.: $400.00
Ster.:   £200.00

HN 2544
A la Mode
Designer: E.J. Griffiths
Height: 12 1/4", 31.1 cm
Colour: Green
Issued: 1974-1979
Series: Haute Ensemble

U.S.:	$225.00
Can.:	$400.00
Ster.:	£200.00

HN 2545
Carmen
Style Two
Designer: E.J. Griffiths
Height: 11 1/2", 29.2 cm
Colour: Blue
Issued: 1974-1979
Series: Haute Ensemble

U.S.:	$325.00
Can.:	$425.00
Ster.:	£200.00

HN 2546
Buddies (matte)
Style One
Designer: E.J. Griffiths
Height: 6", 15.2 cm
Colour: Blue and brown
Issued: 1973-1976

U.S.:	$275.00
Can.:	$375.00
Ster.:	£150.00

HN 2547
R.C.M.P. 1973
Designer: D.V. Tootle
Height: 8", 20.3 cm
Colour: Red
Issued: 1973 in a limited
edition of 1500

U.S.:	$1,000.00
Can.:	$ 800.00
Ster.:	£ 400.00

*

HN 2554
Masque
(Hand holds mask to face)
Designer: D.V. Tootle
Height: 8 1/2", 21.6 cm
Colour: Blue
Issued: 1973-1975
Varieties: HN 2554A

U.S.:	$350.00
Can.:	$500.00
Ster.:	£200.00

HN 2554A
Masque
(Hand holds wand of mask)
Designer: D.V. Tootle
Height: 8 1/2", 21.6 cm
Colour: Blue
Issued: 1975-1982
Varieties: HN 2554

U.S.:	$225.00
Can.:	$450.00
Ster.:	£180.00

HN 2555
R.C.M.P. 1873
Designer: D.V. Tootle
Height: 8 1/4", 21.0 cm
Colour: Red
Issued: 1973 in a limited
edition of 1500

U.S.:	$1,000.00
Can.:	$ 800.00
Ster.:	£ 400.00

*

HN 2671
Good Morning (matte)
Designer: M. Nicoll
Height: 8", 20.3 cm
Colour: Blue, pink
and brown
Issued: 1974-1976

U.S.:	$200.00
Can.:	$375.00
Ster.:	£150.00

*

HN 2677
Taking Things Easy
Designer: M. Nicoll
Height: 6 3/4", 17.2 cm
Colour: Blue, white and brown
Issued: 1975-1987
Varieties: HN 2680

U.S.: $200.00
Can.: $395.00
Ster.: £120.00

HN 2678
The Carpenter
Designer: M. Nicoll
Height: 8", 20.3 cm
Colour: Blue, white and brown
Issued: 1986-1992

U.S.: $300.00
Can.: $365.00
Ster.: £119.00

HN 2679
Drummer Boy
Designer: M. Nicoll
Height: 8 1/2", 21.6 cm
Colour: Multi-coloured
Issued: 1976-1981

U.S.: $450.00
Can.: $695.00
Ster.: £300.00

HN 2680
Taking Things Easy
Designer: M. Nicoll
Height: 6 3/4", 17.2 cm
Colour: Cream and blue
Issued: 1987 to the present
Varieties: HN 2677

U.S.: $275.00
Can.: $395.00
Ster.: £119.00

*

HN 2683
Stop Press
Designer: M. Nicoll
Height: 7 1/2", 19.1 cm
Colour: Brown, blue and white
Issued: 1977-1981

U.S.: $215.00
Can.: $295.00
Ster.: £120.00

*

HN 2693
October
Style One
Designer: M. Davies
Height: 7 3/4", 19.5 cm
Colour: White with blue dress, cosmos flowers
Issued: 1987-1987
Series: Flower of the Month

U.S.: $195.00
Can.: $295.00
Ster.: £120.00

HN 2694
Fiona
Style Two
Designer: M. Davies
Height: 7 1/2", 19.1 cm
Colour: Red and white
Issued: 1974-1981

U.S.: $225.00
Can.: $325.00
Ster.: £120.00

HN 2695
November
Style One
Designer: M. Davies
Height: 7 3/4", 19.7 cm
Colour: White with pink dress, chrysan-themum flowers
Issued: 1987-1987
Series: Flower of the Month

U.S.: $195.00
Can.: $295.00
Ster.: £120.00

HN 2696
December
Style One
Designer: M. Davies
Height: 7 3/4", 19.7 cm
Colour: White with green dress, Christmas rose flowers
Issued: 1987-1987
Series: Flower of the Month

U.S.: $195.00
Can.: $295.00
Ster.: £120.00

HN 2697
January
Style One
Designer: M. Davies
Height: 7 3/4", 19.7 cm
Colour: White with green dress, snowdrop flowers
Issued: 1987-1987
Series: Flower of the Month

U.S.: $195.00
Can.: $295.00
Ster.: £120.00

HN 2698
Sunday Best
Designer: M. Davies
Height: 7 1/2", 19.1 cm
Colour: Pink and white
Issued: 1985 to the present
Varieties: HN 2206

U.S.: $195.00
Can.: $275.00
Ster.: £ 85.00

HN 2699
Cymbals
Designer: M. Davies
Height: 7 1/2", 19.1 cm
Colour: Green and gold
Issued: 1974 in a limited edition of 750
Series: Lady Musicians

U.S.: $ 950.00
Can.: $1,000.00
Ster.: £ 650.00

HN 2700
Chitarrone
Designer: M. Davies
Height: 7 1/2", 19.1 cm
Colour: Blue
Issued: 1974 in a limited edition of 750
Series: Lady Musicians

U.S.: $1,000.00
Can.: $1,150.00
Ster.: £ 650.00

HN 2701
Deborah
Designer: M. Davies
Height: 7 3/4", 19.7 cm
Colour: Green and white
Issued: 1983-1984
Series: Ladies of Covent Garden

U.S.: $450.00
Can.: $450.00
Ster.: £120.00

Commissioned by Amex

HN 2702
Shirley
Designer: M. Davies
Height: 7 1/4", 18.4 cm
Colour: White dress with pink flowers
Issued: 1985 to the present

U.S.: $225.00
Can.: $270.00
Ster.: £ 95.00

HN 2703
February
Style One
Designer: M. Davies
Height: 7 3/4", 19.7 cm
Colour: White with purple dress, violet flowers
Issued: 1987-1987
Series: Flower of the Month

U.S.: $195.00
Can.: $295.00
Ster.: £120.00

HN 2704
Pensive Moments
Designer: M. Davies
Height: 5", 12.7 cm
Colour: Blue
Issued: 1975-1981

U.S.: $225.00
Can.: $375.00
Ster.: £120.00

HN 2705
Julia
Designer: M. Davies
Height: 7 1/2", 19.1 cm
Colour: Gold
Issued: 1975-1990
Varieties: HN 2706

U.S.: $195.00
Can.: $295.00
Ster.: £100.00

HN 2706
Julia
Designer: M. Davies
Height: 7 1/2", 19.1 cm
Colour: Pink and green
Issued: 1985 to the present
Varieties: HN 2705

U.S.: $195.00
Can.: $275.00
Ster.: £ 79.95

HN 2707
March
Style One
Designer: M. Davies
Height: 7 3/4", 19.7 cm
Colour: White with green dress, anemone flowers
Issued: 1987-1987
Series: Flower of the Month

U.S.: $195.00
Can.: $295.00
Ster.: £120.00

HN 2708
April
Style One
Designer: M. Davies
Height: 7 3/4", 19.7 cm
Colour: White with tan dress, sweet pea flowers
Issued: 1987
Series: Flower of the Month

U.S.: $195.00
Can.: $295.00
Ster.: £120.00

HN 2709
Regal Lady
Designer: M. Davies
Height: 7 1/2", 19.1 cm
Colour: Turquoise and cream
Issued: 1975-1983

U.S.: $225.00
Can.: $385.00
Ster.: £100.00

HN 2710
Jean
Style Two
Designer: M. Davies
Height: 5 3/4", 14.6 cm
Colour: White
Issued: 1983-1986
Series: Vanity Fair Ladies

U.S.: $150.00
Can.: $275.00
Ster.: £100.00

HN 2711
May
Style Two
Designer: M. Davies
Height: 7 3/4", 19.7 cm
Colour: White with green dress, lily of the valley flowers
Issued: 1987
Series: Flower of the Month

U.S.: $195.00
Can.: $295.00
Ster.: £120.00

HN 2712
Mantilla
Designer: E.J. Griffiths
Height: 11 1/2", 29.2 cm
Colour: Red, black
and white
Issued: 1974-1979
Series: Haute Ensemble
Varieties: HN3192

U.S.: $425.00
Can.: $495.00
Ster.: £200.00

HN 2713
Tenderness
Designer: E.J. Griffiths
Height: 12", 30.5 cm
Colour: White
Issued: 1982 to the
present
Varieties: HN 2714
Series: Images

U.S.: $150.00
Can.: $165.00
Ster.: £ 59.95

HN 2714
Tenderness
Designer: E.J. Griffiths
Height: 12", 30.5 cm
Colour: Black
Issued: 1982-1992
Varieties: HN 2713
Series: Images

U.S.: $150.00
Can.: $165.00
Ster.: £ 59.95

HN 2715
Patricia
Style Two
Designer: M. Davies
Height: 7 1/2", 19.1 cm
Colour: White
Issued: 1982-1985
Series: Vanity Fair Ladies

U.S.: $225.00
Can.: $450.00
Ster.: £100.00

HN 2716
Cavalier
Style Two
Designer: E.J. Griffiths
Height: 9 3/4", 24.7 cm
Colour: Brown and green
Issued: 1976-1982

U.S.: $250.00
Can.: $395.00
Ster.: £100.00

Flambé pilot piece known

HN 2717
Private, 2nd South Carolina Regiment, 1781
Designer: E.J. Griffiths
Height: 11 1/2", 29.2 cm
Colour: Blue and cream
Issued: 1975 in a limited
edition of 350
Series: Soldiers of the
Revolution

U.S.: $1,200.00
Can.: $1,350.00
Ster.: £ 650.00

HN 2718
Lady Pamela
Designer: D.V. Tootle
Height: 8", 20.3 cm
Colour: Purple
Issued: 1974-1981

U.S.: $225.00
Can.: $300.00
Ster.: £100.00

HN 2719
Laurianne
Designer: D.V. Tootle
Height: 6 1/4", 15.9 cm
Colour: Dark blue
and white
Issued: 1974-1979

U.S.: $175.00
Can.: $275.00
Ster.: £100.00

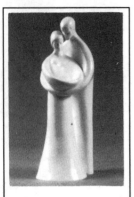

HN 2720
Family
Designer: E.J. Griffiths
Height: 12", 30.5 cm
Colour: White
Issued: 1981 to the present
Varieties: HN 2721
Series: Images

U.S.: $185.00
Can.: $245.00
Ster.: £ 89.95

HN 2721
Family
Designer: E.J. Griffiths
Height: 12", 30.5 cm
Colour: Black
Issued: 1981-1992
Varieties: HN 2720
Series: Images

U.S.: $185.00
Can.: $245.00
Ster.: £ 89.95

HN 2722
Veneta
Designer: W.K. Harper
Height: 8", 20.3 cm
Colour: Green and white
Issued: 1974-1981

U.S.: $175.00
Can.: $325.00
Ster.: £120.00

HN 2723
Grand Manner
Designer: W.K. Harper
Height: 7 3/4", 19.7 cm
Colour: Lavender-yellow
Issued: 1975-1981

U.S.: $225.00
Can.: $300.00
Ster.: £120.00

HN 2724
Clarinda
Designer: W.K. Harper
Height: 8 1/2", 21.6 cm
Colour: Blue and white
Issued: 1975-1981

U.S.: $200.00
Can.: $325.00
Ster.: £120.00

HN 2725
Santa Claus
Designer: W.K. Harper
Height: 9 3/4", 24.7 cm
Colour: Red and white
Issued: 1982 to the present

U.S.: $375.00
Can.: $495.00
Ster.: £155.00

HN 2726
Centurian
Designer: W.K. Harper
Height: 9 1/4", 23.5 cm
Colour: Grey and purple
Issued: 1982-1984

U.S.: $200.00
Can.: $350.00
Ster.: £200.00

HN 2727
Little Miss Muffet
Designer: W.K. Harper
Height: 6 1/4", 15.9 cm
Colour: White and pink
Issued: 1984-1987
Series: Nursery Rhymes

U.S.: $125.00
Can.: $175.00
Ster.: £ 80.00

HN 2728
Rest Awhile
Designer: W.K. Harper
Height: 8", 20.3 cm
Colour: Blue, white and purple
Issued: 1981-1984

U.S.: $225.00
Can.: $300.00
Ster.: £100.00

HN 2729
Song of the Sea
Designer: W.K. Harper
Height: 7 1/4", 18.4 cm
Colour: Blue and grey
Issued: 1982 Canada, 1983 Worldwide -1991

U.S.: $180.00
Can.: $230.00
Ster.: £ 90.00

*

HN 2731
Thanks Doc
Designer: W.K. Harper
Height: 8 3/4", 22.2 cm
Colour: White and brown
Issued: 1975-1990

U.S.: $250.00
Can.: $350.00
Ster.: £120.00

HN 2732
Thank You
Style One
Designer: W.K. Harper
Height: 8 1/4", 21.0 cm
Colour: White, brown and blue
Issued: 1982 Canada, 1983 Worldwide -1986

U.S.: $200.00
Can.: $325.00
Ster.: £100.00

HN 2733
Officer of the Line
Designer: W.K. Harper
Height: 9", 22.9 cm
Colour: Red and yellow
Issued: 1982 Canada, 1983 Worldwide -1986

U.S.: $275.00
Can.: $375.00
Ster.: £150.00

HN 2734
Sweet Seventeen
Designer: D.V. Tootle
Height: 7 1/2", 19.1 cm
Colour: White with gold trim
Issued: 1975 to the present

U.S.: $325.00
Can.: $410.00
Ster.: £109.00

HN 2735
Young Love
Designer: D.V. Tootle
Height: 10", 25.4 cm
Colour: Cream, green, blue and brown
Issued: 1975-1990

U.S.: $600.00
Can.: $795.00
Ster.: £400.00

HN 2736
Tracy
Designer: D.V. Tootle
Height: 7 1/2", 19.1 cm
Colour: White
Issued: 1983 to the present
Series: Vanity Fair Ladies

U.S.: $175.00
Can.: $220.00
Ster.: £ 69.95

HN 2737
Harlequin
Style Two
Designer: D.V. Tootle
Height: 12 1/2", 31.7 cm
Colour: Multi-coloured
Issued: 1982-1992

U.S.: $1,250.00
Can.: $1,350.00
Ster.: £ 650.00

HN 2738
Columbine
Style Three
Designer: D.V. Tootle
Height: 12 1/2", 31.7 cm
Colour: Flowered pink
and blue dress
Issued: 1982-1992

U.S.: $1,250.00
Can.: $1,350.00
Ster.: £ 650.00

HN 2739
Ann
Designer: D.V. Tootle
Height: 7 3/4", 19.7 cm
Colour: White
Issued: 1983-1985
Series: Vanity Fair Ladies

U.S.: $200.00
Can.: $280.00
Ster.: £100.00

HN 2740
Becky
Designer: D.V. Tootle
Height: 8", 20.3 cm
Colour: Green, yellow
and cream
Issued: 1987-1992

U.S.: $185.00 *
Can.: $350.00
Ster.: £ 99.95

HN 2741
Sally
Designer: D.V. Tootle
Height: 5 1/2", 14.0 cm
Colour: Red and lavender
Issued: 1987-1991

U.S.: $175.00
Can.: $225.00
Ster.: £ 80.00

HN 2742
Sheila
Designer: D.V. Tootle
Height: 8 1/4", 21.0 cm
Colour: Pale blue
flowered dress
Issued: 1983 Canada,
1984 Worldwide
-1991

U.S.: $175.00
Can.: $225.00
Ster.: £ 75.00

HN 2743
Meg
Designer: D.V. Tootle
Height: 8", 20.3 cm
Colour: Lavender and
yellow
Issued: 1987-1991

U.S.: $170.00
Can.: $200.00
Ster.: £ 80.00

HN 2744
Modesty
Designer: D.V. Tootle
Height: 8 1/2", 21.6 cm
Colour: White
Issued: 1987-1991

U.S.: $170.00
Can.: $200.00
Ster.: £ 55.00

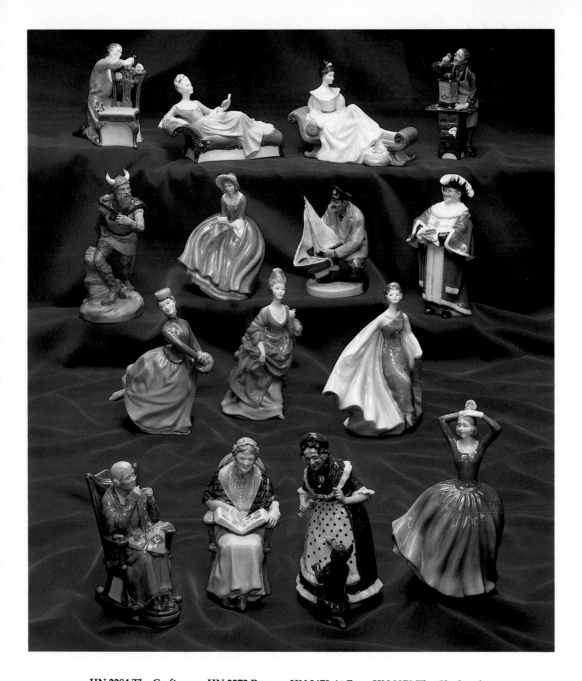

HN 2284 The Craftsman, HN 2272 Repose, HN 2473 At Ease, HN 2279 The Clockmaker

HN 2375 The Viking, HN 2273 Denise, HN 2442 Sailor's Holiday, HN 2280 The Mayor

HN 2318 Grace, HN 2463 Olga, HN 2398 Alexandra (Style One)

HN 2352 A Stich in Time, HN 2321 Family Album, HN 2314 Old Mother Hubbard, HN 2327 Katrina

HN 2866 Mexican Dancer, HN 2803 Indian Temple Dancer, HN 2683, Stop Press, HN 2484 Chelsea Pensioner

HN 2545 Carmen (Style Two), HN 2712 Mantilla, HN 2780 Corporal, 1st New Hampshire Regiment, 1778, HN 2760 Private, Massachusetts Regiment, 1778

HN 2759 Private, Rhode Island Regiment, 1781, HN 2717 Private, 2nd South Carolina Regiment, 1781, HN 2779 Private, 1st Georgia Regiment, 1777

HN 2088 Winter, HN 2143 Friar Tuck, HN 2055 The Leisure Hour, HN2113 Maytime

HN 2119 Town Crier, HN 2118 Good King Wenceslas, HN 2050 Wee Willie Winkie (Style One),
HN 2085 Spring (Style Two), HN 2077 Rowena

HN 2092 Sweet Maid (Style Two), HN 2062 Little Boy Blue (Style One), HN 2074 Marianne,
HN 2063 Little Jack Horner (Style One), HN 2056 Susan (Style One)

HN 2133 Faraway, HN 2060 Jack, HN 2061 Jill, HN 2049 Curly Locks, HN 2047 Once Upon A Time

HN 2163 In The Stocks (Style Two), HN 2149 Love Letter, HN 2256 Twilight, HN 2159 Fortune Teller

HN 2215 Sweet April, HN 2230 Gypsey Dance (Style Two), HN 2156 The Polka, HN 2144 Jovial Monk

HN 2262 Lights Out, HN 2257 Sea Harvest, HN 2186 Harlequin (Style One), HN 2266 Ballard Seller,
HN 2253 Puppetmaker

HN 2248 Tall Story, HN 2185 Columbine (Style Two), HN 2177 My Teddy

HN 2745
Florence
Designer: D.V. Tootle
Height: 8", 20.3 cm
Colour: Purple
Issued: 1987-1992

U.S.: **$250.00**
Can.: **$325.00**
Ster.: **£ 95.00**

HN 2746
May
Style One
Designer: D.V. Tootle
Height: 8", 20.3 cm
Colour: Blue, red
 and green
Issued: 1987-1992
Varieties: HN 3251

U.S.: **$300.00**
Can.: **$375.00**
Ster.: **£119.00**

HN 2747
First Love
Designer: D.V. Tootle
Height: 13", 33.0 cm
Colour: White
Issued: 1987 to the
 present
Series: Images

U.S.: **$150.00**
Can.: **$175.00**
Ster.: **£ 69.95**

HN 2748
Wedding Day
Designer: D.V. Tootle
Height: 12 1/2", 31.7 cm
Colour: White
Issued: 1987 to the
 present
Series: Images

U.S.: **$185.00**
Can.: **$245.00**
Ster.: **£ 99.95**

HN 2749
Lizzie
Designer: D.V. Tootle
Height: 8 1/4", 21.0 cm
Colour: Green, white
 and red
Issued: 1988-1991

U.S.: **$175.00**
Can.: **$225.00**
Ster.: **£ 85.00**

HN 2750
Wedding Vows
Designer: D.V. Tootle
Height: 8", 20.3 cm
Colour: White
Issued: 1988-1992

U.S.: **$250.00**
Can.: **$330.00**
Ster.: **£ 89.95**

HN 2751
Encore
Designer: D.V. Tootle
Height: 10". 25.4 cm
Colour: Lavender, white
 and blue
Issued: 1988 to 1989
Series: Reflections

U.S.: **$225.00**
Can.: **$275.00**
Ster.: **£100.00**

HN 2752
Major, 3rd New Jersey
Regiment, 1776
Designer: E.J. Griffiths
Height: 10", 25.4 cm
Colour: Blue and brown
Issued: 1975 in a limited
 edition of 350
Series: Soldiers of the
 Revolution

U.S.: **$2,000.00**
Can.: **$2,000.00**
Ster.: **£ 750.00**

HN 2753
Serenade
Designer:	E.J. Griffiths
Height:	9", 22.9 cm
Colour:	Cream
Issued:	1983-1985
Series:	Enchantment
U.S.:	**$225.00**
Can.:	**$250.00**
Ster.:	**£100.00**

HN 2754
Private, 3rd North Carolina Regiment, 1778
Designer:	E.J. Griffiths
Height:	11", 27.9 cm
Colour:	Tan
Issued:	1976 in a limited edition of 350
Series:	Soldiers of the Revolution
U.S.:	**$ 900.00**
Can.:	**$1,000.00**
Ster.:	**£ 650.00**

HN 2755
Captain, 2nd New York Regiment, 1775
Designer:	E.J. Griffiths
Height:	10", 25.4 cm
Colour:	Brown
Issued:	1976 in a limited edition of 350
Series:	Soldiers of the Revolution
U.S.:	**$ 900.00**
Can.:	**$1,000.00**
Ster.:	**£ 650.00**

HN 2756
Musicale
Designer:	E.J. Griffiths
Height:	9", 22.9 cm
Colour:	Cream
Issued:	1983-1985
Series:	Enchantment
U.S.:	**$225.00**
Can.:	**$250.00**
Ster.:	**£100.00**

HN 2757
Lyric
Designer:	E.J. Griffiths
Height:	6 1/4", 15.9 cm
Colour:	Cream
Issued:	1983-1985
Series:	Enchantment
U.S.:	**$225.00**
Can.:	**$250.00**
Ster.:	**£100.00**

HN 2758
Linda
Style Two
Designer:	E.J. Griffiths
Height:	7 3/4", 19.7 cm
Colour:	White with pink trim
Issued:	1984 to 1988
Series:	Vanity Fair Ladies
U.S.:	**$160.00**
Can.:	**$225.00**
Ster.:	**£100.00**

HN 2759
Private, Rhode Island Regiment, 1781
Designer:	E.J. Griffiths
Height:	11 3/4", 29.8 cm
Colour:	Grey
Issued:	1977 in a limited edition of 350
Series:	Soldiers of the Revolution
U.S.:	**$ 850.00**
Can.:	**$1,000.00**
Ster.:	**£ 650.00**

HN 2760
Private, Massachusetts Regiment, 1778
Designer:	E.J. Griffiths
Height:	12 1/2", 31.7 cm
Colour:	Blue and tan
Issued:	1977 in a limited edition of 350
Series:	Soldiers of the Revolution
U.S.:	**$ 850.00**
Can.:	**$1,000.00**
Ster.:	**£ 650.00**

HN 2761
Private, Delaware
Regiment, 1776
Designer: E.J. Griffiths
Height: 12", 30.5 cm
Colour: Blue and tan
Issued: 1977 in a limited
edition of 350
Series: Soldiers of the
Revolution
U.S.: $ 850.00
Can.: $1,000.00
Ster.: £ 650.00

HN 2762
Lovers
Designer: D.V. Tootle
Height: 12", 30.5 cm
Colour: White
Issued: 1981 to the
present
Varieties: HN 2763
Series: Images
U.S.: $185.00
Can.: $245.00
Ster.: £ 89.95

HN 2763
Lovers
Designer: D.V. Tootle
Height: 12", 30.5 cm
Colour: Black
Issued: 1981-1992
Varieties: HN 2762
Series: Images
U.S.: $185.00
Can.: $245.00
Ster.: £ 89.95

HN 2764
The Lifeboat Man
Designer: W.K. Harper
Height: 9 1/4", 23.5 cm
Colour: Yellow
Issued: 1987-1991
U.S.: $200.00
Can.: $250.00
Ster.: £ 90.00

HN 2765
Punch and Judy Man
Designer: W.K. Harper
Height: 9", 22.9 cm
Colour: Green and
yellow
Issued: 1981-1990
U.S.: $400.00
Can.: $595.00
Ster.: £100.00

Photograph
Not
Available

HN2766
Autumn Glory
Designer: W.K. Harper
Height: 11 3/4", 29.9 cm
Colour: Blue-grey, tan
grape basket
Issued: 1988 in a limited
edition of 1,000
Series: Reflections
U.S.: $300.00
Can.: $375.00
Ster.: £175.00
Commissioned by Home
Shopping Network, Florida

HN 2767
Pearly Boy
Style Three
Designer: W.K. Harper
Height: 7 1/2", 19.1 cm
Colour: Black, white
and blue
Issued: 1988 to the
present
U.S.: $250.00
Can.: $197.50
Ster.: £ 99.95

HN 2768
Pretty Polly
Designer: W.K. Harper
Height: 6", 15.2 cm
Colour: Pink and white
Issued: 1984-1986
U.S.: $185.00
Can.: $250.00
Ster.: £100.00

HN 2769
Pearly Girl
Style Three
Designer: W.K. Harper
Height: 7 1/2", 19.1 cm
Colour: Black, white
and blue
Issued: 1988 to the
present

U.S.: $250.00
Can.: $197.50
Ster.: £ 99.95

HN 2770
New Companions
Designer: W.K. Harper
Height: 7 3/4", 19.7 cm
Colour: Purple, white
and black
Issued: 1982-1985

U.S.: $210.00
Can.: $300.00
Ster.: £100.00

HN 2771
Charlie Chaplin
Designer: W.K. Harper
Height: 9", 22.9 cm
Colour: Grey
Issued: 1989 in a limited
edition of 5,000
Series: Entertainers

U.S.: $450.00
Can.: $325.00
Ster.: £ 99.50

HN 2772
Ritz Bell Boy
Designer: W.K. Harper
Height: 8", 20.3 cm
Colour: Black
Issued: 1989 to the
present

U.S.: $225.00
Can.: $275.00
Ster.: £ 75.00

HN 2773
Robin Hood
Designer: W.K. Harper
Height: 7 3/4", 19.7 cm
Colour: Green
Issued: 1985-1990

U.S.: $200.00
Can.: $300.00
Ster.: £100.00

HN 2774
Stan Laurel
Designer: W.K. Harper
Height: 9 1/4", 23.5 cm
Colour: Grey-black
Issued: 1990 in a limited
edition of 9,500
Series: Entertainers

U.S.: $300.00
Can.: $395.00
Ster.: £100.00

HN 2775
Oliver Hardy
Designer: W.K. Harper
Height: 10", 25.4 cm
Colour: Black and grey
Issued: 1990 in a limited
edition of 9,500
Series: Entertainers

U.S.: $300.00
Can.: $395.00
Ster.: £100.00

HN 2776
Carpet Seller
(Standing)
Style Three
Designer: W.K. Harper
Height: 9", 22.9 cm
Colour: Flambe
Issued: 1990 to the
present

U.S.: $210.00
Can.: $315.00
Ster.: £ 85.00

HN 2777
Groucho Marx
Designer: W.K. Harper
Height: 9 1/2", 24.1 cm
Colour: Black and grey
Issued: 1991 in a limited
edition of 9,500
Series: Entertainers

U.S.: $275.00
Can.: $330.00 *
Ster.: £117.00

HN 2778
The Bobby
Designer: W.K. Harper
Height: 9", 22.9 cm
Colour: Black
Issued: 1992 to the
present

U.S.: $195.00
Can.: $255.00
Ster.: £ 79.95

HN 2779
Private, 1st Georgia
Regiment, 1777
Designer: E.J. Griffiths
Height: 11", 27.9 cm
Colour: Light brown
Issued: 1975 in a limited
edition of 350
Series: Soldiers of the
Revolution

U.S.: $1,000.00
Can.: $1,000.00
Ster.: £ 650.00

HN 2780
Corporal, 1st New
Hampshire Regiment, 1778
Designer: E.J. Griffiths
Height: 13", 33.0 cm
Colour: Green
Issued: 1975 in a limited
edition of 350
Series: Soldiers of the
Revolution

U.S.: $ 900.00
Can.: $1,000.00
Ster.: £ 650.00

HN 2781
The Lifeguard
Designer: W.K. Harper
Height: 9 1/2", 24.1 cm
Colour: Red, black and
white
Issued: 1992 to the
present

U.S.: $250.00
Can.: $380.00
Ster.: £ 99.95

HN 2782
The Blacksmith
Designer: W.K. Harper
Height: 9", 22.9 cm
Colour: Brown, white
and grey
Issued: 1987-1991

U.S..: $170.00
Can.: $200.00
Ster.: £ 90.00

HN 2783
Good Friends
Designer: W.K. Harper
Height: 9", 22.9 cm
Colour: Blue and brown
Issued: 1985-1990

U.S.: $200.00
Can.: $300.00
Ster.: £100.00

HN 2784
The Guardsman
Designer: W.K. Harper
Height: 9 3/4", 24.8 cm
Colour: Red, black and
white
Issued: 1992 to the
present

U.S.: $250.00
Can.: $380.00
Ster.: £ 99.95

*

HN 2788
Marjorie
Designer: M. Davies
Height: 5 1/4", 13.3 cm
Colour: Pale blue
Issued: 1980-1984

U.S.: $250.00
Can.: $325.00
Ster.: £100.00

HN 2789
Kate
Designer: M. Davies
Height: 7 1/2", 19.1 cm
Colour: Flowered
white dress
Issued: 1978-1987

U.S.: $250.00
Can.: $325.00
Ster.: £100.00

HN 2790
June
Style Three
Designer: M. Davies
Height: 7 3/4", 19.7 cm
Colour: White with pink
dress, roses
Issued: 1987-1987
Series: Flower of the
Month

U.S.: $195.00
Can.: $295.00
Ster.: £100.00

HN 2791
Elaine
Designer: M. Davies
Height: 7 1/2", 19.1 cm
Colour: Blue
Issued: 1980 to the
present
Varieties: HN 3307

U.S.: $325.00
Can.: $410.00
Ster.: £119.00

HN 2792
Christine
Style Two
Designer: M. Davies
Height: 7 1/2", 19.1 cm
Colour: Flowered blue
and white dress
Issued: 1978 to the
present
Varieties: HN 3172

U.S.: $450.00
Can.: $545.00
Ster.: £169.00

HN 2793
Clare
Designer: M. Davies
Height: 7 1/2", 19.1 cm
Colour: Flowered
lavender dress
Issued: 1980-1984

U.S.: $250.00
Can.: $395.00
Ster.: £100.00

HN 2794
July
Style Two
Designer: M. Davies
Height: 7 3/4", 19.7 cm
Colour: White dress,
forget-me-not
flowers
Issued: 1987
Series: Flower of the
Month

U.S.: $195.00
Can.: $295.00
Ster.: £100.00

HN 2795
French Horn
Designer: M. Davies
Height: 6", 15.2 cm
Colour: Purple and
turquoise
Issued: 1976 in a limited
edition of 750
Series: Lady Musicians

U.S.: $ 950.00
Can.: $1,000.00
Ster.: £ 650.00

HN 2796
Hurdy Gurdy
Designer: M. Davies
Height: 6", 15.2 cm
Colour: Turquoise
and white
Issued: 1975 in a limited
edition of 750
Series: Lady Musicians
U.S.: $ 950.00
Can.: $1,000.00
Ster.: £ 650.00

HN 2797
Viola d'Amore
Designer: M. Davies
Height: 6", 15.2 cm
Colour: Pale blue
and yellow
Issued: 1976 in a limited
edition of 750
Series: Lady Musicians
U.S.: $ 950.00
Can.: $1,000.00
Ster.: £ 650.00

HN 2798
Dulcimer
Designer: M. Davies
Height: 6 1/2", 16.5 cm
Colour: Lavender
and cream
Issued: 1975 in a limited
edition of 750
Series: Lady Musicians
U.S.: $ 950.00
Can.: $1,000.00
Ster.: £ 650.00

HN 2799
Ruth
Designer: M. Davies
Height: 6", 15.2 cm
Colour: Green
Issued: 1976-1981
Series: Kate Greenaway
U.S.: $225.00
Can.: $275.00
Ster.: £120.00

HN 2800
Carrie
Designer: M. Davies
Height: 6", 15.2 cm
Colour: Turquoise
Issued: 1976-1981
Series: Kate Greenaway
U.S.: $200.00
Can.: $275.00
Ster.: £120.00

HN 2801
Lori
Designer: M. Davies
Height: 5 3/4", 14.6 cm
Colour: Yellow-cream
Issued: 1976-1987
Series: Kate Greenaway
U.S.: $200.00
Can.: $275.00
Ster.: £120.00

HN 2802
Anna
Designer: M. Davies
Height: 5 3/4", 14.6 cm
Colour: Purple and white
Issued: 1976-1982
Series: Kate Greenaway
U.S.: $225.00
Can.: $225.00
Ster.: £120.00

HN 2803
First Dance
Designer: M. Davies
Height: 7 1/4", 18.4 cm
Colour: Pale blue
Issued: 1977-1992
Varieties: Also called
"Samantha"
HN 3304
U.S.: $300.00
Can.: $395.00
Ster.: £109.00

HN 2804
Nicola
Designer: M. Davies
Height: 7", 17.8 cm
Colour: Red and lilac
Issued: 1987-1987
Varieties: HN 2839; also
            called "Tender
            Moment" HN 3303

U.S.: $275.00
Can.: $300.00
Ster.:   £100.00

HN 2805
Rebecca
Style One
Designer: M. Davies
Height: 7 1/4", 18.4 cm
Colour: Pale blue and
            lavender
Issued: 1980 to the
            present

U.S.: $525.00
Can.: $705.00
Ster.:   £199.00

HN 2806
Jane
Style Two
Designer: M. Davies
Height: 8", 20.3 cm
Colour: Yellow
Issued: 1983-1986

U.S.: $210.00
Can.: $350.00
Ster.:   £100.00

HN 2807
Stephanie
Designer: M. Davies
Height: 7 1/4", 18.4 cm
Colour: Gold
Issued: 1977-1982
Varieties: HN 2811

U.S.: $250.00
Can.: $375.00
Ster.:   £100.00

HN 2808
Balinese Dancer
Designer: M. Davies
Height: 8 3/4", 22.2 cm
Colour: Green and yellow
Issued: 1982 in a limited
            edition of 750
Series: Dancers of the
            World

U.S.: $750.00
Can.: $975.00
Ster.:   £450.00

HN 2809
North American Indian Dancer
Designer: M. Davies
Height: 8 1/2", 21.6 cm
Colour: Yellow
Issued: 1982 in a limited
            edition of 750
Series: Dancers of the
            World

U.S.: $750.00
Can.: $975.00
Ster.:   £450.00

HN 2810
Solitude
Designer: M. Davies
Height: 5 1/2", 14.0 cm
Colour: Cream, blue
            and orange
Issued: 1977-1983

U.S.: $325.00
Can.: $425.00
Ster.:   £100.00

HN 2811
Stephanie
Designer: M. Davies
Height: 7 1/4", 18.4 cm
Colour: Red and white
Issued: 1983 to the
            present
Varieties: HN 2807

U.S.: $300.00
Can.: $395.00
Ster.:   £119.00

HN 2814
Eventide
Designer: W.K. Harper
Height: 7 3/4", 19.7 cm
Colour: Blue, white, red,
yellow and green
Issued: 1977-1991

U.S.: **$275.00**
Can.: **$325.00**
Ster.: **£105.00**

HN 2815
Sergeant, 6th Maryland
Regiment, 1777
Designer: E.J. Griffiths
Height: 13 3/4", 34.9 cm
Colour: Light grey
Issued: 1976 in a limited
edition of 350
Series: Soldiers of the
Revolution

U.S.: **$ 850.00**
Can.: **$1,000.00**
Ster.: **£ 650.00**

HN 2816
Votes for Women
Designer: W.K. Harper
Height: 9 3/4", 24.7 cm
Colour: Gold and grey
Issued: 1978-1981

U.S.: **$250.00**
Can.: **$425.00**
Ster.: **£150.00**

*

HN 2818
Balloon Girl
Designer: W.K. Harper
Height: 6 1/2", 16.5 cm
Colour: Green, white,
grey and red
Issued: 1982 to the
present

U.S.: **$175.00**
Can.: **$305.00**
Ster.: **£ 79.95**

*

HN 2824
Harmony
Designer: R. Jefferson
Height: 8", 20.3 cm
Colour: Grey
Issued: 1978-1984

U.S.: **$225.00**
Can.: **$325.00**
Ster.: **£100.00**

HN 2825
Lady and the Unicorn
Designer: R. Jefferson
Height: 8 3/4", 22.2 cm
Colour: Blue, white
and red
Issued: 1982 in a limited
edition of 300
Series: Myths and
Maidens

U.S.: **$2,500.00**
Can.: **$2,500.00**
Ster.: **£ 850.00**

HN 2826
Leda and the Swan
Designer: R. Jefferson
Height: 9 3/4", 24.7 cm
Colour: Yellow, green,
red and blue
Issued: 1983 in a limited
edition of 300
Series: Myths and
Maidens

U.S.: **$2,000.00**
Can.: **$2,000.00**
Ster.: **£ 850.00**

HN 2827
Juno and the Peacock
Designer: R. Jefferson
Height: 11", 27.9 cm
Colour: Turquoise,
lavender and gold
Issued: 1984 in a limited
edition of 300
Series: Myths and
Maidens

U.S.: **$2,000.00**
Can.: **$2,000.00**
Ster.: **£ 850.00**

HN 2828
Europa and the Bull
Style Two
Designer: R. Jefferson
Height: 10 1/2", 26.5 cm
Colour: Yellow, orange, white and lavender
Issued: 1985 in a limited edition of 300
Series: Myths and Maidens

U.S.:	$2,000.00
Can.:	$2,000.00
Ster.:	£ 850.00

HN 2829
Diana the Huntress
Designer: R. Jefferson
Height: 11 1/4", 28.6 cm
Colour: Green and gold
Issued: 1986 in a limited edition of 300
Series: Myths and Maidens

U.S.:	$2,000.00
Can.:	$2,000.00
Ster.:	£ 850.00

HN 2830
Indian Temple Dancer
Designer: M. Davies
Height: 9 1/4", 23.5 cm
Colour: Gold
Issued: 1977 in a limited edition of 750
Series: Dancers of the World

U.S.:	$1,500.00
Can.:	$ 900.00
Ster.:	£ 450.00

HN 2831
Spanish Flamenco Dancer
Designer: M. Davies
Height: 9 1/2", 24.1 cm
Colour: Red and white
Issued: 1977 in a limited edition of 750
Series: Dancers of the World

U.S.:	$1,800.00
Can.:	$1,500.00
Ster.:	£ 450.00

HN 2832
Fair Lady
Designer: M. Davies
Height: 7 1/4", 18.4 cm
Colour: Red and white
Issued: 1977 to the present
Varieties: HN 2193, 2835

U.S.:	$275.00
Can.:	$335.00
Ster.:	£ 99.95

HN 2833
Sophie
Style One
Designer: M. Davies
Height: 6", 15.2 cm
Colour: Red and grey
Issued: 1977-1987
Series: Kate Greenaway

U.S.:	$175.00
Can.:	$275.00
Ster.:	£120.00

HN 2834
Emma
Style One
Designer: M. Davies
Height: 5 3/4", 14.6 cm
Colour: Pink and white
Issued: 1977-1981
Series: Kate Greenaway

U.S.:	$250.00
Can.:	$275.00
Ster.:	£120.00

HN 2835
Fair Lady
Designer: M. Davies
Height: 7 1/4", 18.4 cm
Colour: Peach
Issued: 1977 to the present
Varieties: HN 2193, 2832

U.S.:	$275.00
Can.:	$335.00
Ster.:	£ 99.95

HN 2836
Polish Dancer
Designer: M. Davies
Height: 9 1/2", 24.1 cm
Colour: Multi-coloured
Issued: 1980 in a limited
edition of 750
Series: Dancers of the
World

U.S.: **$800.00**
Can.: **$900.00**
Ster.: **£450.00**

HN 2837
Awakening
Style Two
Designer: M. Davies
Height: 8 1/2", 21.6 cm
Colour: Black
Issued: 1981 to the
present
Varieties: HN 2875
Series: Images

U.S.: **$ 95.00**
Can.: **$115.00**
Ster.: **£ 39.95**

HN 2838
Sympathy
Designer: M. Davies
Height: 11 3/4", 29.8 cm
Colour: Black
Issued: 1981-1986
Varieties: HN 2876
Series: Images

U.S.: **$200.00**
Can.: **$230.00**
Ster.: **£100.00**

HN 2839
Nicola
Designer: M. Davies
Height: 7", 17.8 cm
Colour: Flowered
lavender dress
Issued: 1978 to the
present
Varieties: HN 2804; also
called "Tender
Moment" HN 3303

U.S.: **$425.00**
Can.: **$540.00**
Ster.: **£159.00**

HN 2840
Chinese Dancer
Designer: M. Davies
Height: 9", 22.9 cm
Colour: Red, green,
purple and
lavender
Issued: 1980 in a limited
edition of 750
Series: Dancers of the
World

U.S.: **$800.00**
Can.: **$900.00**
Ster.: **£450.00**

HN 2841
Mother and Daughter
Designer: E.J. Griffiths
Height: 8 1/2", 21.6 cm
Colour: White
Issued: 1981-1992
Varieties: HN 2843
Series: Images

U.S.: **$185.00**
Can.: **$245.00**
Ster.: **£ 95.00**

HN 2842
Innocence
Style One
Designer: E.J. Griffiths
Height: 7 1/2", 19.1 cm
Colour: Red
Issued: 1979-1983

U.S.: **$175.00**
Can.: **$295.00**
Ster.: **£100.00**

NH 2843
Mother and Daughter
Designer: E.J. Griffiths
Height: 8 1/2", 21.6 cm
Colour: Black
Issued: 1981-1992
Varieties: HN 2841
Series: Images

U.S.: **$185.00**
Can.: **$245.00**
Ster.: **£ 95.00**

HN 2844
Sergeant, Virginia 1st Regiment Continental Light Dragoons, 1777
Designer: E.J. Griffiths
Height: 14 1/4", 36.1 cm
Colour: Brown and green
Issued: 1978 in a limited edition of 350
Series: Soldiers of the Revolution

U.S.:	$4,000.00
Can.:	$4,000.00
Ster.:	£1,200.00

HN 2845
Private, Connecticut Regiment, 1777
Designer: E.J. Griffiths
Height: 11 1/4", 28.5 cm
Colour: Brown and cream
Issued: 1978 in a limited edition of 350
Series: Soldiers of the Revolution

U.S.:	$ 850.00
Can.:	$1,000.00
Ster.:	£ 650.00

HN 2846
Private, Pennsylvania Rifle Battalion, 1776
Designer: E.J. Griffiths
Height: 8", 20.3 cm
Colour: Grey
Issued: 1978 in a limited edition of 350
Series: Soldiers of the Revolution

U.S.:	$ 850.00
Can.:	$1,000.00
Ster.:	£ 650.00
*

HN 2851
Christmas Parcels
Designer: W.K. Harper
Height: 8 3/4", 22.2 cm
Colour: Black
Issued: 1978-1982

U.S.:	$275.00
Can.:	$395.00
Ster.:	£120.00

*

HN 2855
Embroidering
Designer: W.K. Harper
Height: 7 1/4", 18.4 cm
Colour: Grey
Issued: 1980-1990

U.S.:	$225.00
Can.:	$450.00
Ster.:	£100.00

HN 2856
St. George
Style Three
Designer: W.K. Harper
Height: 16", 40.6 cm
Colour: Cream and grey
Issued: 1978 to the present

U.S.:	$13,600.00
Can.:	$15,000.00
Ster.:	£ 4,900.00

HN 2857
Covent Garden
Style Two
Designer: W. K. Harper
Height: 10", 25.4 cm
Colour: Pale blue and white
Issued: 1988-1990
Series: Reflections

U.S.:	$210.00
Can.:	$275.00
Ster.:	£100.00

HN 2858
The Doctor
Designer: W.K. Harper
Height: 7 1/2", 19.1 cm
Colour: Black and grey
Issued: 1979-1992

U.S.:	$375.00
Can.:	$495.00
Ster.:	£139.00

HN 2859
The Statesman
Designer: W.K. Harper
Height: 9 ", 22.9 cm
Colour: Black and grey
Issued: 1988-1990
Varieties: also called
"Sir John A.
MacDonald" ,
HN 2860

U.S.: $175.00
Can.: $200.00
Ster.: £110.00

HN 2860
Sir John A. MacDonald
Designer: W.K. Harper
Height: 9 ", 22.9 cm
Colour: Black and grey
Issued: 1987 -1990
Varieties: Also called
"The Statesman",
HN 2859

U.S.: $250.00
Can.: $350.00
Ster.: £145.00

HN 2861
**George Washington
at Prayer**
Designer: L. Ispanky
Height: 12 1/2", 31.7 cm
Colour: Blue and tan
Issued: 1977 in a limited
edition of 750

U.S.: $1,500.00
Can.: $1,700.00
Ster.: £ 650.00

HN 2862
First Waltz
Designer: M. Davies
Height: 7 1/4", 18.4 cm
Colour: Red
Issued: 1979-1983

U.S.: $350.00
Can.: $425.00
Ster.: £100.00

HN 2863
Lucy
Designer: M. Davies
Height: 6", 15.2 cm
Colour: Blue and white
Issued: 1980-1984
Series: Kate Greenaway

U.S.: $175.00
Can.: $225.00
Ster.: £120.00

HN 2864
Tom
Designer: M. Davies
Height: 5 3/4", 14.6 cm
Colour: Blue and yellow
Issued: 1978-1981
Series: Kate Greenaway

U.S.: $275.00
Can.: $325.00
Ster.: £250.00

HN 2865
Tess
Designer: M. Davies
Height: 5 3/4", 14.6 cm
Colour: Green
Issued: 1978-1983
Series: Kate Greenaway

U.S.: $250.00
Can.: $325.00
Ster.: £150.00

NOTE ON PRICING

Prices are given for three separate and distinct market areas:

Prices are given in the currency of each of these different trading areas.

Prices are not exchange rate calculations but are based on supply and demand in that market.

Prices listed are guidelines to the most current retail values but actual selling prices may vary slightly.

Prices for current figurines are those suggested by Royal Doulton.

Extremely rare or unique figurines have inconsistent retail values and their prices must therefore be determined between buyer and seller.

HN 2866
Mexican Dancer
Designer: M. Davies
Height: 8 1/4", 21.0 cm
Colour: Gold and white
Issued: 1979 in a limited
 edition of 750
Series: Dancers of the
 World

U.S.: $800.00
Can.: $850.00
Ster.: £450.00

HN 2867
Kurdish Dancer
Designer: M. Davies
Height: 8 1/4", 21.0 cm
Colour: Blue
Issued: 1979 in a limited
 edition of 750
Series: Dancers of the
 World

U.S.: $ 950.00
Can.: $1,050.00
Ster.: £ 450.00

HN 2868
Cleopatra
Designer: M. Davies
Height: 7 1/4", 18.4 cm
Colour: White, blue
 and black
Issued: 1979 in a limited
 edition of 750
Series: Les Femmes
 Fatales

U.S.: $1,750.00
Can.: $1,750.00
Ster.: £ 850.00

HN 2869
Louise
Stlye One
Designer: M. Davies
Height: 6", 15.2 cm
Colour: Brown
Issued: 1979-1986
Series: Kate Greenaway

U.S.: $200.00
Can.: $225.00
Ster.: £120.00

HN 2870
Beth
Designer: M. Davies
Height: 5 3/4", 14.6 cm
Colour: Pink and white
Issued: 1979-1983
Series: Kate Greenaway

U.S.: $275.00
Can.: $325.00
Ster.: £120.00

HN 2871
Beat You To It
Designer: M. Davies
Height: 6 1/2", 16.5 cm
Colour: Pink, gold and
 blue
Issued: 1980-1987

U.S.: $350.00
Can.: $525.00
Ster.: £100.00

HN 2872
Young Master
Designer: M. Davies
Height: 7", 17.8 cm
Colour: Purple, grey
 and brown
Issued: 1980-1989

U.S.: $325.00
Can.: $575.00
Ster.: £150.00

HN 2873
The Bride
Style Three
Designer: M. Davies
Height: 8", 20.3 cm
Colour: White with
 gold trim
Issued: 1980-1989

U.S.: $140.00
Can.: $325.00
Ster.: £100.00

HN 2874
The Bridesmaid
Style Four
Designer: M. Davies
Height: 5 1/4", 13.3 cm
Colour: White with
            gold trim
Issued: 1980-1989

U.S.: $100.00
Can.: $195.00
Ster.:   £ 80.00

HN 2875
Awakening
Style Two
Designer: M. Davies
Height: 8 1/2", 21.6 cm
Colour: White
Issued: 1981 to the
            present
Varieties: HN 2837
Series: Images

U.S.: $ 95.00
Can.: $115.00
Ster.:   £ 39.95

HN 2876
Sympathy
Designer: M. Davies
Height: 11 3/4", 29.8 cm
Colour: White
Issued: 1981-1986
Varieties: HN 2838
Series: Images

U.S.: $200.00
Can.: $230.00
Ster.:   £100.00

HN 2877
The Wizard
Designer: A. Maslankowski
Height: 9 3/4", 24.8 cm
Colour: Blue
Issued: 1979 to the
            present
Varieties: HN 3121

U.S.: $400.00
Can.: $465.00
Ster.:   £139.00

HN 2878
Her Majesty
Queen Elizabeth II
Style Two
Designer: E.J. Griffiths
Height: 10 1/2", 26.7 cm
Colour: Blue, red and
            cream
Issued: 1983 in a limited
            edition of 2500

U.S.: $550.00
Can.: $575.00
Ster.:   £325.00

HN 2879
The Gamekeeper
Designer: E.J. Griffiths
Height: 7 1/4", 18.4 cm
Colour: Green, black
            and tan
Issued: 1984-1992

U.S.: $275.00
Can.: $320.00
Ster.:   £ 95.00

*

HN 2881
Lord Olivier as Richard III
Designer: E.J. Griffiths
Height: 11 1/2", 29.2 cm
Colour: Red, blue
            and black
Issued: 1985 in a limited
            edition of 750

U.S.: $ 850.00
Can.: $1,025.00
Ster.:   £ 395.00

HN 2882
HRH Queen Elizabeth
The Queen Mother
Style One
Designer: E.J. Griffiths
Height: 8", 20.3 cm
Colour: Pink
Issued: 1980 in a limited
            edition of 1500

U.S.: $1,500.00
Can.: $1,500.00
Ster.:   £ 650.00

HN 2883
HRH the Prince of Wales
Style One
Designer: E.J. Griffiths
Height: 8", 20.3 cm
Colour: Purple, white and black
Issued: 1981 in a limited edition of 1500

U.S.: $750.00
Can.: $750.00
Ster.: £250.00

HN 2884
HRH the Prince of Wales
Style Two
Designer: E.J. Griffiths
Height: 8", 20.3 cm
Colour: Red and black
Issued: 1981 in a limited edition of 1500

U.S.: $1,000.00
Can.: $1,100.00
Ster.: £ 400.00

HN 2885
Lady Diana Spencer
Designer: E.J. Griffiths
Height: 7 3/4", 19.7 cm
Colour: Blue and white
Issued: 1982 in a limited edition of 1500

U.S.: $600.00
Can.: $600.00
Ster.: £200.00

*

HN 2887
HRH the Princess of Wales
Designer: E.J. Griffiths
Height: 7 3/4", 19.7 cm
Colour: Cream
Issued: 1982 in a limited edition of 1500

U.S.: $1,200.00
Can.: $1,200.00
Ster.: £ 400.00

HN 2888
His Holiness Pope John-Paul II
Designer: E.J. Griffiths
Height: 10", 25.4 cm
Colour: White
Issued: 1982-1992

U.S.: $195.00
Can.: $315.00
Ster.: £ 99.95

HN 2889
Captain Cook
Designer: W.K. Harper
Height: 8", 20.3 cm
Colour: Black and cream
Issued: 1980-1984

U.S.: $450.00
Can.: $495.00
Ster.: £150.00

HN 2890
The Clown
Designer: W.K. Harper
Height: 9", 22.9 cm
Colour: Gold and grey
Issued: 1979 to 1988

U.S.: $250.00
Can.: $375.00
Ster.: £100.00

HN 2891
The Newsvendor
Designer: W.K. Harper
Height: 8", 20.3 cm
Colour: Gold and grey
Issued: 1986 in a limited edition of 2,500
Varieties: Also called "Old Ben" HN 3190

U.S.: $225.00
Can.: $350.00
Ster.: £100.00

HN 2892
The Chief
Designer: W.K. Harper
Height: 7", 17.8 cm
Colour: Gold
Issued: 1979 to 1988

U.S.: $225.00
Can.: $375.00
Ster.: £100.00

Photograph
Not
Available

HN 2893
Monique
Designer: N/A
Height: N/A
Colour: N/A
Issued: 1984
Series: Elegance

U.S.: $450.00
Can.: $450.00
Ster.: £100.00

HN 2894
Balloon Clown
Designer: W.K. Harper
Height: 9 1/4", 23.5 cm
Colour: White and blue
Issued: 1986-1992

U.S.: $225.00
Can.: $325.00
Ster.: £ 89.95

HN 2895
Morning Ma'am
Designer: W.K. Harper
Height: 9", 23.5 cm
Colour: Pale blue
Issued: 1986 to 1989

U.S.: $175.00
Can.: $275.00
Ster.: £100.00

HN 2896
Good Day Sir
Designer: W.K. Harper
Height: 8 1/2", 21.6 cm
Colour: Purple
Issued: 1986 to 1989

U.S. $175.00
Can.: $225.00
Ster.: £100.00

Photograph
Not
Available

HN2897
Francoise
Designer: N/A
Height: N/A
Colour: N/A
Issued: 1984
Series: Elegance

U.S.: $450.00
Can.: $450.00
Ster.: £100.00

HN 2898
Ko-Ko
Style Two
Designer: W.K. Harper
Height: 11 1/2", 29.2 cm
Colour: Yellow and blue
Issued: 1980-1985
Series: Gilbert and
Sullivan

U.S.: $700.00
Can.: $750.00
Ster.: £300.00

HN 2899
Yum-Yum
Style Two
Designer: W.K. Harper
Height: 10 3/4", 27.3 cm
Colour: Green and yellow
Issued: 1980-1985
Series: Gilbert and
Sullivan

U.S.: $700.00
Can.: $750.00
Ster.: £300.00

HN 2900
Ruth, The Pirate Maid
Designer: W.K. Harper
Height: 11 3/4", 29.8 cm
Colour: Brown and blue
Issued: 1981-1985
Series: Gilbert and
         Sullivan

U.S.: $700.00
Can.: $750.00
Ster.: £300.00

HN 2901
The Pirate King
Designer: W.K. Harper
Height: 10", 25.4 cm
Colour: Blue and gold
Issued: 1981-1985
Series: Gilbert and
         Sullivan

U.S.: $700.00
Can.: $750.00
Ster.: £300.00

HN 2902
Elsie Maynard
Style Two
Designer: W.K. Harper
Height: 12", 30.5 cm
Colour: Green and white
Issued: 1982-1985
Series: Gilbert and
         Sullivan

U.S.: $750.00
Can.: $750.00
Ster.: £300.00

HN 2903
Colonel Fairfax
Designer: W.K. Harper
Height: 11 1/2", 29.2 cm
Colour: Red and gold
Issued: 1982-1985
Series: Gilbert and
         Sullivan

U.S.: $750.00
Can.: $750.00
Ster.: £300.00

*

HN 2906
Paula
Designer: P. Parsons
Height: 7", 17.8 cm
Colour: Yellow with
        green trim
Issued: 1980-1986
Varieties: HN 3234

U.S.: $250.00
Can.: $325.00
Ster.: £100.00

HN 2907
The Piper
Designer: M. Abberley
Height: 8", 20.3 cm
Colour: Green
Issued: 1980-1992

U.S.: $455.00
Can.: $550.00
Ster.: £155.00

HN 2908
HMS Ajax
Designer: S. Keenan
Height: 9 3/4", 24.8 cm
Colour: Red, green
        and gold
Issued: 1980 in a limited
        edition of 950
Series: Ships Figureheads

U.S.: $500.00
Can.: $600.00
Ster.: £350.00

HN 2909
Benmore
Designer: S. Keenan
Height: 9 1/4", 23.5 cm
Colour: Blue, red,
        white and gold
Issued: 1980 in a limited
        edition of 950
Series: Ships Figureheads

U.S.: $500.00
Can.: $600.00
Ster.: £350.00

HN 2910
Lalla Rookh
Designer: S. Keenan
Height: 9", 22.9 cm
Colour: Brown, green with gold trim
Issued: 1981 in a limited edition of 950
Series: Ships Figureheads

U.S.: **$600.00**
Can.: **$600.00**
Ster.: **£350.00**

HN 2911
Gandalf
Designer: D. Lyttleton
Height: 7", 17.8 cm
Colour: Green and white
Issued: 1980-1984
Series: Middle Earth

U.S.: **$275.00**
Can.: **$325.00**
Ster.: **£150.00**

HN 2912
Frodo
Designer: D. Lyttleton
Height: 4 1/2", 11.4 cm
Colour: Black and white
Issued: 1980-1984
Series: Middle Earth

U.S.: **$125.00**
Can.: **$190.00**
Ster.: **£120.00**

HN 2913
Gollum
Designer: D. Lyttleton
Height: 3 1/4", 8.3 cm
Colour: Brown
Issued: 1980-1984
Series: Middle Earth

U.S.: **$150.00**
Can.: **$190.00**
Ster.: **£120.00**

HN 2914
Bilbo
Designer: D. Lyttleton
Height: 4 1/2", 11.4 cm
Colour: Brown
Issued: 1980-1984
Series: Middle Earth

U.S.: **$125.00**
Can.: **$190.00**
Ster.: **£120.00**

HN 2915
Galadriel
Designer: D. Lyttleton
Height: 5 1/2", 14.0 cm
Colour: White
Issued: 1981-1984
Series: Middle Earth

U.S.: **$150.00**
Can.: **$190.00**
Ster.: **£120.00**

HN 2916
Aragorn
Designer: D. Lyttleton
Height: 6 1/4", 15.9 cm
Colour: Brown and green
Issued: 1981-1984
Series: Middle Earth

U.S.: **$125.00**
Can.: **$190.00**
Ster.: **£120.00**

HN 2917
Legolas
Designer: D. Lyttleton
Height: 6 1/4", 15.9 cm
Colour: Cream and tan
Issued: 1981-1984
Series: Middle Earth

U.S.: **$125.00**
Can.: **$190.00**
Ster.: **£120.00**

HN 2918
Boromir
Designer: D Lyttleton
Height: 6 3/4", 17.2 cm
Colour: Brown and green
Issued: 1981-1984
Series: Middle Earth

U.S.: **$300.00**
Can.: **$350.00**
Ster.: **£150.00**

HN 2919
Rachel
Designer: P. Gee
Height: 7 1/2", 19.1 cm
Colour: Gold and green
Issued: 1981-1984
Varieties: HN 2936

U.S.: **$300.00**
Can.: **$350.00**
Ster.: **£150.00**

HN 2920
Yearning
Designer: P. Gee
Height: 11 3/4", 29.8 cm
Colour: White
Issued: 1982-1986
Varieties: HN 2921
Series: Images

U.S.: **$200.00**
Can.: **$230.00**
Ster.: **£100.00**

HN 2921
Yearning
Designer: P. Gee
Height: 11 3/4", 29.8 cm
Colour: Black
Issued: 1982-1986
Varieties: HN 2920
Series: Images

U.S.: **$200.00**
Can.: **$230.00**
Ster.: **£100.00**

HN 2922
Gimli
Designer: D. Lyttleton
Height: 5 1/2", 14.0 cm
Colour: Brown and blue
Issued: 1981-1984
Series: Middle Earth

U.S.: **$175.00**
Can.: **$275.00**
Ster.: **£150.00**

HN 2923
Barliman Butterbur
Designer: D. Lyttleton
Height: 5 1/4", 13.3 cm
Colour: Brown, tan and white
Issued: 1982-1984
Series: Middle Earth

U.S.: **$400.00**
Can.: **$450.00**
Ster.: **£200.00**

HN 2924
Tom Bombadil
Designer: D. Lyttleton
Height: 5 3/4", 14.6 cm
Colour: Black and yellow
Issued: 1982-1984
Series: Middle Earth

U.S.: **$500.00**
Can.: **$500.00**
Ster.: **£200.00**

HN 2925
Samwise
Designer: D. Lyttleton
Height: 4 1/2", 11.4 cm
Colour: Black and brown
Issued: 1982-1984
Series: Middle Earth

U.S.: **$475.00**
Can.: **$475.00**
Ster.: **£200.00**

HN 2926
Tom Sawyer
Designer: D. Lyttleton
Height: 5 1/4", 13.3 cm
Colour: Blue
Issued: 1982-1985
Series: Characters
from Children's
Literature
U.S.: $110.00
Can.: $175.00
Ster.: £100.00

HN 2927
Huckleberry Finn
Designer: D. Lyttleton
Height: 7", 17.8 cm
Colour: Tan and brown
Issued: 1982-1985
Series: Characters
from Children's
Literature
U.S.: $110.00
Can.: $175.00
Ster.: £100.00

HN 2928
Nelson
Designer: S. Keenan
Height: 8 3/4", 22.2 cm
Colour: Blue, gold and
green
Issued: 1981 in a limited
edition of 950
Series: Ships Figureheads
U.S.: $600.00
Can.: $750.00
Ster.: £350.00

HN 2929
Chieftain
Designer: S. Keenan
Height: 8 3/4", 22.2 cm
Colour: Green and brown
Issued: 1982 in a limited
edition of 950
Series: Ships Figureheads
U.S.: $950.00
Can.: $950.00
Ster.: £350.00

HN 2930
Pocahontas
Designer: S. Keenan
Height: 8", 20.3 cm
Colour: White, red
and gold
Issued: 1982 in a limited
edition of 950
Series: Ships Figureheads
U.S.: $950.00
Can.: $950.00
Ster.: £300.00

Photograph
Not
Available

HN 2931
Mary Queen of Scots
Style One
Designer: S. Keenan
Height: 9 1/2", 24.1 cm
Colour: Purple, red and
white
Issued: 1983 in a limited
edition of 950
Series: Ships Figureheads
U.S.: $950.00
Can.: $950.00
Ster.: £350.00

Photograph
Not
Available

HN 2932
Hibernia
Designer: S. Keenan
Height: 9 1/2", 24.1 cm
Colour: Black, white
and gold
Issued: 1983 in a limited
edition of 950
Series: Ships Figureheads
U.S.: $950.00
Can.: $950.00
Ster.: £350.00

HN 2933
Kathleen
Style Two
Designer: S. Keenan
Height: 6 1/2", 16.5 cm
Colour: Orange, yellow
and green
Issued: 1983 Canada,
1984 Worldwide
-1987
Varieties: HN 3100
U.S.: $225.00
Can.: $250.00
Ster.: £100.00

HN 2934
Balloon Boy
Designer: P. Gee
Height: 7 1/2", 19.1 cm
Colour: Green and black
Issued: 1984 to the present

U.S.: $175.00
Can.: $295.00
Ster.: £ 79.95

HN 2935
Balloon Lady
Designer: P. Gee
Height: 8 1/4", 21.0 cm
Colour: Purple, gold
and white
Issued: 1984 to the present

U.S.: $195.00
Can.: $315.00
Ster.: £ 99.95

HN 2936
Rachel
Designer: P. Gee
Height: 7 1/2", 19.1 cm
Colour: Red and cream
Issued: 1985 to the present
Varieties: HN 2919

U.S.: $300.00
Can.: $385.00
Ster.: £119.00

HN 2937
Gail
Designer: P. Gee
Height: 7 1/2", 19.1 cm
Colour: Red and cream
Issued: 1986 to the present
Series: Vanity Fair Ladies

U.S.: $300.00
Can.: $385.00
Ster.: £119.00

HN 2938
Isadora
Designer: P. Gee
Height: 8", 20.3 cm
Colour: Lavender
Issued: 1986-1992
Varieties: Also called
"Celeste" HN 3322

U.S.: $275.00
Can.: $350.00
Ster.: £150.00 *

HN 2939
Donna
Designer: P. Gee
Height: 7 3/4", 19.7 cm
Colour: White
Issued: 1986 to the present
Series: Vanity Fair Ladies

U.S.: $185.00
Can.: $220.00
Ster.: £ 69.95

HN 2940
All Aboard
Designer: R. Tabbenor
Height: 9 1/4", 23.5 cm
Colour: Blue, cream
and brown
Issued: 1982-1986

U.S.: $225.00
Can.: $295.00
Ster.: £100.00

HN 2941
Tom Brown
Designer: R. Tabbenor
Height: 6 3/4", 17.2 cm
Colour: Blue and cream
Issued: 1983-1985
Series: Characters
from Children's
Literature

U.S.: $ 95.00
Can.: $150.00
Ster.: £100.00

HN 2942
Prized Possessions
Designer: R. Tabbenor
Height: 6 1/2", 16.5 cm
Colour: Cream, purple
           and green
Issued: 1982-1982
Series: R.D.I.C.C.

U.S.:   **$650.00**
Can.:   **$775.00**
Ster.:   **£350.00**

HN 2943
The China Repairer
Designer: R. Tabbenor
Height: 6 3/4", 17.2 cm
Colour: Blue, white
           and tan
Issued: 1982 Canada,
           1983 Worldwide
           -1988

U.S.:   **$185.00**
Can.:   **$275.00**
Ster.:   **£100.00**

HN 2944
The Rag Doll Seller
Designer: R. Tabbenor
Height: 7", 17.8 cm
Colour: Green, lavender
           and white
Issued: 1983 to the
           present

U.S.:   **$255.00**
Can.:   **$325.00**
Ster.:   **£ 99.95**

HN 2945
Pride and Joy
Designer: R. Tabbenor
Height: 7", 17.8 cm
Colour: Brown, gold
           and green
Issued: 1984-1984
Series: R.D.I.C.C.

U.S.:   **$325.00**
Can.:   **$495.00**
Ster.:   **£300.00**

HN 2946
Elizabeth
Style One
Designer: B. Franks
Height: 8", 20.3 cm
Colour: Green and
           yellow
Issued: 1982-1986

U.S.:   **$350.00**
Can.:   **$425.00**
Ster.:   **£100.00**

*

HN 2952
Susan
Style Two
Designer: P. Parsons
Height: 8 1/2", 21.6 cm
Colour: Blue, black
           and pink
Issued: 1982 to the
           present
Varieties: HN 3050

U.S.:   **$375.00**
Can.:   **$445.00**
Ster.:   **£159.00**

HN 2953
Sleepy Darling
Designer: P. Parsons
Height: 7 1/4", 18.4 cm
Colour: Pale blue
           and pink
Issued: 1981-1981
Series: R.D.I.C.C.

U.S.:   **$250.00**
Can.:   **$400.00**
Ster.:   **£150.00**

HN 2954
Samantha
Style One
Designer: P. Parsons
Height: 7", 17.8 cm
Colour: White
Issued: 1982-1984
Series: Vanity Fair Ladies

U.S.:   **$200.00**
Can.:   **$275.00**
Ster.:   **£100.00**

HN 2955
Nancy
Designer:	P. Parsons
Height:	7 1/2", 19.1 cm
Colour:	White
Issued:	1982 to the present
Series:	Vanity Fair Ladies
U.S.	**$185.00**
Can.:	**$220.00**
Ster.:	**£ 69.95**

HN 2956
Heather
Designer:	P. Parsons
Height:	6", 15.2 cm
Colour:	White
Issued:	1982 to the present
Varieties:	Also called "Marie" HN 3375
Series:	Vanity Fair Ladies
U.S.:	**$185.00**
Can.:	**$220.00**
Ster.:	**£ 69.95**

HN 2957
Edith
Designer:	M. Davies
Height:	5 3/4", 14.6 cm
Colour:	Green and white
Issued:	1982-1985
Series:	Kate Greenaway
U.S.:	**$200.00**
Can.:	**$250.00**
Ster.:	**£120.00**

HN 2958
Amy
Style One
Designer:	P. Parsons
Height:	6", 15.2 cm
Colour:	White and blue
Issued:	1982-1987
Series:	Kate Greenaway
U.S.:	**$125.00**
Can.:	**$250.00**
Ster.:	**£120.00**

HN 2959
Save Some For Me
Designer:	P. Parsons
Height:	7 1/4", 18.4 cm
Colour:	Blue and white
Issued:	1982-1985
Series:	Childhood Days
U.S.:	**$125.00**
Can.:	**$175.00**
Ster.:	**£100.00**

HN 2960
Laura
Designer:	P. Parsons
Height:	7 1/4", 18.4 cm
Colour:	Pale blue and white, yellow flowers
Issued:	1982 Canada, 1984 Worldwide to the present
Varieties:	HN 3136
U.S.:	**$250.00**
Can.:	**$325.00**
Ster.:	**£109.00**

HN 2961
Carol
Designer:	P. Parsons
Height:	7 1/2", 19.1 cm
Colour:	White
Issued:	1982 to the present
Series:	Vanity Fair Ladies
U.S.:	**$185.00**
Can.:	**$220.00**
Ster.:	**£ 69.95**

HN 2962
Barbara
Style Two
Designer:	P. Parsons
Height:	8", 20.3 cm
Colour:	White
Issued:	1982-1984
Series:	Vanity Fair Ladies
U.S.:	**$250.00**
Can.:	**$325.00**
Ster.:	**£100.00**

HN 2963
It Won't Hurt
Designer: P. Parsons
Height: 7 1/2", 19.1 cm
Colour: White, brown and blue
Issued: 1982-1985
Series: Childhood Days

U.S.:	**$110.00**
Can.:	**$175.00**
Ster.:	**£100.00**

HN 2964
Dressing Up
Style One
Designer: P. Parsons
Height: 7 1/2", 19.1 cm
Colour: White and blue
Issued: 1982-1985
Series: Childhood Days

U.S.:	**$150.00**
Can.:	**$175.00**
Ster.:	**£100.00**

HN 2965
Pollyanna
Designer: P. Parsons
Height: 6 1/2", 16.5 cm
Colour: White, grey and tan
Issued: 1982-1985
Series: Characters from Children's Literature

U.S.:	**$125.00**
Can.:	**$195.00**
Ster.:	**£100.00**

HN 2966
And So To Bed
Designer: P. Parsons
Height: 7 1/2", 19.1 cm
Colour: Cream and gold
Issued: 1982-1985
Series: Childhood Days

U.S.:	**$100.00**
Can.:	**$175.00**
Ster.:	**£ 80.00**

HN 2967
Please Keep Still
Designer: P. Parsons
Height: 4 1/2", 11.4 cm
Colour: Yellow and blue
Issued: 1982-1985
Series: Childhood Days

U.S.:	**$140.00**
Can.:	**$175.00**
Ster.:	**£ 80.00**

HN 2968
Juliet
Designer: P. Parsons
Height: 7", 17.8 cm
Colour: Blue and white
Issued: 1983-1984
Series: Ladies Of Covent Garden

U.S.:	**$400.00**
Can.:	**$495.00**
Ster.:	**£150.00**

Commissioned by Amex

HN 2969
Kimberley
Style One
Designer: P. Parsons
Height: 8", 20.3 cm
Colour: Yellow and white
Issued: 1983-1984
Series: Ladies of Covent Garden

U.S.:	**$400.00**
Can.:	**$495.00**
Ster.:	**£150.00**

Commissioned by Amex

HN 2970
And One For You
Designer: A. Hughes
Height: 6 1/2", 16.5 cm
Colour: White and brown
Issued: 1982-1985
Series: Childhood Days

U.S.:	**$110.00**
Can.:	**$175.00**
Ster.:	**£ 80.00**

HN 2971
As Good As New
Designer: A. Hughes
Height: 6 1/2", 16.5 cm
Colour: Blue, green
and tan
Issued: 1982-1985
Series: Childhood Days

U.S.: $110.00
Can.: $175.00
Ster.: £ 80.00

HN 2972
Little Lord Fauntleroy
Designer: A. Hughes
Height: 6 1/4", 15.9 cm
Colour: Blue and white
Issued: 1982-1985
Series: Characters
from Children's
Literature

U.S.: $100.00
Can.: $175.00
Ster.: £ 80.00

*

HN 2974
Carolyn
Style Two
Designer: A. Hughes
Height: 5 1/2", 14.0 cm
Colour: Green
Issued: 1982 Canada,
1984 Worldwide
-1986

U.S.: $225.00
Can.: $300.00
Ster.: £100.00

HN 2975
Heidi
Designer: A. Hughes
Height: 4 1/2", 11.4 cm
Colour: Green and white
Issued: 1983-1985
Series: Characters
from Children's
Literature

U.S.: $150.00
Can.: $175.00
Ster.: £ 80.00

HN 2976
I'm Nearly Ready
Designer: A. Hughes
Height: 7 1/2", 19.1 cm
Colour: Black, white and
brown
Issued: 1983 Canada,
1984 Worldwide
-1985
Series: Childhood Days

U.S.: $150.00
Can.: $170.00
Ster.: £100.00

HN 2977
Magic Dragon
Designer: A. Hughes
Height: 4 3/4", 12.0 cm
Colour: Cream
Issued: 1983-1986
Series: Enchantment

U.S.: $200.00
Can.: $250.00
Ster.: £100.00

HN 2978
The Magpie Ring
Designer: A. Hughes
Height: 8", 20.3 cm
Colour: Cream
Issued: 1983-1986
Series: Enchantment

U.S.: $200.00
Can.: $250.00
Ster.: £100.00

HN 2979
Fairyspell
Designer: A. Hughes
Height: 5 1/4", 13.3 cm
Colour: Cream
Issued: 1983-1986
Series: Enchantment

U.S. $200.00
Can.: $250.00
Ster.: £100.00

HN 2980
Just One More
Designer: A. Hughes
Height: 7", 17.8 cm
Colour: Gold and blue
Issued: 1983 Canada,
            1984 Worldwide
            -1985
Series: Childhood Days

U.S.:   **$100.00**
Can.:   **$175.00**
Ster.:   **£ 80.00**

HN 2981
Stick 'em Up
Designer: A. Hughes
Height: 7", 17.8 cm
Colour: Blue and tan
Issued: 1983 Canada,
            1984 Worldwide
            -1985
Series: Childhood Days

U.S.:   **$100.00**
Can.:   **$175.00**
Ster.:   **£ 80.00**

*

HN 2988
The Auctioneer
Designer: R. Tabbenor
Height: 8 1/2", 21.6 cm
Colour: Black, grey
            and brown
Issued: 1986-1986
Series: R.D.I.C.C.

U.S.:   **$250.00**
Can.:   **$325.00**
Ster.:   **£200.00**

HN 2989
The Genie
Designer: R. Tabbenor
Height: 9 3/4", 24.7 cm
Colour: Blue
Issued: 1983-1990
Varieties: HN 2999

U.S.:   **$175.00**
Can.:   **$250.00**
Ster.:   **£120.00**

HN 2990
Shepherdess
Style Three
Designer: R. Tabbenor
Height: 8", 20.3 cm
Colour: Pale blue, white
            and tan
Issued: 1987-1989
Series: Reflections

U.S.:   **$225.00**
Can.:   **$250.00**
Ster.:   **£100.00**

HN 2991
June
Style Three
Designer: R. Tabbenor
Height: 9", 22.9 cm
Colour: Lavender
            and red
Issued: 1988 to the
            present

U.S.:   **$275.00**
Can.:   **$325.00**
Ster.:   **£ 95.00**

HN 2992
Golfer
Designer: R. Tabbenor
Height: 9 1/2", 24.1 cm
Colour: Blue, white and
            pale brown
Issued: 1988-1991
Series: Reflections

U.S.:   **$225.00**
Can.:   **$300.00**
Ster.:   **£100.00**

HN2993
Old Father Thames
Designer: R. Tabbenor
Height: 5 3/4", 14.6 cm
Colour: Cream with
            gold trim
Issued: 1988 in a limited
            edition of 500

U.S.:   **$175.00**
Can.:   **$250.00**
Ster.:   **£125.00**

HN 2994
Helen
Style Two
Designer: R. Tabbenor
Height: 5", 12.7 cm
Colour: White
Issued: 1985-1987
Series: Vanity Fair Children

U.S.:	**$125.00**
Can.:	**$150.00**
Ster.:	**£ 80.00**

HN 2995
Julie
Designer: R. Tabbenor
Height: 5", 12.7 cm
Colour: White
Issued: 1985 to the
present
Series: Vanity Fair Children

U.S.:	**$110.00**
Can.:	**$150.00**
Ster.:	**£ 39.95**

HN 2996
Amanda
Designer: R. Tabbenor
Height: 5 1/4", 13.3 cm
Colour: White and pink
Issued: 1986 to the
present
Series: Vanity Fair Children

U.S.:	**$ 95.00**
Can.:	**$145.00**
Ster.:	**£ 39.95**

HN 2997
Chic
Designer: R. Tabbenor
Height: 13", 33.0 cm
Colour: Pale blue
Issued: 1987 N.America,
1988 Worldwide
-1990
Series: Reflections

U.S.:	**$160.00**
Can.:	**$200.00**
Ster.:	**£100.00**

HN 2998
Aperitif
Designer: P. Gee
Height: 12", 30.5 cm
Colour: Pale green
Issued: 1988-??
Series: Reflections

U.S.:	**$300.00**
Can.:	**$375.00**
Ster.:	**£100.00**

**Commissioned by Home
Shopping Network, Florida**

HN 2999
The Genie
Designer: R. Tabbenor
Height: 9 3/4", 24.7 cm
Colour: Flambe
Issued: 1989 to the
present
Varieties: HN 2989

U.S.:	**$330.00**
Can.:	**$315.00**
Ster.:	**£ 99.95**

Photograph
Not
Available

HN 3000
Sweet Bouquet
Designer: R. Tabbenor
Height: 13", 33.0 cm
Colour: Blue and white
Issued: 1988-??
Series: Reflections

U.S.:	**$300.00**
Can.:	**$375.00**
Ster.:	**£100.00**

**Commissioned by Home
Shopping Network, Florida**

HN 3001
Danielle
Style Two
Designer: P. Gee
Height: 7", 17.8 cm
Colour: Pink and white
Issued: 1990 to the
present
Series: Vanity Fair Ladies

U.S.:	**$175.00**
Can.:	**$240.00**
Ster.:	**£ 69.95**

HN 3002
Marilyn
Designer: P. Gee
Height: 7 1/4", 18.4 cm
Colour: White dress
            with flowers
Issued: 1985 Canada,
            1986 Worldwide
            to the present

U.S.:   **$250.00**
Can.:   **$280.00**
Ster.:   **£ 95.00**

HN 3003
Lilian In Summer
Designer: P. Gee
Height: 8 1/2", 21.6 cm
Colour: White, blue
            and pink
Issued: 1985
Series: Four Seasons
            (Style Three)

U.S.:   **$250.00**
Can.:   **$295.00**
Ster.:   **£150.00**

Commssioned by Danbury Mint

HN 3004
Emily In Autumn
Style One
Designer: P. Gee
Height: 8", 20.3 cm
Colour: Yellow and white
Issued: 1986
Series: Four Seasons
            (Style Three)

U.S.:   **$250.00**
Can.:   **$300.00**
Ster.:   **£150.00**

Commssioned by Danbury Mint

HN 3005
Sarah In Winter
Designer: P. Gee
Height: 8", 20.3 cm
Colour: Pale green, white
Issued: 1986
Series: Four Seasons
            (Style Three)

U.S.:   **$250.00**
Can.:   **$300.00**
Ster.:   **£150.00**

Commissioned by Danbury Mint

HN 3006
Catherine In Spring
Style Two
Designer: P. Gee
Height: 8 1/2", 21.6 cm
Colour: Pink and white
Issued: 1985
Series: Four Seasons
            (Style Three)

U.S.:   **$250.00**
Can.:   **$300.00**
Ster.:   **£150.00**

Commissioned by Danbury Mint

HN 3007
Mary, Countess Howe
Designer: P. Gee
Height: 9 1/4", 23.5 cm
Colour: Pink and blue
Issued: 1990 in a limited
            edition of 5,000
Series: Gainsborough
            Ladies

U.S.:   **$650.00**
Can.:   **$850.00**
Ster.:   **£230.00**

HN 3008
Sophia Charlotte,
Lady Sheffield
Designer: P. Gee
Height: 10", 25.4 cm
Colour: Yellow, turquoise
Issued: 1991 in a limited
            edition of 5,000
Series: Gainsborough
            Ladies

U.S.:   **$650.00**
Can.:   **$850.00**
Ster.:   **£230.00**

HN 3009
Honourable
Francis Duncombe
Designer: P. Gee
Height: 9 3/4", 24.7 cm
Colour: Blue and yellow
Issued: 1991 in a limited
            edition of 5,000
Series: Gainsborough
            Ladies

U.S.:   **$650.00**
Can.:   **$850.00**
Ster.:   **£230.00**

HN 3010
Isabella,
Countess of Sefton
Designer: P. Gee
Height: 9 3/4", 24.7 cm
Colour: Yellow and black
Issued: 1991 in a limited
              edition of 5,000
Series: Gainsborough
              Ladies
U.S.:   **$650.00**
Can.:   **$850.00**
Ster.:   **£230.00**

HN 3011
My Best Friend
Designer: P. Gee
Height: 8", 20.3 cm
Colour: Pink
Issued: 1990 to the
              present

U.S.:   **$275.00**
Can.:   **$385.00**
Ster.:   **£129.00**

HN 3012
Painting
Designer: P. Parsons
Height: 7 1/4", 18.4 cm
Colour: Purple
Issued: 1987 in a limited
              edition of 750
Series: Gentle Arts
U.S.:   **$1,200.00**
Can.:   **$1,250.00**
Ster.:   **£ 650.00**

HN 3013
James
Designer: P. Parsons
Height: 6", 15.2 cm
Colour: White
Issued: 1983-1987
Series: Kate Greenaway
U.S.:   **$300.00**
Can.:   **$350.00**
Ster.:   **£100.00**

HN 3014
Nell
Designer: P. Parsons
Height: 4", 10.1 cm
Colour: White and pink
Issued: 1982-1987
Series: Kate Greenaway
U.S.:   **$135.00**
Can.:   **$195.00**
Ster.:   **£ 80.00**

HN 3015
Adornment
Designer: P. Parsons
Height: 7 1/4", 18.4 cm
Colour: Pink and lavender
              stripes
Issued: 1989 in a limited
              edition of 750
Series: Gentle Arts
U.S.:   **$1,100.00**
Can.:   **$1,250.00**
Ster.:   **£ 550.00**

HN 3016
The Graduate (female)
Designer: P. Parsons
Height: 8 3/4", 22.2 cm
Colour: Black, pink
              and yellow
Issued: 1984-1992
U.S.:   **$225.00**
Can.:   **$315.00**
Ster.:   **£ 85.00**

HN 3017
The Graduate (male)
Designer: P. Parsons
Height: 9 1/4", 23.5 cm
Colour: Black and grey
Issued: 1984-1992
U.S.:   **$225.00**
Can.:   **$315.00**
Ster.:   **£ 85.00**

HN 3018
Sisters
Designer: P. Parsons
Height: 8 1/2", 21.6 cm
Colour: White
Issued: 1983 to the
           present
Varieties: HN 3019
Series: Images

U.S.:	$ 80.00
Can.:	$160.00
Ster.:	£ 49.95

HN 3019
Sisters
Designer: P. Parsons
Height: 8 1/2", 21.6 cm
Colour: Black
Issued: 1983 to the
           present
Varieties: HN 3018
Series: Images

U.S.:	$ 80.00
Can.:	$160.00
Ster.:	£ 49.95

HN 3020
Ellen
Designer: P. Parsons
Height: 3 1/2", 8.9 cm
Colour: Blue and yellow
Issued: 1984-1987
Series: Kate Greenaway

U.S.:	$325.00
Can.:	$325.00
Ster.:	£120.00

HN 3021
Polly Put The Kettle On
Designer: P. Parsons
Height: 8", 20.3 cm
Colour: White and pink
Issued: 1984-1987
Series: Nursery Rhymes
           (Style Two)

U.S.:	$125.00
Can.:	$175.00
Ster.:	£ 80.00

HN 3024
April Shower
Designer: R. Jefferson
Height: 4 3/4", 12.0 cm
Colour: Cream
Issued: 1983-1986
Series: Enchantment

U.S.:	$200.00
Can.:	$250.00
Ster.:	£100.00

HN 3025
Rumpelstiltskin
Designer: R. Jefferson
Height: 8", 20.3 cm
Colour: Cream
Issued: 1983-1986
Series: Enchantment

U.S.:	$225.00
Can.:	$230.00
Ster.:	£100.00

HN 3026
Carefree
Designer: R. Jefferson
Height: 12 1/4", 31.1 cm
Colour: White
Issued: 1986 to the
           present
Series: Images

U.S.:	$125.00
Can.:	$165.00
Ster.:	£ 59.95

HN 3027
Windswept
Designer: R. Jefferson
Height: 12 1/4", 31.0 cm
Colour: Pale blue
Issued: 1985 No. America
           1987 Worldwide
Series: Reflections

U.S.:	$185.00
Can.:	$225.00
Ster.:	£ 79.95

HN 3028
Panorama
Designer: R. Jefferson
Height: 12 3/4", 32.5 cm
Colour: Pale blue
Issued: 1985 N.America,
1987 Worldwide
-1988
Series: Reflections

U.S.: **$225.00**
Can.: **$250.00**
Ster.: **£110.00**

HN 3029
Carefree
Designer: R. Jefferson
Height: 12 1/4", 31.1 cm
Colour: Black
Issued: 1986 to the
present
Varieties: HN 3026
Series: Images

U.S.: **$125.00**
Can.: **$160.00**
Ster.: **£ 59.95**

HN 3030
Little Bo Peep
Designer: A. Hughes
Height: 8", 20.3 cm
Colour: White with
blue trim
Issued: 1984-1987
Series: Nursery Rhymes
(Style Two)

U.S.: **$125.00**
Can.: **$175.00**
Ster.: **£ 80.00**

HN 3031
Wee Willie Winkie
Style Two
Designer: A. Hughes
Height: 7 3/4", 19.7 cm
Colour: White and blue
Issued: 1984-1987
Series: Nursery Rhymes
(Style Two)

U.S.: **$125.00**
Can.: **$175.00**
Ster.: **£ 80.00**

HN 3032
Tom, Tom, the Piper's Son
Designer: A. Hughes
Height: 7", 17.8 cm
Colour: White, yellow
and pink
Issued: 1984-1987
Series: Nursery Rhymes
(Style Two)

U.S.: **$100.00**
Can.: **$175.00**
Ster.: **£ 80.00**

HN 3033
Springtime
Style Two
Designer: A. Hughes
Height: 8", 20.3 cm
Colour: Yellow, cream
and green
Issued: 1983-1983
Series: R.D.I.C.C and
Four Seasons
(Style Four)

U.S.: **$350.00**
Can.: **$450.00**
Ster.: **£300.00**

HN 3034
Little Jack Horner
Style Two
Designer: A. Hughes
Height: 7", 17.8 cm
Colour: White, yellow
and green
Issued: 1984-1987
Series: Nursery Rhymes
(Style Two)

U.S.: **$100.00**
Can.: **$175.00**
Ster.: **£ 80.00**

HN 3035
Little Boy Blue
Style Two
Designer: A. Hughes
Height: 7 3/4", 19.7 cm
Colour: Blue and white
Issued: 1984-1987
Series: Nursery Rhymes
(Style Two)

U.S.: **$115.00**
Can.: **$175.00**
Ster.: **£ 80.00**

HN 3036
Kerry
Designer: A. Hughes
Height: 5 1/4", 13.3 cm
Colour: White and pale green
Issued: 1986-1992
Series: Vanity Fair Children

U.S.: $100.00
Can.: $145.00
Ster.: £ 39.95

HN 3037
Miranda
Style Two
Designer: A. Hughes
Height: 8 1/2", 21.5 cm
Colour: Cream, yellow and purple
Issued: 1987-1990

U.S.: $225.00
Can.: $275.00
Ster.: £100.00

HN 3038
Yvonne
Designer: A. Hughes
Height: 8 1/2", 21.6 cm
Colour: Turquoise
Issued: 1987 to the present

U.S.: $225.00
Can.: $310.00
Ster.: £ 95.00

HN 3039
Reflection
Designer: A. Hughes
Height: 8", 20.3 cm
Colour: Pale blue, pale brown and white
Issued: 1987 to 1989
Series: Reflections

U.S.: $225.00
Can.: $250.00
Ster.: £100.00

HN 3040
Flower Arranging
Designer: D. Brindley
Height: 7 1/4", 18.4 cm
Colour: Green, purple and pink
Issued: 1988 in a limited edition of 750
Series: Gentle Arts

U.S.: $1,000.00
Can.: $1,250.00
Ster.: £ 600.00

HN 3041
The Lawyer
Designer: P. Parsons
Height: 8 3/4", 22.2 cm
Colour: Grey and black
Issued: 1985 to the present

U.S.: $225.00
Can.: $275.00
Ster.: £ 99.95

HN 3042
Gillian
(With shoulder straps)
Style Two
Designer: P. Parsons
Height: 8 1/4", 21.0 cm
Colour: Green
Issued: 1984-?
Varieties: HN 3042A

U.S.: $175.00
Can.: $200.00
Ster.: £ 80.00

HN 3042A
Gillian
(Without Straps)
Style Two
Designer: P. Parsons
Height: 8 1/4", 21.0 cm
Colour: Green
Issued: ?-1990
Varieties: HN 3042

U.S.: $160.00
Can.: $180.00
Ster.: £ 80.00

HN 3043
Lynsey
Designer: P. Parsons
Height: 4 3/4", 12.0 cm
Colour: White
Issued: 1985 to the
                   present
Series: Vanity Fair
                   Children

U.S.: $110.00
Can.: $150.00
Ster.:   £ 39.95

HN 3044
Catherine
Style Three
Designer: P. Parsons
Height: 5", 12.7 cm
Colour: White
Issued: 1985 to the
                   present
Series: Vanity Fair
                   Children

U.S.: $ 95.00
Can.: $145.00
Ster.:   £ 39.95

HN 3045
Demure
Designer: P. Parsons
Height: 12 3/4", 32.5 cm
Colour: Grey-blue
                   and white
Issued: 1985 N.America,
                   1987 Worldwide
                   -1988
Series: Reflections

U.S.: $225.00
Can.: $250.00
Ster.:   £ 80.00

HN 3046
Debut
Designer: P. Parsons
Height: 12 1/2", 32.0 cm
Colour: Pale blue ,
                   white and green
Issued: 1985 N.America,
                   1987 Worldwide
                   -1989
Series: Reflections

U.S. $225.00
Can.: $250.00
Ster.:   £ 80.00

HN 3047
Sharon
Designer: P. Parsons
Height: 5 1/2", 14.0 cm
Colour: White
Issued: 1984 to the
                   present

U.S.: $195.00
Can.: $240.00
Ster.:   £ 69.95

HN 3048
Tapestry Weaving
Designer: P. Parsons
Height: 7 1/2", 19.1 cm
Colour: Flowered pink
                   dress
Issued: 1985 in a limited
                   edition of 750
Series: Gentle Arts

U.S.: $1,250.00
Can.: $1,250.00
Ster.:   £ 750.00

HN 3049
Writing
Designer: P. Parsons
Height: 7 1/4", 18.4 cm
Colour: Flowered yellow
                   dress
Issued: 1986 in a limited
                   edition of 750
Series: Gentle Arts

U.S.: $1,100.00
Can.: $1,100.00
Ster.:   £ 750.00

HN 3050
Susan
Style Two
Designer: P. Parsons
Height: 8 1/2", 21.6 cm
Colour: Pink and red
Issued: 1986 to the
                   present
Varieties: HN 2952

U.S.: $275.00
Can.: $370.00
Ster.:   £119.00

HN 3051
Country Girl
Designer: A. Hughes
Height: 7 3/4", 19.7 cm
Colour: Blue and white
Issued: 1987 to the
present
Series: Reflections

U.S.: **$150.00**
Can.: **$195.00**
Ster.: **£ 69.95**

HN 3052
A Winter's Walk
Designer: A. Hughes
Height: 12 1/4", 31.1 cm
Colour: Pale blue and white
Issued: 1987 N.America,
1988 Worldwide
to the present
Series: Reflections

U.S.: **$250.00**
Can.: **$315.00**
Ster.: **£109.00**

Photograph
Not
Available

HN 3053
Martine
Designer: N/A
Height: N/A
Colour: N/A
Issued: 1984
Series: Elegance

U.S.: **$ -**
Can.: **$ -**
Ster.: **£ -**

Photograph
Not
Available

HN 3054
Dominique
Designer: N/A
Height: N/A
Colour: N/A
Issued: 1984
Series: Elegance

U.S.: **$ -**
Can.: **$ -**
Ster.: **£ -**

*

Photograph
Not
Available

HN 3056
Danielle
Style One
Designer: N/A
Height: N/A
Colour: N/A
Issued: 1984
Series: Elegance

U.S.: **$ -**
Can.: **$ -**
Ster.: **£ -**

HN 3057
Sir Winston Churchill
Designer: A. Hughes
Height: 10 1/2", 26.7 cm
Colour: White
Issued: 1985 to the
present

U.S.: **$250.00**
Can.: **$305.00**
Ster.: **£ 79.95**

HN 3058
Andrea
Designer: A. Hughes
Height: 5 1/4", 13.3 cm
Colour: Blue and white
Issued: 1985 to the
present
Series: Vanity Fair
Children

U.S.: **$110.00**
Can.: **$150.00**
Ster.: **£ 39.95**

NOTE ON PRICING

Prices are given for three separate and distinct market areas:

Prices are given in the currency of each of these different trading areas.

Prices are not exchange rate calculations but are based on supply and demand in that market.

Prices listed are guidelines to the most current retail values but actual selling prices may vary slightly.

Prices for current figurines are those suggested by Royal Doulton.

Extremely rare or unique figurines have inconsistent retail values and their prices must therefore be determined between buyer and seller.

HN 3059
Sophistication
Designer: A. Hughes
Height: 11 1/2", 29.2 cm
Colour: Pale blue and white
Issued: 1987 N. America,
1988 Worldwide
-1990
Series: Reflections
U.S.: **$225.00**
Can.: **$240.00**
Ster.: **£100.00**

HN 3060
Wintertime
Designer: A. Hughes
Height: 8 1/2", 21.6 cm
Colour: Red and white
Issued: 1985-1985
Series: R.D.I.C.C. and
Four Seasons
(Style Four)
U.S.: **$250.00**
Can.: **$350.00**
Ster.: **£200.00**

HN 3061
Hope
Designer: S. Mitchell
Height: 8 1/4", 21.0 cm
Colour: Pale blue
Issued: 1984 in a limited
edition of 9500
Series: N.S.P.C.C. Charity
U.S.: **$600.00**
Can.: **$750.00**
Ster.: **£250.00**

Photograph
Not
Available

HN 3062
Claudine
Designer: N/A
Height: N/A
Colour: N/A
Issued: 1984
Series: Elegance
U.S.: **$ -**
Can.: **$ -**
Ster.: **£ -**

*

HN 3066
Printemps (Spring)
Designer: R. Jefferson
Height: 11 1/4", 28.6 cm
Colour: White, brown and
green
Issued: 1987 in a limited
edition of 300
Series: Les Saisons
U.S.: **$ 900.00**
Can.: **$1,000.00**
Ster.: **£ 450.00**

HN 3067
Ete (Summer)
Designer: R. Jefferson
Height: 11 3/4", 29.8 cm
Colour: Yellow and green
Issued: 1989 in a limited
edition of 300
Series: Les Saisons
U.S.: **$ 900.00**
Can.: **$1,000.00**
Ster.: **£ 450.00**

HN 3068
Automne (Autumn)
Designer: R. Jefferson
Height: 11 1/2", 29.2 cm
Colour: Lavender and
cream
Issued: 1986 in a limited
edition of 300
Series: Les Saisons
U.S.: **$1,000.00**
Can.: **$1,150.00**
Ster.: **£ 450.00**

HN 3069
Hiver (Winter)
Designer: R. Jeffferson
Height: 11 3/4", 29.8 cm
Colour: White
Issued: 1988 in a limited
edition of 300
Series: Les Saisons
U.S.: **$ 900.00**
Can.: **$1,000.00**
Ster.: **£ 450.00**

HN 3070
Cocktails
Designer: A. Hughes
Height: 11", 28.0 cm
Colour: Pale brown
Issued: 1985 N.America,
1987 Worldwide
to the present
Series: Reflections
U.S.: $225.00
Can.: $265.00
Ster.: £ 95.00

HN 3071
Flirtation
Designer: A. Hughes
Height: 10", 25.4 cm
Colour: Pale blue
Issued: 1985 N.America,
1987 Worldwide
to the present
Series: Reflections
U.S.: $225.00
Can.: $255.00
Ster.: £ 95.00

HN 3072
Promenade
Style Two
Designer: A. Hughes
Height: 13 1/4", 33.5 cm
Colour: Pale brown
Issued: 1985 N.America,
1987 Worldwide
to the present
Series: Reflections
U.S.: $225.00
Can.: $305.00
Ster.: £109.00

HN 3073
Strolling
Designer: A. Hughes
Height: 13 1/2", 34.3 cm
Colour: Pale green and
white
Issued: 1985 N.America,
1987 Worldwide
to the present
Series: Reflections
U.S.: $275.00
Can.: $350.00
Ster.: £109.00

HN 3074
Paradise
Designer: A. Hughes
Height: 14", 35.5 cm
Colour: Pale brown
Issued: 1985 N.America,
1987 Worldwide
to the present
Series: Reflections
U.S.: $225.00
Can.: $255.00
Ster.: £ 95.00

HN 3075
Tango
Designer: A. Hughes
Height: 13", 33.0 cm
Colour: Pale blue and
cream
Issued: 1985 N.America,
1987 Worldwide
to the present
Series: Reflections
U.S.: $225.00
Can.: $295.00
Ster.: £109.00

HN 3076
Bolero
Designer: A. Hughes
Height: 13 1/2", 34.3 cm
Colour: Pale blue and pink
Issued: 1985 N.America,
1987 Worldwide
-1988
Series: Reflections
U.S.: $225.00
Can.: $250.00
Ster.: £100.00

HN 3077
Windflower
Style Three
Designer: A. Hughes
Height: 12 1/4", 31.1 cm
Colour: Pale blue
Issued: 1986 N.America,
1987 Worldwide
to the present
Series: Reflections
U.S.: $195.00
Can.: $225.00
Ster.: £ 95.00

HN 3078
Dancing Delight
Designer: A. Hughes
Height: 12 3/4", 32.0 cm
Colour: Pale brown
Issued: 1986 N.America,
              1987 Worldwide
              -1988
Series: Reflections
U.S.:   **$225.00**
Can.:   **$250.00**
Ster.:   **£100.00**

HN 3079
Sleeping Beauty
Designer: A. Hughes
Height: 4 1/2", 11.4 cm
Colour: Green and white
Issued: 1987-1989
U.S.:   **$250.00**
Can.:   **$295.00**
Ster.:   **£100.00**

HN 3080
Allure
Designer: E. J. Griffiths
Height: 12 1/2", 32.0 cm
Colour: Pale green
Issued: 1985 N.America,
              1987 Worldwide
              - 1988
Series: Reflections
U.S.:   **$225.00**
Can.:   **$250.00**
Ster.:   **£100.00**

*

HN 3082
Faith
Designer: E. J. Griffiths
Height: 8 1/2", 21.6 cm
Colour: Pink
Issued: 1986 in a limited
              edition of 9500
Series: N.S.P.C.C. Charity
U.S.:   **$175.00**
Can.:   **$300.00**
Ster.:   **£100.00**

HN 3083
Sheikh
Designer: E.J. Griffiths
Height: 9 3/4", 24.7 cm
Colour: White
Issued: 1987-1989
Series: Reflections
U.S.:   **$200.00**
Can.:   **$230.00**
Ster.:   **£100.00**

HN 3084
Harvestime
Designer: E.J. Griffiths
Height: 8", 20.3 cm
Colour: Blue and
              blue-grey
Issued: 1988-1990
Series: Reflections
U.S.:   **$225.00**
Can.:   **$250.00**
Ster.:   **£100.00**

HN 3085
Summer Rose
Style One
Designer: E.J. Griffiths
Height: 8 1/2", 21.6 cm
Colour: Blue
Issued: 1987 N.America,
              1988 Worldwide
              to the present
Series: Reflections
U.S.:   **$195.00**
Can.:   **$255.00**
Ster.:   **£109.00**

Photograph
Not
Availab

HN 3086
The Duchess of York
Designer: E.J. Griffiths
Height: 8 1/4", 21.0 cm
Colour: Cream
Issued: 1986 in a limited
              edition of 1500
U.S.:   **$750.00**
Can.:   **$750.00**
Ster.:   **£450.00**

HN 3087
Charity
Designer: E.J. Griffiths
Height: 8 1/2", 21.6 cm
Colour: Yellow and purple
Issued: 1987 in a limited
edition of 9500
Series: N.S.P.C.C. Charity

U.S.: $425.00
Can.: $475.00
Ster.: £100.00

HN 3088
Kate Hannigan
Designer: E.J. Griffiths
Height: 9", 22.9 cm
Colour: Light brown
Issued: 1987 in a limited
edition of 9500

U.S.: $350.00
Can.: $425.00
Ster.: £300.00

HN 3089
Grace Darling
Designer: E.J. Griffiths
Height: 9", 22.9 cm
Colour: Blue, yellow
and rose
Issued: 1987 in a limited
edition of 9500

U.S.: $275.00
Can.: $350.00
Ster.: £250.00

HN 3090
Charisma
Designer: P. Parsons
Height: 12 1/2", 31.7 cm
Colour: Pale blue, white
and brown
Issued: 1986 N.America,
1987 Worldwide
-1990
Series: Reflections

U.S.: $225.00
Can.: $250.00
Ster.: £100.00

HN 3091
Summer's Darling
Designer: P. Parsons
Height: 11 1/2", 29.0 cm
Colour: Pale blue
Issued: 1986 N.America,
1987 Worldwide
to the present
Series: Reflections

U.S.: $250.00
Can.: $315.00
Ster.: £109.00

HN 3092
Cherry Blossom
Designer: P. Parsons
Height: 12 3/4", 32.0 cm
Colour: Pale green and
pale brown
Issued: 1986 N.America,
1987 Worldwide
-1989
Series: Reflections

U.S.: $225.00
Can.: $250.00
Ster.: £100.00

HN 3093
Morning Glory
Designer: P. Parsons
Height: 13", 33.0 cm
Colour: Green and blue
Issued: 1986 N.America,
1987 Worldwide
-1989
Series: Reflections

U.S.: $225.00
Can.: $250.00
Ster.: £100.00

HN 3094
Sweet Perfume
Designer: P. Parsons
Colour: Pale blue
and white
Height: 13", 33.0 cm
Issued: 1986 N.America,
1987 Worldwide
to the present
Series: Reflections

U.S.: $195.00
Can.: $255.00
Ster.: £ 95.00

HN 3095
Happy Birthday
Designer: P. Parsons
Height: 8 1/2", 21.6 cm
Colour: Yellow and white
Issued: 1987 to the present
Series: Special Occasions

U.S.: $275.00
Can.: $360.00
Ster.: £109.00

HN 3096
Merry Christmas
Designer: P. Parsons
Height: 8 1/2", 21.6 cm
Colour: Green and white
Issued: 1987-1992
Series: Special Occasions

U.S.: $275.00
Can.: $360.00
Ster.: £ 99.95

HN 3097
Happy Anniversary
Style One
Designer: P. Parsons
Height: 6 1/2", 16.5 cm
Colour: Purple and white
Issued: 1987 to the present
Series: Special Occasions

U.S.: $225.00
Can.: $360.00
Ster.: £109.00

HN 3098
Dorothy
Designer: P. Parsons
Height: 7", 17.8 cm
Colour: Grey
Issued: 1987-1990

U.S.: $225.00
Can.: $295.00
Ster.: £100.00

HN 3099
Queen Elizabeth I
Designer: P. Parsons
Height: 9", 22.9 cm
Colour: Red and gold
Issued: 1986 U.K., 1987 Worldwide in a limited edition of 5000
Series: Queens of the Realm

U.S.: $550.00
Can.: $675.00
Ster.: £250.00

HN 3100
Kathleen
Style Two
Designer: S. Keenan
Height: 6 1/2", 16.5 cm
Colour: Purple, cream and pink
Issued: 1986-1986
Varieties: HN 2933

U.S.: $225.00
Can.: $275.00
Ster.: £100.00

*

HN 3105
The Love Letter
Style Two
Designer: R. Jefferson
Height: 12", 30.5 cm
Colour: Pale blue and pale brown
Issued: 1986 N.America, 1987 Worldwide -1988
Series: Reflections

U.S.: $225.00
Can.: $250.00
Ster.: £100.00

HN 3106
Secret Moment
Designer: R. Jefferson
Height: 12 1/4", 31.1 cm
Colour: Pale blue, green flowers
Issued: 1986 N.America 1987 Worldwide -1988
Series: Reflections

U.S.: $225.00
Can.: $250.00
Ster.: £100.00

HN 3107
Daybreak
Designer: R. Jefferson
Height: 11 3/4", 29.8 cm
Colour: White, pale green
borders with
yellow flowers
Issued: 1986 N.America,
1987 Worldwide
-1988
Series: Reflections
U.S.: $225.00
Can.: $250.00
Ster.: £100.00

HN 3108
Enchanting Evening
Designer: R. Jefferson
Height: 11 3/4", 29.8 cm
Colour: Pale pink
Issued: 1986 N.America,
1987 Worldwide
to the present
Series: Reflections
U.S.: $195.00
Can.: $255.00
Ster.: £ 89.95

HN 3109
Pensive
Designer: R. Jefferson
Height: 13", 33.0 cm
Colour: White with yellow
flowers on skirt
Issued: 1986 N.America,
1987 Worldwide
-1988
Series: Reflections
U.S.: $225.00
Can.: $250.00
Ster.: £100.00

HN 3110
Enigma
Designer: R. Jefferson
Height: 12 3/4", 32.0 cm
Colour: Cream
Issued: 1986 N.America,
1987 Worldwide
to the present
Series: Reflections
U.S.: $195.00
Can.: $255.00
Ster.: £ 79.95
*

HN 3115
Idle Hours
Designer: A. Maslankowski
Length: 12 1/4", 31.1 cm
Colour: Blue-white and
pale green
Issued: 1986 N.America,
1987 Worldwide
-1988
Series: Reflections
U.S.: $250.00
Can.: $275.00
Ster.: £100.00

HN 3116
Park Parade
Designer: A. Maslankowski
Height: 11 3/4", 29.8 cm
Colour: Pale green
and pale blue
Issued: 1987 N.America,
1988 Worldwide
to the present
Series: Reflections
U.S.: $225.00
Can.: $305.00
Ster.: £109.00

HN 3117
Indian Maiden
Designer: A. Maslankowski
Height: 12", 30.5 cm
Colour: Pale tan and
pale blue
Issued: 1987-1991
Series: Reflections
U.S.: $250.00
Can.: $275.00
Ster.: £100.00

HN 3118
Lorraine
Designer: A. Maslankowski
Height: 7 3/4", 19.7 cm
Colour: Blue
Issued: 1988 to the
present
U.S.: $275.00
Can.: $360.00
Ster.: £109.00

HN 3119
Partners
Designer: A. Maslankowski
Height: 6 3/4", 17.2 cm
Colour: Black, blue
and grey
Issued: 1990-1992
Series: Clowns
U.S.: $250.00
Can.: $395.00
Ster.: £119.00

Photograph
Not
Available

HN 3120
Spring Walk
Designer: A. Maslankowski
Height: 13", 32.9 cm
Colour: Blue with
white poodle
Issued: 1990 to the
present
Series: Reflections
U.S.: $225.00
Can.: $350.00
Ster.: £109.00

HN 3121
Wizard
Designer: A. Maslankowski
Height: 10", 25.4 cm
Colour: Flambe
Issued: 1990 to the
present
Varieties: HN 2877
U.S.: $195.00
Can.: $225.00
Ster.: £ 99.95

HN 3122
My First Pet
Designer: A. Maslankowski
Height: 4 1/2", 11.4 cm
Colour: Blue and white
Issued: 1991 to the
present
Series: Vanity Fair
Children
U.S.: $ 95.00
Can.: $135.00
Ster.: £ 45.00

HN 3123
Sit
Designer: A. Maslankowski
Height: 4 1/2", 11.4 cm
Colour: White and yellow
Issued: 1991 to the
present
Series: Vanity Fair
Children
U.S.: $ 95.00
Can.: $135.00
Ster.: £ 45.00

HN 3124
Thinking of You
Designer: A. Maslankowski
Height: 6 3/4", 17.1 cm
Colour: White
Issued: 1991 to the
present
Varieties: Sentiments
U.S.: $ 85.00
Can.: $105.00
Ster.: £ 39.95

HN 3125
Queen Victoria
Designer: P. Parsons
Height: 8", 20.3 cm
Colour: Pink and white
Issued: 1987 U.K., 1988
Worldwide in a
limited edition
of 5000
Series: Queens of the
Realm
U.S.: $1,500.00
Can.: $1,500.00
Ster.: £ 500.00

HN 3126
Storytime
Designer: P. Parsons
Height: 6", 15.2 cm
Colour: Pale blue
Issued: 1987 to the
present
Series: Reflections
U.S.: $225.00
Can.: $285.00
Ster.: £ 85.00

HN 3127
Playmates
Designer: P. Parsons
Height: 8 1/2", 21.6 cm
Colour: Pale blue,
green and white
Issued: 1987 to the
present
Series: Reflections
U.S.: **$225.00**
Can.: **$285.00**
Ster.: **£ 79.95**

HN 3128
Tomorrow's Dreams
Designer: P. Parsons
Height: 6 1/2", 16.5 cm
Colour: White and green
Issued: 1987 to the
present
Series: Reflections
U.S.: **$250.00**
Can.: **$295.00**
Ster.: **£ 85.00**

HN 3129
Thankful
Designer: P. Parsons
Height: 8 1/2", 21.6 cm
Colour: White
Issued: 1987 to the
present
Varieties: HN 3135
Series: Images
U.S.: **$ 95.00**
Can.: **$115.00**
Ster.: **£ 43.00**

HN 3130
Sisterly Love
Designer: P. Parsons
Height: 8 1/2", 21.6 cm
Colour: Pale blue
and white
Issued: 1987 to the
present
Series: Reflections
U.S.: **$195.00**
Can.: **$245.00**
Ster.: **£ 79.95**

*

HN 3132
Good Pals
Designer: P. Parsons
Height: 6 1/4", 15.9 cm
Colour: Pale blue
and white
Issued: 1987 to the
present
Series: Reflections
U.S.: **$195.00**
Can.: **$275.00**
Ster.: **£ 85.00**

HN 3133
Dreaming
Designer: P. Parsons
Height: 9", 22.9 cm
Colour: Pale pink
Issued: 1987 to the
present
Series: Reflections
U.S.: **$150.00**
Can.: **$195.00**
Ster.: **£ 69.95**

HN 3134
Ballet Class
Designer: P. Parsons
Height: 6", 15.2 cm
Colour: White and tan
Issued: 1987 N.America,
1988 Worldwide
to the present
Series: Reflections
U.S.: **$250.00**
Can.: **$295.00**
Ster.: **£ 85.00**

HN 3135
Thankful
Designer: P. Parsons
Height: 8 1/2", 21.6 cm
Colour: Black
Issued: 1987 to the
present
Varieties: HN 3129
Series: Images
U.S.: **$ 95.00**
Can.: **$115.00**
Ster.: **£ 43.00**

HN 3136
Laura
Designer: P. Parsons
Height: 7 1/4", 18.4 cm
Colour: Dark blue and white
Issued: 1988-1988
Varieties: HN 2960

U.S.: $225.00
Can.: $295.00
Ster.: £100.00

HN 3137
Summertime
Designer: P. Parsons
Height: 8", 20.3 cm
Colour: White and blue
Issued: 1987-1987
Series: R.D.I.C.C and Four Seasons (Style Four)

U.S.: $200.00
Can.: $295.00
Ster.: £100.00

HN 3138
Eastern Grace
Designer: P. Parsons
Height: 12", 30.5 cm
Colour: Cream
Issued: 1988-1989
Series: Reflections

U.S.: $225.00
Can.: $250.00
Ster.: £100.00

HN 3139
Free As The Wind
Designer: P. Parsons
Height: 9 1/2". 24.1 cm
Colour: Pale blue
Issued: 1988 N. America, 1989 Worldwide to the present
Series: Reflections

U.S.: $225.00
Can.: $305.00
Ster.: £109.00

HN 3140
Gaiety
Designer: P. Parsons
Height: 10 1/4". 26.0 cm
Colour: Pale green and pale blue
Issued: 1988-1990
Series: Reflections

U.S.: $225.00
Can.: $275.00
Ster.: £100.00

HN 3141
Queen Anne
Designer: P. Parsons
Height: 9". 22.9 cm
Colour: Green, red and white
Issued: 1988 U.K., 1989 Worldwide; limited edition of 5000
Series: Queens of the Realm

U.S.: $450.00
Can.: $600.00
Ster.: £300.00

HN 3142
Mary Queen of Scots
Style Two
Designer: P. Parsons
Height: 9". 22.9 cm
Colour: Blue and purple
Issued: 1989 U.K., 1990 Worldwide; limited edition of 5000
Series: Queens of the Realm

U.S.: $750.00
Can.: $750.00
Ster.: £300.00

HN 3143
Rosemary
Style Two
Designer: P. Parsons
Height: 7 1/2", 19.1 cm
Colour: White dress with pink flowers
Issued: 1988-1991

U.S.: $220.00
Can.: $275.00
Ster.: £ 90.00

HN 3144
Florence Nightingale
Designer: P. Parsons
Height: 8 1/4", 21.0 cm
Colour: Red
Issued: 1988 in a limited
edition of 5,000

U.S.: $1,000.00
Can.: $1,000.00
Ster.: £ 400.00

HN 3145
Rose Arbour
Designer: D. Brindley
Height: 12", 30.5 cm
Colour: Pale blue and white
Issued: 1987 N.America,
1988 Worldwide
-1990
Series: Reflections

U.S.: $225.00
Can.: $240.00
Ster.: £100.00

*

HN 3155
Water Maiden
Designer: A. Hughes
Height: 12", 30.5 cm
Colour: Blue
Issued: 1987 N. America,
1988-1991
Series: Reflections

U.S.: $200.00
Can.: $250.00
Ster.: £ 75.00

HN 3156
Bathing Beauty
Designer: A. Hughes
Height: 9 3/4", 24.7 cm
Colour: Pale grey
Issued: 1987-1989
Series: Reflections

U.S.: $350.00
Can.: $280.00
Ster.: £100.00

HN 3157
Free Spirit
Designer: A. Hughes
Height: 10 1/2", 26.5 cm
Colour: White
Issued: 1987-1992
Varieties: HN 3159
Series: Images

U.S.: $150.00
Can.: $175.00
Ster.: £ 65.00

*

HN 3159
Free Spirit
Designer: A. Hughes
Height: 10 1/2", 26.5 cm
Colour: Black
Issued: 1987-1992
Varieties: HN 3157
Series: Images

U.S.: $150.00
Can.: $175.00
Ster.: £ 65.00

HN 3160
Shepherd
Style Five
Designer: A. Hughes
Height: 8 1/2", 21.6 cm
Colour: Grey-blue
and black
Issued: 1988-1989
Series: Reflections

U.S.: $225.00
Can.: $230.00
Ster.: £100.00

HN 3161
The Gardener
Designer: A. Hughes
Height: 8 1/4", 21.0 cm
Colour: Blue and pale
brown
Issued: 1988 N. America,
1989 Worldwide
-1991
Series: Reflection

U.S.: $???
Can.: $???
Ster.: £ 99.00

HN 3162
Breezy Day
Designer: A. Hughes
Height: 8 1/2", 21.6 cm
Colour: Pale blue, pale
           brown and white
Issued: 1988-1990
Series: Reflections

U.S.: $225.00
Can.: $295.00
Ster.:   £100.00

HN 3163
Country Maid
Designer: A. Hughes
Height: 8 1/4", 21.0 cm
Colour: Blue, pink, white
           and black
Issued: 1988-1991

U.S.: $150.00
Can.: $200.00
Ster.:   £ 65.00

HN 3164
Farmer's Wife
Style Two
Designer: A. Hughes
Height: 8 3/4", 22.2 cm
Colour: Brown and blue
Issued: 1988-1991

U.S.: $150.00
Can.: $200.00
Ster.:   £ 75.00

HN 3165
August
Style One
Designer: M. Davies
Height: 7 3/4", 19.7 cm
Colour: White and blue
           dress, poppies
Issued: 1987
Series: Flower of the
           Month

U.S.: $195.00
Can.: $295.00
Ster.:   £100.00

HN 3166
September
Style One
Designer: M. Davies
Height: 7 3/4", 19.7 cm
Colour: White and yellow
           dress, michaelmas
           daisies
Issued: 1987
Series: Flower of
           the Month

U.S.: $195.00
Can.: $295.00
Ster.:   £100.00

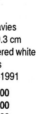

HN 3167
Hazel
Style Two
Designer: M. Davies
Height: 8", 20.3 cm
Colour: Flowered white
           dress
Issued: 1988-1991

U.S.: $200.00
Can.: $275.00
Ster.:   £ 90.00

HN 3168
Jemma
Designer: M. Davies
Height: 7 1/4", 18.4 cm
Colour: Red and blue
Issued: 1988-1991

U.S.: $200.00
Can.: $275.00
Ster.:   £100.00

HN 3169
Jessica
Designer: M. Davies
Height: 7", 17.8 cm
Colour: White
Issued: 1988 to the
           present
Series: Vanity Fair Ladies

U.S.: $185.00
Can.: $240.00
Ster.:   £ 79.95

HN 3170
Caroline
Designer: M. Davies
Height: 7 1/2", 19.1 cm
Colour: White dress with
blue flowers
Issued: 1988-1992
U.S.: $250.00
Can.: $280.00
Ster.: £ 89.95

*

HN 3172
Christine
Style Two
Designer: M. Davies
Height: 7 1/2", 19.1 cm
Colour: Pink and white
Issued: 1988 in a limited
edition of 1,000
Varieties: HN 2792
U.S.: $250.00
Can.: $280.00
Ster.: £100.00

HN 3173
Natalie
Designer: M. Davies
Height: 8", 20.3 cm
Colour: Yellow and
white
Issued: 1989 to the
present
Series: Vanity Fair Ladies
U.S.: $185.00
Can.: $240.00
Ster.: £ 79.95

HN 3174
Southern Belle
Designer: M. Davies
Height: 4", 10.1 cm
Colour: Red and
yellow
Issued: 1988 to the
present
Series: Miniatures
U.S.: $150.00
Can.: $185.00
Ster.: £ 49.95

HN 3175
Sweet Violets
Designer: D.V. Tootle
Height: 10 1/4", 26.0 cm
Colour: Pale blue and
white
Issued: 1988-1989
Series: Reflections
U.S.: $225.00
Can.: $250.00
Ster.: £100.00

HN 3176
Young Dreams
Designer: D.V. Tootle
Height: 6 1/4", 15.9 cm
Colour: Pink
Issued: 1988 to the
present
U.S.: $275.00
Can.: $325.00
Ster.: £ 95.00

HN 3177
Harriet
Designer: D.V. Tootle
Height: 7 1/4", 18.4 cm
Colour: Pink
Issued: 1988-1991
U.S.: $225.00
Can.: $275.00
Ster.: £ 95.00

HN 3178
Polly
Designer: D.V. Tootle
Height: 8", 20.3 cm
Colour: Green and
lavender
Issued: 1988-1991
U.S.: $200.00
Can.: $275.00
Ster.: £ 99.00

HN 3179
Eliza
Style Two
Designer: D. V. Tootle
Height: 7 1/2", 19.1 cm
Colour: Red and lilac
Issued: 1988-1992

U.S.:	$250.00
Can.:	$330.00
Ster.:	£ 95.00

HN 3180
Phyllis
Style Two
Designer: D.V. Tootle
Height: 7 1/4", 18.4 cm
Colour: Red, white and purple
Issued: 1988-1991

U.S.:	$200.00
Can.:	$275.00
Ster.:	£ 95.00

HN 3181
Moondancer
Designer: D.V. Tootle
Height: 11 3/4", 29.8 cm
Colour: Blue, white and pale green
Issued: 1988-1990
Series: Reflections

U.S.:	$250.00
Can.:	$275.00
Ster.:	£100.00

HN 3182
Stargazer
Designer: D.V. Tootle
Height: 10 1/2", 26.7 cm
Colour: Blue and pale blue
Issued: 1988-1990
Series: Reflections

U.S.:	$250.00
Can.:	$275.00
Ster.:	£100.00

HN 3183
Tumbler
Designer: D.V. Tootle
Height: 9", 22.9 cm
Colour: Pink and yellow
Issued: 1989 to the present
Series: Reflections

U.S.:	$210.00
Can.:	$295.00
Ster.:	£ 75.00

HN 3184
Joy
Designer: D.V. Tootle
Height: 6 3/4", 17.2 cm
Colour: Blue and pink
Issued: 1988-1990
Series: Reflections

U.S.:	$250.00
Can.:	$265.00
Ster.:	£100.00

HN 3185
Traveller's Tale
Designer: E.J. Griffiths
Height: 9 1/4", 23.5 cm
Colour: Pale blue and pale green
Issued: 1988-1989
Series: Reflections

U.S.:	$250.00
Can.:	$250.00
Ster.:	£100.00

HN 3186
Entranced
Designer: E.J. Griffiths
Height: 7 1/4", 18.4 cm
Colour: Green, white and tan
Issued: 1988-1989
Series: Reflections

U.S.:	$225.00
Can.:	$230.00
Ster.:	£100.00

Photograph Not Available	Photograph Not Available		

HN 3187
Balloons
Designer: E.J. Griffiths
Height: 8 1/2", 21.6 cm
Colour: Pale blue
Issued: 1988-in a limited edition of 1,000
Series: Reflections
U.S.: $325.00
Can.: $375.00
Ster.: £100.00

HN 3188
Debutante
Style Two
Designer: E.J. Griffiths
Height: 12", 30.5 cm
Colour: Grey-pink
Issued: 1988 in a limited edition of 1,000
Series: Reflections
U.S.: $325.00
Can.: $375.00
Ster.: £100.00

HN3189
HM Queen Elizabeth,
The Queen Mother
Style Two
Designer: E.J. Griffiths
Height: 8", 20.3 cm
Colour: Lavender, blue and pink
Issued: 1990 in a limited edition of 2,500
U.S.: $700.00
Can: $750.00
Ster.: £300.00

HN 3190
Old Ben
Designer: M. Nicholl
Height: 8 1/2", 21.6 cm
Colour: Green, brown and blue
Issued: 1990 in a limited editon of 1,500
Varieties: also called "Newsvendor" HN 2891
U.S.: $175.00
Can.: $225.00
Ster.: £ 75.00

HN 3191
Brothers
Designer: E.J. Griffiths
Height: 8 1/4", 21.0 cm
Colour: White
Issued: 1991 to the present
Series: Images
U.S.: $ 80.00
Can.: $160.00
Ster.: £ 39.95

HN 3192
Mantilla
Designer: E.J. Griffiths
Height: 11 1/2", 29.2 cm
Colour: Red, black and white
Issued: 1992-1992
Varieties: Re-issue of HN 2712
U.S.: $350.00 *
Can.: $795.00
Ster.: £180.00

Expo '92, Seville, Spain *

HN 3195
The Farmer
Designer: A. Hughes
Height: 9", 22.9 cm
Colour: Brown and white
Issued: 1988-1991
U.S.: $150.00
Can.: $200.00
Ster.: £ 75.00

HN 3196
The Joker
Style One
Designer: A. Hughes
Height: 9 1/4", 23.5 cm
Colour: White
Issued: 1988-1990
Series: Reflections
U.S.: $200.00
Can.: $265.00
Ster.: £100.00

<table>
<tr><td>

Photograph
Not
Available

HN 3197
Ballerina
Style Two
Designer: A. Hughes
Height: 14", 35.5 cm
Colour: White and biege
Issued: 1988 in a limited
edition of 1,000
Series: Reflections
U.S.: $325.00
Can.: $375.00
Ster.: £ 90.00

</td><td>

HN 3198
Vanessa
Style Two
Designer: A. Hughes
Height: 8 1/2", 21.6 cm
Colour: Green and black
Issued: 1989-1990
U.S.: $175.00
Can.: $225.00
Ster.: £100.00

</td><td>

HN 3199
Maxine
Designer: A. Hughes
Height: 8 1/2", 21.6 cm
Colour: Pink and purple
Issued: 1989-1990
U.S.: $175.00
Can.: $225.00
Ster.: £100.00

</td><td>

HN 3200
Gloria
Style Two
Designer: A. Hughes
Height: 8 3/4", 22.2 cm
Colour: Pink
Issued: 1989-1990
U.S.: $175.00
Can.: $225.00
Ster.: £100.00

</td></tr>
<tr><td>

HN 3201
Liberty
Designer: A. Hughes
Height: 8 1/4", 21.0 cm
Colour: White, blue
and red
Issued: 1989-1990
U.S.: $175.00
Can.: $225.00
Ster.: £100.00

</td><td>

HN 3202
The Boy Evacuee
Designer: A. Hughes
Height: 8 1/2", 21.6 cm
Colour: Green and blue
Issued: 1989 in a limited
edition of 9,500
Series: Children of the
Blitz
U.S.: $350.00
Can.: $400.00
Ster.: £125.00

</td><td>

HN 3203
The Girl Evacuee
Designer: A. Hughes
Height: 8", 20.3 cm
Colour: Red, blue
and brown
Issued: 1989 in a limited
edition of 9,500
Series: Children of the
Blitz
U.S.: $350.00
Can.: $400.00
Ster.: £125.00

</td><td>

HN 3204
Emily
Style Two
Designer: A. Hughes
Height: 8 1/4", 21.0 cm
Colour: White and blue
Issued: 1989 to the
present
Series: Vanity Fair Ladies
U.S.: $195.00
Can.: $240.00
Ster.: £ 95.00

</td></tr>
</table>

HN 3205
Veronica
Style Three
Designer: A. Hughes
Height: 8", 20.3 cm
Colour: White and pink
Issued: 1989-1992
Series: Vanity Fair Ladies

U.S.: $185.00
Can.: $240.00
Ster.: £ 69.95

HN 3206
Teresa
Style Two
Designer: A. Hughes
Height: 7 3/4", 19.7 cm
Colour: White with
flowers
Issued: 1989-1992

U.S.: $225.00
Can.: $290.00
Ster.: £ 89.95

HN 3207
Louise
Style Two
Designer: A. Hughes
Height: 7 1/2", 19.1 cm
Colour: Red
Issued: 1990 to the
present

U.S.: $250.00
Can.: $315.00
Ster.: £109.00

HN 3208
Emma
Style Three
Designer: A. Hughes
Height: 4 1/4", 10.8 cm
Colour: Red
Issued: 1990 to the
present
Series Miniatures

U.S.: $150.00
Can.: $185.00
Ster.: £ 49.95

HN 3209
Claire
Designer: A. Hughes
Height: 8 1/2", 21.6 cm
Colour: Red
Issued: 1990-1992

U.S.: $225.00
Can.: $230.00
Ster.: £ 75.00

HN 3210
Christening Day
Designer: P.A. Northcroft
Height: 8 1/2", 21.6 cm
Colour: White, baby's
shawl blue
Issued: 1988-1990
Varieties: HN 3211
Series: Special Occasions

U.S.: $200.00
Can.: $230.00
Ster.: £100.00

HN 3211
Christening Day
Designer: P.A. Northcroft
Height: 8 1/2", 21.6 cm
Colour: White, baby's
shawl pink
Issued: 1988-1990
Varieties: HN 3210
Series: Special Occasions

U.S.: $200.00
Can.: $230.00
Ster.: £100.00

HN 3212
Christmas Morn
Designer: M. Davies
Height: 4", 10.1 cm
Colour: Red and white
Issued: 1988 to the
present
Series: Miniatures
Varieties: HN 3245

U.S.: $150.00
Can.: $185.00
Ster.: £ 49.95

HN 3213
Kirsty
Designer: M. Davies
Height: 3 3/4", 9.5 cm
Colour: Red
Issued: 1988 to the present
Series: Miniatures
Varieties: HN 3246

U.S.: $150.00
Can.: $165.00
Ster.: £ 49.95

HN 3214
Elaine
Designer: M. Davies
Height: 4", 10.1 cm
Colour: Blue
Issued: 1988 to the present
Series: Miniatures
Varieties: HN 3247

U.S.: $150.00
Can.: $185.00
Ster.: £ 49.95

HN 3215
Ninette
Designer: M. Davies
Height: 3 1/2", 8.9 cm
Colour: Cream and lavender
Issued: 1988 to the present
Series: Miniatures
Varieties: HN 3248

U.S.: $225.00
Can.: $145.00
Ster.: £ 43.00

HN 3216
Fair Lady
Designer: M. Davies
Height: 3 3/4", 9.5 cm
Colour: Lemon and blue
Issued: 1988 to the present
Series: Miniatures
Varieties: HN 3336

U.S.: $125.00
Can.: $145.00
Ster.: £ 43.00

HN 3217
Joan
Style Two
Designer: M. Davies
Height: 8", 20.3 cm
Colour: Yellow and green
Issued: 1988 in a limited edition of 2,000
Varieties: Also called "Adrienne", HN 2152, 2304

U.S.: $350.00
Can.: $400.00
Ster.: £100.00

HN 3218
Sunday Best
Designer: M. Davies
Height: 3 3/4", 9.5 cm
Colour: Green and blue
Issued: 1988 to the present
Series: Miniatures
Varieties: HN 3312

U.S.: $135.00
Can.: $165.00
Ster.: £ 49.95

HN 3219
Sara
Designer: M. Davies
Height: 3 3/4", 9.5 cm
Colour: Pink and green
Issued: 1988 to the present
Series: Miniatures
Varieties: HN 3249

U.S.: $125.00
Can.: $145.00
Ster.: £ 43.00

HN 3220
Fragrance
Designer: M. Davies
Height: 3 3/4", 9.5 cm
Colour: Gold
Issued: 1988-1992
Series: Miniatures
Varieties: HN 3250

U.S.: $150.00
Can.: $165.00
Ster.: £ 49.95

HN 3221
Country Rose
Designer: M. Davies
Height: 8 1/2", 21.6 cm
Colour: White dress, red flowers
Issued: 1989 to the present

U.S.: $225.00
Can.: $280.00
Ster.: £ 95.00

*

HN 3223
Pamela
Style Two
Designer: M. Davies
Height: 7", 17.8 cm
Colour: White and blue
Issued: 1989-1989
Varieties: HN 2479
Series: Vanity Fair Ladies

U.S.: $175.00
Can.: $225.00
Ster.: £100.00

*

Photograph
Not
Available

HN 3226
Innocence
Style Two
Designer: P. Parsons
Height: 7 3/4", 19.7 cm
Colour: N/A
Issued: In a limited edition of 9,500

U.S.: $225.00
Can.: $275.00
Ster.: £120.00

*

HN 3228
Devotion
Designer: P. Parsons
Height: 9 1/2", 24.1 cm
Colour: Pale green
Issued: 1989 to the present
Series: Reflections

U.S.: $250.00
Can.: $325.00
Ster.: £109.00

HN 3229
The Geisha
Designer: P. Parsons
Height: 9 1/2", 24.1 cm
Colour: Flambe
Issued: 1989-1989
Series: R.D.I.C.C.

U.S.: $250.00
Can.: $280.00
Ster.: £150.00

HN 3230
HM Queen Elizabeth the Queen Mother as the Duchess of York
Designer: P. Parsons
Height: 9", 22.9 cm
Colour: Pale blue and pink
Issued: 1989 in a limited edition of 9,500

U.S.: $500.00
Can.: $750.00
Ster.: £265.00

HN 3231
Autumntime
Designer: P. Parsons
Height: 8", 20.3 cm
Colour: Golden brown
Issued: 1989
Series: R.D.I.C.C. Four Seasons (Style Four)

U.S.: $225.00
Can.: $250.00
Ster.: £120.00

HN 3232
Anne Bolelyn
Designer: P. Parsons
Height: 8", 20.3 cm
Colour: Red and grey
Issued: 1990 in a limited edition of 9,500

U.S.: $650.00
Can.: $850.00
Ster.: £225.00

HN 3233
Catherine of Aragon
Designer: P. Parsons
Height: 6 1/2", 16.5 cm
Colour: Green, blue
and white
Issued: 1990 in a limited
edition of 9,500

U.S.: $650.00
Can.: $700.00
Ster.: £225.00

HN3234
Paula
Designer: P. Parsons
Height: 7", 17.8 cm
Colour: White and blue
Issued: 1990 to the
present
Series: Vanity Fair Ladies
Varieties: HN 2906

U.S.: $175.00
Can.: $265.00
Ster.: £ 75.00

HN 3235
Mother and Baby
Designer: P. Parsons
Height: 7 1/2", 19.1 cm
Colour: White and blue
Issued: 1991 to the
present
Varieties: HN 3348, 3353

U.S.: $250.00
Can.: $325.00
Ster.: $109.00

HN 3236
Falstaff
Designer: C.J. Noke
Height: 3 3/4", 9.5 cm
Colour: Brown, yellow
and lavender
Issued: 1989 to the
present
Series: Miniatures

U.S.: $140.00
Can.: $210.00
Ster.: £ 50.00

*

HN 3244
Southern Belle
Designer: M. Davies
Height: 4", 10.1 cm
Colour: Turquoise with
22 kt gold trim
Issued: 1989
Series: M. Doulton
Signature
Collection
Varieties: HN 3174

U.S.: $125.00
Can.: $150.00
Ster.: £ 59.00

HN 3245
Christmas Morn
Designer: M. Davies
Height: 3 1/2", 8.9 cm
Colour: Green, blue, white,
with 22 kt gold trim
Issued: 1991
Series: M. Doulton
Signature
Collection
Varieties: HN 3212

U.S.: $125.00
Can.: $150.00
Ster.: £ 69.00

HN 3246
Kirsty
Designer: M. Davies
Height: 3 3/4", 9.5 cm
Colour: Purple with
22 kt gold trim
Issued: 1989
Series: M. Doulton
Signature
Collection
Varieties: HN 3213

U.S.: $125.00
Can.: $150.00
Ster.: £ 59.00

HN 3247
Elaine
Designer: M. Davies
Height: 4", 10.1 cm
Colour: Blue with
22kt gold trim
Issued: 1989
Series: M. Doulton
Signature
Collection
Varieties: HN 3213

U.S.: $125.00
Can.: $150.00
Ster.: £ 59.00

HN 3248
Ninette
Designer: M. Davies
Height: 3 1/2", 8.9 cm
Colour: Red and green,
22 kt gold trim
Issued: 1989
Series: M. Doulton
Signature
Collection
Varieties: HN 3215

U.S.:	**$125.00**
Can.:	**$150.00**
Ster.:	**£ 59.00**

HN 3249
Sara
Designer: M. Davies
Height: 3 3/4", 9.5 cm
Colour: Blue and pink,
22 kt gold trim
Issued: 1989
Series: M. Doulton
Signature
Collection
Varieties: HN 3219

U.S.:	**$125.00**
Can.:	**$150.00**
Ster.:	**£ 59.00**

HN 3250
Fragrance
Designer: M. Davies
Height: 3 3/4", 9.5 cm
Colour: Red with
22 kt gold trim
Issued: 1989
Series: M. Doulton
Signature
Collection
Varieties: HN 3220

U.S.:	**$125.00**
Can.:	**$150.00**
Ster.:	**£ 59.00**

HN 3251
May
Style One
Designer: D.V. Tootle
Height: 8", 20.3 cm
Colour: Blue, red and pink
Issued: 1989 in an
un-numbered
limited edition
of 2,000
Varieties: HN 2746

U.S.:	**$250.00**
Can.:	**$280.00**
Ster.:	**£125.00**

HN 3252
Fiona

Style Three
Designer: D.V. Tootle
Height: 7", 17.8 cm
Colour: Red
Issued: 1989-1992

U.S.:	**$325.00**
Can.:	**$410.00**
Ster.:	**£119.00**

HN 3253
Cheryl
Designer: D.V. Tootle
Height: 7 1/2", 19.1 cm
Colour: Red and white
Issued: 1989 to the
present

U.S.:	**$350.00**
Can.:	**$445.00**
Ster.:	**£129.00**

HN 3254
Happy Anniversary
Style Two
Designer: D.V. Tootle
Height: 12", 30.5 cm
Colour: White
Issued: 1989 to the
present
Series: Images

U.S.:	**$275.00**
Can.:	**$285.00**
Ster.:	**£ 95.00**

HN 3255
Madeleine
Designer: D.V. Tootle
Height: 7 1/2", 19.1 cm
Colour: Blue, pink
and cream
Issued: 1989 to the
present

U.S.:	**$275.00**
Can.:	**$335.00**
Ster.:	**£ 95.00**

HN 3256
Queen Victoria and
Prince Albert
Designer: D.V. Tootle
Height: 9 1/4", 20.3 cm
Colour: Yellow-pink,
           cream and red
Issued: 1990 in a limited
           edition of 2,500

U.S.:   **$1,250.00**
Can.:   **$1,250.00**
Ster.:   **£ 450.00**

HN 3257
Sophie
Style Two
Designer: D.V. Tootle
Height: 8", 20.3 cm
Colour: Blue and red
Issued: 1990 to the
           present

U.S.:   **$350.00**
Can.:   **$435.00**
Ster.:   **£139.00**

HN 3258
Dawn
Style Two
Designer: D.V. Tootle
Height: 8", 20.3 cm
Colour: Purple, red
           and white
Issued: 1990-1992

U.S.:   **$225.00**
Can.:   **$290.00**
Ster.:   **£ 99.95**

HN 3259
Ann
Style Two
Designer: D.V. Tootle
Height: 8", 20.3 cm
Colour: Pink, green
           and blue
Issued: 1990 to the
           present

U.S.:   **$375.00**
Can.:   **$440.00**
Ster.:   **£129.00**

HN 3260
Jane
Style Three
Designer: D.V. Tootles
Height: 7 3/4", 19.7 cm
Colour: Green, blue
           and yellow
Issued: 1990 to the
           present

U.S.:   **$275.00**
Can.:   **$330.00**
Ster.:   **£119.00**

HN 3261
The Town Crier
Designer: M. Davies
Height: 4", 10.1 cm
Colour: Purple, green
           and black
Issued: 1989 to the
           present
Series: Miniatures

U.S.:   **$160.00**
Can.:   **$175.00**
Ster.:   **£ 50.00**

HN 3262
Good King Wenceslas
Designer: M. Davies
Height: 4", 10.1 cm
Colour: Black and
           lavender
Issued: 1989 to the
           present
Series: Miniatures

U.S.:   **$160.00**
Can.:   **$175.00**
Ster.:   **£ 50.00**

HN 3263
Beatrice
Designer: M. Davies
Height: 7", 17.8 cm
Colour: Blue flowered
           dress
Issued: 1989 to the
           present

U.S.:   **$250.00**
Can.:   **$280.00**
Ster.:   **£ 89.95**

HN 3264
Alison
Designer: M. Davies
Height: 7 1/2", 19.1 cm
Colour: White and pastel pink
Issued: 1989 to the present
Varieties: HN 2336
U.S.: **$195.00**
Can.: **$285.00**
Ster.: **£ 79.95**

HN 3265
Lisa
Designer: M. Davies
Height: 7 1/2", 19.1 cm
Colour: White and rose
Issued: 1989 to the present
Varieties: HN 2310, 2394
U.S.: **$195.00**
Can.: **$275.00**
Ster.: **£ 79.95**

HN 3266
Diana
Style Two
Designer: M. Davies
Height: 8", 20.3 cm
Colour: Pink, blue and white
Issued: 1990-1990
Varieties: HN 2468
U.S.: **$225.00**
Can.: **$300.00**
Ster.: **£125.00**

HN3267
Salome
Style Two
Designer: M. Davies
Height: 9 1/2", 24.1cm
Colour: Red, blue, lavender and green
Issued: 1990 in a limited edition of 1,000
U.S.: **$850.00**
Can.: **$950.00**
Ster.: **£550.00**

HN 3268
Buttercup
Designer: M. Davies
Height: 4", 10.1 cm
Colour: Green
Issued: 1990 to the present
Series: Miniatures
U.S.: **$110.00**
Can.: **$165.00**
Ster.: **£ 49.95**

HN 3269
Christine
Designer: M. Davies
Height: 3 3/4", 9.5 cm
Colour: Orange and pink
Issued: 1990 to the present
Series: Miniatures
Varieties: HN 3337
U.S.: **$125.00**
Can.: **$165.00**
Ster.: **£ 49.95**

HN3270
Karen
Designer: M. Davies
Height: 4", 10.1 cm
Colour: Red
Issued: 1990 to the present
Series: Miniatures
Varieties: HN 3338
U.S.: **$150.00**
Can.: **$195.00**
Ster.: **£ 49.95**

HN 3271
Guy Fawkes
Designer: C.J. Nokes
Height: 4", 10.1 cm
Colour: Red and black
Issued: 1989 to the present
Series: Miniatures
U.S.: **$150.00**
Can.: **$175.00**
Ster.: **£ 45.00**

HN 3272
Dick Turpin
Designer: G. Tongue
Height: 12", 30.5 cm
Colour: Brown and black
Issued: 1989 in a limited
edition of 5,000

U.S.: $750.00
Can.: $900.00
Ster.: £450.00

HN 3273
Annabel
Designer: R. Tabbenor
Height: 6", 15.2 cm
Colour: White and blue
Issued: 1989-1992

U.S.: $325.00
Can.: $410.00
Ster.: £119.00

HN 3274
Over The Threshold
Designer: R. Tabbenor
Height: 12", 30.5 cm
Colour: White
Issued: 1989 to the
present
Series: Images

U.S.: $275.00
Can.: $325.00
Ster.: £ 95.00

HN 3275
Will He - Won't He
Designer: R. Tabbenor
Height: 9", 22.9 cm
Colour: Green
Issued: 1990 to the
present
Series: Clowns

U.S.: $225.00
Can.: $295.00
Ster.: £ 89.95

HN3276
Teeing Off
Designer: R. Tabbenor
Height: 9", 22.9 cm
Colour: Yellow and
green
Issued: 1990 to the
present

U.S.: $175.00
Can.: $295.00
Ster.: £ 99.95

HN 3277
The Carpet Seller
(Sitting)
Style Four
Designer: R. Tabbenor
Height: 7 1/2", 19.0 cm
Colour: Flambe
Issued: 1990 to the
present

U.S.: $195.00
Can.: $315.00
Ster.: £ 85.00

HN 3278
Lamp Seller
Designer: R. Tabbenor
Height: 9", 22.9 cm
Colour: Flambe
Issued: 1990 to the
present

U.S.: $325.00
Can.: $475.00
Ster.: £125.00

HN 3279
The Winning Put
Designer: R. Tabbenor
Height: 8", 20.3 cm
Colour: Blue and yellow
Issued: 1991 to the
present

U.S.: $175.00
Can.: $265.00
Ster.: £ 99.95

HN 3280
Brisdemaid
Style Five
Designer: R. Tabbenor
Height: 8 1/2", 21.6 cm
Colour: White
Issued: 1991 to the
           present
Series: Images
U.S.:   **$ 80.00**
Can.:   **$150.00**
Ster.: **£ 39.95**

HN 3281
Bride and Groom
Designer: R. Tabbenor
Height: 6 1/4", 15.9 cm
Colour: White
Issued: 1991 to the
           present
Series: Images
U.S.:   **$ 80.00**
Can.:   **$105.00**
Ster.: **£ 37.00**

HN 3282
First Steps
Style Two
Designer: R. Tabbenor
Height: 10", 25.4 cm
Colour: White
Issued: 1991 to the
           present
Series: Images
U.S.:   **$125.00**
Can.:   **$160.00**
Ster.: **£ 69.95**

HN 3283
Tumbling
Designer: D. V. Tootle
Height: 8 3/4", 22.2 cm
Colour: White, yellow,
           blue and green
Issued: 1990 to the
           present
Series: Clowns
Varieties: HN 3289
U.S.:   **$195.00**
Can.:   **$295.00**
Ster.: **£ 85.00**

HN 3284
The Bride
Style Four
Designer: D. V. Tootle
Height: 8 1/4", 21.0 cm
Colour: White
Issued: 1990 to the
           present
U.S.:   **$225.00**
Can.:   **$300.00**
Ster.: **£109.00**

HN 3285
The Bride
Style Four
Designer: D. V. Tootle
Height: 8 1/4", 21.0 cm
Colour: Ivory
Issued: 1990 to the
           present
U.S.:   **$225.00**
Can.:   **$300.00**
Ster.: **£109.00**

HN 3286
Alexandra
Style Two
Designer: D. V. Tootle
Height: 7 3/4", 19.7 cm
Colour: Orange
Issued: 1990 to the
           present
U.S.:   **$275.00**
Can.:   **$395.00**
Ster.: **£119.00**

*

HN 3289
Tumbling
Designer: D.V. Tootle
Height: 8 3/4", 22.2 cm
Colour: Pink and blue
Issued: 1991 in a limited
           edition of 2,500
Varieties: HN 3283
U.S.:   **$250.00**
Can.:   **$300.00**
Ster.: **£125.00**

National Playing Fields Association

HN 3290
Lauren
Designer: D.V. Tootle
Height: 8", 20.3 cm
Colour: Mauve and yellow
Issued: 1992-1992
Varieties: Also called "Ann", HN 3259

U.S.: $175.00 *
Can.: $275.00 *
Ster.: £ 94.99

*

HN 3293
Tip-toe
Designer: A. Hughes
Height: 9", 22.9 cm
Colour: Black, white and yellow
Issued: 1990 to the present
Series: Clowns

U.S.: $195.00
Can.: $295.00
Ster.: £ 85.00

HN 3294
Daddy's Joy
Designer: A. Hughes
Height: 8", 20.3 cm
Colour: Pink, yellow and white
Issued: 1990 in a limited edition of 12,500

U.S.: $350.00
Can.: $400.00
Ster.: £150.00

HN 3295
The Homecoming
Designer: A. Hughes
Height: 7", 17.8 cm
Colour: Blue, pink and green
Issued: 1990 in a limited edition of 9,500
Series: Children of the Blitz

U.S.: $375.00
Can.: $425.00
Ster.: £150.00

HN 3296
Fantasy
Designer: A. Hughes
Height: 12 1/2", 31.7 cm
Colour: White with four white cats
Issued: 1990 to the present
Series: Reflections

U.S.: $225.00
Can.: $350.00
Ster.: £109.00

HN 3297
Milestone
Designer: A. Hughes
Height: 7 1/4", 18.4 cm
Colour: Red and blue
Issued: 1990 to the present
Series: Childhood

U.S.: $275.00
Can.: $375.00
Ster.: £129.00

HN 3298
Hold Tight
Designer: A. Hughes
Height: 8 1/2", 21.6 cm
Colour: Red, blue and green
Issued: 1990 to the present
Series: Childhood

U.S.: $350.00
Can.: $550.00
Ster.: £159.00

*

HN 3299
Welcome Home
Designer: A. Hughes
Height: 8 1/2", 21.6 cm
Colour: Grey and turquoise
Issued: 1991 in a limited edition of 9,500
Series: Children of the Blitz

U.S.: $375.00
Can.: $375.00
Ster.: £150.00

HN 3300
Dressing Up
Style Two
Designer: A. Hughes
Height: 6 3/4", 17.5 cm
Colour: Yellow and blue
Issued: 1991 in a limited
            edition of 9,500

U.S.:	$175.00 *
Can.:	$225.00 *
Ster.:	£ 99.50

HN 3301
Santa's Helper
Designer: A. Hughes
Height: 6 1/2", 16.5 cm
Colour: Green, red
            and white
Issued: 1991 to the
            present

U.S.$	$215.00 *
Can.:	$260.00 *
Ster.:	$117.00

HN 3302
Please Sir
Designer: A. Hughes
Height: 8", 20.3 cm
Colour: Blue, grey
            and beige
Issued: 1992 in a limited
            edition of 7,500

U.S.$	$270.00 *
Can.:	$330.00 *
Ster.:	$147.50

"National Childrens Home"

HN 3303
Tender Moment
Designer: M. Davies
Height: 7", 17.8 cm
Colour: Pink
Issued: 1990 to the
            present
Series: Vanity Fair Ladies
Varieties: Also called "Nicola"
            HN 2839, 2804

U.S.:	$175.00
Can.:	$240.00
Ster.:	£ 79.95

HN 3304
Samantha
Style Two
Designer: M. Davies
Height: 7 1/2", 19.1 cm
Colour: White/green dress ,
            flowered border
Issued: 1990 to the
            present
Varieties: Also called "First
            Dance" HN 3802

U.S.:	$185.00
Can.:	$270.00
Ster.:	£ 95.00

HN 3305
Kathy
Stlye Two
Designer: M. Davies
Height: 7 1/4", 18.4 cm
Colour: Blue /white dress,
            flowered border
Issued: 1990 to the
            present
Varieties: Also called "Lynne"
            HN 2329

U.S.:	$195.00
Can.:	$270.00
Ster.:	£ 95.00

HN 3306
Megan
Designer: J. Bromley
Height: 7 1/2 ", 19.0 cm
Colour: White and yellow
Issued: 1992 to the
            present
Series: Vanity Fair Ladies

U.S.:	$150.00
Can.:	$210.00
Ster.:	£ 69.95

HN3307
Elaine
Designer: M. Davies
Height: 7 1/4", 18.4 cm
Colour: Pink
Issued: 1990 to the
            present
Varieties: HN 2791

U.S.:	$210.00
Can.:	$315.00
Ster.:	£119.00

HN 3308
Sara
Designer: M. Davies
Height: 7 3/4", 19.7 cm
Colour: Blue, pink
and white
Issued: 1990 to the
present
Varieties: HN 2265
U.S.: **$235.00**
Can.: **$375.00**
Ster.: **£149.00**

HN3309
Summer Rose
Style Two
Designer: M. Davies
Height: 7 1/2", 19.1 cm
Colour: White with
pink flowers
Issued: 1991 to the
present
Variations: Also called
"Denise" HN 2477
U.S.: **$195.00**
Can.: **$265.00**
U.S.: **£ 89.95**

HN 3310
Diana
Designer: M. Davies
Height: 4 1/4", 10.8 cm
Colour: Pale pink and blue
Issued: 1991 to the
present
Series: Miniatures
U.S.: **$125.00**
Can.: **$155.00**
Ster.: **£ 49.95**

HN 3311
Fragrance
Designer: M. Davies
Height: 7 1/4", 18.4 cm
Colour: Red
Issued: 1991-1991
Varieties: HN 2334
U.S.: **$195.00**
Can.: **$225.00**
Ster.: **£ 80.00**

HN 3312
Sunday Best
Designer: M. Davies
Height: 3", 7.6 cm,
Colour: Green, blue and
white, gold trim
Issued: 1991-91
Series: M. Doulton
Signature
Collection
Varieties: HN 3218
U.S.: **$125.00**
Can.: **$150.00**
Ster.: **£ 69.00**

HN 3313
Morning Breeze
Designer: P. Gee
Height: 8", 20.3 cm
Colour: Mottled blue
and orange
Issued: 1990 to the
present
U.S.: **$235.00**
Can.: **$375.00**
Ster.: **£119.00**

HN 3314
Confucious
Designer: P. Gee
Height: 9", 22.9 cm
Colour: Flambe
Issued: 1990 to the
present
U.S.: **$165.00**
Can.: **$250.00**
Ster.: **£ 85.00**

HN 3315
Waiting For A Train
Designer: P. Gee
Height: 8 1/2", 21.6 cm
Colour: Cashmere coat,
black hat,
"biscuit" finish
Issued: 1991 in a limited
edition of 9,500
U.S.: **$185.00** *
Can.: **$225.00** *
Ster.: **£ 99.00**

HN 3316
Amy
Style One
Designer: P. Gee
Height: 8" 20.3 cm
Colour: Blue and rose
Issued: 1991-1991
Series: Figure of the Year

U.S.:	**$275.00**
Can.:	**$325.00**
Ster.:	**£110.00**

HN 3317
Countess of Harrington
Designer: P. Gee
Height: 9 1/2", 24.3 cm
Colour: Pale green
Issued: 1992 in a limited
edition of 5,000
Series: Reynolds Ladies

U.S.:	**$550.00**
Can.:	**$750.00**
Ster.:	**£275.00**

HN 3318
Lady Worsley
Designer: P. Gee
Height: 9 1/2", 24.3 cm
Colour: Red, black and gold
Issued: 1992 in a limited
edition of 5,000
Series: Reynolds Ladies

U.S.:	**$550.00**
Can.:	**$750.00**
Ster.:	**£275.00**

HN 3319
Mrs. Hugh Bonfoy
Designer: P. Gee
Height: 9 1/2", 24.3 cm
Colour: Blue-pink
Issued: 1992 in a limited
edition of 5,000
Series: Reynolds Ladies

U.S.:	**$550.00**
Can.:	**$750.00**
Ster.:	**£275.00**

HN 3320
Countess Spencer
Designer: P. Gee
Height: 9 1/2", cm
Colour: Red, blue and white
Issued: 1993 in a limited
edition of 5,000
Series: Reynolds Ladies

U.S.:	**$550.00**
Can.:	**$750.00**
Ster.:	**£275.00**

HN 3321
Gail
Designer: P. Gee
Height: 3 3/4", cm
Colour: Red and white
Issued: 1992 to the
present
Series: Miniatures

U.S.:	**$125.00**
Can.:	**$195.00**
Ster.:	**£ 49.95**

HN 3322
Celeste
Style Two
Designer: P. Gee
Height: 8", 20.3 cm
Colour: Yellow
Issued: 1992
Varieties: Also called
"Isadora" HN 2938

U.S.:	**$185.00 ***
Can.:	**$225.00 ***
Ster.:	**£ 99.99**

*

HN3335
A Jester
Designer: C.J. Noke
Height: 4", 10.1 cm
Colour: Brown and
purple
Issued: 1990-1990
Series: Miniatures, RDICC

U.S.:	**$150.00**
Can.:	**$175.00**
Ster.:	**£ 95.00**

HN 3336
Fair Lady
Designer: M. Davies
Height: 3 1/2", 8.9 cm
Colour: Red, white, purple,
2 kt gold trim
Issued: 1991
Series: M. Doulton
Signature
Collection
Varieties: HN 3216

U.S.:	S150.00
Can.:	$175.00
Ster.:	£ 69.00

HN 3337
Christine
Designer: M. Davies
Height: 3 1/2", 8.9 cm
Colour: Yellow, black, white
with 22 kt gold trim
Issued: 1991
Series: M. Doulton
Signature
Collection
Varieties: HN 3269

U.S.:	$150.00
Can.:	$175.00
Ster.:	£ 69.00

HN 3338
Karen
Designer: M. Davies
Height: 3 /12", 8.9 cm
Colour: Purple with
22 kt gold trim
Issued: 1991
Series: M. Doulton
Signature
Collection
Varieties: HN 3270

U.S.:	$150.00
Can.:	$175.00
Ster.:	£ 69.00

HN 3341
January

Style Two
Designer: M. Davies
Height: 8", 20.3 cm
Colour: White with pale
blue; snowdrops
Issued: 1991
Series: Wild Flower of
the Month

U.S.:	$175.00
Can.:	$235.00
Ster.:	£ 75.00

HN 3342
February
Style Two
Designer: M. Davies
Height: 7 1/2", 19.0 cm
Colour: White with pink,
wood anemone
flowers
Issued: 1991-1991
Series: Wild Flower of
the Month

U.S.:	$225.00
Can.:	$295.00
Ster.:	£ 75.00

HN 3343
March
Style Two
Designer: M. Davies
Height: 7 1/2", 19.0 cm
Colour: White, violet
flowers
Issued: 1991
Series: Wild Flower of
the Month

U.S.:	$175.00
Can.:	$235.00
Ster.:	£ 75.00

HN 3344
April
Style Two
Designer: M. Davies
Height: 7 1/2", 19.0 cm
Colour: White with blue,
primrose flowers
Issued: 1991
Series: Wild Flower of
the Month

U.S.:	$175.00
Can.:	$235.00
Ster.:	£ 75.00

HN 3345
May
Style Three
Designer: M. Davies
Height: 7 1/2", 19.0 cm
Colour: White with Lady's
Smock flowers
Issued: 1991
Series: Wild Flower of
the Month

U.S.:	$175.00
Can.:	$235.00
Ster.:	£ 75.00

HN 3346
June
Style Four
Designer: M. Davies
Height: 7 1/2", 19.0 cm
Colour: White with briar rose flowers
Issued: 1991
Series: Wild Flower of the Month

U.S.: $225.00
Can.: $295.00
Ster.: £ 75.00

HN 3347
July
Style Two
Designer: M. Davies
Height: 7 1/2", 19.0 cm
Colour: White with hare bell flowers
Issued: 1991
Series: Wild Flower of the Month

U.S.: $225.00
Can.: $295.00
Ster.: $ 75.00

HN 3348
Mother and Baby
Designer: P. Parsons
Height: 7 1/2", 19.0 cm
Colour: White with pink
Issued: 1991 to the present
Varieties: HN 3235, 3353

U.S.: $250.00
Can.: $325.00
Ster.: £109.00

HN 3349
Jane Seymour
Designer: P. Parsons
Height: 9", 22.9 cm
Colour: Orange and blue
Issued: 1991 in a limited edition of 9,500
Series: Six Wives of Henry VIII

U.S.: $395.00 *
Can.: $475.00 *
Ster.: £215.00

HN 3350
Henry VIII
Style Three
Designer: P. Parsons
Height: 9 1/2", 24.0 cm
Colour: Gold-brown and red
Issued: 1991 in a limited edition of 1991

U.S.: $1,250.00
Can.: $1,450.00
Ster.: £ 650.00

HN 3351
Congratulations
Designer: P. Gee
Height: 11", 27.9 cm
Colour: White
Issued: 1991 to the present
Series: Images

U.S.: $155.00 *
Can.: $260.00
Ster.: £ 85.00

Photograph
Not
Available

HN 3352
Marie Curie
Designer: N/A
Height: N/A
Colour: N/A
Issued: To be released by Lawleys in 1993 in a limited edition of 9,500

U.S.: $ -
Can.: $ -
Ster.: £ -

NOTE ON PRICING

Prices are given for three separate and distinct market areas:

Prices are given in the currency of each of these different trading areas.

Prices are not exchange rate calculations but are based on supply and demand in that market.

Prices listed are guidelines to the most current retail values but actual selling prices may vary slightly.

Prices for current figurines are those suggested by Royal Doulton.

Extremely rare or unique figurines have inconsistent retail values and their prices must therefore be determined between buyer and seller.

HN 3353
Mother and Baby
Designer: P. Parsons
Height: 7 1/2", 19.0 cm
Colour: White
Issued: 1991 to the
present
Series: Vanity Fair Series
Varieties: HN 3235, 3348

U.S.: **$185.00** *
Can.: **$230.00**
Ster.: **£100.00** *

HN 3354
Yours Forever
Designer: P. Parsons
Height: 8", 20.3 cm
Colour: Yellow and pink
Issued: 1992 - Canada
1993 - Worldwide
to the present

U.S.: **$180.00**
Can.: **$250.00**
Ster.: **£ 79.95**

HN 3355
Just For You
Designer: P. Parsons
Height: 8 1/4", 21 cm
Colour: White
Issued: 1992 to the
present

U.S.: **$195.00**
Can.: **$310.00**
Ster.: **£ 85.00**

HN 3356
Anne of Cleves
Designer: P. Parsons
Height: 6 1/4", 15.9 cm
Colour: Green and gold
Issued: 1991 in a limited
edition of 9,500
Series: Six Wives of
Henry VIII

U.S.: **$395.00**
Can.: **$475.00**
Ster.: **£215.00**

HN 3357
Marie
Style Three
Designer: P. Parson
Height: 6", 15.2 cm
Colour: Pink and yellow
Issued: 1992
Varieties: Also called
"Heather" HN 2956

U.S.: **$140.00** *
Can.: **$170.00** *
Ster.: **$ 74.95**

HN 3358
Loyal Friend
Designer: V. Annand
Height: 8 1/4", 20.9 cm
Colour: Pale green and
white
Issued: 1991 to the
present
Series: Childhood

U.S.: **$255.00** *
Can.: **$370.00**
Ster.: **£139.00**

HN 3359
L'Ambitieuse
Designer: V. Annand
Height: 8 1/4 ", 20.9 cm
Colour: Rose and pale blue
Issued: 1991 in a limited
edition of 5,000
Series: RDICC

U.S.: **$295.00**
Can.: **$350.00**
Ster.: **£125.00**

HN 3360
Katie
Designer: V. Annand
Height: 8 1/4", 21.0 cm
Colour: Yellow and pink
Issued: 1992 to the
present

U.S.: **$275.00**
Can.: **$375.00**
Ster.: **£109.00**

*

HN 3368
Alice
Style Two
Designer: N. Pedley
Height: 8 1/4", 21.0 cm
Colour: Light blue and pink
Issued: 1992 to the
present

U.S.: $275.00
Can.: $350.00
Ster.: £119.00

HN 3369
Hannah
Designer: N. Pedley
Height: 8 1/4", 19.0 cm
Colour: Pale pink, yellow
and blue
Issued: 1991 to the
present

U.S.: $250.00
Can.: $350.00
Ster.: £119.00

HN 3370
Bunny's Bedtime
Designer: N. Pedley
Height: 6", 15.2 cm
Colour: Pale blue,
pink ribbon
Issued: 1991 in a limited
edition of 9,500
Series: RDICC

U.S.: $200.00
Can.: $220.00
Ster.: £125.00

HN 3371
Puppy Love
Designer: N. Pedley
Height: 7 1/2", 19.0 cm
Colour: Yellow-orange
and brown
Issued: 1991 in a limited
edition of 9,500
Series: Age of Innocence

U.S.: $275.00
Can.: $400.00
Ster.: £139.00

HN 3372
Making Friends
Designer: N. Pedley
Height: 5 1/2", 14.o cm
Colour: Pinkish yellow
and white
Issued: 1991 in a limited
edition of 9,500
Series: Age of Innocence

U.S.: $275.00
Can.: $450.00
Ster.: £139.00

HN 3373
Feeding Time
Designer: N. Pedley
Height: 7", 17.8 cm
Colour: yellow and white
Issued: 1991 in a limited
edition of 9,500
Series: Age of Innocence

U.S.: $250.00
Can.: $400.00
Ster.: £139.00

HN 3374
Linda
Style Two
Designer: V. Annand
Height: 8 1/4", 21.0 cm
Colour: Blue-green
and white
Issued: 1990 - Canada
1991 - Worldwide
to the present

U.S.: $275.00
Can.: $375.00
Ster.: £119.00

HN 3375
Mary
Style Two
Designer: N. Pedley
Height: 8 1/2", 21.6 cm
Colour: Blue and white
Issued: 1992 to the
present
Series: Figure of the Year

U.S.: $225.00
Can.: $395.00
Ster.: £ 99.95

HN 3376
Single Red Rose
Designer: N. Pedley
Height: 8", 20.3 cm
Colour: Red
Issued: 1992 to the
present

U.S.:	$250.00
Can.:	$420.00
Ster.:	£109.00

HN 3377
First Outing
Designer: N. Pedley
Height: 7 1/2", 19.0 cm
Colour: Peach and white
Issued: 1992 in a limited
edition of 9,500
Series: Age of Innocence

U.S.:	$275.00
Can.:	$450.00
Ster.:	£139.00

HN 3378
Summer's Day
Style Two
Designer: T. Potts
Height: 8 1/3", 21.6 cm
Colour: Rose and white
Issued: 1992 to the
present

U.S.:	$250.00
Can.:	$330.00
Ster.:	£ 99.95

Photograph
Not
Available

HN 3379
Kimberley
Style Two
Designer: T. Potts
Height: 8 1/2", 21.6 cm
Colour: White and blue
Issued: 1992 Canada
1993 - Worldwide
to the present
Series: Vanity Fair Ladies

U.S.:	$150.00
Can.:	$220.00
Ster.:	£100.00
●

HN 3388
Forget-Me-Not
Style Two
Designer: A. Maslankowski
Height: 6", 15.2 cm
Colour: White
Issued: 1991 to the
present
Series: Sentiments

U.S.:	$ 85.00
Can.:	$105.00
Ster.:	£ 39.95

HN 3389
Loving You
Designer: A. Maslankowski
Height: 6 1/4", 15.8 cm
Colour: White
Issued: 1991 to the
present
Series: Sentiments

U.S.:	$ 85.00
Can.:	$105.00
Ster.:	£ 39.95

HN 3390
Thank You
Style Two
Designer: A. Maslankowski
Height: 6 1/4", 15.8 cm
Colour: White
Issued: 1991 to the
present
Series: Sentiments

U.S.:	$ 85.00
Can.:	$105.00
Ster.:	£ 39.95

HN 3391
Reward
Designer: A. Maslankowski
Height: 4 1/2", 11.4 cm
Colour: White and pink
Issued: 1992 to the
present
Series: Vanity Fair
Children

U.S.:	$ 95.00
Can.:	$140.00
Ster.:	£ 45.00

HN 3392
Christopher Columbus
Designer:	A. Maslankowski
Height:	12", 30.5 cm
Colour:	Green, brown and red
Issued:	1992 in a limited edition of 1,492
U.S.:	**$1,950.00**
Can.:	**$2,600.00**
Ster.:	**£ 750.00**

HN 3393
With Love
Designer:	A. Maslankowski
Height:	6", 15.2 cm
Colour:	White
Issued:	1992 to the present
Series:	Sentiments
U.S.:	**$ 85.00**
Can.:	**$105.00**
Ster.:	**£ 39.95**

HN 3394
Sweet Dreams
Style Two
Designer:	A. Maslankowski
Height:	6", 15.2 cm
Colour:	White
Issued:	1992 to the present
Series:	Sentiments
U.S.:	**$ 85.00**
Can.:	**$105.00**
Ster.:	**£ 39.95**

HN 3395
Little Ballerina
Designer:	A. Maslankowski
Height:	6", 15.2 cm
Colour:	White
Issued:	1992 to the present
U.S.:	**$110.00**
Can.:	**$135.00**
Ster.:	**£ 35.00**

HN 3396
Buddies
Style Two
Designer:	A. Maslankowski
Height:	4 1/4", 10.8 cm
Colour:	Pink and beige
Issued:	1992 to the present
Series:	Vanity Fair Children
U.S.:	**$ 80.00**
Can.:	**$137.50**
Ster.:	**£ 45.00**

HN 3397
Let's Play
Designer:	A. Maslankowski
Height:	4", 10.0 cm
Colour:	Pale green and white
Issued:	1992 to the present
Series:	Vanity Fair Children
U.S.:	**$110.00**
Can.:	**$135.00**
Ster.:	**£ 45.00**

HN 3398
The Ace
Designer:	R. Tabbenor
Height:	10", 25.4 cm
Colour:	White
Issued:	1991 to the present
U.S.:	**$195.00**
Can.:	**$275.00**
Ster.:	**£ 89.95**

HN 3399
Father Christmas
Designer:	R. Tabbenor
Height:	9", 22.9 cm
Colour:	Red and white
Issued:	1992 to the present
U.S.:	**$185.00 ***
Can.:	**$275.00**
Ster.:	**£ 99.95**

HN 3400
God Bless You
Designer: R. Tabbenor
Height: 8", 20.3 cm
Colour: White
Issued: 1992 to the
           present
Series: Images
U.S.:   **$55.00** *
Can.:   **$90.00**
Ster.: **£29.95**

HN 3401
Gardening Time
Designer: R. Tabbenor
Height: 5", 12.7 cm
Colour: Yellow, blue
           and green
Issued: 1992 to the
           present
U.S.:   **$250.00**
Can.:   **$330.00**
Ster.: **£ 99.95**

HN 3402
Samurai Warrior
Designer: R. Tabbenor
Height: 9", 22.7 cm
Colour: Flambe
Issued: 1992 in a limited
           edition of 950
U.S.:   **$450.00**
Can.:   **$715.00**
Ster.: **£175.00**

*

HN 3408
August
Style Two
Designer: M. Davies
Height: 8", 20.3 cm
Colour: White with green,
           poppy flowers
Issued: 1991
Series: Wild Flower
           of the Month
U.S.:   **$175.00**
Can.:   **$235.00**
Ster.: **£ 75.00**

HN 3409
September
Style Two
Designer: M. Davies
Height: 8", 20.3 cm
Colour: White with pink,
           blue flowers
Issued: 1991
Series: Wild Flower
           of the Month
U.S.:   **$175.00**
Can.:   **$235.00**
Ster.: **£ 75.00**

HN 3410
October
Style Two
Designer: M. Davies
Height: 8", 20.3 cm
Colour: White with blue,
           buttercup flowers
Issued: 1991
Series: Wild Flower
           of the Month
U.S.:   **$175.00**
Can.:   **$235.00**
Ster.: **£ 75.00**

HN 3411
November
Style Two
Designer: M. Davies
Height: 8", 20.3 cm
Colour: White with blue,
           pink campion
           flowers
Issued: 1991
Series: Wild Flower
           of the Month
U.S.:   **$175.00**
Can.:   **$235.00**
Ster.: **£ 75.00**

HN 3412
December
Style Two
Designer: M. Davies
Height: 8", 20.3 cm
Colour: White with pink trim;
Christmas rose flowers
Issued: 1991-1991
Series: Wild Flower
           of the Month
U.S.:   **$175.00**
Can.:   **$235.00**
Ster.: **£ 75.00**
*

HN 3414
Rebecca
Style Two
Designer: M. Davies
Height: 3 1/2", 8.9 cm
Colour: Pale blue and pink
Issued: 1992 to the
present
Series: Miniatures
U.S.: $100.00 *
Can.: $195.00
Ster.: £ 49.95

HN 3415
Janette
Designer: M. Davies
Height: 7 1/2" 19.1 cm
Colour: Blue and green
Issued: 1992
Varieties: Also called
"Kirsty" HN 2381
U.S.: $165.00 *
Can.: $200.00 *
Ster.: £ 89.99

HN 3416
Victoria
Designer: M. Davies
Height: 6 1/2", 16.5 cm
Colour: Blue and rose
design, 22kt gold
highlights
Issued: 1992 only at
Doulton Road Show
Events in the UK
Varieties: HN 2471
U.S.: $230.00 *
Can.: $350.00 *
Ster.: £125.00

HN 3417
Ninette
Designer: M. Davies
Height: 7 1/2", 19.1 cm
Colour: Deep orange dress
with green sleeves,
22kt gold highlights
Issued: 1992
Varieties: HN 2379 only at
Doulton Road Show
Events in the UK
U.S.: $275.00 *
Can.: $335.00 *
Ster.: £149.00

HN 3418
Bedtime
Style Two
Designer: N. Pedley
Height: 7 1/4", 18.4 cm
Colour: Pink-yellow
Issued: 1992 in a limited
edition of 9,500
U.S.: $250.00 *
Can.: $300.00 *
Ster.: £136.00

HN 3419
Angela
Style Three
Designer: N. Pedley
Height: 8 1/2", 21.6 cm
Colour: Blue, pink and white
Issued: 1992
U.S.: $195.00
Can.: $395.00
Ster.: £ 95.00

HN 3420
Ashley
Designer: N. Pedley
Height: 8", 20.3 cm
Colour: Lavender
Issued: 1992 to the
present
Series: Vanity Fair Ladies
U.S.: $150.00
Can.: $220.00
Ster.: £ 59.95

*

HN 3428
Discovery
Designer: A. Munslow
Height: 12", 30.5 cm
Colour: Matte white
Issued: 1992-1992
Series: RDICC
U.S.: $160.00 *
Can.: $185.00
Ster.: £ 85.00 *

HN 3429
Napoleon at Waterloo
Designer:	A. Maslankowski
Height:	11 1/2", 29.2 cm
Colour:	Black, cream and green
Issued:	1992 in a limited edition of 1,500
U.S.:	$1,900.00
Can.:	$2,750.00
Ster.:	£ 995.00

*

HN 3439
The Skater
Style Two
Designer:	P. Gee
Height:	8", 20.3 cm
Colour:	Red
Issued:	1992 to the present
U.S.:	$295.00
Can.:	$420.00
Ster.:	£119.00

HN 3440
HM Queen Elizabeth II
Designer:	P. Gee
Height:	7 1/2", 19.0 cm
Colour:	Yellow and pink
Issued:	1992 in a limited edition of 3,500
U.S.:	$425.00
Can.:	$550.00
Ster.:	£250.00

*

HN 3459
King Charles I
Designer:	Charles Noke and Harry Tittensor
Height:	16 3/4", 42.5 cm
Colour:	Red, dark blue, and white
Issued:	1992 in a limited edition of 350
Varieties:	HN 404, 2084
U.S.:	$3,025.00 *
Can.:	$5,025.00
Ster.:	£1,642.00

M SERIES

M1
Victorian Lady
Designer: L. Harradine
Height: 3 3/4", 9.5 cm
Colour: Pink and green
Issued: 1932-1945
Varieties: M 2, 25

US: $450.00
Can.: $575.00
Ster.: £250.00

M 2
Victorian Lady
Designer: L. Harradine
Height: 3 3/4", 9.5 cm
Colour: Lavender
           and green
Issued: 1932-1945
Varieties: M 1, 25

US: $450.00
Can.: $575.00
Ster.: £250.00

M 3
Paisley Shawl
Designer: L. Harradine
Height: 4", 10.1 cm
Colour: Lavender
Issued: 1932-1938
Varieties: M 4, 26

US: $500.00
Can.: $575.00
Ster.: £250.00

M 4
Paisley Shawl
Designer: L. Harradine
Height: 4", 10.1 cm
Colour: Purple and
           green
Issued: 1932-1945
Varieties: M 3, 26

US: $425.00
Can.: $500.00
Ster.: £250.00

M 5
Sweet Anne
Designer: L. Harradine
Height: 4", 10.1 cm
Colour: Lavender
           and green
Issued: 1932-1945
Varieties: HN 6, 27

US: $450.00
Can.: $500.00
Ster.: £250.00

M 6
Sweet Anne
Designer: L. Harradine
Height: 4", 10.1 cm
Colour: Blue
Issued: 1932-1945
Varieties: HN 5, 27

US: $500.00
Can.: $600.00
Ster.: £250.00

M 7
Patricia
Designer: L. Harradine
Height: 4", 10.1 cm
Colour: Pink and
           green
Issued: 1932-1945
Varieties: HN 8, 28

US: $600.00
Can.: $700.00
Ster.: £300.00

M 8
Patricia
Designer: L. Harradine
Height: 4", 10.1 cm
Colour: Orange and
           yellow
Issued: 1932-1938
Varieties: HN 7, 28

US: $550.00
Can.: $650.00
Ster.: £300.00

M 9
Chloe
Designer: L. Harradine
Height: 2 3/4", 7.0 cm
Colour: Pink
Issued: 1932-1945
Varieties: HN 10, 29

US: **$550.00**
Can.: **$650.00**
Ster.: **£300.00**

M 10
Chloe
Designer: L. Harradine
Height: 2 3/4", 7.0 cm
Colour: Lavender
Issued: 1932-1945
Varieties: HN 9, 29

US: **$550.00**
Can.: **$650.00**
Ster.: **£300.00**

M 11
Bridesmaid
Designer: L. Harradine
Height: 3 3/4", 9.5 cm
Colour: Pink and
lavender
Issued: 1932-1938
Varieties: M 12, 30

US: **$650.00**
Can.: **$700.00**
Ster.: **£250.00**

M 12
Bridesmaid
Designer: L. Harradine
Height: 3 3/4", 9.5 cm
Colour: Yellow and
lavender
Issued: 1932-1945
Varieties: M 11, 30

US: **$425.00**
Can.: **$500.00**
Ster.: **£250.00**

M 13
Priscilla
Designer: L. Harradine
Height: 4", 10.1 cm
Colour: Green and
yellow
Issued: 1932-1938
Varieties: M 14, 24

US: **$650.00**
Can.: **$700.00**
Ster.: **£300.00**

M 14
Priscilla
Designer: L. Harradine
Height: 4", 10.1 cm
Colour: Lavender
and pink
Issued: 1932-1945
Varieties: M 13, 24

US: **$475.00**
Can.: **$575.00**
Ster.: **£300.00**

M 15
Pantalettes
Designer: L. Harradine
Height: 3 3/4", 9.5 cm
Colour: Lavender
Issued: 1932-1945
Varieties: M 16, 31

US: **$600.00**
Can.: **$700.00**
Ster.: **£300.00**

M 16
Pantalettes
Designer: L. Harradine
Height: 3 3/4", 9.5 cm
Colour: Pink
Issued: 1932-1945
Varieties: M 15, 31

US: **$475.00**
Can.: **$600.00**
Ster.: **£300.00**

M 17
Shepherd
Designer: Unknown
Height: 3 3/4", 9.5 cm
Colour: Purple, pink
and green
Issued: 1932-1938
Varieties: M 19

US:	$3,000.00
Can.:	$3,000.00
Ster.:	£1,000.00

M 18
Shepherdess
Designer: Unknown
Height: 3 1/2", 8.9 cm
Colour: Green and
lavender
Issued: 1932-1938
Varieties: M 20

US:	$3,000.00
Can.:	$3,000.00
Ster.:	£1,000.00

M 19
Shepherd
Designer: Unknown
Height: 3 3/4", 9.5 cm
Colour: Purple, green
and brown
Issued: 1932-1938
Varieties: M 17

US:	$3,000.00
Can.:	$3,000.00
Ster.:	£1,000.00

M 20
Shepherdess
Designer: Unknown
Height: 3 3/4", 9.5 cm
Colour: Yellow
Issued: 1932-1938
Varieties: M 18

US:	$3,000.00
Can.:	$3,000.00
Ster.:	£1,000.00

M 21
Polly Peachum
Designer: L. Harradine
Height: 2 1/4", 5.7 cm
Colour: Pink
Issued: 1932-1945
Varieties: M 22, 23

US:	$600.00
Can.:	$700.00
Ster.:	£250.00

M 22
Polly Peachum
Designer: L. Harradine
Height: 2 1/4", 5.7 cm
Colour: Red and blue
Issued: 1932-1938
Varieties: M 21, 23

US:	$900.00
Can.:	$900.00
Ster.:	£300.00

M 23
Polly Peachum
Designer: L. Harradine
Height: 2 1/4", 5.7 cm
Colour: Purple, pink
and white
Issued: 1932-1938
Varieties: M 21, 22

US:	$1,500.00
Can.:	$1,500.00
Ster.:	£ 500.00

M 24
Priscilla
Designer: L. Harradine
Height: 3 3/4", 9.5 cm
Colour: Red
Issued: 1932-1945
Varieties: M 13, 14

US:	$550.00
Can.:	$600.00
Ster.:	£300.00

M 25
Victorian Lady
Designer: L. Harradine
Height: 3 3/4", 9.5 cm
Colour: Lavender
           and pink
Issued: 1932-1945
Varieties: M 1, 2

US:	**$550.00**
Can.:	**$575.00**
Ster.:	**£250.00**

M 26
Paisley Shawl
Designer: L. Harradine
Height: 3 3/4", 9.5 cm
Colour: Green
Issued: 1932-1945
Varieties: M 3, 4

US:	**$575.00**
Can.:	**$575.00**
Ster.:	**£250.00**

M 27
Sweet Anne
Designer: L. Harradine
Height: 4", 10.1 cm
Colour: Red, blue and
           yellow
Issued: 1932-1945
Varieties: M 5, 6

US:	**$500.00**
Can.:	**$600.00**
Ster.:	**£250.00**

M 28
Patricia
Designer: L. Harradine
Height: 4", 10.1 cm
Colour: Lavender
Issued: 1932-1945
Varieties: M 7, 8

US:	**$600.00**
Can.:	**$650.00**
Ster.:	**£350.00**

M 29
Chloe
Designer: L. Harradine
Height: 2 3/4", 7.0 cm
Colour: Pink and yellow
Issued: 1932-1945
Varieties: M 9, 10

US:	**$650.00**
Can.:	**$700.00**
Ster.:	**£250.00**

M 30
Bridesmaid
Designer: L. Harradine
Height: 3 3/4", 9.5 cm
Colour: Pink and
           lavender
Issued: 1932-1945
Varieties: M 11, 12

US:	**$425.00**
Can.:	**$500.00**
Ster.:	**£250.00**

M 31
Pantalettes
Designer: L. Harradine
Height: 4", 10.1 cm
Colour: Green and
           blue
Issued: 1932-1945
Varieties: M 15, 16

US:	**$675.00**
Can.:	**$750.00**
Ster.:	**£300.00**

M 32
Rosamund
Designer: L. Harradine
Height: 4 1/4", 10.8 cm
Colour: Yellow
Issued: 1932-1945
Varieties: M 33

US:	**$850.00**
Can.:	**$975.00**
Ster.:	**£400.00**

M 33
Rosamund
Designer: L. Harradine
Height: 4", 10.1 cm
Colour: Red
Issued: 1932-1945
Varieties: M 32

US: $850.00
Can.: $975.00
Ster.: £400.00

M 34
Denise
Designer: L. Harradine
Height: 4 1/2", 11.4 cm
Colour: Green, red
and blue
Issued: 1933-1945
Varieties: M 35

US: $1,000.00
Can.: $1,000.00
Ster.: £ 400.00

M 35
Denise
Designer: L. Harradine
Height: 4 1/2", 11.4 cm
Colour: Blue and pink
Issued: 1933-1945
Varieties: M 34

US: $1,250.00
Can.: $1,250.00
Ster.: £ 400.00

M 36
Norma
Designer: L. Harradine
Height: 4 1/2", 11.4 cm
Colour: Red adn green
Issued: 1933-1945
Varieties: M 37

US: $1,250.00
Can.: $1,250.00
Ster.: £ 400.00

M 37
Norma
Designer: L. Harradine
Height: 4 1/2", 11.4 cm
Colour: Blue, red
and white
Issued: 1933-1945
Varieties: M 36

US: $1,500.00
Can.: $1,500.00
Ster.: £ 400.00

M 38
Robin
Designer: L. Harradine
Height: 2 1/2", 6.4 cm
Colour: Pink and
lavender
Issued: 1933-1945
Varieties: M 39

US: $ 900.00
Can.: $1,000.00
Ster.: £ 400.00

M 39
Robin
Designer: L. Harradine
Height: 2 1/2", 6.4 cm
Colour: Blue and green
Issued: 1933-1945
Varieties: M 38

US: $ 900.00
Can.: $1,000.00
Ster.: £ 400.00

M 40
Erminie
Designer: L. Harradine
Height: 4", 10.1 cm
Colour: White and
pink
Issued: 1933-1945

US: $1,000.00
Can.: $1,200.00
Ster.: £ 400.00

M 41
Mr. Pickwick
Designer: L. Harradine
Height: 4", 10.1 cm
Colour: Yellow and
  black
Issued: 1932-1983
Series: Dickens
  Miniatures
  US: $100.00
  Can.: $125.00
  Ster.: £ 40.00
■

M 42
Mr. Micawber
Designer: L. Harradine
Height: 4", 10.1 cm
Colour: Yellow and black
Issued: 1932-1983
Series: Dickens
  Miniatures
  US: $100.00
  Can.: $125.00
  Ster.: £ 40.00

M 43
Mr. Pecksniff
Designer: L. Harradine
Height: 4 1/4", 10.8 cm
Colour: Black
Issued: 1932-1982
Series: Dickens
  Miniatures
  US: $100.00
  Can.: $125.00
  Ster.: £ 40.00

M 44
Fat Boy
Designer: L. Harradine
Height: 4 1/4", 10.8 cm
Colour: Blue and white
Issued: 1932-1983
Series: Dickens
  Miniatures
  US: $100.00
  Can.: $125.00
  Ster.: £ 40.00

M 45
Uriah Heep
Designer: L. Harradine
Height: 4", 10.1 cm
Colour: Black
Issued: 1932-1983
Series: Dickens
  Miniatures
  US: $100.00
  Can.: $125.00
  Ster.: £ 40.00

M 46
Sairey Gamp
Designer: L. Harradine
Height: 4", 10.1 cm
Colour: Green
Issued: 1932-1983
Series: Dickens
  Miniatures
  US: $100.00
  Can.: $125.00
  Ster.: £ 40.00

M 47
Tony Weller
Designer: L. Harradine
Height: 4", 10.1 cm
Colour: Green, black,
  red and yellow
Issued: 1932-1981
Series: Dickens
  Miniatures
  US: $100.00
  Can.: $125.00
  Ster.: £ 40.00

M 48
Sam Weller
Designer: L. Harradine
Height: 4", 10.1 cm
Colour: Yellow and
  brown
Issued: 1932-1981
Series: Dickens
  Miniatures
  US: $100.00
  Can.: $125.00
  Ster.: £ 40.00

M 49
Fagin
Designer: L. Harradine
Height: 4", 10.1 cm
Colour: Brown
Issued: 1932-1983
Series: Dickens
            Miniatures

US: $100.00
Can.: $125.00
Ster.: £ 40.00

M 50
Stiggins
Designer: L. Harradine
Height: 4", 10.1 cm
Colour: Black
Issued: 1932-1981
Series: Dickens
            Miniatures

US: $100.00
Can.: $125.00
Ster.: £ 40.00

M 51
Little Nell
Designer: L. Harradine
Height: 4 1/4", 10.8 cm
Colour: Pink
Issued: 1932-1983
Series: Dickens
            Miniatures

US: $100.00
Can.: $125.00
Ster.: £ 40.00

M 52
Alfred Jingle
Designer: L. Harradine
Height: 3 3/4", 9.5 cm
Colour: Black and white
Issued: 1932-1981
Series: Dickens
            Miniatures

US: $100.00
Can.: $125.00
Ster.: £ 40.00

M 53
Buz Fuz
Designer: L. Harradine
Height: 4", 10.1 cm
Colour: Black and
            red
Issued: 1932-1983
Series: Dickens
            Miniatures

US: $100.00
Can.: $125.00
Ster.: £ 40.00

M 54
Bill Sykes
Designer: L. Harradine
Height: 4 1/4", 10.8 cm
Colour: Black and brown
Issued: 1932-1981
Series: Dickens
            Miniatures

US: $100.00
Can.: $125.00
Ster.: £ 40.00

M 55
Artful Dodger
Designer: L. Harradine
Height: 4 1/4", 10.8 cm
Colour: Black and brown
Issued: 1932-1983
Series: Dickens
            Miniatures

US: $100.00
Can.: $125.00
Ster.: £ 40.00

M 56
Tiny Tim
Designer: L. Harradine
Height: 3 3/4", 9.5 cm
Colour: Black and brown
Issued: 1932-1983
Series: Dickens
            Miniatures

US: $100.00
Can.: $125.00
Ster.: £ 40.00

*

M 64
Veronica
Designer: L. Harradine
Height: 4 1/2", 10.8 cm
Colour: Pink
Issued: 1934-1949
Varieties: M 70

  US: $1,000.00
  Can.: $1,100.00
  Ster.:   £ 400.00

M 65
June
Designer: L. Harradine
Height: 4 1/4", 10.8 cm
Colour: Pink and
             lavender
Issued: 1935-1949
Varieties: M 71

  US: $700.00
  Can.: $800.00
  Ster.:   £400.00

M 66
Monica
Designer: L. Harradine
Height: 3", 7.6 cm
Colour: Blue and pink
Issued: 1935-1949
Varieties: M 72

  US: $1,100.00
  Can.: $1,200.00
  Ster.:   £ 400.00

M 67
Dainty May
Designer: L. Harradine
Height: 4", 10.1 cm
Colour: Turquoise
             and pink
Issued: 1935-1949
Varieties: M 73

  US: $1,000.00
  Can.: $1,200.00
  Ster.:   £ 400.00

M 68
Mirabel
Designer: L. Harradine
Height: 4", 10.1 cm
Colour: Pink and
             green
Issued: 1936-1949
Varieties: M 74

  US: $ 900.00
  Can.: $1,100.00
  Ster.:   £ 450.00

M 69
Janet
Designer: L. Harradine
Height: 4", 10.1 cm
Colour: Blue and
             white
Issued: 1936-1949
Varieties: M 75

  US: $850.00
  Can.: $975.00
  Ster.:   £400.00

M 70
Veronica
Designer: L. Harradine
Height: 4 1/4", 10.8 cm
Colour: Green
Issued: 1936-1949
Varieties: M 64

  US: $1,250.00
  Can.: $1,250.00
  Ster.:   £ 400.00

M 71
June
Designer: L. Harradine
Height: 4 1/4", 10.8 cm
Colour: Lavender and
             green
Issued: 1936-1949
Varieties: M 65

  US: $900.00
  Can.: $975.00
  Ster.:   £400.00

M 72
Monica
Designer: L. Harradine
Height: 3", 7.6 cm
Colour: Blue and white
Issued: 1936-1949
Varieties: M 66

US: **$1,100.00**
Can.: **$1,200.00**
Ster.: **£ 400.00**

M 73
Dainty May
Designer: L. Harradine
Height: 4", 10.1 cm
Colour: Pink and
turquoise
Issued: 1936-1949
Varieties: M 67

US: **$1,200.00**
Can.: **$1,200.00**
Ster.: **£ 400.00**

M 74
Mirabel
Designer: L. Harradine
Height: 4", 10.1 cm
Colour: Turquoise
and red
Issued: 1936-1949
Varieties: M 68

US: **$ 900.00**
Can.: **$1,100.00**
Ster.: **£ 450.00**

M 75
Janet
Designer: L. Harradine
Height: 4", 10.1 cm
Colour: Purple
Issued: 1936-1949
Varieties: M 69

US: **$700.00**
Can.: **$850.00**
Ster.: **£400.00**

M 76
Bumble
Designer: L. Harradine
Height: 4", 10.1 cm
Colour: Green and
red
Issued: 1939-1982
Series: Dickens
Miniatures

US: **$100.00**
Can.: **$125.00**
Ster.: **£ 40.00**

M 77
Captain Cuttle
Designer: L. Harradine
Height: 4", 10.1 cm
Colour: Yellow and
black
Issued: 1939-1982
Series: Dickens
Miniatures

US: **$100.00**
Can.: **$125.00**
Ster.: **£ 40.00**

M 78
Windflower
Designer: L. Harradine
Height: 4", 10.1 cm
Colour: Blue and
green
Issued: 1939-1949
Varieties: M 79

US: **$1,200.00**
Can.: **$1,400.00**
Ster.: **£ 600.00**

M 79
Windflower
Designer: L. Harradine
Height: 4", 10.1 cm
Colour: Blue and
green
Issued: 1939-1949
Varieties: M 78

US: **$1,200.00**
Can.: **$1,400.00**
Ster.: **£ 600.00**

M 80
Goody Two Shoes
Designer: L. Harradine
Height: 4", 10.1 cm
Colour: Pink and blue
Issued: 1939-1949
Varieties: M 81

US: $1,250.00
Can.: $1,250.00
Ster.: £ 450.00

M 81
Goody Two Shoes
Designer: L. Harradine
Height: 4", 10.1 cm
Colour: Lavender
and pink
Issued: 1939-1949
Varieties: M 80

US: $1,100.00
Can.: $1,250.00
Ster.: £ 450.00

M 82
Bo-Peep
Designer: L. Harradine
Height: 4", 10.1 cm
Colour: Pink
Issued: 1939-1949
Varieties: M 83

US: $1,100.00
Can.: $1,200.00
Ster.: £ 450.00

M 83
Bo-Peep
Designer: L. Harradine
Height: 4", 10.1 cm
Colour: Purple
Issued: 1939-1949
Varieties: M 82

US: $1,100.00
Can.: $1,200.00
Ster.: £ 450.00

M 84
Maureen
Designer: L. Harradine
Height: 4", 10.1 cm
Colour: Pink
Issued: 1939-1949
Varieties: M 85

US: $1,100.00
Can.: $1,250.00
Ster.: £ 600.00

M 85
Maureen
Designer: L. Harradine
Height: 4", 10.1 cm
Colour: Purple
Issued: 1939-1949
Varieties: M 84

US: $1,100.00
Can.: $1,250.00
Ster.: £ 600.00

M 86
Mrs. Bardell
Designer: L. Harradine
Height: 4 1/4", 10.8 cm
Colour: Green
Issued: 1949-1982
Series: Dickens
Miniatures

US: $ 80.00
Can.: $125.00
Ster.: £ 40.00

M 87
Scrooge
Designer: L. Harradine
Height: 4", 10.1 cm
Colour: Brown
Issued: 1949-1982
Series: Dickens
Miniatures

US: $ 80.00
Can.: $125.00
Ster.: £ 40.00

M 88
David Copperfield
Designer: L. Harradine
Height: 4 1/4", 10.8 cm
Colour: Black and tan
Issued: 1949-1983
Series: Dickens
                 Miniatures

US: $ 80.00
Can.: $125.00
Ster.:   £ 40.00

M 89
Oliver Twist
Designer: L. Harradine
Height: 4 1/4", 10.8 cm
Colour: Black and tan
Issued: 1949-1983
Series: Dickens
                 Miniatures

US: $ 80.00
Can.: $125.00
Ster.:   £ 40.00

M 90
Dick Swiveller
Designer: L. Harradine
Height: 4 1/4", 10.8 cm
Colour: Black and tan
Issued: 1949-1981
Series: Dickens
                 Miniatures

US: $ 80.00
Can.: $125.00
Ster.:   £ 40.00

M 91
Trotty Veck
Designer: L. Harradine
Height: 4 1/4", 10.8 cm
Colour: Black and brown
Issued: 1949-1982
Series: Dickens
                 Miniatures

US: $ 80.00
Can.: $125.00
Ster.:   £ 40.00

INDEX

A

A la Mode, HN 2544
A Penny's Worth, HN 2408
A Winter's Walk, HN 3052
Abdullah, HN 1410, 2104
Ace, HN 3398
A'Courting, HN 2004
Adele, HN 2480
Adornment, HN 3015
Adrienne, HN 2152, 2304. Also called Joan (Style Two),
    HN 3217
Affection, HN 2236
Afternoon Tea, HN 1747, 1748
Age of Chivalry: see Sir Edward, Sir Ralph, Sir Thomas
Age of Innocence: see Feeding Time, First Outing, Making
    Friends, Puppy Love
Aileen, HN 1645, 1664, 1803
Ajax, HMS, HN 2908
Alchemist, HN 1259, 1282
Alexandra (Style One), HN 2398
Alexandra (Style Two), HN 3286
Alfred Jingle, HN 541; M 52
Alice (Style One), HN 2158
Alice (Style Two), HN 3368
Alison, HN 2336, 3264
All Aboard, HN 2940
All-A-Blooming, HN 1457, 1466
Allure, HN 3080
Amanda, HN 2996
Amy (Style One), HN 2958
Amy (Style Two), HN 3316
And One For You, HN 2970
And So To Bed, HN 2966
Andrea, HN 3058
Angela (Style One), HN 1204, 1303
Angela (Style Two), HN 2389
Angela (Style Three), HN 3419
Angelina, HN 2013
Ann (Style One), HN 2739
Ann (Style Two), HN 3259
Anna, HN 2802
Annabel, HN 3273
Annabella, HN 1871, 1872, 1875
Anne Bolelyn, HN 3232
Anne of Cleves, HN 3356
Annette, HN 1471, 1472, 1550
Anthea, HN 1526, 1527, 1669
Antoinette (Style One), HN 1850, 1851
Antoinette (Style Two), HN 2326
Aperitif, HN 2998
Apple Maid, HN 2160
April (Style One), HN 2708
April (Style Two), HN 3344
April Shower, HN 3024
Arab, HN 33, 343, 378. Also called The Moor, HN 1308,
    1366, 1425, 1657, 2082
Aragorn, HN 2916
Artful Dodger, HN 546; M 55
As Good As New, HN 2971
Ascot, HN 2356

Ashley, HN 3420
At Ease, HN 2473
Auctioneer, HN 2988
August (Style One), HN 3165
August (Style Two), HN 3408
Automne, HN 3068
Autumn (Style One), HN 314, 474
Autumn (Style Two), HN 2087
Autumn Breezes, HN 1911, 1913, 1934, 2131, 2147
Autumn Breezes (Miniature) HN 2176, 2180
Autumn Glory, HN 2766
Autumntime, HN 3231
Awakening (Style One), HN 1927
Awakening (Style Two), HN 2837, 2875

B

Baba, HN 1230, 1243-1248
Babette, HN 1423, 1424
Babie, HN 1679, 1842, 2121
Baby Bunting, HN 2108
Baby, HN 12
Bachelor, HN 2319
Balinese Dancer, HN 2808
Ballad Seller, HN 2266
Ballerina (Style One), HN 2116
Ballerina (Style Two), HN 3197
Ballet Class, HN 3134
Balloon Boy, HN 2934
Balloon Clown, HN 2894
Balloon Girl, HN 2818
Balloon Lady, HN 2935
Balloon Man, HN 1954
Balloon Seller, HN 479, 486, 548, 583, 697
Balloon Seller, (Miniature), HN 2130
Balloons, HN 3187
Barbara (Style One), HN 1421, 1432, 1461
Barbara (Style Two), HN 2962
Barliman Butterbur, HN 2923
Basket Weaver, HN 2245
Bather (Style One), HN 597, 687, 781, 782, 1238, 1708
Bather (Style Two), HN 773, 774, 1227
Bathing Beauty, HN 3156
Beachcomber, HN 2487
Beat You To It, HN 2871
Beatrice, HN 3263
Becky, HN 2740
Bedtime (Style One), HN 1978
Bedtime (Style Two), HN 3418
Bedtime Story, HN 2059
Beethoven, HN 1778
Beggar (Style One), HN 526, 591
Beggar (Style Two), HN 2175
Beggar's Opera: see The Beggar, Captain MacHeath,
    The Highwayman, Lucy Lockett, Polly Peachum
Belle (Style One), HN 754, 776
Belle (Style Two), HN 2340
Belle o' the Ball, HN 1997
Benmore, HN 2909
Bernice, HN 2071
Bess, HN 2002, 2003

Beth, HN 2870
Betsy, HN 2111
Betty (Style One), HN 402, 403, 435, 438, 477, 478
Betty (Style Two), HN 1404, 1405, 1435, 1436
Biddy, HN 1445, 1500, 1513
Biddy Penny Farthing, HN 1843
Bilbo, HN 2914
Bill Sykes, HN 537, M 54
Blacksmith, HN 2782
Blacksmith of Williamsburg, HN 2240
Blighty, HN 323
Blithe Morning, HN 2021, 2065
Blossom, HN 1667
Blue Beard (Style One), HN 75, 410,
Bluebeard (Style Two), HN 1528, 2105
Bluebird, HN 1280
Boatman, HN 2417
Bobby, HN 2778
Bolero, HN 3076
Bon Appetit, HN 2444
Bon Jour, HN 1879, 1888
Bonnie Lassie, HN 1626, 1626A
Bo-Peep (Style One), HN 777, 1202, 1327, 1328
Bo-Peep (Style Two), HN 1810, 1811
Bo-Peep, M 82, 83
Boromir, HN 2918
Boudoir, HN 2542
Bouquet, HN 406, 414, 422, 428, 429, 567, 794
Boy Evacuee, HN 3202
Boy from Williamsburg, HN 2183
Boy on Crocodile, HN 373
Boy on Pig, HN 1369
Boy with Turban, HN 586, 587, 661, 662, 1210, 1212, 1213,
    1214, 1225
Breezy Days, HN 3162
Breton Dancer, HN 2383
Bride (Style One), HN 1588, 1600, 1762, 1841
Bride (Style Two), HN 2166
Bride (Style Three), HN 2873
Bride (Style Four), HN 3284, 3285
Bride and Groom, HN 3281
Bridesmaid (Style One), HN 1433, 1434, 1530
Bridesmaid (Style Two), HN 2148
Bridesmaid (Style Three), HN 2196
Bridesmaid (Style Four), HN 2874
Bridesmaid (Style Five), HN 3280
Bridesmaid, M 11, 12, 30
Bridget, HN 2070
Broken Lance, HN 2041
Brothers, HN 3191
Buddies (Style One), HN 2546
Buddies (Style Two), HN 3396
Bumble, M 76
Bunny, HN 2214
Bunny's Bedtime, HN 3370
Buttercup, HN 2309, 2399
Buttercup (Miniature), HN 3268
Butterfly, HN 719, 720, 730, 1203; Also called Butterfly
    Girl, HN 1456
Butterfly Girl, HN 1456; Also called Butterfly, HN 719,
    720, 730, 1203

Buz Fuz, HN 538; M 53

C

"Called Love, a Little Boy", HN 1545
Calumet, HN 1428, 1689, 2068
Camellia, HN 2222
Camilla, HN 1710, 1711
Camille, HN 1586, 1648, 1736
Captain (Style One), HN 778
Captain (Style Two), HN 2260
Captain Cook, HN 2889
Captain Cuttle, M 77
Captain MacHeath, HN 464, 590, 1256
Captain, 2nd New York Regiment, 1775, HN 2755
Carefree, HN 3026, 3029
Carmen (Style One), HN 1267, 1300
Carmen (Style Two), HN 2545
Carnival, HN 1260, 1278
Carol, HN 2961
Caroline, HN 3170
Carolyn (Style One), HN 2112
Carolyn (Style Two), HN 2974
Carpenter, HN 2678
Carpet Seller (Style One), HN 1464
Carpet Seller (Style Two), HN 1464A
Carpet Seller (Style Three), HN 2776
Carpet Seller (Style Four), HN 3277
Carpet Vendor (Style One), HN 38, 76, 350
Carpet Vendor (Style Two), HN 38A, 348,
Carrie, HN 2800
Cassim (Style One), HN 1231, 1232
Cassim (Style Two), HN 1311, 1312
Catherine (Style One), HN 2395
Catherine (Style Two), HN 3006
Catherine (Style Three), HN 3044
Catherine of Aragon, HN 3233
Cavalier (Style One), HN 369
Cavalier (Style Two), HN 2716
Celeste (Style One), HN 2237
Celeste (Style Two), HN 3322
Celia, HN 1726, 1727
Cellist, HN 2226
Cello, HN 2331
Centurion, HN 2726
Cerise, HN 1607
Characters from Children's Literature: see Heidi,
    Huckleberry Finn, Little Lord Fauntleroy, Pollyanna,
    Tom Brown, Tom Sawyer
Charisma, HN 3090
Charity, HN 3087
Charley's Aunt (Style One), HN 35, 640
Charley's Aunt (Style Two), HN 1411, 1554
Charley's Aunt (Style Three), HN 1703
Charlie Chaplin, HN 2771
Charlotte, HN 2421, 2423
Charmian, HN 1568, 1569, 1651
Chelsea Pair (woman), HN 577, 578
Chelsea Pair (man), HN 579, 580
Chelsea Pensioner, HN 689
Cherie, HN 2341

Cheryl, HN 3253
Cherry Blossom, HN 3092
Chic, HN 2997
Chief, HN 2892
Chieftain, HN 2929
Child from Williamsburg, HN 2154
Child on Crab, HN 32
Child Study (Style One), HN 603A, 603B, 1441
Child Study (Style Two), HN 604A, 604B, 1442, 1443
Child Study (Style Three), HN 605A, 605B
Child's Grace, HN 62, 62A, 510
Childhood Days: see And One For You, And So To Bed,
    As Good As New, Dressing Up, I'm Nearly Ready,
    I't Won't Hurt, Just One More, Please Keep Still,
    Save Some For Me, Stick 'em Up
Childhood Series: Loyal Friends
Children of the Blitz: see The Boy Evacuee, The Girl
    Evacuee, The Homecoming, Welcome Home
China Repairer, HN 2943
Chinese Dancer, HN 2840
Chitarrone, HN 2700
Chloe, HN 1470, 1476, 1479, 1498, 1765, 1956; M 9, 10, 29
Choice, HN 1959, 1960
Choir Boy, HN 2141
Chorus Girl, HN 1401
Christening Day, HN 3210, 3211
Christine (Style One), HN 1839, 1840
Christine (Style Two), HN 2792, 3172
Christine (Miniature), HN 3269, 3337
Christmas Morn, HN 1992
Christmas Morn, (Miniature) HN 3212, 3245
Christmas Parcels, HN 2851
Christmas Time, HN 2110
Christopher Columbus, HN 3392
Chu Chin Chow, HN 450, 460, 461
Cicely, HN 1516,
Circe, HN 1249, 1250, 1254, 1255
Cissie, HN 1808, 1809
Clare, HN 2793
Claribel, HN 1950, 1951
Clarinda, HN 2724
Claire, HN 3209
Clarissa (Style One), HN 1525, 1687
Clarissa (Style Two), HN 2345
Claudine, HN 3062
Clemency, HN 1633, 1634, 1643
Cleopatra, HN 2868
Clockmaker, HN 2279
Clothilde, HN 1598, 1599
Cloud, HN 1831
Clown, HN 2890
Clowns: see The Joker, Partners, Slapdash,Tip-toe,
    Tumbling, Will He-Won't He
Clownette, HN 1263; also called Lady Clown, HN 717,
    718, 738, 770
Coachman, HN 2282
Cobbler (Style One), HN 542, 543, 682
Cobbler (Style Two), HN 681, 1251, 1283
Cobbler (Style Three), HN 1705, 1706
Cocktails, HN 3070
Collinette, HN 1998, 1999

Colonel Fairfax, HN 2903
Columbine (Style One), HN 1296, 1297, 1439
Columbine (Style Two), HN 2185
Columbine (Style Three), HN 2738
Coming of Spring, HN 1722, 1723
Confucious, HN 3314
Congratulations, HN 3351
Constance, HN 1510, 1511
Contemplation, HN 2213, 2241
Contentment, HN 395, 396, 421, 468, 572, 685, 686, 1323
Cookie, HN 2218
Coppelia, HN 2115
Coquette, HN 20, 20A, 37
Coralie, HN 2307
Corinthian, HN 1973
Corporal, 1st. New Hampshire Regiment, 1778, HN 2780
Countess of Harrington, HN 3317
Countess Spencer, HN 3320
Country Girl, HN 3051
Country Lass, HN 1991A; Also called Market Day,
    HN 1991
Country Love, HN 2418
Country Maid, HN 3163
Country Rose, HN 3221
Court Shoemaker, HN 1755
Courtier, HN 1338
Covent Garden (Style One), HN 1339
Covent Garden (Style Two), HN 2857
Cradle Song, HN 2246
Craftsman, HN 2284
Crinoline, HN 8, 9, 9A, 21, 21A, 413, 566, 628
Crinoline Lady, HN 650, 651, 652, 653, 654, 655
Crouching Nude, HN 457
Cup of Tea, HN 2322
Curly Knob, HN 1627
Curly Locks, HN 2049
Curtsey, HN 57, 57B, 66A, 327, 334, 363, 371, 518, 547, 629,
    670
Cymbals, HN 2699
Cynthia (Style One), HN 1685, 1686, 1686A
Cynthia (Style Two), HN 2440

D

Daddy's Joy, HN 3294
Daffy-Down-Dilly, HN 1712, 1713
Dainty May, HN 1639, 1656; M 67, 73
Daisy, HN 1575, 1961
Damaris, HN 2079
Dancers of the World: see Balinese Dancer, Breton Dancer,
    Chinese Dancer, Indian Temple Dancer, Kurdish
    Dancer, Mexican Dancer, North American Indian
    Dancer, Philippine Dancer, Polish Dancer, Scottish
    Highland Dancer, Spanish Flamenco Dancer, West
    Indian Dancer, Indian Temple
Dancing Delight, HN 3078
"Dancing Eyes and Sunny Hair" HN 1543
Dancing Figure, HN 311
Dancing Years, HN 2235
Dandy, HN 753
Danielle (Style One), HN 3056,

Danielle (Stye Two), HN 3001
Daphne, HN 2268
Dapple Grey, HN 2521
Darby, HN 1427, 2024
Darling (Style One), HN 1, 1319, 1371, 1372
Darling (Style Two), HN 1985
David Copperfield, M 88
Dawn (Style One), HN 1858, 1858A
Dawn (Style Two), HN 3258
Daybreak, HN 3107
Daydreams, HN 1731, 1732, 1944,
Deauville, HN 2344
Debbie, HN 2385, 2400
Deborah, HN 2701
Debut, HN 3046
Debutante (Style One), HN 2210
Debutante (Style Two), HN 3188
December (Style One), HN 2696
December (Style Two), HN 3412
Deidre, HN 2020,
Delicia, HN 1662, 1663, 1681
Delight:, HN 1772, 1773
Delphine, HN 2136
Demure, HN 3045
Denise (Style One), HN 2273; M 34, 35
Denise (Style Two), HN 2477
Derrick, HN 1398
Despair, HN 596
Detective, HN 2359
Devotion, HN 3220
Diana (Style One), HN 1716, 1717, 1986
Diana (Style Two), HN 2468, 3266
Diana (Miniature), HN 3310
Diana the Huntress, HN 2829
Dick Swiveller, M 90
Dick Turpin, HN 3272
Dickens Characters: see Alfred Jingle, The Artful Dodger,
    Bill Sykes, Bumble, Buz Fuz, Captain Cuttle, David
    Copperfield, Dick Swiveller, Fagin, The Fat Boy, Little
    Nell, Mr. Micawber, Mr. Pickwick, Mrs. Bardell,
    Oliver Twist, Pecksniff, Sairey Gamp, Sam Weller,
    Scrooge, Stiggins, Tiny Tim, Tony Weller, Trotty Veck,
    Uriah Heep
Digger (Australian), HN 322, 353
Digger (New Zealand), HN 321
Diligent Scholar, HN 26
Dimity, HN 2169
Dinky-Do, HN 1678, 2120
Discovery, HN 3428
"Do You Wonder...", HN 1544
Doctor, HN 2858
Dolly Vardon, HN 1514, 1515
Dolly (Style One), HN 355
Dolly (Style Two), HN 469. Also called "The Little
    Mother" (Style One)
Dominique, HN 3054
Donna, HN 2939
Dorcas, HN 1490, 1491, 1558
Doreen, HN 1363, 1389, 1390
Doris Keene as Cavallini (Style One), HN 90, 467
Doris Keene as Cavallini (Style Two), HN 96, 345

Dorothy, HN 3098
Double Jester, HN 365
Dreaming, HN 3133
Dreamland, HN 1473, 1481
Dreamweaver, HN 2283
Dressing Up (Style One), HN 2964
Dressing-Up (Style Two), HN 3300
Drummer Boy, HN 2679
Dryad of the Pines, HN 1869
Duchess of York, HN 3086
Dulcie, HN 2305
Dulcimer, HN 2798
Dulcinea, HN 1343, 1419
Dunce, HN 6, 310, 357

E

Easter Day, HN 1976, 2039
Eastern Grace, HN 3138
Edith, HN 2957
Elaine, HN 2791, 3307
Elaine (Miniature), HN 3214, 3247
Eleanor of Provence, HN 2009
Eleanore, HN 1753, 1754
Elegance, HN 2264
Elegance: see Claudine, Danielle (Style One), Dominique,
    Francoise, Martine, Monique
Elfreda, HN 2078
Eliza (Style One), HN 2543, 2543A
Eliza (Style Two), HN 3179
Elizabeth (Style One), HN 2946
Elizabeth (Style Two), HN 2465
Elizabeth Fry, HN 2, 2A
Ellen, HN 3020
Ellen Terry as Queen Catherine, HN 379
Elsie Maynard (Style One), HN 639
Elsie Maynard (Style Two), HN 2902
Elyse, HN 2429, 2474
Embroidering, HN 2855
Emily (Style One), HN 3004
Emily, (Style Two), HN 3204
Emir, HN 1604, 1605; Also called
    Ibrahim, HN 2095
Emma (Style One), HN 2834
Emma (Style Two), HN 3208
Enchanting Evening, HN 3108
Enchantment: See April Shower, Fairyspell, Lyric, Magic
    Dragon, The Magpie Ring, Musicale, Queen of the
    Dawn, Queen of the Ice, Rumpelstiltskin, Serenade,
    Sonata
Enchantment, HN 2178
Encore, HN 2751
Enigma, HN 3110
Entranced, HN 3186
Ermine Coat, HN 1981
Ermine Muff, HN 54, 332, 671
Erminie, M 40
Esmeralda, HN 2168
Estelle, HN 1566, 1802
Ete (Summer), HN 3067
Eugene, HN 1520, 1521

Europa and the Bull (Style One), HN 95
Europa and the Bull (Style Two), HN 2828
Eve, HN 2466
Evelyn, HN 1622, 1637
Eventide, HN 2814

F

Fagin, HN 534, M 49
Fair Lady, HN 2193, 2832, 2835
Fair Lady (Miniature), HN 3216, 3336
Fair Maiden, HN 2211, 2434
Fairy (Style One), HN 1324
Fairy, (Style Two), HN 1374, 1380, 1532
Fairy, (Style Three), HN 1375, 1395, 1533
Fairy, (Style Four), HN 1376, 1536
Fairy, (Style Five), HN 1377
Fairy, (Style Six), HN 1378, 1396, 1535
Fairy, (Style Seven), HN 1379, 1394, 1534
Fairy, (Style Eight), HN 1393
Fairyspell, HN 2979
Faith, HN 3082
Falstaff (Style One), HN 571, 575, 608, 609, 619, 638, 1216, 1606
Falstaff (Style Two), HN 618, 2054
Falstaf (Miniature), HN 3236
Family Album, HN 2321
Family, HN 2720, 2721
Fantasy, HN 3296
Faraway, HN 2133
Farmer, HN 3195
Farmer's Boy, HN 2520
Farmer's Wife (Style One), HN 2069
Farmer's Wife (Style Two), HN 3164
Fat Boy (Style One), HN 530
Fat Boy (Style Two), HN 555, 1893
Fat Boy (Style Three), HN 2096
Fat Boy, M 44
Father Christmas, HN 3399
Favourite, HN 2249
February (Style One), HN 2703
February (Style Two), HN 3342
Feeding Time, HN 3373
Fiddler, HN 2171
Figure of the Year see: Amy, Mary
Fiona (Style One), HN 1924, 1925, 1933
Fiona (Style Two), HN 2694
Fiona (Style Three), HN 3252
First Dance, HN 2803
First Love, HN 2747
First Outing, HN 3377
First Steps (Style One), HN 2242
First Steps (Style Two), HN 3282
First Waltz, HN 2862
Fisherwoman, HN 80, 349, 359, 631
Mrs. Fitzherbert, HN 2007
Fleur, HN 2368, 2369
Fleurette, HN 1587
Flirtation, HN 3071
Flora, HN 2349
Florence, HN 2745

Florence Nightingale, HN 3144
Flounced Skirt, HN 57A, 66, 77, 78, 333
Flower Arranging, HN 3040
Flower of Love, HN 2460
Flower of the Month: see January, February, March, April, May, June, July, August, September, October, November, December
Flower Seller, HN 789
Flower Seller's Children, HN 525, 551, 1206, 1342, 1406
Flute, HN 2483
Foaming Quart, HN 2162
Folly, HN 1335, 1750
Forget-Me-Not (Style One), HN 1812, 1813
Forget-Me-Not (Style Two), HN 3388
Fortune Teller, HN 2159
Forty Winks, HN 1974
Four O'Clock, HN 1760
Four Seasons (Style One) see: Spring (Style One), Summer (Style One), Autumn (Style One), Winter (Style One)
Four Seasons (Style Two) see: Spring (Style Three), Summer (Style Two), Autumn (Style Two), Winter (Style Two)
Four Seasons (Style Three) see: Catherine in Spring (Style Two), Lilian in Summer, Emily in Autumn (Style One), Sarah in Winter
Four Seasons (Style Four) see: Springtime (Style Two), Summertime, Autumntime, Wintertime
Fragrance, HN 2334, 3311
Fragrance (Miniature), HN 3220, 3250
Francine, HN 2422
Francoise, HN 2897
Frangçon, HN 1720, 1721
Free As The Wind, HN 3139
Free Spirit, HN 3157, 3159
French Horn, HN 2795
French Peasant, HN 2075
Friar Tuck, HN 2143
Frodo, HN 2912
Fruit Gathering, HN 449, 476, 503, 561, 562, 706, 707

G

Gaffer, HN 2053
Gaiety, HN 3140
Gail, HN 2937
Gail (Miniature), HN 3321
Gainsborough Hat, HN 46, 46A, 47, 329, 352, 383, 453, 675, 705
Gainsborough Ladies: see Honourable Francis Duncombe, Isabella, Countess of Sefton, Mary, Countess Howe Sophia Charlotte, Lady Sheffield
Galadriel, HN 2915
Gamekeeper. HN 2879
Gandalf, HN 2911
Gardener, HN 3161
Gardening Time, HN 3401
Gay Morning, HN 2135
Geisha (Style One), HN 354, 376, 376A, 387, 634, 741, 779, 1321, 1322
Geisha (Style Two), HN 1223, 1234, 1292, 1310
Geisha (Style Three), HN 3229

Genevieve, HN 1962
Genie, HN 2989, 2999
Gentle Arts: see Adornment, Flower Arranging, Painting,
    Spinning, Tapestry Weaving, Writing
Gentleman from Williamsburg, HN 2227
Gentlewoman, HN 1632
George Washington at Prayer, HN 2861
Georgiana, HN 2093
Georgina, HN 2377
Geraldine, HN 2348
Gilbert and Sullivan: see Colonel Fairfax, Elsie Maynard
    (Style Two), Ko-Ko (Style Two), The Pirate King, Ruth
    the Pirate Maid, Yum-Yum (Style Two)
Gillian (Style One), HN 1670 1670A
Gillian (Style Two), HN 3042, 3042A
Gimli, HN 2922
Girl Evacuee, HN 3203
Girl with Yellow Frock, HN 588
Giselle, HN 2139
Giselle, The Forest Glade, HN 2140
Gladys, HN 1740, 1741
Gleaner, HN 1302
Gloria (Style One), HN 1488, 1700
Gloria (Style Two), HN 3200
Gnome, HN 319, 380, 381
God Bless You, HN 3400
Golden Days, HN 2274
Golfer, HN 2992
Gollum, HN 2913
Gollywog, HN 1979, 2040
Good Catch, HN 2258
Good Day Sir, HN 2896
Good Friends, HN 2783
Good King Wenceslas, HN 2118
Good King Wenceslas (Miniature), HN 3262
Good Morning, HN 2671
Good Pals, HN 3132
Goody Two Shoes, HN 1889, 1905, 2037; M 80, 81
Goosegirl (Style One), HN 425, 436, 437, 448, 559, 560
Goose Girl (Style Two), HN 2419
Gossips, HN 1426, 1429, 2025
Grace, HN 2318
Grace Darling, HN 3089
Graduate (female), HN 3016
Graduate (male), HN 3017
Grand Manner, HN 2723
Grandma, HN 2052, 2052A
Granny, HN 1804, 1832
Granny's Heritage, HN 1873, 1874, 2031
Granny's Shawl, HN 1642, 1647
Greta, HN 1485
Gretchen, HN 1397, 1562
Grief, HN 595
Griselda, HN 1993
Grizel, HN 1629
Grossmith's 'Tsang Ihang', HN 582
Groucho Marx, HN 2777
Guardsman, HN 2784
Guy Fawkes (Miniature), HN 3271
Guy Fawkes, HN 98, 347, 445
Gwendolen, HN 1494, 1503, 1570

Gwynneth, HN 1980
Gypsy Dance (Style One), HN 2157
Gypsy Dance (Style Two), HN 2230

H

Hannah, HN 3369
Happy Anniversary (Style One), HN 3097
Happy Anniversary (Style Two), HN 3254
Happy Birthday, HN 3095
"Happy Joy, Baby Boy..." HN 1541
Harlequin (Style One), HN 2186
Harlequin (Style Two), HN 2737
Harlequinade, HN 585, 635, 711, 780
Harlequinade Masked, HN 768, 769, 1274, 1304
Harmony, HN 2824
Harp, HN 2482
Harriet, HN 3177
Harvestime, HN 3084
Haute Ensemble: See A La Mode, Boudoir, Carmen (Style
    Two), Eliza (Style One), Mantilla
Hazel (Style One), HN 1796, 1797
Hazel (Style Two), HN 3167
He Loves Me, HN 2046
Heart to Heart, HN 2276
Heather, HN 2956
Heidi, HN 2975
Helen (Style One), HN 1508, 1509, 1572
Helen (Style Two), HN 2994
Helen of Troy, HN 2387
Helmsman, HN 2499
Henrietta Maria, HN 2005
Henry Irving As Cardinal Wolsey, HN 344
Henry Lytton As Jack Point, HN 610
Henry VIII (Style One), HN 370, 673
Henry VIII (Style Two), HN 1792
Henry VIII (Style Three), HN 3350
Her Ladyship, HN 1977
"Here A Little Child I Stand..." HN 1546
Herminia, HN 1644, 1646, 1704
Hermione, HN 2058
Hibernia, HN 2932
Highwayman, HN 527, 592, 1257
Hilary, HN 2335
Hinged Parasol, HN 1578, 1579
His Holiness Pope John-Paul II, HN 2888
Hiver (Winter), HN 3069
HM Queen Elizabeth, The Queen Mother (Style Two),
    HN 3189
HM Queen Elizabeth, The Queen Mother As The Duchess
    of York, HN 3230
HM Queen Elizabeth II (Style One), HN 2502
HM Queen Elizabeth II (Style Two), HN 2878
HM Queen Elizabeth II (Style Three), HN 3440
Hold Tight, HN 3298
Home Again, HN 2167
Homecoming, HN 3295
Honey, HN 1909, 1910, 1963
Hope, HN 3061
Hornpipe, HN 2161
Hostess of Williamsburg, HN 2209

HRH Prince Philip, Duke of Edinburgh, HN 2386
HRH The Prince of Wales (Style One), HN 2883
HRH The Prince of Wales (Style Two), HN 2884
HRH The Princess of Wales, HN 2887
HRH Queen Elizabeth, The Queen Mother (Style One),
    HN 2882
Huckleberry Finn, HN 2927
Hunting Squire, HN 1409; Also called Squire, HN 1814
Hunts Lady, HN 1201
Huntsman (Style One), HN 1226
Huntsman (Style Two), HN 1815; Also called John Peel,
    HN 1408
Huntsman (Style Three), HN 2492
Hurdy Gurdy, HN 2796

I

I'm Nearly Ready, HN 2976
Ibrahim, HN 2095; Also called Emir, HN 1604, 1605
Idle Hours, HN 3115
Images: see Awakening (Style Two), Bride and Groom,
    Bridesmaid, Carefree, Congratulations, Contemplation,
    Family, First Love, First Steps (Style Two), Free Spirit,
    God Bless You, Happy Anniversary (Style Two),
    Lovers, Mother and Daughter, Over the Threshold,
    Peace, Sisters, Sympathy, Tenderness, Thankful,
    Tranquility, Wedding Day, Yearning
In Grandma's Days, HN 339, 340 388, 442; Also called
    Lilac Shawl HN 44, 44A and Poke Bonnet HN 362,
    612, 765
In The Stocks (Style One), HN 1474, 1475
In The Stocks (Style Two), HN 2163
Indian Brave, HN 2376
Indian Maiden, HN 3117
Indian Temple Dancer, HN 2830
Innocence (Style One), HN 2842
Innocence (Style Two), HN 3226
Invitation, HN 2170
Iona, HN 1346
Irene, HN 1621, 1697, 1952
Irish Colleen, HN 766, 767
Irishman, HN 1307
Isabella, Countess of Sefton, HN 3010
Isadora, HN 2938
It Won't Hurt, HN 2963
Ivy, HN 1768, 1769

J

Jack, HN 2060
Jack Point, HN 85, 91, 99, 2080
Jacqueline (Style One), HN 2000, 2001
Jacqueline (Style Two), HN 2333
James, HN 3013
Jane (Style One), HN 2014
Jane (Style Two), HN 2806
Jane (Style Three), HN 3260
Jane Seymour, HN 3349
Janet (Style One), HN 1537, 1538, 1652, 1737
Janet (Style Two), HN 1916, 1964

Janet, M 69, 75
Janette, HN 3415
Janice, HN 2022, 2165
Janine, HN 2461
January (Style One), HN 2697
January (Style Two), HN 3341
Japanese Fan, HN 399, 405, 439, 440
Jasmine, HN 1862, 1863, 1876
Jean (Style One) HN 1877, 1878, 2032
Jean (Style Two) HN 2710
Jemma, HN 3168
Jennifer (Style One), HN 1484
Jennifer (Style Two), HN 2392
Jersey Milkmaid, HN 2057; Also called The Milkmaid,
    HN 2057A
Jessica, HN 3169
Jester (Style One), HN 45, 71, 71A, 320, 367, 412, 426, 446,
    552, 616, 627, 1295, 1702, 2016
Jester (Style Two), HN 45A, 45B, 55, 308, 630, 1333
Jester (Miniature), HN 3325
Jill, HN 2061
Joan (Style One), HN 1422, 2023
Joan (Style Two), HN 3217. Also called Adrienne,
    HN 2152, 2304
Joanne, HN 2373
John Peel, HN 1408; Also called Huntsman, HN 1815
Joker (Style One), HN 3196
Joker (Style Two), HN 2252
Jolly Sailor, HN 2172
Jovial Monk, HN 2144
Joy, HN 3184
Judge and Jury, HN 1264
Judge, HN 2443, 2443A
Judith (Style One), HN 2089
Judith (Style Two), HN 2278, 2313
Julia, HN 2705, 2706
Julie, HN 2995
Juliet, HN 2968
July (Style One), HN 2794
July (Style Two), HN 3347
June (Style One), HN 1690, 1691, 1947, 2027; M 65, 71
June (Style Two), HN 2790
June (Style Three), HN 2991
June (Style Four), HN 3346
Juno and the Peacock, HN 2827
Just For You, HN 3355
Just One More, HN 2980

K

Karen (Style One), HN 1994
Karen (Style Two), HN 2388
Karen (Miniature), HN 3270, 3338
Kate, HN 2789
Kate Greenaway: See Amy, Anna, Beth, Carrie, Edith,
    Ellen, Emma, Georgina, James, Kathy, Lori, Louise,
    Lucy, Nell, Ruth, Sophie, Tess, Tom
Kate Hannigan, HN 3088
Kate Hardcastle, HN 1718, 1719, 1734, 1861, 1919, 2028
Katharine, HN 61, 74, 341, 471, 615, 793
Katie, HN 3360

Kathleen (Style One), HN 1252, 1253, 1275, 1279, 1291, 1357, 1512
Kathleen, (Style Two), HN 2933, 3100
Kathy (Style One), HN 2346
Kathy (Style Two), HN 3305
Katrina, HN 2327
Kay, HN 2155
Kelly, HN 2478
Kerry, HN 3036
Kimberley (Style One), HN 2969
Kimberley (Style Two), HN 3379
King Charles, HN 404, 2084, 3459
Kirsty, HN 2381
Kirsty (Miniature), HN 3213, 3246
Kitty, HN 1367
Ko-Ko (Style One), HN 1266, 1286
Ko-Ko (Style Two), HN 2898
Kurdish Dancer, HN 2867

L

La Sylphide, HN 2138
Ladies of Covent Garden: see
    Catherine (Style One), Deborah, Juliet, Kimberley
Lady and Blackamoor (Style One), HN 374
Lady and Blackamoor (Style Two), HN 375, 377, 470
Lady and the Unicorn, HN 2825
Lady Anne, HN 83, 87, 93
Lady Anne Nevill, HN 2006
Lady April, HN 1958, 1965
Lady Betty, HN 1967
Lady Charmian, HN 1948, 1949
Lady Clare, HN 1465
Lady Clown, HN 717, 718, 738, 770. Also called Clownette, HN 1263
Lady Diana Spencer, HN 2885
Lady Fayre, HN 1265, 1557
Lady from Williamsburg, HN 2228
Lady Jester (Style One), HN 1221, 1222, 1332
Lady Jester (Style Two), HN 1284, 1285
Lady Musicians: see Cello, Chitarrone, Cymbals, Dulcimer, Flute, French Horn, Harp, Hurdy Gurdy, Lute, Viola d'Amore, Violin, Virginals
Lady of the Elizabethan Period (Style One), HN 40, 40A, 73, 411,
Lady of the Elizabethan Period (Style Two), HN 309
Lady of the Fan, HN 48, 52, 53, 53A, 335, 509
Lady of the Georgian Period, HN 41, 331, 444, 690, 702
Lady of the Snows, HN 1780, 1830
Lady Pamela, HN 2718
Lady with Ermine Muff, HN 82
Lady with Rose, HN 48A, 52A, 68, 304, 336, 515, 517, 584, 624
Lady with Shawl, HN 447, 458, 626, 678, 679
Lady without Bouquet, HN 393, 394
Lady Worsley, HN 3318
Ladybird, HN 1638, 1640
Laird, HN 2361
Lalla Rookh, HN 2910
Lambeth Walk, HN 1880, 1881
Lambing Time, HN 1890

L'Ambitieuse, HN 3359
Lamp Seller, HN 3278
Land of Nod, HN 56, 56A, 56B
Last Waltz, HN 2315, 2316
Laura, HN 2960, 3136
Lauren, HN 3290
Laurianne, HN 2719
Lavender Woman, HN 22, 23, 23A, 342, 569, 744
Lavinia, HN 1955
Lawyer, HN 3041
Leading Lady, HN 2269
Leda and the Swan, HN 2826
Legolas, HN 2917
Leisure Hour, HN 2055
Les Femmes Fatales: see Cleopatra, Eve, Helen of Troy, Lecrezia Borgia, Queen of Sheba, T'zu-hsi, Empress Dowager
Les Saisons: see Printemps (Spring), Ete (Summer), Automne (Autumn), Hiver (Winter),
Lesley, HN 2410
Let's Play, HN 3397
Liberty, HN 3201
Lido Lady, HN 1220, 1229
Lifeboat Man, HN 2764
Lifeguard, HN 2781
Lights Out, HN 2262
Lilac Shawl, HN 44, 44A; Also called in Grandma's Days, HN 339, 340, 388, 442 and The Poke Bonnet, HN 362, 612, 765
Lilac Time, HN 2137
Lilian, HN 3003
Lily, HN 1798, 1799
Linda (Style One), HN 2106
Linda (Style Two), HN 2758
Linda (Style Three), HN 3374
Lisa, HN 2310, 2394, 3265
Lisette, HN 1523, 1524, 1684
Little Ballerina, HN 3395
Little Bo Peep, HN 3030
Little Boy Blue (Style One), HN 2062
Little Boy Blue (Style Two), HN 3035
Little Bridesmaid, See Bridesmaid (Style One), HN 1433, 1434, 1530
"Little Child So Rare And Sweet" (Style One), HN 1540
"Little Child So Rare And Sweet" (Style Two), HN 1542
Little Jack Horner (Style One), HN 2063
Little Jack Horner (Style Two), HN 3034
Little Lady Make Believe, HN 1870
Little Land, HN 63, 67
Little Lord Fauntleroy, HN 2972
Little Miss Muffet, HN 2727
Little Mistress, HN 1449
Little Mother (Style One), HN 389, 390; Also called Dolly, HN 469
Little Mother (Style Two), HN 1418, 1641; Also called Young Widow, HN 1399
Little Nell, HN 540; M 51
Lizana, HN 1756, 1761
Lizzie, HN 2749
Lobster Man, HN 2317, 2323
London Cry, Strawberries, HN 749, 772

London Cry, Turnips and Carrots, HN 752, 771
Long John Silver, HN 2204
Lord Olivier as Richard III, HN 2881
Loretta, HN 2337
Lori, HN 2801
Lorna, HN 2311
Lorraine, HN 3118
Louise (Style One), HN 2869
Louise (Style Two), HN 3207
Love Letter (Style One), HN 2149
Love Letter (Style Two), HN 3105
Lovers, HN 2762, 2763
Loving You, HN 3389
Loyal Friends, HN 3358
Lucrezia Borgia, HN 2342
Lucy, HN 2863
Lucy Ann, HN 1502, 1565
Lucy Lockett (Style One), HN 485, 524
Lucy Lockett (Style Two), HN 695, 696
Lunchtime, HN 2485
Lute, HN 2431
Lydia, HN 1906, 1907, 1908
Lynne, HN 2329
Lynsey, HN 3043
Lyric, HN 2757

M

Macaw, HN 1779, 1829
Madaleine, HN 3255
Madonna of the Square, HN 10, 10A, 11, 14, 27, 326, 573,
    576, 594, 613, 764, 1968, 1969, 2034
Magic Dragon, HN 2977
Magpie Ring, HN 2978
Maisie, HN 1618, 1619
Major, 3rd New Jersey Regiment, 1776, HN 2752
Make Believe, HN 2224, 2225
Making Friends, HN 3373
Mam'selle, HN 658, 659, 724, 786
Man in Tudor Costume, HN 563
Mandarin, (Style One), HN 84, 316, 318, 382, 611, 746, 787,
    791
Mandarin, (Style Two), HN 366, 455, 641
Mandarin, (Style Three), HN 601
Mandy, HN 2476
Mantilla, HN 2712, 3192
March (Style One), HN 2707
March (Style Two), HN 3343
Margaret (Style One), HN 1989
Margaret (Style Two), HN 2397
Margaret of Anjou. HN 2012
Margery, HN 1413
Margot, HN 1628, 1636, 1653
Marguerite, HN 1928, 1929, 1930, 1946
Marianne, HN 2074
Marie (Style One), HN 401, 434, 502, 504, 505, 506
Marie (Style Two), HN 1370, 1388, 1417, 1489, 1531, 1635,
    1655
Marie (Style Three), HN 3357
Marie Curie, HN 3352
Marietta, HN 1341, 1446, 1699

Marigold, HN 1447, 1451, 1555
Marilyn, HN 3002
Marion, HN 1582, 1583
Mariquita, HN 1837
Marjorie, HN 2788
Market Day, HN 1991; Also called Country Lass,
    HN 1991A
Marriage of Art and Industry, HN 2261
Martine, HN 3053
Mary (Style One), HN 2374
Mary (Style Two), HN 3375
Mary, Countess Howe, HN 3007
Mary Had A Little Lamb, HN 2048
Mary Jane, HN 1990
Mary, Mary, HN 2044
Mary Queen of Scots (Style One), HN 2931
Mary Queen of Scots (Style Two), HN 3142
Mask Seller, HN 1361, 2103
Mask, HN 656, 657, 729, 733, 785, 1271
Masque, HN 2554, 2554A
Masquerade (man) (Style One), HN 599, 636, 683
Masquerade (woman) (Style One), HN 600, 600A, 637, 674
Masquerade (Style Two), HN 2251, 2259
Master Sweep, HN 2205
Master, HN 2325
Matador and Bull, HN 2324
Matilda, HN 2011
Maureen (Style One), HN 1770, 1771; M 84, 85
Maureen (Style Two), HN 2481
Maxine, HN 3199
May (Style One), HN 2746, 3251
May (Style Two), HN 2711
May (Style Three), HN 3345
Mayor, HN 2280
Maytime, HN 2113
Meditation, HN 2330
Meg, HN 2743
Megan, HN 3306
Melanie, HN 2271
Melissa, HN 2467
Melody, HN 2202
Memories, HN 1855, 1856, 1857, 2030
Mendicant, HN 1355, 1365
Mephisto, HN 722, 723
Mephistopheles and Marguerite, HN 755, 775
Meriel, HN 1931, 1932
Mermaid, HN 97, 300
Merry Christmas, HN 3096
Meryll, HN 1917; Also called Toinette, HN 1940
Mexcian Dancer, HN 2866
Michael Doulton Signature Collection: see Autumn
    Breezes, Christine, Christmas Morn, Elaine, Fair Lady,
    Fragrance, Karen, Kirsty, Ninette, Sara, Southern Belle,
    Sunday Best
Michele, HN 2234
Middle Earth: see Aragorn, Barliman Butterbur, Bilbo,
    Boromir, Frodo, Galadriel, Gandalf, Gimli, Gollum,
    Legolas, Samwise, Tom Bombadil
Midinette (Style One), HN 1289, 1306
Midinette (Style Two), HN 2090,
Midsummer Noon, HN 1899, 1900, 2033

Milady, HN 1970
Milestone, HN 3297
Milking Time, HN 3, 306
Milkmaid, HN 2057A; Also called Jersey Milkmaid, HN 2057
Millicent, HN 1714, 1715, 1860
Miniatures: see Autumn Breezes, The Balloon Seller, Buttercup, Christine, Christmas Morn, Diana, Elaine, Fair Lady, Falstaff, Fragrance, Gail, Good King Wenceslas, Guy Fawkes, A Jester, Karen, Kirsty, Ninette, The Old Balloon Seller, Rebecca, Sara, Southern Belle, Sunday Best, Top 'o The Hill, The Town Crier
Minuet, HN 2019, 2066
Mirabel, HN 1743, 1744; M 68, 74
Miranda (Style One), HN 1818, 1819
Miranda (Style Two), HN 3037
Mirror, HN 1852, 1853
Miss 1926, HN 1205, 1207
Miss Demure, HN 1402, 1440, 1463, 1499, 1560
Miss Fortune, HN 1897, 1898
Miss Muffet, HN 1936, 1937
Miss Winsome. HN 1665, 1666
M'Lady's Maid, HN 1795, 1822
Modena, HN 1845, 1846
Modern Piper, HN 756
Modesty, HN 2744
Moira, HN 1347
Molly Malone, HN 1455
Monica, HN 1458, 1459, 1467; M 66, 72
Monique, HN 2893
Monte Carlo, HN 2332
Moondancer, HN 3181
Moor, HN 1308, 1366, 1425, 1657, 2082; Also called An Arab, HN 33, 343, 378
Moorish Minstrel, HN 34, 364, 415, 797
Moorish Piper Minstrel, HN 301, 328, 416
Morning Breeze, HN 3313
Morning Glory, HN 3093
Morning Ma'am, HN 2895
Mother and Baby, HN 3235, 3348, 3353
Mother and Daughter, HN 2841, 2843
Mother's Help, HN 2151
Motherhood, HN 28, 30, 303
Mr. Micawber (Style One), HN 532
Mr. Micawber (Style Two), HN 557, 1895
Mr. Micawber (Style Three), HN 2097
Mr. Micawber, M 42
Mr. Pickwick (Style One), HN 529
Mr. Pickwick (Style Two), HN 556, 1894
Mr. Pickwick (Style Three), HN 2099
Mr. Pickwick, M 41
Mrs. Bardell, M 86
Mrs. Fitzherbert, HN 2007
Mrs. Hugh Bonfoy, HN 3319
Musicale, HN 2756
My Best Friend, HN 3011
My First Pet, HN 3122
My Love, HN 2339
My Pet, HN 2238
My Pretty Maid, HN 2064

My Teddy, HN 2177
Myfanwy Jones, HN 39, 92, 456, 514, 516, 519, 520, 660, 668, 669, 701, 792; Also called The Welsh Girl
Myths and Maidens: see Diana the Huntress, Europa and the Bull (Style Two), Juno and the Peacock, Lady and the Unicorn, Leda and the Swan

N

Nadine, HN 1885, 1886
Nana, HN 1766, 1767
Nancy, HN 2955
Nanny, HN 2221
Napoleon at Waterloo, HN 3429
Natalie, HN 3173
Negligee, HN 1219, 1228, 1272, 1273, 1454
Nell, HN 3014
Nell Gwynn, HN 1882, 1887
Nelson, HN 2928
New Bonnet, HN 1728, 1957
New Companions, HN 2770
Newhaven Fishwife, HN 1480
Newsboy, HN 2244
Newsvendor, HN 2891
Nicola, HN 2804, 2839
Nina, HN 2347
Ninette, HN 2379, 3417
Ninette (Miniature), HN 3215, 3248
Noelle, HN 2179
Norma, M 36, 37
North American Indian Dancer, HN 2809
November (Style One), HN 2695
November (Style Two), HN 3411
Nude on Rock, HN 593
Nude Study, HN 606A, 606B
Nursery Rhymes (Style One) see: Curly Locks, He Loves Me, Jack, Jill, Little Boy Blue (Style One), Little Jack Horner (Style One), Mary, Mary, Mary Had A Little Lamb, My Pretty Maid, Once Upon A Time, She Loves Me Not, Wee Willie Winkie (Style One),
Nursery Rhymes (Style Two) see: Little Bo Peep, Little Boy Blue (Style Two), Little Jack Horner (Style Two), Little Miss Muffet, Polly Put The Kettle On, Tom, Tom, the Piper's Son, Wee Willie Winkie (Style Two)

O

October (Style One), HN 2693
October (Style Two), HN 3410
Odds and Ends, HN 1844
Officer of the Line, HN 2733
Old Balloon Seller, HN 1315
Old Balloon Seller (Miniature), HN 2129
Old Balloon Seller and Bulldog, HN 1791, 1912
Old Ben, HN 3190
Old Father Thames, HN 2993
Old King, HN 358, 623, 1801, 2134
Old King Cole, HN 2217
Old Lavender Seller, HN 1492, 1571
Old Man, HN 451

Old Meg, HN 2494
Old Mother Hubbard, HN 2314
Olga, HN 2463
Oliver Hardy, HN 2775
Oliver Twist, M 89
Olivia (Style One), HN 1995
Olivia (Style Two), HN 2197
Omar Khayyam (Style One), HN 408, 409
Omar Khayyam (Style Two), HN 2247
Omar Khayyam and the Beloved, HN 407, 419, 459, 598
Once Upon a Time, HN 2047
One of the Forty (Style One), HN 417, 490, 495, 501, 528, 648, 677, 1351, 1352
One of the Forty (Style Two), HN 418, 494, 498, 647, 666, 704, 1353
One of the Forty (Style Three), HN 423
One of the Forty (Style Four), HN 423A
One of the Forty (Style Five), HN 423B
One of the Forty (Style Six), HN 423C
One of the Forty (Style Seven), HN 423D
One of the Forty (Style Eight), HN 423E
One of the Forty (Style Nine), HN 427
One of the Forty (Style Ten), HN 480, 493, 497, 499, 664, 714
One of the Forty (Style Eleven), HN 481, 483, 491, 646, 667, 712, 1336, 1350
One of the Forty (Style Twelve), HN 482, 484, 492, 645, 663, 713
One of the Forty (Style Thirteen), HN 496, 500, 649, 665, 1354
One That Got Away, HN 2153
Orange Lady, HN 1759, 1953
Orange Seller, HN 1325
Orange Vendor, HN 72, 508, 521, 1966
Organ Grinder, HN 2173
Out for a Walk, HN 86, 443, 748
Over the Threshold, HN 3274
Owd Willum, HN 2042

P

Painting, HN 3012
Paisley Shawl (Style One), HN 1392, 1460, 1707, 1739, 1987
Paisley Shawl (Style Two), HN 1914, 1988
Paisley Shawl, M 3, 4, 26
Palio, HN 2428
Pamela (Style One), HN 1468, 1469, 1564
Pamela (Style Two), HN 2479, 3223
Pan on Rock, HN 621, 622
Panorama, HN 3028
Pantalettes, HN 1362, 1412, 1507, 1709; M 15, 16, 31
Paradise, HN 3074
Parisian, HN 2445
Park Parade, HN 3116
Parson's Daughter, HN 337, 338, 441, 564, 790, 1242, 1356, 2018
Partners, HN 3119
Past Glory, HN 2484
Patchwork Quilt, HN 1984
Patricia (Style One), HN 1414, 1431, 1462, 1567; M7, 8, 28
Patricia (Style Two), HN 2715

Paula, HN 2906, 3234
Pauline (Style One), HN 1444
Pauline (Style Two), HN 2441
Pavlova, HN 487, 676
Peace, HN 2433, 2470
Pearly Boy (Style One), HN 1482, 1547
Pearly Boy (Style Two), HN 2035
Pearly Boy (Style Three), HN 2767
Pearly Girl (Style One), HN 1483, 1548
Pearly Girl (Style Two), HN 2036
Pearly Girl (Style Three), HN 2769
Pecksniff (Style One), HN 535; M43
Pecksniff (Style Two), HN 553, 1891
Pecksniff (Style Three), HN 2098
Pedlar Wolf, HN 7
Peggy, HN 1941, 2038
Penelope, HN 1901, 1902
Penny, HN 2338, 2424
Pensive, HN 3109
Pensive Moments, HN 2704
Perfect Pair, HN 581
Period Figures in English History: see Eleanor of Province; Henrietta Maria; The Lady Anne Nevill; Margaret of Anjou; Matilda; Mrs.Fitzherbert; Phillippa of Hainault; The Young Miss Nightingale
Philippa of Hainault, HN 2008
Philippine Dancer, HN 2439
Phyllis (Style One), HN 1420, 1430, 1486, 1698
Phyllis (Style Two), HN 3180
Picardy Peasant (man), HN 13, 17, 19
Picardy Peasant (woman), HN 4, 5, 17A, 351, 513
Picnic, HN 2308
Pied Piper, HN 1215, 2102
Pierrette (Style One), HN 642, 643, 644, 691, 721, 731, 732, 784
Pierrette (Style Two), HN 795, 796
Pierrette (Style Three), HN 1391, 1749
Pillow Fight, HN 2270
Pinkie, HN 1552, 1553
Piper, HN 2907
Pirate King, HN 2901
Pirouette, HN 2216
Playmates, HN 3127
Please Keep Still, HN 2967
Please Sir, HN 3302
Poacher, HN 2043
Pocahontas, HN 2930
Poke Bonnet, HN 362, 612, 765; Also called In Grandma's Days, HN 339, 340, 388, 442; and Lilac Shawl, HN 44, 44A
Polish Dancer, HN 2836
Polka, HN 2156
Polly, HN 3178
Polly Peachum (Style One), HN 463, 465, 550, 589, 614, 680, 693
Polly Peachum (Style Two), HN 489, 549, 620, 694, 734
Polly Peachum (Style Three), HN 698, 699, 757-762
Polly Peachum, M 21, 22, 23
Polly Put The Kettle On, HN 3021
Pollyanna, HN 2965
Potter, HN 1493, 1518, 1522

Premiere, HN 2343, 2343A
Pretty Lady, HN 69, 70, 302, 330, 361, 384, 565, 700, 763, 783
Pretty Polly, HN 2768
Pride and Joy, HN 2945
Primroses, HN 1617
Prince of Wales, HN 1217
Princess, HN 391, 392, 420, 430, 431, 633
Princess Badoura, HN 2081
Printemps (Spring), HN 3066
Priscilla, HN 1337, 1340, 1495, 1501, 1559; M 13, 14, 24
Private, 1st Georgia Regiment, 1777, HN 2779
Private, 2nd South Carolina Regiment, 1781, HN 2717
Private, 3rd North Carolina Regiment, 1778, HN 2754
Private, Connecticut Regiment, 1777, HN 2845
Private, Delaware Regiment, 1776, HN 2761
Private, Massachusetts Regiment, 1778, HN 2760
Private, Pennsylvania Rifle Battalion, 1776, HN 2846
Private, Rhode Island Regiment, 1781, HN 2759
Prized Possession, HN 2942
Professor, HN 2281
Promenade (Style One), HN 2076
Promenade (Style Two), HN 3072
Proposal (woman), HN 715, 716, 788
Proposal (man), HN 725, 1209
Prudence, HN 1883, 1884
Prue, HN 1996
Puff and Powder, HN 397, 398, 400, 432, 433
Punch and Judy Man, HN 2765
Puppetmaker, HN 2253
Puppy Love, HN 3371
Pussy, HN 18, 325, 507
Pyjams, HN 1942

Q

Quality Street, HN 1211, 1211A
Queen Anne, HN 3141
Queen Elizabeth I, HN 3099
Queen of Sheba, HN 2328
Queen of the Dawn, HN 2437
Queen of the Ice, HN 2435
Queen Victoria, HN 3125
Queen Victoria and Prince Albert, HN 3256
Queens of the Realm: see Queen Elizabeth I,
    Queen Victoria, Queen Anne, Mary Queen of Scots

R

R.C.M.P. 1873, HN 2555
R.C.M.P. 1973, HN 2547
R.D.I.C.C.: see The Auctioneer, Autumntime, Bunny's
    Bedtime, Discovery, The Geisha, Jester, L'Ambitieuse,
    Pride and Joy, Prized Possessions, Sleepy Darling,
    Springtime (Style Two), Summertime, Top o' The Hill,
    Wintertime,
Rachel, HN 2919, 2936
Rag Doll, HN 2142
Rag Doll Seller, HN 2944
Rebecca, HN 2805
Rebecca (Miniature), HN 3414

Reflection, HN 3039
Reflections: see Allure, Aperitif, Autumn Glory, Ballet
    Class, Balloons, Bathing Beauty, Bolero, Breezy Day,
    Charisma, Cherry Blossom, Chic, Cocktails, Country
    Girl, Covent Garden (Style Two), Dancing Delight,
    Daybreak, Debut, Debutante, Demure, Devotion,
    Dreaming, Eastern Grace, Enchanting Evening, Encore,
    Enigma, Entranced, Fantasy, Flirtation, Free As The
    Wind, Gaiety, The Gardner, Golfer, Good Pals,
    Harvestime, Idle Hours, Indian Maiden, The Joker, Joy,
    The Love Letter (Style Two), Moondancer, Morning
    Glory, Panorama, Paradise, Park Parade, Pensive,
    Playmates, Promenade (Style Two), Reflection, Rose
    Arbour, Secret Moment, Sheikh, Shepherd (Style Five),
    Shepherdess (Style Three), Sisterly Love, Sophistication,
    Spring Walk, Stargazer, Storytime, Strolling, Summer
    Rose, Summer's Darling, Sweet Bouquet, Sweet
    Perfume, Sweet Violets, Tango, Tomorrow's Dreams,
    Traveller's Tale, Tumbler, Water Maiden, Windflower
    (Style Three), Windswept, A Winter's Walk
Reflections, HN 1820, 1821, 1847, 1848
Regal Lady, HN 2709
Regency, HN 1752
Regency Beau, HN 1972
Rendezvous, HN 2212
Repose, HN 2272
Rest Awhile, HN 2728
Return of Persephone, HN 31
Reverie, HN 2306
Reward, HN 3391
Reynolds Ladies: Countess of Harrington, Countess
    Spencer, Lady Worsley, Mrs. Hugh Bonfoy
Rhapsody, HN 2267
Rhoda, HN 1573, 1574, 1688
Rhythm, HN 1903, 1904
Rita, HN 1448, 1450
Ritz Bell Boy, HN 2772
River Boy, HN 2128
Robert Burns, HN 42
Robin, M 38, 39
Robin Hood, HN 2773
Rocking Horse, HN 2072
Romance, HN 2430
Romany Sue, HN 1757, 1758
Rosabell, HN 1620
Rosalind, HN 2393
Rosamund (Style One), HN 1320
Rosamund (Style Two), HN 1497, 1551
Rosamund, M 32, 33
Rose, HN 1368, 1387, 1416, 1506, 1654, 2123
Rose Arbour, HN 3145
Roseanna, HN 1921, 1926
Rosebud (Style One), HN 1580, 1581
Rosebud (Style Two), HN 1983
Rosemary (Style One), HN 2091
Rosemary (Style Two), HN 3143
Rosina, HN 1358, 1364, 1556
Rowena, HN 2077
Royal Governor's Cook, HN 2233
Ruby, HN 1724, 1725
Rumpelstiltskin, HN 3025

Rustic Swain, HN 1745, 1746
Ruth, HN 2799
Ruth, The Pirate Maid, HN 2900

S

Sabbath Morn, HN 1982
Sailor's Holiday, HN 2442
Sairey Gamp (Style One), HN 533; M 46
Sairey Gamp (Style Two), HN 558, 1896
Sairey Gamp (Style Three), HN 2100
Sally, HN 2741
Salome (Style One), HN 1775, 1828
Salome (Style Two), HN 3267
Sam Weller, HN 531; M 48
Samantha (Style One), HN 2954
Samantha (Style Two), HN 3304
Samurai Warrior, HN 3402
Samwise, HN 2925
Sandra, HN 2275, 2401
Santa Claus, HN 2725
Santa's Helper, HN 3301
Sara, HN 2265, 3308
Sara (Miniature), HN 3219, 3249
Sarah, HN 3005
Saucy Nymph, HN 1539
Save Some For Me, HN 2959
Schoolmarm, HN 2223
Scotch Girl, HN 1269
Scotties, HN 1281, 1349
Scottish Highland Dancer, HN 2436
Scribe, HN 305, 324, 1235
Scrooge, M 87
Sea Characters: see The Boatman, The Captain, A Good
    Catch, Helmsman, The Lobster Man, Sailor's Holiday,
    Sea Harvest, The Seafarer, Shore Leave, Tall Story
Sea Harvest, HN 2257
Sea Sprite (Style One), HN 1261
Sea Sprite (Style Two), HN 2191
Seafarer, HN 2455
Seashore, HN 2263
Seasons (Style One): see Spring, Summer, Autumn, Winter
Seasons (Style Two): see Spring, Summer,Autumn, Winter
Seasons (Style Three): see Catherine in Spring (Style Two),
    Lilian in Summer, Emily in Autumn (Style One),
    Sarah in Winter
Seasons (Style Four): see Springtime (Style Two),
    Summertime, Autumntime, Wintertime
Les Saisons (Style Five): see Printemps (Spring),
    Ete (Summer), Automne (Autumn), Hiver (Winter)
Secret Moment, HN 3106
Secret Thoughts, HN 2382
Sentimental Pierrot, HN 36, 307
Sentiments: Forget-Me-Not, Loving You, Sweet Dreams,
Thank You, Thinking of You, With Love
Sentinel, HN 523
September (Style One), HN 3166
September (Style Two), HN 3409
Serena, HN 1868
Serenade, HN 2753
Sergeant, 6th Maryland Regiment, 1777, HN 2815

Sergeant, Virginia 1st Regiment Continental Light
    Dragoons, 1777, HN 2844
Sharon, HN 3047
She Loves Me Not, HN 2045
Sheikh, HN 3083
Sheila, HN 2742
Shepherd (Style One), HN 81, 617, 632
Shepherd (Style Two), HN 709
Shepherd (Style Three), HN 751
Shepherd (Style Four), HN 1975
Shepherd (Style Five), HN 3160
Shepherd, M 17, 19
Shepherdess (Style One), HN 708
Shepherdess (Style Two), HM 735, 750
Shepherdess (Style Three), HN 2990
Shepherdess (Style Four), HN 2420
Shepherdess, M 18, 20
Ship's Figureheads: see HMS Ajax, Benmore, Chieftain,
    Hibernia, Lalla Rookh, Mary Queen of Scots, Nelson,
    Pocahontas
Shirley, HN 2702
Shore Leave, HN 2254
Shy Anne, HN 60, 64, 65, 568
Shylock, HN 79, 317
Sibell, HN 1668, 1695, 1735
Siesta, HN 1305
Silks and Ribbons, HN 2017
Silversmith of Williamsburg, HN 2208
Simone, HN 2378
Single Red Rose, HN 3376
Sir Edward, HN 2370
Sir John A. MacDonald, HN 2860;
    also called The Statesman, HN 2859
Sir Ralph, HN 2371
Sir Thomas, HN 2372
Sir Thomas Lovell, HN 356
Sir Walter Raleigh, HN 1742, 1751, 2015
Sir Winston Churchill, HN 3057
Sisterly Love, HN 3130
Sisters, HN 3018, 3019
Sit, HN 3123
Six Wives of Henry VIII: Anne Bolelyn, Anne of Cleves,
    Jane Seymour
Skater (Style One), HN 2117
Skater (Style Two), HN 3439
Slapdash, HN 2277
Sleep, HN 24, 24A, 25, 25A, 424, 692, 710
Sleeping Beauty, HN 3079
Sleepy Darling, HN 2953
Sleepy Scholar, HN 15, 16, 29
Sleepyhead, HN 2114
Smiling Buddha, HN 454
Snake Charmer, HN 1317
Soiree, HN 2312
Soldiers of the Revolution: see Private, 2nd South Carolina
    Regiment, 1781; Major, 3rd New Jersey Regiment, 1776;
    Private 3rd North Carolina Regiment, 1778; Captain,
    2nd New York Regiment, 1775; Private, Rhode Island
    Regiment, 1781; Private Massachusets Regiment, 1778;
    Private, Delaware Regiment, 1776; Private, 1st Georgia
    Regiment, 1777; Corporal, 1st New Hampshire

Regiment, 1778; Sergeant, 6th Maryland Regiment, 1777; Sergeant, Virginia 1st Regiment Continental Light Dragoons, 1777; Private, Connecticut Regiment, 1777; Private Pennsylvania Rifle Battalion, 1776
Solitude, HN 2810
Sonata, HN 2438
Song of the Sea, HN 2729
Sonia, HN 1692, 1738
Sonny, HN 1313, 1314
Sophia Charlotte, Lady Sheffield, HN 3008
Sophie (Style One), HN 2833
Sophie (Style Two), HN 3257
Sophistication, HN 3059
Southern Belle, HN 2229, 2425
Southern Belle (Miniature), HN 3174, 3244
Special Occasions: see Christening Day (Blue), Christening Day (Pink), Happy Anniversary (Style One), Happy Birthday, Merry Christmas
Spanish Flamenco Dancer, HN 2831
Spanish Lady, HN 1262, 1290, 1293, 1294, 1309
Spinning, HN 2390
Spirit of the Wind, HN 1777, 1825
Spook, HN 50, 51, 51A, 51B, 58, 512, 625, 1218
Spooks, HN 88, 89, 372
Spring (Style One), HN 312, 472
Spring (Style Two), HN 1774, 1827
Spring (Style Three), HN 2085
Spring Flowers, HN 1807, 1945
Spring Morning, HN 1922, 1923
Springtime (Style One), HN 1971
Springtime (Style Two), HN 3033
Spring Walk, HN 3120
Squire, HN 1814; Also called Hunting Squire, HN 1409
St. George (Style One), HN 385, 386, 1800, 2067
St. George (Style Two), HN 2051
St. George (Style Three), HN 2856
Stan Laurel, HN 2774
Stargazer, HN 3182
Statesman The, HN 2859: Also called Sir John A. MacDonald, HN 2860
Stayed At Home, HN 2207
Stephanie, HN 2807, 2811
Stick 'em Up, HN 2981
Stiggins, HN 536; M 50
Stitch in Time, HN 2352
Stop Press, HN 2683
Storytime, HN 3126
Strolling, HN 3073
Suitor, HN 2132
Summer (Style One), HN 313, 473
Summer (Style Two), HN 2086
Summer Rose (Style One), HN 3085
Summer Rose (Style Two), HN 3309
Summer's Darling, HN 3091
Summer's Day (Style One), HN 2181
Summer's Day (Style Two), HN 3378
Summertime, HN 3137
Sunday Best, HN 2206, 2698
Sunday Best (Miniature), HN 3218, 3312
Sunday Morning, HN 2184
Sunshine Girl, HN 1344, 1348

Susan (Style One), HN 2056
Susan (Style Two), HN 2952, 3050
Susanna, HN 1233, 1288, 1299
Suzette, HN 1487, 1577, 1585, 1696, 2026
Sweet and Fair, HN 1864, 1865
Sweet and Twenty (Style One), HN 1298, 1360, 1437, 1438, 1549, 1563, 1649
Sweet and Twenty (Style Two), HN 1589, 1610
Sweet Anne, HN 1318, 1330, 1331, 1453, 1496, 1631, 1701; M 5, 6, 27
Sweet and Twenties: see Deauville, Monte Carlo
Sweet April, HN 2215
Sweet Bouquet, HN 3000
Sweet Dreams (Style One), HN 2380
Sweet Dreams (Style Two), HN 3394
Sweet Lavender, HN 1373
Sweet Maid (Style One), HN 1504, 1505
Sweet Maid (Style Two), HN 2092
Sweet Perfume, HN 3094
Sweet Seventeen, HN 2734
Sweet Sixteen, HN 2231
Sweet Suzy, HN 1918
Sweet Violets, HN 3175
Sweeting, HN 1935, 1938
Swimmer, HN 1270, 1326, 1329
Sylvia, HN 1478
Sympathy, HN 2838, 2876
Symphony, HN 2287

T

Tailor, HN 2174
Taking Things Easy, HN 2677, 2680
Tall Story, HN 2248
Tango, HN 3075
Tapestry Weaving, HN 3048
Teatime, HN 2255
Teeing Off, HN 3276
Teenager, HN 2203
Teenagers: see Columbine, Faraway, Harlequin, Melody, Sea Sprite, Sweet Sixteen, Teenager, Wood Nymph
Tender Moment, HN 3303
Tenderness, HN 2713, 2714
Teresa (Style One), HN 1682, 1683
Teresa (Style Two), HN 3206
Tess, HN 2865
Tete-a-Tete (Style One), HN 798, 799
Tete-a-Tete (Style Two), HN 1236, 1237
Thank You (Style One), HN 2732
Thank You (Style Two), HN 3390
Thankful, HN 3129, 3135
Thanks Doc, HN 2731
Thanksgiving, HN 2446
Thinking of You, HN 3124
This Little Pig, HN 1793, 1794, 2125
Tildy, HN 1576, 1859
Tinkle Bell, HN 1677
Tinsmith, HN 2146
Tiny Tim, HN 539; M 56
Tip-Toe, HN 3293
To Bed, HN 1805, 1806

Toinette, HN 1940; Also called Meryll, HN 1917
Tom, HN 2864
Tom Bombadil, HN 2924
Tom Brown, HN 2941
Tom Sawyer, HN 2926
Tom, Tom, The Piper's Son, HN 3032
Tomorrow's Dreams, HN 3128
Tony Weller (Style One), HN 346, 368, 684
Tony Weller (Style Two), HN 544; M 47
Tootles, HN 1680
Top o' the Hill, HN 1833, 1834, 1849, 2127
Top o' the Hill (Miniature), HN 2126
Town Crier (Miniature), HN 3261
Town Crier, HN 2119
Toymaker, HN 2250
Toys, HN 1316
Tracy, HN 2736
Tranquility, HN 2426, 2469
Travellers' Tale, HN 3185
Treasure Island, HN 2243
Trotty Veck, M 91
Tulips, HN 466, 488, 672, 747, 1334
Tumber The, HN 3183
Tumbling, HN 3283, 3289
Tuppence a Bag, HN 2320
Twilight, HN 2256
Two-a-Penny, HN 1359
T'zu-hsi, Empress Dowager, HN 2391

U

Uncle Ned, HN 2094
Under the Gooseberry Bush, HN 49
"Upon Her Cheeks She Wept.", HN 59, 511, 522
Uriah Heep (Style One), HN 545; M 45
Uriah Heep (Style Two), HN 554, 1892
Uriah Heep (Style Three), HN 2101

V

Valerie, HN 2107
Vanessa (Style One), HN 1836, 1838
Vanessa (Style Two), HN 3198
Vanity, HN 2475
Vanity Fair Children: see Amanda, Andrea, Buddies, Catherine (Style Three), Helen (Style Two), Julie, Kerry, Let's Play, Lynsey, My First Pet, Reward, Sit
Vanity Fair Ladies: see Angela (Style Two), Ann, Ashley, Barbara (Style Two), Carol, Danielle (Style Two), Denise (Style Two), Donna, Emily (Style Two), Gail, Heather, Jean (Style Two), Jessica, Joanne, Kimberley, Linda (Style Two), Margaret (Style Two), Mary, Maureen (Style Two), Megan, Mother and Baby, Nancy, Natalie, Pamela (Style Two), Patricia (Style Two), Samantha, Tracy, Veronica (Style Three)
Veneta, HN 2722
Vera, HN 1729, 1730
Verena, HN 1835, 1854
Veronica (Style One), HN 1517, 1519, 1650, 1943
Veronica (Style Two), HN 1915

Veronica (Style Three), HN 3205
Veronica, M 64, 70
Victoria, HN 2471, 3416
Victorian Lady, HN 726, 727, 728, 736, 739, 740, 742, 745, 1208, 1258, 1276, 1277, 1345, 1452, 1529; M 1, 2, 25
Viking, HN 2375
Viola d'Amore, HN 2797
Violin, HN 2432
Virginals, HN 2427
Virginia, HN 1693, 1694
Vivienne, HN 2073
Votes For Women, HN 2816

W

Waiting For A Train, HN 3315
Wandering Minstrel, HN 1224
Wardrobe Mistress, HN 2145
Water Maiden, HN 3155
Wayfarer, HN 2362
Wedding Day, HN 2748
Wedding Morn, HN 1866, 1867
Wedding Vows, HN 2750
Wee Willie Winkie (Style One), HN 2050
Wee Willie Winkie (Style Two), HN 3031
Welcome Home, HN 3299
Welsh Girl, HN 39, 92, 456, 514, 516, 519, 520, 660, 668, 669, 701, 792. Also called Myfanwy Jones
Wendy, HN 2109
West Indian Dancer, HN 2384
West Wind, HN 1776, 1826
Wigmaker of Williamsburg, HN 2239
Wildflower of the Month: see January, February, March, April, May, June, July, August, September, October, November, December
Will He-Won't He, HN 3275
Williamsburg, Figures of: see A Child from Williamsburg, Boy from Williamsburg, Blacksmith of Williamsburg, Gentleman from Williamsburg, Hostess of Williamsburg, Lady from Williamsburg, Royal Governor's Cook, Silversmith of Williamsburg, Wigmaker of Williamsburg
Willy-Won't He, HN 1561, 1584, 2150
Windflower (Style One), HN 1763, 1764, 2029
Windflower (Style Two), HN 1920, 1939
Windflower (Style Three), HN 3077
Windflower, M 78, 79
Windmill Lady, HN 1400
Windswept, HN 3027
Winner, HN 1407
Winning Put, HN 3279
Winsome, HN 2220
Winter (Style One), HN 315, 475
Winter (Style Two), HN 2088
Wintertime, HN 3060
Wistful, HN 2396, 2472
With Love, HN 3393
Wizard, HN 2877, 3121
Woman Holding Child, HN 462, 570, 703, 743
Woman of the Time of Henry VI, HN 43
Wood Nymph, HN 2192

Writing, HN 3049

Y

Yearning, HN 2920, 2921
Yeoman of the Guard, HN 688, 2122
Young Dreams, HN 3176
Young Knight, HN 94
Young Love, HN 2735

Young Master, HN 2872
Young Miss Nightingale, HN 2010
Young Mother with Child, HN 1301
Young Widow, HN 1399; Also called Little Mother
  (Style Two), HN 1418, 1641
Yours Forever, HN 3354
Yum-Yum (Style One), HN 1268, 1287
Yum-Yum (Style Two), HN 2899
Yvonne, HN 3038

HN 76 THE CARPET VENDOR (Style One)

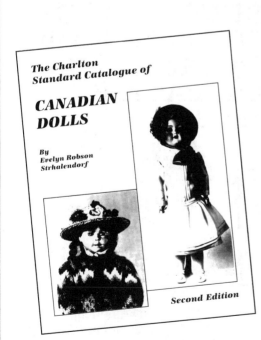

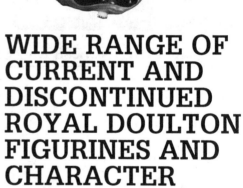
344

At The British Toby, Doulton is *all* we buy, sell or trade.

We offer a wide selection of discontinued and special commission Figurines, Character Jugs, Animals, Bunnykins, Seriesware, and Advertising ware.

Complete range of currently produced Figurines, Character Jugs, Bunnykins, and Animals.

Mail order is our specialty—and we welcome the chance to help you find the rarest in Doulton.

Selection, quality, pricing, Doulton knowledge and customer satisfaction have combined to make us Canada's Largest Doulton Dealer.

We buy single pieces or entire collections. Appraisals undertaken. To receive our bimonthly BT InfoLetter please call or write:

Call 416-472-TOBY
Toll free in Canada & USA 1-800-263-TOBY

Main Store (Open Tuesday through Saturday):
10 Centre Street, Markham, Ontario L3P 2N8

Harbourfront Antique Market (Open weekends):
390 Queen's Quay W., Toronto M5V 3A6

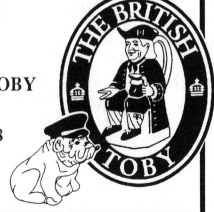